WORK IN A METRO

This volume is about why 'work' changed to become more precarious around the turn of the century. This happened not just in the developed world but also inside sectors that were demarcated as organized and modern within developing countries like India. In these sectors, unlike the greater part of the Indian economy, insecure jobs were uncommon before winds of change made them normal. This shift had occurred before the great global financial crisis of 2008.

Between 2005-8 a survey based on over thousand structured interviews with workers in offices, factories, shops and establishments (below the supervisory rank) in Mumbai was undertaken. This is the innovative segment of the book which tries to measure and quantify some of these changes and their associations. It is designed to investigate the central proposition of the 'Insecurity Hypothesis' (IH), which is that the economic risk of increased and global competition was being progressively passed on from the employer to the employee. This was happening through shortened job tenure, erratic remuneration, variable work, contingent employment, and institutional changes that remove or reduce protection, bargaining power of employees in the work place everywhere. The corollary is that widespread and unremitting work (and income related) insecurity is an expedient competitive strategy but a damaging socio-economic phenomenon.

Anuradha Kalhan has taught economics in Mumbai for thirty years and has a PhD in the subject from the University of Mumbai. She has been an active member of the Bombay University and College Teachers Union, a member of its executive committee and an elected member of the Senate of University of Mumbai. She was a Fellow at Nehru Memorial Museum & Library, New Delhi in 2013-15. As an independent researcher she now divides her time between California, Scotland, Mumbai and Pune.

WORK IN A METRO

Intense, Flexible, Insecure

ANURADHA KALHAN

Routledge
Taylor & Francis Group
LONDON AND NEW YORK

First published 2018
by Routledge
4 Park Square, Milton Park, Abingdon, Oxon OX14 4RN
605 Third Avenue, New York, NY 10017

First issued in paperback 2023

Routledge is an imprint of the Taylor & Francis Group, an informa business

Publisher's Note
The publisher has gone to great lengths to ensure the quality of this reprint but points out that some imperfections in the original copies may be apparent.

Print edition not for sale in South Asia (India, Sri Lanka, Nepal, Bangladesh, Afghanistan, Pakistan or Bhutan)

British Library Cataloguing in Publication Data
A catalogue record for this book is available from the British Library

Library of Congress Cataloging in Publication Data
A catalog record for this book has been requested

ISBN: 978-1-03-265319-8 (pbk)
ISBN: 978-1-138-48489-4 (hbk)
ISBN: 978-1-351-05047-0 (ebk)

DOI: 10.4324/9781351050470

Typeset in Minion Pro 11/13
by Ravi Shanker, Delhi 110 095

MANOHAR

For my students and for my daughter
who encounter this new world of work . . .

Contents

Preface

This book is about how work in the city became what it is now intense, flexible and insecure. It is rare these days to talk about work or jobs and find someone who doesn't complain about the maladies of their work or their workplace. They grumble about pace, frenzy, hours, vagaries, terms of contract, ethics and the very meaning of their work. This gripe is reiterated across sectors considered organized and through age profiles. For many at mid-life, caught in the vortex of accelerating changes at the workplace, adjustment is excruciating. Older people outside the work force, are astonished by long and hectic hours the young have to put in when they do eventually find suitable work; unable to comprehend the new kind of work or the new workplace.

For, there are so many workers who are 'solo entrepreneurs' without well-defined work or workplace. They used to be called self-employed or footloose. Just as many people work on trifling contracts. Of course, there are by now millions across the globe who want to work but either do not have suitable skills or do not find decent work. They may string along more than one job to make ends meet. They may even stay solvent if they are the indomitable type. There are eccentric new kinds too, who are well educated, can find work, have skills to do the work but have withdrawn from work unable to cope with its frantic nature. They live off accumulated savings or their parents; they may be learning to calm down, waiting to find a better job or retraining for yet another.

Then there are the grim winners who work all day, have little time and few associations outside the one organization that they serve . . . as though Rip van Winkle had fallen asleep mid-way during the Industrial Revolution to wake up much better educated, better clothed, somewhat better fed but unrested and with no memory of the any other way of being.

All these kinds of workers are found in both, first- and third-world cities today. They work within sectors that are called formal and organized. Third-world countries like India had a phase of planned development and formal job creation; islands of a few coveted, stable jobs still exist twenty-five years after liberalization but for the rest insecurity and work intensification rules. Workers in the third world were told that there was no alternative to globalization for stimulating economic growth, job creation and well-being. Globalization was presented as an almost mythical goliath striding the globe, forcing corporations to become efficient, cut costs and states to shrink for wealth and job creation.

Twenty-five years later, the consequences for labour markets even in developing countries, have not been cheery. Not quite as many stable decent jobs have been created as promised, insecurity is the rule. Certainly not all economies across the globe have created the same level of unemployment and insecurity but the tendency for unstable jobs, and rise in insecurity is ubiquitous.

Many who grew up in big cities of the developing world in the second half of the twentieth century came to accept that work involved intense exertions but it was a means of self-realization and security. Work gave people social identity, work ethics defined personality, and workplaces also gave people friends, associations, trade unions. Family was only one of the steady, fraternal entities that they belonged to. For those fortunate enough to access education and formal-sector jobs, work was ascent into a modern world with prospects for not just security but social mobility. That process seems to have been rather arrested now. Its impact on a fragile social cohesion is uncertain.

In the days leading up to the global recession of 2008, social theorists in the developed world talk of the end of the work society and the emergence of the multi-active risk society and argue that people are no longer identified by the work they do but by what they consume, aspire to consume or what they believe in and these are all so diverse as to make societies plural. They said that cultural identity, differing lifestyles based on commodity preferences, opinions that range from creationism, vegetarianism, environmentalism to the criticality of gay rights fashioned a multicultural, divergent, tolerant society quite unlike the industrial society that preceded it. No single feature of this society was robust enough to pull it together. Its counterpart in the developing world is emerging (often comprising young people whose parents had greater job, income or locational stability than they are likely to have) but it is unlikely to be as tolerant as its counterpart in the developed world because the combined effect of rising levels of education, absence of decent work, lack of social security, falling standards of living and self-worth create a dreadful spiral indeed.

Anthropologists suggest that the labour of acquiring skills played a part in the transition from ape to man. In a brilliant lecture titled, 'History as Progress', E.H. Carr (1990) also says 'the essence of man as a rational being is the ability to develop his potential capacities by accumulating the experience of past generations'. Thus, 'History is progress through the transmission of acquired skills from one generation to another' (p. 114). Workplaces used to be the modern skill building and skill diffusion grounds. Could the loss of skills from increasingly insecure employment feed into inability to acquire future skills? Could this vicious circularity have implications for local economies, social reproduction and human development?

Historically, division of work stimulated new skills and secured and sustained modern, urban civilization. It gave people their social context. Could this new, troubled, insecure world of work completely fragment society in the guise of plurality? Could this be the reason why even the nuclear family is crumbling?

The book plan is as follows: the first two chapters are an introduction to the concept, theme and correlates of insecurity in labour markets as a result of globalization; the third is the survey of a thousand workers to scale their insecurity, the survey is in the organized sector in the metropolis of Mumbai undertaken over 2005-7. The background of the city, why it is an appropriate location to examine workplace changes and key concepts operationalized in the survey are explained. The subsequent chapters develop the theoretical connections of the central theme to concerns of skill development, human resource management and trade unions. Each chapter places India in the world.

The epilogue revisits the world of work seven years later. In the interlude the Great Recession of 2007-8 had occurred, unemployment and insecurity worsened. The causes of the recession that began in the American financial sector are known now and across the globe well-coordinated macro-economic policies that followed signaled a decisive shift in political economy in country after country. The speed and direction of state policies repudiate, the 'orchestrated global scare' [to use Ulrich Beck's (2000) phrase] that the nation-state had becomes helpless, effete in the era of globalization. In hardly any country has the size of the government's budget actually shrunk, infact to the contrary. Instead globalization has dismantled the old accountabilities and apparatus of the nation state and brazenly made it the sentinel of international finance capital. On the other side rampant deficiency of decent work and elite capture of state power began to infuriate and unite what had appeared to be a very plural, tolerant society. One sequence of reaction began with the Occupy Wall Street movement for a more egalitarian society and spread across. Another contending reaction took the form of nationalist right wing movements, mainly against other races, religions or immigrants.

Mumbai 2016 ANURADHA KALHAN

Acknowledgements

The deepest gratitude is owed to those who participated in the fieldwork. All the workers in Mumbai who filled out long questionnaires; my students who fanned out to support the field-work, employees' organizations and trade unions that supported, gave valuable advice and attention so that we could improve our methods and questionnaire. They collectively made an apparently impossible idea possible.

Shrikant Bhosle as an untiring field-worker deserves a special mention. Huge amount of data would have been insurmountable without the technical support of R.C. Sharma (ex-TISS), M.M. Sharma (ex-CDAC) and V. Parab.

Dr A.R. Nadkarni of the Department of Economics, University of Mumbai, was the guiding spirit of the project. Dr D.M. Harver, Head, Department of Economics, Jai Hind College provided valuable editing support towards the end, when I was tiring of the enormous task. The University Grants Commission funded the quest in part.

I think both curiosity and angst drove us all through the long-drawn-out process. Questions raised and answers discovered on the field were often based on an exchange of ideas about the 'change' that was engulfing all of us at our own workplaces. I thank all for pitching in generously, selflessly.

Terms, catchphrases, concepts and hypotheses that are the foundation of this book and those that provoked fieldwork in Mumbai are credited in the references. But as in every extensive endeavour of this kind there may be many whose ideas were so much a part of contemporary discourse and wisdom that they have not been cited. Every scholar that has endeavoured before me, to understand this world of work, is acknowledged here with deep gratitude. They made it possible.

Anuradha Kalhan

CHAPTER 1

Introduction: Insecurity Hypothesis

> There is no security on this earth, there is only opportunity.
>
> GENERAL DOUGLAS MACARTHUR

To claim that there is no security on this earth but only opportunity would have seemed rather fitting to an army general. That it should be an appropriate description of a society in peace time, not even ostensibly at war with itself, would have been unthinkable even a few decades ago. This book explores why and how the world of work changed across the globe making work more intense, flexible, insecure; its correlates and possible consequences for society. It examines the broad trends up to 2007-8. Field work in Mumbai between 2005-7 is used to measure these changes in work. The global recession that followed only intensified adverse trends in labour markets. These are highlighted in the epilogue.

The central proposition of the 'Insecurity Hypothesis' (IH) is that the economic risk of increased global competition is being progressively passed on from the employer to the employee, through shortened job tenure, erratic remuneration, variable work, contingent employment, and institutional changes that remove or reduce the protection and bargaining power of the employee in the workplace.

The corollary is that widespread insecurity is damaging. In the short run, it promotes an employment relationship based on opportunism, distrust, and low commitment. The medium to long-term consequence is that the employers under-invest in skill formation and training because of shortening tenures of work. Training and upgrading skills are, however, critical to competitive advantage. Widespread employment-related insecurity weakens institutions of collective bargaining like trade unions that act as networks of trust and cooperation. Feeble trade unions become both a cause and a consequence of mounting insecurity. In the long-term, it undermines productivity and economic performance because in times of rapid economic and technological change insufficient management of social and human capital can become the limiting factor to growth. This last facet has implications for developing countries like India where the impact of increasing global competition may be increasingly passed on to the workers without regard to the medium to long-term consequences.

Literature on the global economy refers to dramatic changes after the late-1970s. The transformation that swept the world began in the industrialized countries, and reached the developing countries before the end of the century. These changes had two clearly discernible aspects. First there was a greater reliance on market forces that ushered in a move to deregulate the commodity and factor markets, reduce import barriers, reduce income taxes, bring in privatization and replace central planning with price mechanism. Second, there was an extension of globalization defined as increase in economic and financial linkage among countries.

This chapter, therefore, provides a background to the central theme of 'Insecurity Hypothesis'. The nature, history, processes of globalization and the resulting trends in the labour markets in leading OECD countries like Britain, United States, and Japan are reviewed over the last two decades of the twentieth century. A rising proportion of unemployment in the workforce and deterioration in quality of employment occurred in the period following large-scale restructuring. And this offers an insight into the long-term repercussions for the labour markets in both the developed and developing countries. Common tendencies across the OECD countries are summed up and the multifaceted link between high rates of unemployment and worker insecurity are pointed out.

Since the study examines the Insecurity Hypothesis in the Indian context on the basis of sample study evidence, the impact of the liberalization and restructuring process on the labour market in India after 1991, is also reviewed. The evidence there also indicates deterioration in organized sector employment in India, though the evidence is over a shorter span of time compared to the OECD countries. Some similarity between the trends in the developed and organized sector in the developing countries is evident.

Section 1.1 deals entirely with globalization and restructuring; Section 1.2 discusses trends in unemployment and insecurity thereof; Section 1.3 sums up common long-term symptoms of restructuring in OECD countries; 1.4 outlines the background in post-liberalization India; 1.5 describes economic reforms and their impact on labour; 1.6 is a background to the ultimate sample study, and 1.7 concludes the introduction.

1.1 Globalization and Restructuring

During the period 1945-70 the OECD countries enjoyed what in retrospect appears a golden period in terms of labour market performance – an era of full employment policies, job security, rising real incomes and a drive for increasing equality of opportunity. The Keynesian welfarist model of demand management on the one hand, and redistributive tax and transfer payments on the other seemed to have been the foundation of that golden era. There were recessions but for the most part these led to short-term frictions and many of the advanced countries seemed to have achieved a workable blend of economic efficiency and social equity. In stark contrast to that period, the years 1980-2004 have been one of intense upheavals. Profound changes took place in the closing decades of the twentieth century in both the capitalist and socialist economies of the developed world.[1] The intensity and pace of change is different but analogous outcomes are perceptible.

Cumulatively these changes have, over time, qualitatively transformed the nature of global interdependence. Interdependence now goes far beyond expansion of international trade that had occurred in the preceding two hundred years. The components of these changes include the growth and relative importance of FDI, the internationalization of the financial markets, the development and diffusion of communication and transport technology, deregulation and liberalization, and privatization of the public sector. These changes are often loosely referred to as globalization. International economic interdependence is driven more by the movement of capital and the movement of goods. This process has only gained momentum over time, led by multinational corporations. According to the *World Investment Report 2000* of the United Nations Conference on Trade and Development, international trade in the 1980s had grown at half the rate of FDI. The global sales of foreign operations of multinationals in 1999 amounted to $14,000 billion. This was nearly twice as high as the value of world exports.

The creation of the WTO and its institutional arrangements has pressed the rate of change to create a global market for goods and capital. Many of the developing countries have also moved towards integration; some under pressure from the IMF and the World Bank. Although globalization has been presented as a purely technological inevitability there are ideological elements that have fashioned its development; often referred to as neo-liberal in inspiration. These ideological forces have been sharply contested. The repudiation has been led on two fronts, academic research into the impact of globalization on inequalities, poverty and labour market, and the voice/felt experiences of the working class. Trade unions have described the experience of globalization as a 'race to the bottom'.

Some serious long-term trends were emerging, e.g. in the earlier period, OECD unemployment averaged less than 10 million but by the early 1990s it had increased to over 35 million. There are rising regional disparities within the OECD, Europe being worse affected than the USA and Japan.[2] Over and above this there is increasing evidence of deteriorating quality of employment across the OECD.[3] The labour market has reflected changes induced by globalization and there is mounting evidence that the labour markets of both developed and developing countries have become characterized by increasing uncertainty, joblessness, insecurity, risk and inequality. For instance, the term 'informal sector' was first used in the 1970s to describe the urban self-employment and casual labour present in the less developed countries as a result of insufficient development. The term was then imported into the developed country literature in the 1980s to explain the phenomenon that occurred in their labour markets due to restructuring and deindustrialization. By the 1990s terms like flexible employment, casual work, part-time workers, temporary workers, contract or agency workers, were being used to describe the terms of employment in the developed and developing countries alike.[4] The important difference was that in the developed countries these changes applied to a smaller segment of labour markets compared to the developing countries where informal employment was and remains the norm.

To get a perspective on the sweeping nature of change at the end of the twentieth century, it is important to place it in the context of some major events of the earlier period in the century, such as, the Great Depression of 1930s, the New Deal, Keynesian demand management policies, the Second World War, the fortification of the Welfare State, and the rise of mega-corporations and government – industry collaboration, the birth and expansion of multinationals, the oil crisis of the mid-1970s, rise of the Japanese economy, stagflation in the OECD countries, recurring balance-of-payment crisis in the developing countries, slowdown in global trade, collapse of the Soviet Union, and the more recent establishment of the WTO, and the related trends towards economic liberalization.[5] Regulated capitalism and the Bretton Woods system of institutions (like the IMF, World Bank, GATT) established to regulate international economy, contributed to the unprecedented period of sustained growth in the world capitalist economies from the Second World War to the early 1970s, but in the later parts of the 1970s the global economy entered a crisis. Global economic growth fell to 2.5 per cent, half of its rate in the former decade. Profit rates in the seven richest industrial countries fell from 17 per cent in 1965 to 11 per cent in 1980; and for manufacturing alone they fell from 25 to 12 per cent (profit defined as net operating surplus divided by net capital stock at current prices).[6] The corporations experienced the economic crisis as an intensification of international competition. The IMF chairman Jacques Delarosiere declared in 1984 that there was a clear pattern of substantial and progressive long-term decline in the rate of return to capital and corporations increasingly saw the national regulatory systems as a barrier to their increasing profits.

The solution came to be seen as cutting labour and other costs, and in the words of the IMF chairman: 'of a gradual reduction in the rate of increase in real wages over the medium term if we are to restore adequate investment incentive'.[7] The cost reduction strategy included challenging national policies, which adversely increased their cost, moving operations to lower cost location, transforming their own structure and creating a new system of global economic governance which supported their aim. There is a strong interconnection between capital mobility and reducing cost of production. The mobility offers the opportunity to move to low-cost areas and pit workers of different nations against one another, while using the threat of moving-out as a clout, corporations can extract wage and regulatory concessions. They can escape or dilute environment regulations, consumer safety standards, and labour regulations.

In the earliest stages of restructuring, there occurred off-shoring of operations, relocation to the export promoting zones of the Third World countries, and, these were generally in military dictatorship and authoritarian developing states. Some of these became what was known as newly-industrialized countries (NICs), e.g. Asian Tigers like Korea and Singapore and later Vietnam and China.[8] Mobility of capital was amplified by the development of global capital market in financial instruments; and these markets tied together by modern data and communication technologies have grown very rapidly and severely limit the ability of national governments to pursue independent policies. So much so that some economists have begun to suggest that the pace of private capital mobility has become unacceptably and uncontrollably rapid, causing too much dislocation and a deepening sense of insecurity.[9]

The vertically integrated large firms that dominated the world markets up to the 1970s restructured themselves into geographic-boundary spanning networks of firms linking together big and small companies working in different industries, regions and countries. The locus of ultimate power and control remains concentrated with the MNC, key government agencies, big banks and fiduciaries, research hospitals and major universities with close ties to business. This emerging paradigm of reconstruction is 'networked production' and is described as concentration of control combined with decentralization of production. The more the economy is globalized the more it is accessible only to companies with a global reach.[10] Businesses unable to or unwilling to globalize are at a disadvantage. Lean production, downsizing, outsourcing and spatially extensive networks, core vs. peripheral workers, and strategic alliances across the globe are all strategies to seek flexibility to cope with global competition. This restructuring polarizes the labour market into sectors of low-wage contingent workers in which people work for a living but do not earn a living wage vs. highly-paid supervisors and managers and highly skilled knowledge workers. The process of globalization led by the MNCs and their domestic counterparts tends to lead to more homogenized production processes, technology, management systems, organization and product mixes across the world regardless of local factor endowment. This process also universalizes the problem of labour displacement and deteriorating conditions of work. The Director General's Report of the International Labour Conference (2006) points out that 'Job creating potential of FDI can be overstated. Empirical research in the developing countries does not show a strong employment and labour market effects. A rising share of FDI in total investment reduces the overall employment elasticity while shifting the overall pattern of labour demand.' As a result countries across the globe both with large and growing populations and modest and declining populations have had to contend with frequent throwback of a disturbingly large part of the labour force into informal employment or open unemployment. Little wonder then that the twenty-first century opened with global unemployment and inadequate employment gripping over one billion people, according to the ILO *World Employment Report*.[11]

These recent changes have altered the entire matrix of social, political, and economic relationships established in the post-

Second World War period, particularly between the employers and workers. These radically-altered relationships need to be comprehended thoroughly since they have the seeds of social and political upheavals. They are of special significance if the developing economies are to respond adequately to safeguard their core economic and political interests, and beyond that to handle the change as an opportunity for development and not just growth.

I once asked a trade union leader how he would define a member of the working class in this age where the workforce is fragmented with so many without steady wage income, and many who are earning part of their income from capital, dividend, rent and part from work and a few who earned so much from their work that they transcended the class. The ready solution he suggested was that if more than half the current annual income came from work of any kind there should be no objective doubt about class location. The rest always depended on 'state of one's consciousness'. On a more serious note the definition of labour or worker as a class is necessary in a discussion of economic restructuring occurring on a global scale. Definition is critical to be able to distinguish systemic features from the structural features of the working class. The survey undertaken later also uses this concept to cover workers in a wide sense and includes workers from factories and establishments, high and low skills, but below the supervisory and managerial levels. According to Kolko, structural components are variables determining the nature of a class at a point in time or in a place. For instance, work could be in any sector of economy: industrial or service, skilled or unskilled, under or over paid; worker could be of any race or gender. The systemic features include labour as a commodity in the production process; its vulnerability; exploitation and class struggle. The most important and constant structural features of the working class are their role in the production process and their vulnerability as an expendable commodity. Working class, a systemic feature, extends beyond the industrial workers, which is an occupational category. The core distinction is the social position as wage earner irrespective of the type of employment or unemployment it is engaged in.[12]

Its characteristic feature is the sale of labour for wages/salaries, productive and non-productive; and the origin of income as linked to the relations of production. More income does not change the inherent vulnerability of workers as 'commodity' or their relations of exploitation. Their bargaining power attained during cyclic peaks of prosperity crumbles in times of crisis – workers' middle class living standard has never been secure. The reality of labour in capitalistic system is to be vulnerable, expendable and increasingly superfluous.

The restructuring process has been accompanied by rising rates of unemployment, as have been studied by the ILO. By the twenty-first century the consequences of restructuring had become a major source of concern for labour organizations all over the world. In the European Union, the unemployment rate was 11 per cent in July 1996; by 2002 it was down to an average of 8 per cent.[13] In Central and Eastern Europe it was at 11 per cent in 1996 and shows no sign of decline. Among the Latin American countries there was a surge in unemployment towards double-digit levels by 1994-5 and remained at about 10 per cent in 2002.[14] The ILO has problems of securing comparable data on Africa and Asia, but indicators are of persistent poverty and underemployment. A review of the employment effects of reforms shows that except for Sri Lanka, the entire South Asian region experienced declining employment growth especially in the private organized sector during the 1980s and 1990s. Even the Far Eastern economies, like Taiwan, experienced the periodic pressures of relocation of capital as a result of globalization; some 174,000 companies ceased to operate and left their workers without jobs or back wages and severance pays between 1993 and 1995. More than half the workers were women and had to seek lower paid employment further down the flexible work chain or remain unemployed.[15] The post-1997 Asian crisis had drastic impact on employment and its quality.

New evidence of an endemic and systemic problem of employment and more significantly 'decent employment' in the global economy has come in the report of the 95th session of the International Labour Conference held in Geneva from 30 May to 16 June 2006. It notes that from 1995 to 2005 the number of unemployed people worldwide increased from 157.3 million to 191.8 million, an increase of 21.9 per cent. The people with no work at all is thus at its highest ever and has upped the unemployment rate from 6 to 6.3 per cent of the global workforce. This is happening despite robust global economic growth. Half of the unemployed are youth between the ages of 15-24 years as the global economy is failing to deliver new jobs for those entering the job markets.[16]

The global production system firmly entrenched by the twenty-first century has some 65,000 multinational enterprises with foreign affiliates as the main actors behind these new production systems. They organize global supply chains that link firms across countries to enterprises in the unorganized sectors, to outsourcing subcontractors who work outside the factory system and among networks of home workers. Usually the high-end/high-value-added work like R&D, design, brand building is undertaken in the developed countries while the lower end work is outsourced globally with minimal manufacturing and inventory costs in JIT delivery systems. Global production systems are the most pronounced in high-tech industries like electronics, semiconductors, components and parts; in the service sector like software, information technology-enabled back office operations, call-centre services and in labour-intensive consumer goods industries like garments, shoes, costume jewellery/trinkets. The global production systems are also extending to consumer durables. All this has occurred without the framework of global rules to govern FDI. The impact of this reorganization has been profound for the labour markets across the globe.[17] Changes in one part reverberate in another rapidly.

Since the mid-1970s the trend in all industrialized capitalist countries has been (a) export of lower skill jobs to less-regulated/low-cost regions, (b) shift from high-wage factory work to low-wage service occupations for increasing percentage of workforce, (c) increase in part-time and temporary employment, and (d) preponderance of low-wage women workers in occupations with expanding employment. This trend is likely to repeat itself in the organized segments of labour markets in the developing world with some noticeable differences since the developing countries had a small, organized, high-wage, modern sector and a large unorganized/informal, low-wage, low-capital and primitive technology sector. The shifts in patterns of labour demand driven by low costs could lead to an expansion of the latter.

The ILO had estimated that in the last twenty years of the twentieth century one-third more people would enter the labour force each year, at a time of shrinking employment worldwide compared to the period 1950-75 when employment was expanding.

An analysis of this background by different sources indicates prospects of deteriorating job security, e.g. even the OECD reports that the structural conditions of working class in developed and in due course developing countries, following the capitalist system, have deteriorated rapidly as they are forced to bear the brunt of restructuring in their societies.[18]

1.2 Unemployment Trends and Insecurity

Unemployment trends in the last quarter of the twentieth century in major OECD countries are described, and coupled with insecurity.

1.2.1 *Trends*

One might assume that the rate of unemployment and the absolute number of unemployed alone would be the most important indicator of the level of workforce insecurity. But the relationship is more complex. Unemployment rates tend to hide the deterioration in the terms and conditions of employment, the stagnation in real wage rates, the more aggressive policies of human resource management, and the diminished status of workers' trade unions for those who are employed.

The last decades of the twentieth century were a period of such intense change in the terms and conditions of employment in the OECD countries – most, if not all, of the labour market certainty of long post-war boom were undermined. A specter of mass unemployment was haunting the OECD countries.

Whatever be the manifestation of unemployment – social exclusion, stagnant real wages, and inequality – it was evident that on a broad canvas, things were getting worse and some of the evidence presented strongly indicates that the official figures may have substantially underestimated the problem.[19] Labour markets had become characterized by increasing uncertainty, insecurity, risk and inequality. At an aggregate scale there was a distinctive international geography to the OECD job problem. The growth of unemployment has been much more pronounced in the EU compared to the USA and Japan. These international differences have been the focus of analytic scrutiny by economists like Burgess (1994), Freeman (1993), and Krugman (1994).[20] The problem has also been studied by leading international organizations like the European Commission (1993), OECD (1994), and ILO (1995).[21] And within the EU there have been marked regional differences in unemployment rate. In the 1950s and 1960s the unemployed in OECD averaged less than 10 million. In the mid-1970s recession they stood at 18 million, by early 1980s the number rose to 30 million; and by 1990 to 35 million. Thus in two decades – from 1972 to 1992 – the number of unemployed tripled. The unemployment rates in the EU, USA and Japan are given below in Table 1.1. That the problem was and remains serious in its implication can be gauged from the tenor of the Green Paper on European Social Policy: 'No democratic state or union of states can function without efforts towards economic cohesion and solidarity between poor and rich regions and between fortunate and disadvantaged social groups'.[22] Years later the Director General's report of the 95th International Labour Conference (2006), commenting on the historically high absolute number of unemployed globally, says that 'the absence of work, the quality of work, voice at work, continued gender discrimination, and unacceptably high youth unemployment are at the heart of politics today'.

As per Table 1.1, the unemployment rate in the USA in 1985 was 8.1 per cent; by 1990 it was 5.2 per cent and by 1994 it was 5.4 per cent, reflecting a marginal decline during the decade. In 2005 official unemployment rates stood at 5 per cent having dipped to as low as 4.2 per cent in 2001. The only country to have reverted

Table 1.1: Unemployment Rates in EU, USA, Japan 1970-94, Over the Period of Restructuring

Country	*1970*	*1975*	*1980*	*1985*	*1990*	*1994*
Japan	1.1	1.8	2.0	2.4	2.1	3.0
EU	2.4	3.6	5.1	8.7	7.6	10.8
USA	5.8	8.4	6.5	8.1	5.2	5.4

Source: OECD (1994).

back to the 1970s level of unemployment by the mid-1990s was the USA. Much has been said about the flexibility of labour markets in the USA and the declining strength of unions, which has made this lower rate of unemployment possible.

In the UK unemployment rate in 1985 was 12 per cent of the labour force; by 1990 it dropped to 7 per cent, and by 1995 it was 8 per cent of the labour force. The UK labour market has moved more rapidly towards flexibility than its European counterparts, especially French and German.

Unemployment rate for Japan in 1985 was 2.5 per cent; by 1990 it had fallen to 2 per cent and rose to 3 per cent by 1995. Japan has also grappled with the problem and slowly adapted to the need for greater flexibility since then.

1.2.2 *Some Indications from USA: Restructuring Impact on the Labour Market*

Four million jobs were added in the US during the period 1958-68 but 2.3 million jobs disappeared in manufacturing since 1980, and, most of these were in high-wage organized sectors. A labour department study argued that industrial workers were earning more than their counterparts in the service sector but the work-force was shrinking. In newer industries such as electronics, assembly jobs were few and low paying.[23] In 1994 the official unemployment stood at 6.5 per cent. Many economists regarded unemployment at such levels necessary to prevent inflation. In a February 1994 poll, one-fourth of respondents said that they had personally experienced lay-offs, pay-cuts, reduction in hours worked in the previous two years and two-fifth worried that they may face the same in the next two years.[24] But Martin Feldstein of Harvard University, then head of the National Bureau of Economic Research, stated, 'we are essentially at full employment today', but according to the MIT economist Lester Thurow: 'in the USA if one adds together the officially unemployed, discouraged workers who have stopped actively looking for work, and those part-time workers who want fulltime job, 15 per cent of the labour force is looking for work'.[25]

Writing in 2005, Paul Krugman also critically examined the official statistics on employment from the Labour Statistics Department, which state that the US economy had fully recovered from a recession it experienced after 2001 when unemployment rate was 4.2 per cent.[26] This rose to a peak of 6.3 per cent in 2003 and then fell to 5 per cent in 2005. However, average weekly earnings have been flat for 2000-5. When the economy is generating jobs, economists expect to see strong growth in the wage rates, pay rolls reported by employers, and in the number of people who say that they have jobs. But American economists are seeing none of these corollaries of a tightening job market yet. In the same article Krugman quotes a study by Katharine Bradbury of the Federal Reserve Bank of Boston who suggests that millions of Americans who should be in the workforce are not. The addition of these hypothetical participants would raise the unemployment rate by one to over three percentage points. These Americans are not participating in the labour market. The reasons could fall into two categories. One that many more people would continue to look for jobs if they still rationally expected to find decent work – these are referred to as 'discouraged workers'. On the other hand, workers may be staying away from the job market to improve their education and skills so as to improve their wages in future. The reported rise in the number of middle-aged workers dropping out of the workforce (hence the declining WFPR) to go back to school, and the declining real wage rate for the unskilled may be pointers to the fact that low-end jobs are disappearing from the economy and new jobs which can be regarded as 'decent' are growing only in the higher skill segments. And that was before the Great Recession of 2008 set in. Many of these tends in the labour market got aggravated after that and are discussed in the Epilogue.

1.2.3 *Some Indications from UK: Impact of Restructuring on the Labour Market*

In his presidential address to the Royal Economic Society, Stephan Nickell observed that relative poverty (measured as percentage of people earning less than 60 per cent of the median household income, adjusted for composition of households) has risen massively in Britain since 1979, mainly because of increasing worklessness and growing income dispersion.[27] Proportion of people living in working age households, who are poor rose from 13 per cent in 1979 to 24.4 per cent in 1999.[28] The economic force underlying this is the significant shift in demand against the unskilled. Over 20 per cent of the population in the working age has very low skills (close to illiterate). This increases worklessness among the low skilled, depresses their wages and later reduces their children's opportunities for improving skills. This is reflected in the fact that in the UK, if an individual was not employed in 1996, the probability of his living in a household where no one else worked was 50 per cent higher than in any other OECD country; and 70 per cent of workers in poor households are low paid. The irony is that compared to 1979, higher levels of poverty, worklessness and relatively low unemployment rates coexist now in the UK.

Human capital theories indicate that job termination incurs a permanent loss of firm, specific human capital, while an unemployment spell not only precludes the accumulation but may also bring about a deterioration of general skills. Future earnings in employment will therefore be lower than if unemployment had not occurred. In cases where productivity is not easily measurable or observable, future employers may offer lower wages based on past unemployment as a signal of low productivity. So the best predictor of an individual's future risk of unemployment is his past history of unemployment: which tends to bring future unemployment for individuals. This phenomenon is referred to as Unemployment Scarring.[29]

Early studies of Unemployment Scarring were done in the USA and focused on the effects of job displacements on subsequent earnings. They originated in the aftermath of the massive job losses particularly in manufacturing which followed the overvaluing of the dollar in the mid-1980s. Special surveys collected data on pre- and post-displacement earnings, job characteristics and on the intervening period of unemployment. These gave clear prima facie evidence of reduction in post-displacement earnings. However, there was no corresponding information for those who had not lost their jobs. Hence there was no control group to base inferences on. Such studies were later done in Britain to study the scarring effect of unemployment of men in the 1980s and 1990s.

The issue gained social and economic significance following the changes that swept the labour markets in the 1980s, which persisted and are visible twenty years later. The level of unemployment rose sharply in the period 1979-81 as a result of sharp increase in redundancies and fall in recruitment. The duration of unemployment spells lengthened along with an increase in long-term unemployment. By 1986, half of the men aged over twenty-five years on the unemployment register had been unemployed for more than a year. The experience gradually spread to groups not earlier exposed to it – managers, professionals, skilled craftsmen, and supervisory staff. The brunt of the recession of the early 1980s was however borne by the traditional manufacturing industry. By the early 1990s, the recession impacted the service industry and as a consequence of these developments, redundancy became widely perceived as a risk to employment. This came with a rise in male inactivity and growth of female part-time jobs. By 1998 the ratio of males in the working age who were inactive (2.3 million) was more than double the number unemployed (1 million).

The findings of the wage scarring studies are based on different data sources like:

1. British Panel Household Survey (BPHS), which is a random sample of 55,000 households undertaken every year since 1991.
2. New Earnings Survey Panel (NESP), which is a 1 per cent random sample of earnings of all employees in employment, in the pay week of April each year.

3. Joint Unemployment and Vacancies Operating Systems (JUVOS). This is a 5 per cent sample of claimants of all unemployment-related benefits. The NESP samples are linked to JUVOS.

Wage scarring studies find significant wage penalties to employment interruption in line with American evidence.[30] The wage penalty is estimated to be about 6 per cent during the first year of re-entry, increasing within the next three years of the same employment spell to over 14 per cent before declining. The second study finds a weaker impact of unemployment on subsequent earnings; an average earning setback of 10 per cent eroded over two years. But unemployment duration has a higher impact on future wages.[31]

The costs of unemployment, especially long spells and repeated unemployment, are greater than the immediate loss of earnings, and are therefore higher than just the loss of immediate earnings. An example will be the deterioration in skills. The policy options being recommended by the studies are:

1. Macro-economic policies should focus on increasing levels of employment since that is the first best attack on scarring.
2. In-work benefits should be provided to firms to promote employment and skills.
3. Time limit of welfare measures should be fixed to encourage workers to seek re-employment or training.
4. Improve educational attainment and assist transition from school to work of 'at risk' groups of men/women to prevent repeated rounds of unemployment and poor labour market outcomes.

1.2.3 *Some Restructuring Impact on the Labour Market: Indications from Japan*

Researchers while analysing the sign of revival in the Japanese economy, which was in recession since the 1990s, say that one of the main reasons for revival is the change in the terms and conditions of employment.[32] Japan was earlier known, rather exaggeratedly, as a country of lifetime employment. In return for loyalty and commitment, big employers typically offered a lifetime of commitment to their workers, with generous fringe benefits, pay rise according to age and seniority and association with company unions. Even after the recession set in, most big and medium companies continued in the old ways, with the employees asked to take pay and bonus cuts rather than job loss, with the result that new recruitment slowed down, e.g. less than half new graduates were hired in 2003 as against 1997. Eventually changes in the employment laws enabled firms to exercise flexibility by hiring labour part-time or on contracts. The law treated full-time contracts up to three years as temporary. A part-time worker on average gets less than half the full-time hourly wages. Lowest contract workers can expect hourly wages between 6-800 yen per hour, which is well below the British legal minimum wage and the cost of living in Japan is one of the highest in the world. In 1990, non-regular workers made up 18.8 per cent of the labour force, while in 2005 the figure was 30 per cent, which in Japan with a workforce of 65 million means roughly 20 million people.

These workers are predominantly women, young and low-skilled. Canon, a successful electronics firm, still firmly maintains a lifetime commitment for its core workers, who account for only 30 per cent of the staff, while 70 per cent of the factory staff works on non-regular terms, up from 50 per cent in 2000.[33] And this was only 10 per cent in 1990. In 1998 worker-pay equaled 73 per cent of corporate earnings, and by 2004 the proportion had dropped to 64 per cent. As long the wages were falling and the new employment being created was of cheaper and less secure sort, there was little chance that the economic growth would be sustainable, because lower wage meant declining domestic demand. Labour flexibility came at a price; while it boosted profits it weakened the consumption demand. In recent years, households choosing to save less of their income have sustained this demand. In 1990, the Japanese were saving one-third of their disposable income; in 2005 they were saving only 5 per cent. It was only in the April 2005 employment data that the full-time employment began to grow faster than non-regular employment and even this, partly, represents growth in full-time contract work.

1.2.4 *Common Long-term Symptoms*

Globalization and restructuring has produced some common and pervasive symptoms over the long term in OECD countries.

TECHNOLOGY HAS A PERVASIVE IMPACT ON RESTRUCTURING OF ECONOMY AND WORK

Peter Drucker writes, rather provocatively, that in the post-industrial society, labour is really not an asset; it is neither an imperative ingredient nor a core input for manufacturing operations.[34] Labour as an expendable commodity is rendered surplus or shifted to low-wage jobs of uncertain duration – part-time or temporary. Women have entered low-wage jobs where employment expansion is high. In this process the capital gains in profitability while the workers consistently lose income. He says: that in the 1960s the integrated steel industry (ore to steel) in America employed 120,000 workers. Within a decade this had been reduced to 20,000 workers without affecting steel production, which in fact slightly increased. A full 83 per cent of the workforce became redundant. This was done by closing some older, unprofitable, so-called 'smoke stack' factories, introducing a new equipment, but primarily by introducing a new generation of automated and high-optimized steel plants. Such technology breakthroughs are a creation of sustained endeavour of high-skilled knowledge workers. He further observes that since the output of these mills is higher it reflects a productivity gain of about 700 per cent in a decade.

Drucker further notes that the mini steel mills that start with scrap iron are five to six times more efficient and he cites one such mill that employed only 90 skilled specialists. He sums up by noting that the continued productivity growth requires highly skilled and highly formally educated specialists. The others will be needed in reasonable numbers but in secondary and tertiary roles, where they will accordingly attract low wages.

In Japan where the total population of 120 million is expected to shrink to 86 million and grow old, the optimal strategy is to outsource the manufacturing to developing countries with guarantees for quality and timely deliveries, and to concentrate on marketing, R&D, and design at home; namely the high value-added niches of the postmodern economy. Given that smart design can ensure that manufacturing operations need low-skilled or unskilled workers, and as long as there is an excess of these in the developing countries, the Japanese foresee no risk in securing the services of cheap overseas labour. In fact, they advocate that it is a better and a more responsible way of supporting the development processes there.

Competing with labour anywhere in the world simply means, over a period – however long or however gradual the process – establishment of global average income commensurate with skill levels. The transition cost must be borne by the workers both in the developed and developing countries.

SERVICE WORK

in most OECD countries the service sector seems to be the one creating most jobs. In the USA, based on its Department of Labour's Bureau of Labour Statistics reports, by 1986, 81 per cent of new jobs were in the services compared with 66 per cent in 1985 and 52 per cent in 1984.[35] This trend accelerated in 1987 when 94 per cent of new jobs were in services. Since 1970 three-fifths of the 8.1 million new jobs, service and non-service, have paid $7,000 a year or less. This compels employees to seek more than one job at any time. Such trends have been confirmed by many time series studies which point out that goods output accounted for 65 per cent of the GDP and 38 per cent of employment in 1939; since then it has fallen 54 per cent of the GDP and 28 per cent of employment in 1979. In 2004 only 43 per cent of the GDP and 17 per cent of employment originated in the goods producing industry.[36]

In manufacturing the percentage of service jobs as opposed to production jobs has increased. In 1978 it was 23 per cent in USA, 35 per cent in FRG, and 25 per cent in Sweden. In the 1980s, non-production workers made up 80 per cent of the new employment in manufacturing in the USA. Even though automation in banking, finance, marketing, insurance and other white-collar job-areas has resulted in requiring fewer people for the same work, these growing sectors remain the main new job creators. With falling wages, women have entered in low-end service jobs like data entry and health care. The trend is relentless and global. The share of global industrial employment was 28.7 per cent in 1995 and fell to 24.8 in 2005. Over the same period the global service employment has increased from 34.4 to 39 per cent. In developed countries service employment increased by 5.3 percentage points, to equal 71.4 per cent.[37]

INFORMAL SECTOR WORK

As a result of restructuring, in 1988, one-fourth of all employed were part-time workers in the USA and of these 17 per cent wanted full-time work but could not find it. Most part-time workers are in the production sector, though a third of jobs in the retail and service sector are also part-time. Attention has been drawn to the need to expand the limits of National Income Accounting from goods production to service measurement, informal sector and non-market activities. Part-time is also the trend in other OECD countries, in 1988, 12 per cent of all employed in the FRG were part-time and 25 per cent in Sweden. In Japan it is termed as the 'secret weapon' of its competitive success.[38] After restructuring and after a 15-year slowdown in Japan the number of non-regular workers rose from 18.8 per cent of the labour force in 1990 to 30 per cent.[39] Temporary workers are technically the same as part-time workers except that they are entitled to fewer benefits.

Labour markets in the OECD countries had become increasingly segmented into core (stable) and peripheral (insecure) workforce with widening inequality in skill, training and income, and marked with the gradual disappearance of manufacturing from the high-wage into low-wage countries. In the low-wage LDCs, even up to the 1980s, the growth of the informal sector was looked upon as a healthy sign of growing non-agricultural economic activity and employment. But by the late 1990s, it was clear that normalization was a critical component of globalization with its low-wage, high-insecurity implications. Its main effect was to undermine organized labour and facilitate the development of 'disorganized capitalism'.[40]

WOMEN WORKERS

In 1985 women in all OECD countries occupied 60-85 per cent of service jobs, often to counter the falling real-income of the family. Their percentage in the labour force rose from 36.5 per cent in 1960 to 54 per cent in 1985 with married women between 25-34 years of age accounting for the most increase from 28 to 65 per cent.[41] According to the Bureau of Labour Statistics, female labour force participation rates in the USA rose from about 34 per cent in 1950 to 59 per cent in 2004. The pattern is similar to one witnessed in Indonesia during the Asian crisis of 1997-9, where wages fell by 41 per cent but the overall employment rose with women joining in large numbers.[42]

In LDCs, over 80 per cent of workers in new industries are women, mostly between 16 and 24 years of age. They get about half the wage of men and work the longest hours. Many studies have chronicled the near subsistence wages and poor working conditions. Most countries have so-called 'underground' economies that operate outside the state social security, minimum wage, and legal employment rules. And often these are integrated with the formal sectors and serve as a mechanism for lowering the latter's costs.[43] Studies show that as the labour shifts from rural to urban areas and feeds into this 'underground' sector, so do the workers from better jobs when they are laid off. The real-wages fall regardless of the state of the national economy.

WORK AND WAGES

Wages in production are the highest, significantly lower in the services and surprisingly least for workers in very high-tech electronics manufacturing units and garment industries. Gains won during prosperous years are lost during recession and long spells of unemployment, which only highlights the treatment of labour as an expendable commodity. Capital, pursuing profits determinedly makes higher-wage jobs redundant with the introduction of automation or relocating itself to cheaper areas. At a social level, the issues of income distribution come down to the social holding patterns of the capital or the operative politics of income distribution. Democracies in the sense of government by the people, of the people, and for the people have not secured security or stability (only spells of comfort) for the workers who obviously constituted an overwhelming majority – their vulnerability has endured. Governments by and large have been pro-profit.

In the USA, real wages rose until 1973, and then declined for the next two decades. In 1980 they were at the 1960 levels and more than 12 per cent below the peak of 1972-3. And these were expected to fall further during 1987.[44] Unions having to make concessions on wages and benefits numbered 159 in 1982 and 430 in 1983. In 1982, some 38 per cent unionized workers took wage cuts and 15 per cent had no increase. Unions in France and Italy made similar concessions. When businesses restructure with automation or closure, wages fall and benefits shrink, as seen in all OECD countries.[45] The trends of flat or declining real wages are persisting in robust economic growth situations and well into 2006.

WORK AND PRODUCTIVITY

Productivity has been viewed as a question either of how much more can be produced with a given amount of labour (cost), or, when the demand is slack how labour costs can be reduced. This can also be viewed as a measure of 'rate of exploitation'. The US still had the highest absolute productivity, though the growth rate in productivity has been declining over the last two decades of the twentieth century. Of the ten official causes of decline in productivity only three relate to workers – the so-called declining work ethics, equal opportunity law, and the union 'featherbedding'. Recurring investment is supposed to be the key factor in raising productivity and decline in investment is attributed to high taxes, wages and falling profits. However in OECD countries, there has been a marked rise in mergers and takeovers rather than fresh investments.

The earlier American advantage in productivity has diminished. The labour productivity in foreign manufacturing subsidiaries was 92 per cent of the USA during the 1970s. In some it was even higher because of the intensity of work (long hours of work, 10 to 11 hours or more per day). According to OECD, the technologies transferred tend to be the most efficient ones, because in some developing countries with a much disciplined workforce, the equipment can be operated longer. The work hours tend to be 20-30 per cent more than the OECD average. For instance, the Korean working week has varied between 50-60 hours per week over recent years.

WORK AND UNIONS

Restructuring of employment had major impact on labour organization. OECD wrote in 1995: 'Labour power as measured by union membership and strike activity has fallen to its lowest post-war levels in most countries'.[46] By 1983, unionized industries had the highest unemployment and more companies discouraged unions. Surprisingly one French union official noted that the socialist governments had an effect of reducing labour protest against austerity measure. As he stated: 'Ten years ago, if we had seen the kind of layoffs we're seeing now or the cuts in purchasing power, we would have shut down the big companies and waged war on the capitalists – and tried to change the government to the boot. Today there's an appreciation that a reaction like that doesn't fit the time.' Another official of the Trade Union Institute in Brussels observed in 1985, 'Somehow the governments in Europe feel now that they ought to be tougher. Many of the problems would exist even if there were socialist governments in every capital, because the economic crisis cannot be escaped.'[47]

While labour organizations have the potential of strengthening forces of production, redistribution and liberating workers from dangerous and monotonous work, the technology and capital now, as in the past, is used as a weapon against the labour. And if the cost of labour-substituting technology falls as fast as the cost of labour, it will continue to replace labour.

One study of the US Congress highlighted the inability of weakened unions to redistribute incomes; it concluded that the holdings of the top half of the population jumped from 15 per cent of total wealth in 1976, to about 38 per cent in 1983, i.e. it more than doubled in just seven years of neoliberal policies.[48] Their effort to keep the labour flexible and wages low for reasons of profit stands in sharp contrast.

Once again the trend of declining union membership is relentless in the OECD countries and recent ILO statistics confirm it, for example, union membership in the USA declined from 15 per cent in 1995 to 13 per cent in 2005.

For the foreseeable future labour can continue to expect the ongoing pressures because business and governments are in agreement on the future directions that globalization should take.

1.3 Background: Post-Liberalization Years in India

The policy package of liberalization, privatization and globalization (that led to economic restructuring and eventually changed the labour markets of major OECD countries in the 1980s) came to India in the 1990s. Some of these policies, initiated in the 1980s, had intensified the process of domestic deregulation and competition. The impact of these policies on the Indian economy has been widely debated and the verdict is mixed. The impact on employment and the labour markets is not entirely encouraging. Some symptoms and trends similar to those observed in the OECD countries can be discerned with respect to the organized sector employment. This is the only sector, however small, that had striven for and obtained some rights and a measure of security.

Popularly known as the Washington/Neo-liberal Consensus, these policies have common ingredients globally:

1. Opening the economy to world trade and financial flows through reduced tariff barriers and financial sector liberalization – the

peak tariff rates were reduced from 300 per cent in 1990 to 30 per cent in 2002.
2. Privatization of the public sector.
3. Deregulation of the commodity and factor markets to increase competition.
4. Regulation to maintain macro-economic stability by controlling inflation and fiscal deficit.

Tables 1.2 and 1.3 will underscore the opening up of the Indian economy. As can be seen, the rates of growth of both exports and imports have more than doubled as a result of changes in the external sector policies. The rate of increase in imports continue to exceed exports, and the trade deficit which in 1991 was US$ 5,932 million mounted to US$ 14,306 million in 2003-4. Exports as a percentage of GDP increased from 4.6 to 10.4 per cent. The

Table 1.2: Rate of Change in the Value of India's Foreign Trade since 1991

Year	*Rate of change in export (in per cent)*	*Rate of change import (in per cent)*
1990-1	9.2	13.5
1991-2	-1.5	-19.4
1992-3	3.8	12.7
1993-4	20.0	6.5
1994-5	18.4	22.9
1995-6	20.8	28.0
1996-7	5.3	6.7
1997-8	4.6	6.0
1998-9	-5.1	2.2
1999-2000	10.8	17.2
2000-1	21.0	1.7
2001-2	-1.6	1.7
2002-3	20.3	19.4
2003-4	21.1	27.3

Source: Government of India, *Economic Survey 2004-5*, New Delhi, 2005. Statement 7.1 (B), p. S79.

Table 1.3: Exports as Percentage of GDP

Exports as per cent of GDP	
Period	*Per cent of GDP*
1980-1	4.6
1990-1	5.8
1992-3	7.3
1993-4	8.3
1994-5	8.3
1995-6	9.1
1996-7	8.9
1997-8	8.7
1998-9	8.3
1999-2000	8.4
2000-1	9.8
2001-2	9.4
2002-3	10.3
2003-4	10.4

Source: Statistical Outline of India, Tata Services, Department of Economics and Statistics, Mumbai.

Note: The final figures may differ from balance of payment data, owing to different systems of evaluation.

net inflows of FDI grew from $ 586 million to 3,420 million (584 per cent) and FII from $ 1,665 to $ 10,918 million (656 per cent).

India's total merchandise trade as a percentage of GDP increased from 29 per cent in 2004-5 to almost 42 per cent in 2013-14. Exports grew from 12 to 17 per cent of GDP. The process of external sector growth continued after 2008 but with increasing uncertainty (indiabudget.nic.in/es2014). The secular trends have not changed for example exports as percentage of GDP were 23.59 per cent in 2014. Having doubled as a percentage of GDP since 2004. Imports also increased as a percentage of GDP to their highest level in 2012 at 31.24 per cent according to World Bank estimates. Foreign Direct Investments at 1.66 per cent of GDP in 2014 had peaked at about 3.5 per cent of GDP in the period before the recession of 2008. Net foreign flows have also grown. Among

Table 1.4: Net Inflow in Capital Account in 1990s (Million US$)

Year	*Net-FDI*	*Net-FII*
1993-4	586	1,665
1995-6	1,954	2,009
1996-7	2,651	1,926
1998-9	2,380	-390
1999-2000	2,093	2,135
2001-2	4,734	1,505
2002-3	3,217	377
2003-4	3,420	10,918

Source: Government of India, Economic Survey 2004-5, New Delhi, 2005. Table 6.2, p. 109.

Note: As can be seen in Table 1.4, both FDI and FII increased after the policy change, with the FII showing a sharper rise.

countries with Current Account Deficit (CAD) India has the second largest foreign reserve after Brazil. Significantly 39 per cent of factor input in India's exports is labour, skilled and unskilled. Hence uncertainty in global markets is bound to be passed on to the labour market. Most scholars today describe the Indian economy as integrated into the world economy. This was not the case before 1991.

There are by now a number of studies that attempt to evaluate the impact of these and other policies associated with liberalization over a decade of its introduction. There is a lack of consensus, however, on the performance of the economy in the post-liberalization period, about the change in rates of growth, levels of poverty, inequality and on employment generation in the post- and pre-reform periods. The debate is also concerned with the extent of rise in the long-term trend rate of employment elasticity of growth before and after 1991. Contributions to this debate have come from several economists.[49] Some of these contributions are reviewed in the following sections.

1.4 Economic Reforms and its Impact on the Labour

Rapid pace of reforms in trade, FDI policy and industrial policy influences the production process in different sectors of the economy and also the structure of the economy. With growing competition, enterprises tend to focus more on increasing efficiency, reducing the cost of production, introducing new technologies, increasing the productivity of labour and reducing the cost of labour. As FDI inflows assume more importance there could be an intensification of these tendencies.[50] There is a shift in the demand for labour from the unskilled to the trainable and the skilled category. The structural shifts impact various segments of the labour market in different ways. Eventually they impact the quantity and quality of employment in different segments of the labour market. The trends are highlighted below.

The emerging overall evidence on employment has been both confused and dismal. One of the earliest influential papers on the sharp declining trend in workforce growth during the post-reform period reported in the 50th and 55th NSSO rounds, was by Sundram (2001).[51] His estimates suggested that based on Usual Principal and Subsidiary Status (UPSS), the workforce growth during the period 1993-2000 was 0.81 per cent as against a 1.75 per cent estimated growth of population. The constitution of several committees in a span from 2000-5 by the GOI is indicative of the concern.

Montek Singh Ahluwalia headed the first of these committees constituted in 1999, and in 2001 it submitted its findings 'Report of the Task Force on Employment Opportunities'. It emphasized the virtues of organized sector employment with the service sector taking the lead. It estimated that the growth rate of employment was at 0.98 per cent in the period 1993-2000. And it was 2.04 per cent in the period 1983-93 using NSSO data on UPSS employment.

In May 2002, the S.P. Gupta Committee submitted its report 'Special Group on Targeting Ten Million Employment Opportunities per Year'. It recommended a big push to the unorganized sector with agriculture at the core. It estimated a growth rate of employment of 1.07 per cent for the period 1993-2000. Based on the NSSO data on Current Daily Status (CDS), the growth rate was 2.7 per cent in the previous period of 1983-93.

A third group, 'Working Group on Employment Monitoring', headed by Y.K. Alag was set up. According to it, employment elasticity had fallen from 0.41 per cent in the period 1983-93, to 0.15 per cent in the 1993-2000 period. The comment of the GOI in this context is worth noting: 'the overall decline in the employment elasticity is to a large extent due not only to changes in the broad nine sector composition of output, but also in the inter sectoral composition and technology impacts of labour capital substitution. Capital intensity in the Indian economy in almost all the sectors including small unorganized and services appears to be increasing over time.'

These quoted studies have used data generated by the NSSO, preferring to use the concept and measurement of Usual Status Unemployment rather than the Weekly and Daily Status estimates. These studies also do not examine the absolute number of unemployed both in terms of the aggregated and the disaggregated state-level situations. They also do not examine more precisely the relationship between the rates of growth and the rate of unemployment. This is important if we are to rely on accelerated growth rates of 8-9 per cent to resolve the issues of unemployment as recommended by the Task Force on Unemployment (2001) of the Tenth Five Year Plan.

There has been some debate about the studies quoted above, both about the methodology and the implications. How much of the deceleration in the rate of growth of employment and absolute amounts of unemployment in the post-1991 period is a result of impact of globalization-related policies on the labour markets, and how much is due to the secular long-term trend?[52]

In this context the study by Baumik (2003) is important. The main sources of data used are the quinquennial survey on employment and unemployment as conducted by the NSSO.[53] Out of the six surveys conducted since 1972-3 following identical concepts and methodology, Baumik uses the Current Daily Status (CDS) data from the years 1983 (NSSO 38th round), 1993-4 (50th round), and 1999-2000 (55th round) to study the periods before and after liberalization. The conclusions of the study show that there has been a significant increase in the number of unemployed in the country in the post-liberalization period. The number of unemployed actually declined in the period, from 21.61 million in 1983 to 20.24 million in 1993. It increased to 26.43 million in 1999-2000. The increase at the all-India level in the absolute number of unemployed in the post-reform period has been visible across regions and sex of the labour force. The annual compound growth rate of the total unemployed was - 0.62 per cent in the pre-reform period; it became 4.55 per cent in the post-reform period. For rural India, the figures were -1.16 per cent in the pre-reform period, which increased to 5.13 per cent in the post-reform period; and the agricultural rural sector experienced a greater increase in this increased unemployment.

The NSDP growth rate in 9 out of the 15 observed states was higher in the post-reform years compared to the pre-reform period. But this rise was due to growth in the tertiary sector and to a smaller extent in the secondary sector. Further, in the pre-reform period, the states that had a higher rate of growth of NSDP had a lower growth rate of unemployment. But in the post-reform period the higher rates of growth of NSDP have not been associated with lower rates of growth of unemployment. What perhaps matters is the quality and composition of growth from the point of view of employment. Each region and sector will have to be examined for possible policy interventions to generate employment.

This conclusion is reinforced in another study done by Bhattacharya (2003), based on NSSO data using alternative measures of employment UPSS, CDS, and CWS. It indicates that while there was a mild acceleration in the output rate during the post-reform period, there has been a sharp deceleration in the employment growth rate during the same year.[54] Employment elasticities across all sectors changed for the worst, declining even in the primary sector besides in the secondary and tertiary sectors. This is evident at the all-India level with some variation across states.

In another paper Baumik (2003) uses NSSO data to study the trends and dimensions of casualization of the workforce nationwide and statewide over the period 1983-2002.[55] The rate of casualization is taken as another index of the health of the labour market. Increasing rate of casualization for any given rate of unemployment is an indication of the deteriorating quality of work. The casual worker is vulnerable to changing market conditions, is denied employment and income security and does not have the protection of labour legislation on wages or welfare. The casual worker is also likely to be in the informal sector, a low wage worker, frequently unemployed and poor.[56] The process of liberalization has also been linked to the process of casualization by researchers in India.[57] The NSSO data divides all usual status workers into three categories:

1. Self-employed (SE): Work on their own farm, or non-farm employed; profits represent their income.
2. Regular workers (RW): Work for others, get a regular wage/salary. No periodic renewal of contract.
3. Casual workers (CW): Work for others, get a periodic time or piece wage, subject to renewal of contract. Contract may be formal or informal.

The percentage distribution of workers by mode of employment at the all-India level reveals that more than half of all the workers have been self-employed but the percentage of SE workers has been showing a declining trend over the period 1983-2002 from 57.3 to 54.7 per cent. The percentage of regular workers remains almost unchanged. CW has increased from 28.9 to 31.1 per cent. In the rural areas where the percentage of SE is the highest, their percentage has declined from 61.5 per cent in 1983 to 58.3 per cent in 2002. The percentage of CW in rural India increased from 31.5 to 35.4 per cent in 2001-2.

In the urban areas both SE and RW are equally important. In 2002, 39.3 per cent workers were in RE and 43.2 per cent were SE. The percentage of RE did not change over the study period while the per cent of SE increased marginally. There was no marked increase in the casualization of labour in urban areas over the period; their percentage was 18.1 per cent in 1983, which declined to 17.5 per cent in 2001-2. The year-on-year fluctuations in the percentage of CW in the urban areas was significant but no trend of increase in the rate of casualization was noted. If the gender basis was examined, the data clearly revealed a relatively higher rate of casualization among women workers in both rural and urban areas.

The overall trend, i.e. rural plus urban, points to a higher rate of casualization after 1991 compared to the earlier period. Along with this, there was a decline in SE. It was visible in rural areas after the early 1990s and continued all through the following period. At the state level too, the trends were similar. The CW rate (CW to total workers) is correlated to levels of unemployment, poverty and diversification of the economy. Bhatt (2003) supports Baumik's conclusions. Based on data from the economic survey 2001-2 and NSSO rounds Bhatt concludes that the structure of workforce had changed; while the workforce in agriculture and allied activities had fallen, that in manufacturing had increased very marginally. There was also a sharp increase in the workforce in trade, hotels and restaurants over the period 1993-2000.[58] The share of casual workers rose from 26.3 per cent in 1990-1 (when it was its lowest in the years 1983-2000) to 32.4 per cent. The rise of casual workers in the organized sector, as well, was mainly due to the fact that most of the private organizations were appointing contract workers rather than regular salaried workers.

Endorsing this aspect of increasing casualization is another study.[59] Using data released in the 56th Round Unorganized Manufacturing Sector 2000-1 (UMS) the authors Unni and Rani (2003) compare the organized with the unorganized sector and note that although in the early stages of reforms (1989-95) the growth of value-addition, employment and capital in the organized manufacturing sector (OMS) as a whole surged ahead, in the later phase, growth rates declined (1994-2001). On the other hand, the growth of the unorganized manufacturing sector had peaked during the period 1978-85 and it tapered off in the early reform period. But in the later reform period 1994-2001 it was the UMS that picked up in terms of rate of growth of value-addition and employment. Employment, especially in the unorganized manufacturing sector (UMS), grew at 2.2 per cent per annum during the latter period while in the organized sector the growth of employment slowed down from 2.1 per cent in the early phase of liberalization to 0.7 per cent in the latter phase. Within the UMS there were interesting trends that may indicate increasing flexibilization and casualization.

There are three employment classes of the UMS:

i. Own account manufacturing enterprises (OAME): Enterprises with no hired workers on a regular basis.
ii. Non-directory manufacturing enterprises (NDME): One hired help at least, on a regular basis.
iii. Directory manufacturing enterprises (DME): Ten or more workers and at least one hired help.

Of the above three types, the rate of growth of value added and employment was the highest in the NDME in the later phase; their share in the total value added and employment in the unorganized sector also increased. Overall the share of large-size DMEs decreased. The growth of non-traditional NDME like chemicals, electrical machinery, fabricated metals, machinery, equipment, communication equipment auto parts, etc., were higher than the traditional NDME like food, paper, fibre, wood, etc. The non-traditional, however, registered a slower rate of growth of employment compared to the traditional NDME implying that they became less labour intensive. Further there was a slight increase in the proportion of women workers in the unorganized sector; there was also an increase in the proportion of part-time workers from 10.5 per cent in 1989-90 to 15.7 per cent in 2000-1. There was also an increase in the proportion of family labour from 64 to 70 per cent. Within the unorganized sector too, high performing industries increased the flexibility of their workforce as they tried to reduce costs.

Yet another micro-level case study by Panda (2001) that analysed the modality of this change was based on six firms in the automobile industry. It also concluded that the decline in the growth rate of employment after liberalization was evident in four out of the six firms.[60] In the case of the automobile industry including cars, light commercial, and medium and heavy commercial vehicles, the author defined the liberalization period from the early 1980s onwards. Thus in the study the regulated period was 1960 to 1979, while the post-regulation period was 1980-90. In the period after the 1980s firms enjoyed greater freedom with respect to expansion of capacity, degree of vertical integration, output mix, technological choice, foreign collaborations and import of capital goods. All the firms in the case study brought in new technology through foreign collaborations and imports. There was a major technological shift in this segment of the industry and its impact on rate of growth of employment was broadly negative. The growth in the levels of total factor productivity did not bring about an increase in the levels of employment of firms. Instead the growth in productivity was through labour saving. Changes in employment were sensitive to wage rates (measured as a ratio of wages to price of product) and degree of vertical integration of the firm.

Deshpande (2003), however, takes the opposite point of view using the NSSO and census figures, and she concludes that a comparison of unemployment rates averaged for the three NSSO surveys of 1977-8, 1983 and 1987-8 with the post-reform period surveys of 1993-4 and 1999-2000 show that average unemployment rates based on the workforce participation rates (WPR) were lower in the post-liberalization period by all standards of measurement, i.e. usual status, weekly status, current daily status.[61] The number of days on which UPS could get work if classified by daily status increased after 1991. WPR of rural men did not change while that of urban men increased in the post-reform period compared to the pre-reform period. While urban women were as active, the rural women were slightly less so. There was no major change in the education-specific WPR, although the participation of primary- and middle-school educated females increased in urban areas while there was a decline in the participation rates of educated rural women. Participation of children declined more rapidly during the period 1993-2000. Using census figures, Deshpande shows continuing shift of workforce away from agriculture. She also concludes that the real wages of both casual and regular workers increased faster in the 1990s than in the earlier sub-periods. She supports her argument with data relating to poverty estimates of the Planning Commission (GOI, 2002), which indicate that poverty levels fell more rapidly in the 1990s than the 1980s.

For the organized manufacturing sector employment, Nagaraj's (2004) most widely quoted study uses data from the Annual Survey of Industries (ASI) to show that there was practically no increase in employment during the 1980s in the sector, but in the 1990s there was a short boom for four years (1992-6) followed by retrenchment, and between 1995-6 and 2001-2, 1.3 million employees, i.e. 13 per cent of the workforce lost its jobs.[62] In principle, these job losses should get reflected in labour bureau data for 'layoffs and retrenchment'; but they do not because of increasing under-reporting. Thus employment in 2001-2 was roughly the same as it was eight years earlier and the use of contingent labour had increased. Some of these jobs shed could have reappeared in the unorganized informal sector, with growing subcontracting of production, and auxiliary services like transport, security, cleaning, and canteen. Therefore in the aggregate the extent of job losses may not be as severe as it appears in the first instance. But undoubtedly, these changes in the labour use do represent a fall in the quality of employment in terms of stagnant real wages and greater job insecurity.

According to the ASI, during 1980-2001 productivity per worker increased by over 100 per cent. The job losses were widespread across industries and states. Of 15 major industries 11, which were representing 80 per cent of the workforce, witnessed fall in employment during 1996-2001. Similarly employment declined in this sector in 13 out of 17 major states in India. It was mostly workers (low skilled) who lost their jobs while the employment of supervisory staff registered a steady gain. In the period 1980-2001 the annual growth rate of employment for workers was 0.9 and 2.2 per cent for supervisors. To provide a perspective, during 1981-2002, real gross value added (output) in registered manufacturing had grown at 7.9 per cent per year without any long-term acceleration after the 1991 reforms. Real wages (nominal wages deflated by consumer price index) had roughly stagnated during the 1990s, while the real emolument of supervisors went up by 77 per cent during 1992-2001.

Also during the post-1991 period the ceiling on managerial salary was removed and the survey clubbed managers with supervisors. Education and skill levels probably explain the divergence in earnings, reflecting the industrial sector growing in technological complexity and witnessing changes in the structural composition of the sector. The 15 per cent fall in employment in six years in latter half of the 1990s had occurred without the intervention of labour laws or large-scale resistance from the organized labour. This strengthens the argument that the claims of labour market rigidity do not appear to be valid. Also a rigid labour market could not have permitted rapid output and productivity growth with only a modest real wage growth (average per capita annual income growth in the 1990s was only 3 per cent). Shedding of excess labour was one of the initiatives of industrial restructuring in the face of increased domestic and external competition under the changed policy regime. And wage-rental ratio declined quite sharply from index value 100 in 1980 to 60 in 2001, with the sharpest drop in 1990 suggesting rapid modernization of and diversification in the production structure. This can also contribute to explaining the increase in labour productivity in the organized manufacturing sector. Table 1.5 underlines the observations made above about rising capital intensity and productivity but only a modest growth in real incomes.

Yet another comprehensive review of the depressing impact of economic reforms on the labour market and social security in India which endorses the views of a majority of scholars in the field is offered in by Panchamukhi et al. (2004).[63]

In this background of globalization and structural changes, unease about the direction of labour market changes pervades the commentary of the international agencies and individual researchers in a range of countries.[64] This perspective is a coherent set of statements about the nature, causes, and effects of recent changes in employments relation summed up as the 'Insecurity Thesis'. The central proposition of the thesis as mentioned earlier is that employment and income insecurity are deepening and widening in the labour market. This thesis includes amongst its key propositions that the economic risk of increased competition

Table 1.5: Performance of Organized Manufacturing Sector 1981-2001

	1981	*1991*	*2000-1*	*Per cent change 1981-91*	*Per cent change 1991-2001*
Number of workers in million	5.5	5.7	5.7	3.6	-
Real wages/worker Index	00	18.2	34.0	18.2	13.1
Product wage/worker	100	165.4	210	65.4	27.2
Wage Rental ratio	100	80.6	60.6	-19.4	-24.8
Labour productivity index	100	219.1	395.7	119.1	80.6
Capital stock/worker	100	183.3	423.8	83.3	131.2
Per capita net national product	145.2	198.5	278.1	36.7	40.1

Source: Annual Survey of Industry as quoted by R. Nagraj – 'Fall in Organized Manufacturing Employment'.

Notes: 1. Workers are defined by the ASI to include all persons employed directly or through any agency whether for wages or not and engaged in any manufacturing process or maintaining any part of machinery or the premises or any other kind of work connected with the manufacturing process incidental or related to the subject of the process.

2. The labour engaged in repair and maintenance of fixed assets for own-use of the factory is included. Similarly workers employed for generating electricity, producing coal, etc., are included. Excluded from this are supervisors, managers, administrative staff, storekeepers, and personnel in welfare, sales, purchase and security staff.

is being transferred increasingly from employers to employees through shortened job tenures, and contingent employment and remuneration. That insecurity is damaging to long-term economic performance through its promotion of employment relationship founded on opportunism, mistrust, and low commitment, and the emergence of an insecure workforce imposes a cost on both the individual firm and the society. These and associated claims constitute a deeply critical assessment of current labour market changes and adherents of the thesis have proposed a variety of radical reforms to reverse or mitigate the perceived slide towards insecure employment. The hypothesis is reconnoitered more comprehensively in the following chapters (Ch. 3).

1.5 Background to Sample Study

The purpose of the present study is to interrogate the 'Insecurity Thesis' in the Indian context. The situation in India, like in other developing countries, is such that over 90 per cent of the workforce is employed in the unorganized sector where uncertain tenures, contingent employment and remunerations are the norm; the study, none the less for reasons given later, focuses on the organized sector workers. Methodologically the study attempts to objectify and measure insecurity from the worker's point of view. In doing so support has been taken from many studies undertaken in OECD countries,[65] the case being that the modernization agenda in developing countries is closely linked to the expansion of the organized sector. If liberalization and globalization is creating pressures to reverse the trend as far as employment in the organized sector is concerned, then the implications of the phenomenon for the workers and the labour market at large must be evaluated.

The organized sector workers in India represent the cream of the workforce in terms of job security, skills and training necessary for a modern enterprise. The study based on a sample survey of manufacturing and service sector workers in the Greater Mumbai (GM) region and Thane, is centred entirely on the workers in the organized-registered sector. The sample frame was first provided by the tables on Distribution of Factories and Average Daily Employment by major Groups and Regions in Greater Mumbai - 1992 provided by the Director of Industrial Safety and Health, MS, Mumbai and the tables on Distribution of Establishments and Employment Therein by Wards – 1994 sourced from the Municipal Corporation of Greater Mumbai. The study uses the term 'Factory' as defined by the Annual Survey of Industries, 'Establishment' as listed by the BMC, 'Bank' as scheduled by RBI, and 'Registered Companies' as registered with the Registrar of Companies.

The survey using the questionnaire method and firm-based sampling seeks to measure the experience of insecurity, since

1991, among workers, lower administrative staff like clerks, sales staff, all below the level of supervisors in the factory and below the management cadre in the establishments. It also attempts to measure their current state of insecurity (2005). Besides this, to further probe the 'Insecurity Hypothesis', the questionnaire seeks to evaluate the state of human resource management at the firm level and the condition of employee unions. These two are the most significant associational variables determining insecurity.

Skill formation is, now, generally accepted as the main collective goal of the economic policy and an effective system of vocational education and training is viewed as a necessary condition for the maintenance of competitive advantage in the context of increased global competition. Competitive advantage can be lost even as wages rise in an industry and work can be relocated to other countries. The speed at which this may occur increases under the WTO regime. It is possible to introduce compensatory restructuring, provided the period over which industry loses its comparative advantage is long enough to introduce new industries, products, technologies and skills necessary in the workforce. The 'Insecurity Hypothesis' suggests that more contingent employment relationship actually inhibits on-the-job skill formation.[66] It may also inhibit the ability of the individual worker to invest in general continued education in the absence of a supportive institutional infrastructure and social security nets. The questionnaire in the present study seeks information about the acquisition of additional education, skills and training both on and off the job and relates this to the state of insecurity of the worker.

Since the survey is based in Mumbai some background about the state and the metropolis is obligatory to indicate its suitability as a location for such a survey.

1.5.1 *Indications from Maharashtra and Mumbai Metropolitan Region (MMR)*

Growth rate of aggregate employment in the state of Maharashtra by Current Daily Status (CDS) was 2.86 per cent in the pre-reform period of 1983-94 and fell to 1.26 per cent in the post-reform period of 1993-2000. By Current Weekly Status (CWS), the rate was 2.76 per cent, and fell to 1.53 per cent over the same periods. And by the UPSS it was 2.29 per cent and 1.05 per cent in the pre- and post-reform period. This is a clear indication of a decline in employment growth. Growth of primary sector employment by CDS was 2.86 per cent in the pre- and -0.21 per cent in the post-reform period. By CWS measure the growth of primary sector employment was 2.81 per cent and 0.36 per cent in the respective periods. By UPSS it was 1.33 and 0.14 per cent. Growth of manufacturing sector employment by CDS was 0.60 and 4.42 per cent. By CWS it was 0.81 and 2.13 per cent in the respective periods. By UPSS measures it was 2.53 and 1.64 per cent in the same periods. The decline was also evident in the tertiary sector. As per the CDS employment was growing at 4.31 per cent in the pre-reform period 1983-93 and at 2.28 per cent in the post-reform period. By CWS it was growing at 4.18 per cent in the pre- and 3.60 per cent in the post-reform period and by UPSS 4.88 and 2.69 per cent respectively. A trend that persisted, for example according to the NSSO estimates also quoted by ILO, the increase in total employment in India from 2004-10 (a relatively high growth period was only 1.1 million). It revived in the period 2009-10 to 2011-12 but slowed again. Unemployment rates rose and LFPR fell. Maharashtra was however among the high growth rate states in the post-reform period; the average annual growth rate of its GDSP was 7.72 per cent in the period 1983-94 and lower at 6.11 per cent in the later period.

Within Maharashtra, Mumbai is the largest employment centre with a population of approximately 12 million by the 2001 Census of India. It is 100 per cent urban and 87 per cent of the population is literate. The workforce in the city increased from 53 to 60 per cent of the population. The 2001 census also showed a dramatic decline in the number of full-time workers and a proportionate increase of casual and daily-wage workers. The NSSO data from 1999-2000 corroborated this trend and showed that a significant percentage of the urban unemployed were earlier regular wage earners. The proportion of main workers, which corresponds to the concept of UPS, has increased by less than one-percentage point between the two censuses of 1991 and 2001 from 35 to 35.9 per cent.

The city experienced structural changes in its economy before 1991. A rapid decline in the manufacturing sector employment and an increase in the service sector employment began prior to 1991. Factory employment declined from 1,674 per lakh of population in 1991-2 to 1,285 per lakh in 2004. Further, there is growing evidence of declining employment in the organized public and private sectors. Increasing flexibilization and casualization of employment in the region is a result of the overall trend and has occurred in the background of rising unemployment in the metropolis as reported by the census of 2001. As a percentage of the labour force, unemployment in Maharashtra rose from 1.1 per cent in 1991 to 6.4 per cent in 2001. In Mumbai it rose from 2.7 to 11.7 per cent over the same period. The national average was 7.2 per cent in 2001. When, the census adds the number of marginal workers seeking employment to the unemployed, the number of unemployed rises to 6.7 lakh or 14 per cent of the workforce. In Mumbai 23 per cent of the workforce in the age group of 20 to 24 years was unemployed, while the figure was 6 per cent in 1991 for the same age group. This group is regarded as the most flexible segment of the workforce.

In the post-liberalization period there is indication of a continued deterioration in the state of employment. In the circumstances GM becomes a suitable location to probe the Insecurity Hypothesis because it has a large organized sector which has experienced more than two decades of restructuring. The restructuring process accelerated in the post-liberalization period.

1.6 Conclusion

In contrast to the labour market trends in OECD countries in the period 1945-70, the following period 1970-2005 was marked by sharp deterioration in labour market conditions. Restructuring and new global production systems have left the working class increasingly insecure, uncertain, and informalized in the OECD countries appraised. There is evidence of significant wage penalties to interruptions in employment in UK and noteworthy changes in the terms and conditions of employment even in Japan. Besides this there are common trends over all, like flat real wage rates, non-standard, flexible employment, service jobs, and increasing employment of under-paid women.

India also presents a less than encouraging picture when the pre- and post-reform periods are compared in terms of workforce growth, falling growth rate of employment, declining employment elasticity, significant increase in the number of unemployed and casualization based on NSSO figures examined by many scholars. Data from the states also confirms the trends. Maharashtra and more specifically Mumbai provide an appropriate background to conduct a survey to evaluate insecurity of the organized sector workers and examine the relationship of insecurity with human resource policies at the firm level and the role of trade unions and the ability of the workers to upgrade their skills.

Chapter 3 will make a comprehensive statement of the Insecurity Hypothesis and indicate why the insecurity hypothesis has acquired the status of a social theory. Chapters 4, 5 and 6 will review correlates of the hypothesis. Chapter 6 elaborates the methodology of the current study and the survey, and presents the analysis. The final chapter will present the main conclusions and some policy options that emerge.

Notes

1. Robert Soloman (1999): *Transformations of the World Economy*, Macmillan Press, London.
2. Ron Martin (1998): 'Regional Dimensions of European Unemployment Crisis', in Paul Lawless, Ron Martin and Sally Hardy (eds.), *Unemployment and Social Exclusion*, Jessica Kingsley Publishers & Regional Studies Association, England.
3. Joyce Kolko, (1988): *Restructuring the World Economy*, Pantheon, New York.
4. E. Ozveren (2005): 'Polyani Chayanov and Lessons for the Study of the Informal Sector', *The Journal of Economic Issues*, vol. 39, no. 3. September, pp. 765-76.
5. Harry Dahms (2000): 'Introduction', in Harry Dahms (ed.), *The*

Transformations of Capitalism, Society and State in Modern Times, McMillan Press, London.
6. Bennet Harrison (1994): *Lean and Mean... the Changing Landscape of Corporate Power in the Age of Flexibility*, Basic Books, New York, pp. 125-6.
7. Howard Wachtel, (1986): *Money Mandarins: the Making of a New Supra National Economic Order*, Pantheon, New York, p. 137.
8. J. Brecher and Tim Costello (1994): *Global Village or Global Pillage*, Southend Press, Boston.
9. B. Bluestone and Bennett Harrison (1982): *The Deindustrialization of America*, Basic Books, New York.
10. Harrison (1994): *Lean and Mean...*, p. 171.
11. Jeremy Rifkin (2004): *The End of Work: The Decline of the Global Labour Force and the Dawn of the Post-Market Era*, Penguin, New York.
12. Joyce Kolko (2000): 'Restructuring and the Working Class', in Harry Dahms (ed.), *The Transformations of Capitalism, Society and State in Modern Times*, Macmillan Press, London, p. 275.
13. ILO (1997): *World Employment: National Policies in a Global Context*, ILO, Geneva.
    ILO (2004): 'A Fair Globalization: Creating Opportunities for All', *Report of the World Commission on the Social Dimensions of Globalization*, ILO, Geneva.
14. Ibid.
15. L. Cheng (1999): 'Globalization and Woman's Paid Work in Asia', *International Social Science Journal*, no. 160, UNESCO.
16. ILO (2006): *Report of the International Labour Conference*, ILO, Geneva.
17. ILO (1999): *World Employment Report*, ILO-Geneva, pp. 15-17.
    ILO (1999): *Decent Work: Report of the Director General*, ILO, Geneva.
18. A. Sohlamon and David Turnham (1994): 'What can the Developing Countries Learn from the OECD Labour Markets', *Technical Paper* 93, OECD, Paris.
19. Paul Lawless (1998): 'The Policy Challenge', in Paul Lawless, Ron Martin and Sally Hardy (eds.), *Unemployment and Social Exclusion*, Jessica. Kingsley Publishers and Regional Studies Association, England.
20. S. Burgess (1994): 'Where did Europe Fail: A Disaggregated Experiment of Net Job Generation in USA and Europe', Discussion

Paper 192, Centre for Economic Performance, London School of Economics.

R. Freeman (1993): 'Labour Market Institutions and Economic Performance', *Economic Policy*, vol. 3, no. 1, April.

R. Freeman (1993): 'Labour Market Institutions and Policies: Help or Hindrance to Economic Development', *Annual Conference on Development Economic-1992*, Supplement to the World Bank Research Observer, March.

P. Krugman (1994): 'Inequality and the Political Economy of Eurosclerosis', *Discussion Paper 8*, London: Centre for Policy Research.

21. European Commission (1993): 'Growth Competitiveness and Employment – The Challenges and the Way Forward into the 21st Century', *Bulletin of the European Community*, Supplement 6/93, Brussels.

    ILO (1995): *World Employment Report*, ILO, Geneva.

    OECD (1994): *The OECD Job Study: Fact, Analysis, Strategy.*

    Job Study Part 1, 'Labour Market Trend and Underlying Forces of Change'.

    Job Study Part 2, 'Adjustment Potential of Labour Markets'.
22. OECD (1993): *Green Paper: European Social Policy Options for the Union*, COMPOM 551, OECD, Paris, p. 21.
23. US Bureau of Labour (1988): *Labour Statistics Report*, US Department of Labour, Bureau of Labour Statistics.
24. *New York Times* (1994): 10 March.
25. *New York Times* (1994): 28 March, 6 May.
26. Paul Krugman (2005): 'The Drop out Puzzle', in *The Hindu*, 19 July.
27. S. Nickell (2004): 'Poverty and Worklessness in Britain', *The Economic Journal*, vol. 14, no. 494, March, *The Journal of the Royal Economic Society.*
28. R. Dickens and D.T. Ellwood (2000): 'Wither Poverty in Britain and United States', *Center for Economic Performance Report no. 506*, London School of Economics.
29. Wiji Arulampalam, Paul Gregg and Mary Gregory (2001): 'Unemployment Scarring', *The Economic Journal*, 111, November.
30. Wiji Arulampalam (2001): 'Is Unemployment Really Scarring?' *The Economic Journal*, 111, November.
31. Mary Gregory and Robert Jukes (2001): 'Unemployment and Subsequent Earnings: Estimating Scarring Among British Men 1984-94', *The Economic Journal* 111, November, pp. 607-25.

32. Bill Emmott (2005): 'The Sun Also Rises', www//economist.com/survey/audio, p. 56.
33. Mitarai Fugio (2005): 'Survey of Japan', *Economist*, 8-14 October, p. 4.
34. Peter Drucker (1993): *Post-capitalist Society*, Butterworth Heinemann, London.
35. US Bureau of Labour (1989): *Labour Statistics Report*, US Department of Labour, Bureau of Labour Statistics.
36. K.S. Abraham (2005): 'What We Don't Know Could Hurt Us: Some Reflections on the Measurement of Economic Activity', *Journal of Economic Perspectives*, vol. 19, no. 3, pp. 3-18.
37. ILO (2006): *Director Generals Report on the 95th International Labour Conference*, ILO, Geneva
38. *Far Eastern Economic Review* (1985): 19 December, p. 57.
39. Bill Emmott (2005): 'The Sun Also Rises', *Economist*, 8 October, pp. 4-7.
40. R. Munck (2002): *Globalization and Labour*, Madhya Books, Delhi, p. 82.
41. Joyce Kolko (2000): 'Restructuring and the Working Class', in Harry Dahms (ed.), *The Transformations of Capitalism, Society and State in Modern Times*, Macmillan Press, London.
42. Gordon Blanchard and Rizwanul Islam (2001): *East Asia Labour Mark*ets, ILO, Geneva.
43. Joyce Kolko (2000): 'Restructuring and the Working Class', in Harry Dahms (ed.), *The Transformations of Capitalism, Society and State in Modern Times*, Macmillan Press, London, p. 284.
44. Ibid.
45. Ibid.
46. *International Herald Tribune* (1985): A Report, 23 January.
47. Joyce Kolko (2000): 'Restructuring and the Working Class', in Harry Dahms (ed.), *The Transformations of Capitalism, Society and State in Modern Times*, Macmillan Press, London, p. 292.
48. US Congress, Joint Economic Committee (1986): *The Concentration of Wealth in the United States: Trends in the Distribution of Wealth among American Families*, Washington DC, 1986, p. 44.
49. Montek S. Ahluwalia (2000): 'Economic Performance of State in Post-Reform Period', *Economic and Political Weekly*, vol. 35, no. 19, 6 May.

    R. Nagraj (2000): 'Indian Economy Since 1980: Virtuous Growth or Polarization', *Economic and Political Weekly*, vol. 35, no. 32, 5 August, pp. 2831-9.

Abhijit Sen (1996): 'Economic Reforms, Employment and Poverty', *Economic and Political Weekly*, vol. 31, nos. 35-7 Special Number, pp. 213-22.

50. V.R. Panchamukhi, Nagesh Kumar and Ram Upendar Das (2004): 'Economic Reforms and Implications for Labour Markets', in R. Agarwal, N. Kumar and Ribond Michelle (eds.), *Reforms Labour Markets and Social Security in India*, Oxford University Press, New Delhi.
51. K. Sundram (2001): 'Employment-Unemployment Situation in the 1990s', *Economic and Political Weekly*, vol. 36, no. 11, 17 March, pp. 931-40.

    K. Sundram (2001): 'Employment and Poverty in the 1990s', *Economic and Political Weekly*, August, pp. 3039-49.
52. Pravin Visaria (2002): 'Workforce and Employment in India 1961-94', in B.S. Minhas (ed.), *National Income Accounts & Data Systems*, Oxford University Press, New Delhi.

    Abhijit Sen (1996): 'Economic Reforms, Employment and Poverty', *Economic and Political Weekly*, vol. 31, nos. 35-7, Special, pp. 213-22.

    K. Sundram (2001): 'Employment-Unemployment Situation in the 1990s: Some Results from NSS 55TH Round Survey', *Economic and Political Weekly*, vol. 36, no. 11, March, pp. 931-40.

    Gaurav Datt (1999): 'Has Poverty Declined Since Economic Reforms? Statistical Data Analysis', *Economic and Political Weekly*, vol. 34, no. 50, December.
53. S.K. Bhaumik (2003): 'Unemployment in India – The Post-Liberalization Era', *Indian Journal of Labour Economics*, vol. 46, no. 1, pp. 69-94.
54. B.B. Bhattacharya and S. Sakthivel (2003): 'Economic Reforms and Jobless Growth in India in the 1990s', *Indian Journal of Labour Economics*, vol. 46, no. 4, pp. 845-76.
55. S.K. Baumik (2003): 'Casualisation of the Workforce in India, 1983-2002', *Indian Journal of Labour Economics*, vol. 46, no. 4, pp. 907-26.
56. Amitabh Kundu (1997): 'Trends and Patterns of Female Employment in India: A Case of Organized Informalization', *Indian Journal of Labour Economics*, vol. 40, no. 3, July-September.
57. S. Deshpande and L.K. Deshpande (1998): 'Impact of Liberalization on Labour Markets in India', *Economic and Political Weekly*, vol. 33, no. 22, May.

    R.R. Birada and S.T. Bagalkoti (2001): 'Changing Facets of Employment in Rural India: Emerging Issues & Challenges', *Indian Journal of Agricultural Economics*, vol. 56, no. 3, July-September.

58. P.R. Bhatt (2003): 'Changes in Workforce Structure in India', *Indian Journal of Labour Economics*, vol. 46, no. 4, pp. 877-86.
59. Jeemol Unni and Uma Rani (2003): 'Changing Structure of Workforce in the Unorganized Manufacturing', *Indian Journal of Labour Economics*, vol. 46, no. 4, pp. 983-97.
60. Hrushikesh Panda (2001): 'Technology, Factor Substitution and Employment Generation at the Firm Level: A Case of Automobile Industry in India', *Indian Journal of Labour Economics*, vol. 44, no. 2, pp. 205-21.
61. Sudha Deshpande (2003): 'Changing Employment Structure in Large States in India: What do NSSO Data Show?', *Indian Journal of Labour Economics*, vol. 46, no. 4, pp. 811-44.
62. R. Nagraj (2004): 'Fall in Organized Manufacturing Employment', *Economic and Political Weekly*, vol. 39, no. 30, July, pp. 3387-90.
63. V.R. Panchamukhi, Nagesh Kumar and Ram Upendra Das (2004): 'Economic Reforms and Implications for Labour Markets', in R. Agarwal, N. Kumar and Ribond Michelle (eds.), *Reforms, Labour Markets, and Social Security in India*, Oxford University Press, New Delhi.
64. Guy Standing (1997): 'Globalization, Labour Flexibility and Insecurity: In the Era of Market Regulation', *European Journal of Industrial Relations*, 3, 1, pp. 43-55.
    K. Barker and K. Christensen (1998): *Contingent Work . . . American Employment Relations in Transition*, Cornell University Press, Ithaca New York.
    OECD (1997): *Employment Outlook*, OECD, Paris.
65. Peter Robinson (2000): 'Insecurity and the Flexible Work Force: Measuring the Ill Defined' in Edmond Heery and John Solomon (eds.), *Insecure Work Force*, Routledge, London, New York.
    A. Felstead, B. Burchell and F. Greene (1998): 'Insecurity at Work: Is Job Insecurity Really Much Worse than Before', *New Economy*, 5, 3, pp. 180-4.
    OECD (1997): 'Is Job Insecurity on the Increase in OECD Countries?' *Employment Outlook*, OECD, Paris.
    A. Gosling et al. (1997): 'The Dynamics of Low Pay and Unemployment in Early 1990s Britain', *Institute for Fiscal Studies*, Working Paper, London.
    P. Gregg and J. Wadsworth (1996): *Feeling Insecure? An Analysis of Job Tenure from 1975-1995*, Employment Policy Institute, Autumn, London.

P. Teasdale (1998): 'Incidence and Repeat Spells of Unemployment . . . An Analysis Using Claimant Data', *Labour Market Trends*, 106, 11, pp. 555-62.
S. Nickell, P. Jones and G. Quintini (2002): 'A Picture of Job Insecurity Facing British Men', *The Economic Journal*, vol. 112, no. 476, pp. 1-27.
W. Arulampalam, P. Gregg and M. Gregory (2001): 'Introduction. Unemployment Scarring', *The Economic Journal*, vol. 111, no. 475, pp. F577-84.
M. Gregory and R. Jukes (2001): 'Unemployment and Subsequent Earning . . . Estimating Scarring Among British Men 1984-94', *The Economic Journal*, vol. 111, no. 475, pp. F607-25.
K.F. Schene and Matthew Job Slaughter (2001): *Globalization and the Perceptions of American Workers*, Institute for International Economics, Washington, March.

66. C. Crouch (1997): 'Skill-Based Full Employment: The Latest Philosopher's Stone', *The British Journal of Industrial Relations*, 35, 3, pp. 367-84.
W. Screeck (1989): 'Skill and the Limit of Neo Liberalism: The Enterprise of the Future as the Place for Learning', *Work, Employment Society*, 3, 1, pp. 89-104.
P. Cappelli et al. (1997): *Change at Work*, Oxford University Press, New York.

CHAPTER 2

The Insecurity Hypothesis and Flexibilization of Labour Markets

> Nothing as fundamental as 'work' changes without changing us and other things around us.
>
> ANON.

> All fixed, fast-frozen relations, with their train of ancient and venerable prejudices and opinions, are swept away.
>
> MARX

Here security is a multi-dimensional concept, which includes (1) labour market security – state-guaranteed employment or income, (2) employment security – protection from arbitrary dismissal, retrenchment and layoff or in cases of accident or sickness, (3) job security – protection of an occupation or skill, (4) skill reproduction security – improved access to training and apprenticeship, (5) income security – protection of real incomes, (6) representational security – protection of collective voice of labour. Policy has to continue to address these issues.

The central claim of the Insecurity Hypothesis is that insecurity is deepening and widening even across sectors traditionally considered secure in terms of the above dimensions, e.g., the public sector, unionized sectors and white-collared service sector.

Section 2.1 states the Insecurity Hypothesis, its corollaries and consequences. Section 2.2 highlights the policy implications, 2.3 elaborates on the types of flexibility, while 2.4 provides a critique of the flexibility. Section 2.5 describes some empirical studies on Insecurity Hypothesis (IH) in the UK, USA and India; the measured variables, and their principal findings, and 2.7 sums up the discussion, key aspects of the IH, and evidence on flexibility.

2.1 Statement of the Hypothesis

By the end of the 1980s and into the early 1990s sustained increase in global competition and recurrent recessions lead to broadly three types of organizational transitions in the OECD countries – restructuring and downsizing, mergers and acquisitions, and privatization.[1] These changes came about as an attempt to increase sagging comparative productivity, which at that point was receiving increasing attention in economic debates.

Unease about the direction of change in the labour market set off by these organizational transformations pervades a wide range of opinions today and is commonplace for the workforce of even the developed world to be described as increasingly insecure.[2] This view is global in scope and embraces international commentators in a range of countries and over a wide range of interests.[3] For some, we live in the 'age of insecurity' and risk, and as a consequence, instability/continual change has become the defining feature of contemporary social life.[4] Underlying this viewpoint is a coherent set of statements about the nature, causes, and effects of recent changes in employment relations, which is referred to as the 'Insecurity Hypothesis'. Reports of this are available from a number of empirical studies, many of which were conducted in OECD countries like the UK, USA and a few in developing countries like India.

From these studies, it is possible to extract the concepts and the measures of insecurity experienced by workers. Concepts that are frequently used to empirically examine insecurity as a process are increasing spells of unemployment, shorter job tenures, increasing number of job changes, increasing working hours, wage scarring (declining real wage rates experienced after spells of unemployment), increasing contingent employment and institutional and legal changes that reduce the job protection available to workers. For the workers there is an association between various kinds of flexibilities – organizational, technological and functional, numerical, and wage. Similarly, there is a correspondence between flexibility and insecurity, just as there are wide-ranging and often detrimental psychological, social, political, and economic consequences of increasing job insecurity. The empirical work done as latter part of this study draws conceptually from the empirical effort in the studies quoted in this chapter. (Some of these studies are summarized in the chapter.)

As stated, the central proposition of the IH is that the economic risk of increased global competition is being progressively passed on from the employer to the employee, through shortened job tenure, erratic remuneration, variable work, contingent employment, and institutional changes that remove or reduce the protection and bargaining power of employee in the workplace.

The corollary is that widespread insecurity is damaging. In the short run, it promotes an employment relationship based on opportunism, distrust, and low commitment. The medium- to long-term consequence is that the employers under-invest in skill formation and training because of shortening tenures of work. Training and upgrading skills is however critical to competitive advantage. Additionally, widespread employment-related insecurity weakens institutions of collective action bargaining like trade unions that act as networks of trust and cooperation. The feeble trade union becomes both a cause and a consequence of mounting insecurity. In the long term, it undermines productivity and economic performance because in times of rapid economic and technological change insufficient management of social and human capital can become the limiting factor to growth. This last facet has implications for developing countries like India where the impact of increasing global competition may be frequently passed on to the workers, both organized and the majority unorganized) without regard to the medium- and long-term economic, social and political consequences of heightened insecurity.

The IH has a breadth of coverage because it seeks to connect developments in the world of work with changes beyond. All its expressions taken together make it a coherent social theory with inputs from labour economics, development economics, social psychology, sociology, political economy and political science.

2.1.1 *Prominent Propositions of the Hypothesis*

A decline in employment and job security over time is the central claim of IH and this insecurity can be defined and measured. Some of its indicators are lower median job tenures, increase in involuntary job separations, growth in the use of contingent workers such as fixed-term contract, freelance, agency and temporary workers and the use of variable performance-linked pays, which are neither consolidated nor pensionable, and the rising work flexibility in affected countries.[5] Substantiated from the point of view of the experience of the worker/employee, insecurity has all or some of the following indicators: increasing spells of unemployment, increasing number of jobs changed due to organizational decisions, increasing time period spent searching for another job, increasing time period of unemployment, decreasing or stagnant real wages, increasing hours of work, increasing contingent employment, etc. All or many of these symptoms may occur together to make the worker insecure.

Employment in the developed countries has become insecure or unstable in the sense that both continued employment and level of remuneration have become less stable and are dependent on factors outside the control of the employee. A clear shift has taken place from the earlier dominant pattern in which internal labour markets shielded workers from market forces.[6] The OECD report presents an analysis of nine EU countries, which reveals that the difficulty of finding replacement work has risen since the early 1980s, even when the effects of economic cycles are taken into account.[7] Apart from the rising incidence of job insecurity, the OECD report also notes that earnings when the new job is found may be substantially lower than in the previous job. The difference is substantial and enduring even in the UK and USA.[8] Both the risks of job separation and its cost have increased. These trends have repercussions for labour markets in both developing and developed countries.

The trend towards insecure employment has been compounded by changes in factors external to the labour market and national systems of employment regulation. The external factors at work here are the heightened global competition, rising rates of unemployment caused by structural and technological changes in the economy. The national systems of regulation have moved towards creating flexible labour markets. In Britain, for example, this included changes in benefit systems that have increased pressure on men to accept flexible terms of employment, the attenuation of individual employment rights, increase in the qualifying period for the right to not be unfairly dismissed (from six months to two years), severe and continuous decline in trade union density and coverage by bargaining power.[9]

The incidence of both instability and feelings of insecurity is changing. Previously-secure groups are now finding themselves in a precarious position. The current list includes middle managers, public service professionals, and other professionals like teachers, nurses, doctors and older workers. Each of these categories may continue to enjoy higher security than private sector workers, non-management, non-permanent employees, younger workers, and most women workers, but it is asserted that their relative position is becoming less favourable. The trend is secular and not temporary or sector specific.[10] These trends are in the direction of what has been termed the contingent workforce – an army of blue-collar, white-collar and managerial temps.[11]

This trend is likely to replicate itself even in the organized manufacturing and service sectors in the developing countries, so that educated, skilled employees who were thought of as secure may no longer feel so. The process of creeping insecurity may begin with just longer hours of work (extending beyond the eight-hour work day), work intensification and multi-tasking.

2.1.2 *Explanatory Factors*

Increase in workforce insecurity has been traced to two causal factors:

1. Globalization of the economy: In an era of 'market deregulation' the capitalist economies have entered a new stage of development at the heart of which is increasing competition and a new

model of management characterized by identification of 'core-competencies' and restructuring for flexibility.[12] All operations and services outside this core competency can be performed by non-core contingent workforce.[13]
2. National systems of capitalism: These promote dominance by a system of financial interest and the short-term management of company assets in the interest of shareholder values. This argument hinges upon corporate governance and financing. It emphasizes different experiences of labour across national economies because it highlights the significance of national systems of labour market regulation in increasing or moderating the pressure of insecurity.[14]

2.1.3 *The Consequences*

The consequences of increasing insecurity in the workforce are wide ranging and they have economic, psychological, social and political facets:

1. Altering the psychological contract at work such that the workplace begins to resemble a spot market where workers are encouraged to focus on their immediate self-interest and employers undertake to do the same.[15] Several disadvantages of this breakdown of the psychological contract include low levels of employee commitment, unwillingness to work beyond contract, and high transaction cost associated with the monitoring and enforcement of contracts. Rightsizing, restructuring and downsizing were corporate slogans in the 1980s and 1990s in the USA, especially in the manufacturing sector. It was supposed to be the fastest and the easiest way to cut business costs, be more competitive, and raise profits. There is mounting evidence that such labour policy had backfired. Firms that had downsized not only failed to record a sustained increase in earnings but found their ability to compete eroded even further. One of the unintended effects of downsizing was that employees who survived were insecure, had to work longer and felt less loyal towards the firm. They

also reported a loss of creativity under high levels of stress. The American Management Association, in 1992, surveyed more than 500 firms who had downsized since 1987.[16] More than 75 per cent reported that employee morale had collapsed. Two-thirds showed no increase in efficiency and less than half showed any increase in profits.

2. This also works as a disincentive for employers to invest in training and employee involvement.[17] Cappelli (1997) argues that new forms of high-performance work organization for global competition, require committed, flexible, and highly trained employees, the very factors whose growth is hampered by worker insecurity. Paradoxically, an essential precondition for business strategy, which emphasizes quality enhancement, productivity growth, and flexibility, is a stable, secure, and trained workforce.[18]
3. The skill premium has increased since the end of the last century, unlike the earlier part of the century when it fell as a result of the Fordist organization of production.[19] When production had become organized in large mass-producing plants, jobs became routinized favouring less-skilled workers. Manufacturing could absorb a large number of workers from the rural sector. The nature of technological change was different in the second half of the twentieth century. The recent experience of manufacturing is that flexible numerically controlled machines have allowed plants to operate at a smaller scale. Batch production has replaced mass production. Each batch may be highly customized and require workers who can manipulate the machines to perform the wide variety of tasks that it can perform. In data samples from 1977 to 1994 downsizing is related to decrease in plant size, increase in the average industry wage, productivity and employment of more skilled rather than unskilled labour.[20]

The emergence of more insecure workforce is associated with a range of wider social ills, but most significantly, skill development in the system of production. Skill formation has been identified as the main collective goal of economic policy and an effective system of vocational educational training is viewed as a necessary condition for maintenance of a high wage economy in the context of increased global competition.[21] The emergence of more flexible systems of production actually requires increased involvement of enterprises in the design and development of programmes of training and development. But a more contingent employment relationship and collapse of internal labour market inhibit skill development. The risk of uncertain product markets is passed on via outsourcing, subcontracting, JIT inventory systems, network of subsidiary firms and contingent labour strategies. Just as all production inputs are being purchased on the market and only in sufficient quantities, so too the labour market is being shaped along similar lines where labour is purchased on the market on an as-needed basis as contingent labour force via labour contractors. In addition, employers now require labour to enter the labour market with a threshold or at least a minimum set (above minimal, i.e. very low or negligible) of generalized skills, which labour is increasingly acquiring via temporary agency training programmes or vocational schools. This reduces the employer's investment in labour skills and therefore reduces the employer's interest in holding on to employees.[22] Therefore, a smaller workforce is being compelled to work more intensively, being both speeded-up and stretched-out, while millions of unemployed accept worse jobs or no jobs. So the profits increase as employment and wages decline.[23] A reverse process of de-skilling might set in and create low wage equilibriums. Low wages based on low skills is not a viable long-run competitive advantage strategy in a democracy. 'The threat of being fired instills fear which inhibits learning and systemic improvements; furthermore incentive, quota and piecework system of pays all foster competition rather than team work among workers and undermine morale because of their inherent arbitrary nature'.[24] Insecurity hypothesis and its impact on 'lifelong learning', 'empowerment': education and training, in other words learning, are the basis of individual, organizational, and national growth. Since the skill, knowledge and experience of each individual contributes to economic growth of the organization and cumulatively the national economy, economists talk in terms of human capital as the primary requirement for national economic development. The main effect of accumulative knowledge and capital has been to accelerate change. This has reduced the number of low-skill jobs and increased the number of high-skill ones, so that the acquisition of knowledge is today the key to value addition and wealth creation globally, just as control over raw materials was in the age of industrial capitalism.

4. Social scientists see society being deeply divided into three knowledge-based classes – the symbolic analyst who creates and manipulates knowledge, a service class to support them and a large number of people who have no economic role at all. There is a tendency like never before to polarize the working class. Social scientists declare that technological and organizational changes in the post-industrial economy are occurring so rapidly that there is an urgent and growing need to constantly train and retrain workers to prevent any long-term exclusion/marginalization of workers from the market. As it stands, in 1993, the OECD job study survey had estimated that the average individual leaving school in the developed world would have five separate jobs in a working life, for each job major retraining would be required.
5. The critical question therefore is who will bear the cost of this learning and relearning over a lifetime? Will the cost be passed on to an increasingly insecure workforce that will have to bear it to be re-employable? Since education is a very long-term investment, the typical market-driven firm will train its employees only if urgently required for the briefest period and this is most likely in the case of absence of long-term retention and employment. It is even more likely in the case of low-skilled peripheral/non-permanent workers. Hence, the possibility of cumulative causations that keeps the low skilled in a trap, unemployable and poor. There is a further likelihood of the developing countries getting trapped in a vicious cycle of cheap labour advantage in global trade-low

skill-low productivity-low wage circuit, unless state policy induces/compels firms to train and upgrade workforce.[25]

6. Lifelong learning and empowerment needs a dynamic process of devolving power and responsibility downward in organizations to harness creative energies of workforce. The essence of empowerment lies in the growth of knowledge, training, analytical skills, experience and motivation of workers.[26] Empowerment becomes increasingly possible as the education levels rise. Organizations grow and technology and processes become more complex. A class of workers called professionals comes to exist, and, they exercise power within organizations. Empowerment occurs simultaneously in the social and business processes with the spread of education. Nowadays, human resource policy makers talk of the Dawn of the 'Age of Learning' and the necessity of lifelong learning in a knowledge-driven society. At a micro level, this translates into the character of HRM policies of the firm and its culture that may or may not induce lifelong learning. It implies that workers will have to learn throughout their working life and view every new task as an opportunity to learn afresh.[27]
7. Firms in England and USA, for example, were spending 1 to 2 per cent of their salary bills on formal training in 1994-5. In addition, informal training would amount to six times the amount spent on formal training. Training or staff development is itself a growing industry. It caters to a growing number of firms and other organizations that may need outside help/decentralized training to prevent staff obsolescence in a competitive market.[28] Employment stability, measured as the average employment tenure, is now considered important for achieving high levels of productivity. While a degree of job mobility is necessary for increasing productivity, this has to be distinguished from employment instability and insecurity. The prime source of productivity growth is technological change. Technological change relies on innovation, which is itself influenced by an array of institutions, the quality and quantity of human capital, spending on R&D, competitive pressures in the market and levels of investment in general.

8. That changes in the organization of work and production have a profound effect on productivity has been long acknowledged, from Adam Smith 250 years ago in his study of the growth of division of labour, specialization and rising productivity in the factory system down to present discussions about generating high-performance work systems. Human capital theory also tells us that much of how workers learn to do their job better comes from formal training plus the training they receive on the job from more experienced workers, simply called learning by doing. The employer has no incentive to invest in workers' training if the contract between the employer and worker is an uncertain and short one. Workers on the other hand have no reason to develop and acquire more productive ways of doing things as either teams or individuals if they fear that they will work themselves out of a job. Employment stability promotes productivity growth and the reverse is also true that productivity growth can improve employment stability with the help of appropriate institutional arrangements like in-place employment protection legislation.[29] However, labour productivity gains have occurred despite increasing insecurity. This is a result of increasing investments in ICT, ITeS, and intelligent machines.
9. Increasingly insecure workforce is also associated with polarization of labour market. At one end are the high-skill, high-wage workers, and at the other, low-skill, low-wage insecure workforce, the latter numerically larger than the former. This increasing inequality in income and wealth reduces social cohesion and has been linked to criminality, family breakdown, political alienation and breakdown of the democratic fabric.[30]
10. The increasingly insecure workforce is making a demand for protective regulation, because, the job and everything organized around the job – the friends at work, the after-work meeting places, even group transport – are losing their social function. These are becoming as permanently temporary as the work itself. The new workplace is destabilizing the family, degrading the very institution critical for social reproduction.[31]

11. It is being argued that while there are new and increasing threats, there are opportunities as well for trade unionism. Trade unions have to effect a realignment of their policies and structures. For example, pursuit of collective bargain in which job security is exchanged for union cooperation for raising productivity and company performance has to be circumvented. Also, unions must pay increasing attention to organizing contingent workforce in old and new sectors of economy. Since the demographic characteristics of the current workforce includes large number of women, migrants and the youth, these segments must be adequately represented within union policymaking.[32] Unionizing new service sector establishments is another challenge.
12. Social scientists, sociologists and political scientists have also suggested that this central problem of our day, 'personal economic insecurity of working people', might be distancing a growing percentage of population from conventional politics and fostering support for extremist politics of all types.[33] This is a view that is supported by a growing number of social commentators.

    Based on the pattern of development in Gujarat and Maharashtra in the last two decades similar relationships have been studied in India as well.[34] For example, the growth of identity politics and vandalism in Maharashtra in the shape of the politics of a political party called the Shiv Sena over the period 1966-84 is studied by Shaikh (2005) and linked to the slowdown in the growth of jobs in Mumbai's textile mills, immigration into Mumbai, growth of the partially, temporary and self-employed in a growing informal economy and the increasing economic insecurity of workers.[35] According to the author: this transformation of the workers' psyche away from class-based formations to right-wing, identity-based regional chauvinism that occurs in the Central Mumbai heartland of left unions speaks a lot for the possible consequences of insecurity. The Shiv Sena grew to capture the Municipal Corporation of Mumbai; later it aligned itself with right-wing national party BJP, rode the wave of communal violence and Hindu nationalism that swept India in the post-Babri Masjid period. It ruled over the state of Maharashtra between 1994-9.

The French riots of November 2005 and Los Angeles riots earlier have also been attributed to the same process of alienation, polarization, and insecurity.[36] Silver (2003) also makes a similar observation when she says that insecure labour may have good reason to seek identity in non-class boundaries and borders, e.g. race, citizenship, and gender as a way of making claims for privileged protection from the maelstrom created by the desocialization of the state. Just because capital finds it in its interest to treat labour as interchangeable commodities, the workers may not find it in their interest to accept this paradigm.[37] The initial impact of globalization could well mean an intensification of identity-based rather than class-based politics.

13. One of the effects of the spread of insecure employment is work intensification, i.e. reduction in access to holiday, sick pay, increase in hours of work, and abuse of managerial authority.[38] This intensification is directly connected with loss of social capital, democratic practice and space.

    Social scientists have also attributed the loss of social capital, i.e. public indifference to socio-political causes and declining public participation in collective action to new work conditions like work intensification and insecurity. The middle class is wedged between intense pressures to maintain their standard of living and an increasingly insecure labour market.[39]

14. Costs for employees of job insecurity extend beyond the workplace and includes physical and psychological stress, and ill health, which is as great as that associated with unemployment.[40] All industrial countries have experienced sizeable changes in their labour markets over the past two decades and one of the most significant and recurrent themes in this upheaval has been the reduction of employee security. Many social psychologists have also examined the phenomenon and from their perspective job insecurity is very stressful. It affects the motivation and attitudes of employees, and it spills over into family, the basic unit of

social reproduction.[41] The psychological effects of stress are often visible in the decreased quality of life and decreased levels of psychological well-being like increased anxiety level and depression, a sense of uselessness, lack of self-confidence and dissatisfaction with one's environment. Studies have shown that anticipation or concern about job loss may be as damaging as job loss itself.[42] Job insecurity has been found to be associated with increasing medical consultation for psychological distress. In studies on job insecurity in the OECD countries, psychological well-being has been measured on a number of scales and indicators and found to be negatively related to insecurity.[43] Macho cultures in lean and mean work places requiring long hours of work in an insecure job environment are especially hard on women with young children.[44]

15. Insecurity ultimately has consequence for the social reproduction of labour. Social reproduction refers to all those activities and processes by which human beings are sustained materially and psychologically, directly and indirectly. In simple terms, it means how labour power is reproduced over every generation to sustain economic activity, which in turn sustains it. These activities and processes of social reproduction have been historically embedded in social and cultural structures like the tribe, the family, community, market, and state. Economists focus on production and not on social reproduction, which is assumed to be autonomous. In fact, the process by which labour is produced and maintained even as a commodity has not been considered important enough even in Marxist literature. This tends to assign the social organization of childbirth, infant care, and domestic socialization to the realm of nature or some intermediate location and sees the real dynamic of society as stemming from production. The concept therefore figures mainly in feminist discourses and sociology. But if one takes labour power seriously as a productive force in all modes of production, the question of the specific relations within which it is produced and reproduced must be centrally addressed.[45]

In the period before the Industrial Revolution and the reorientation of values that held the individuals responsible for sustaining themselves, the individual was not threatened by starvation unless the community as a whole was in a likewise predicament.[46] The unpaid domestic labour of women also serves to lower the cost of all wage labour.[47] Historically the ties of reciprocity took care of social reproduction. In the period after that, instability of market conditions brought about the dilution of community ties and increasing insecurity. And it became apparent that the capitalist system was unable to provide for the reproduction of its own labour force. 'Because workers have only one way to live under capitalism – by selling their own labour power – a reserve army necessitates some mechanism for maintaining the unemployed and those earning poverty wages in a condition in which they are ready to work when capital calls.' It must be pointed out that social reproduction requires not just physical reproduction of labour in required quantities for work, but, with higher/diverse levels of knowledge and skills commensurate with technology. Hence, social reproduction presupposes training and up-skilling as well. As long as the cost of maintaining these reserve armies of workers can be diffused through religious charity, community reciprocity or the welfare state the market system can survive.

Under capitalism, social reproduction refers to the reproduction of the capital wage labour relationship and thereby the construction of labour power as a commodity. However, there are three peculiarities of labour: first the commodity labour power is inseparable from the human being, as Marx said that labour power is the capacity of a living person to labour, which in turn depends on labour's productive consumption. Second, there is a historical, social, and cultural basis of determining the value of labour power. It would differ in time and place. Third, of all the commodities produced in a capitalistic society labour is the only one that cannot be produced capitalistically based on wage labour and the extraction of surplus value. It is produced outside the ambit of the market in the household and family, which may be penetrated by the market and state but lies outside it.[48]

The state interfaces social reproduction through industrial

policies, labour market regulations, and social and redistribution policies. The welfare state can be understood in that context. It sought to stabilize and reproduce the workforce to meet the needs of an increasingly well organized and highly productive factory organization, which had evolved over 150 years since Adam Smith first wrote about it. The welfare system was to provide the reserve army and the non-wage earning dependents of wage earners – family unit within which labour is reproduced – some form of security.[49] The welfare state was a struggle within capitalism for a transfer of value led by the workers themselves for whom the insufficiency and insecurity of wage is a threat to survival and reproduction.[50]

Globalization and the restructuring of production have changed the premise of the state. The state is now a partner with the capital to weaken the welfare structures that made social reproduction possible in capitalism. That has set into process cumulative causative forces that bring down the price of labour even below its real cost for super-profits. A process of recasualization/normalization has set in across the globe and workers from developed/developing countries, both skilled and unskilled, are experiencing the pressures. Non-standard employment, with uncertain or limited duration, i.e. work assignment other than full-time-wage job, is a commonly used source of flexibility by firms now. The casual, informal worker works at low wages outside the parameters of state-mandated labour regulations regarding wages, lay-off wages, retrenchment compensation, work hours, work environment, health insurance and any other forms of security. The only recourse now for social reproduction for these contingent workers is the family, since community solidarity, NGOs and self-help groups are proving to be inadequate.[51]

Globalization of economy and the accompanying deregulation of financial, product markets has thus significantly altered the employment patterns and aggravated insecurity. These changes are most obvious in wide-ranging, multi-dimensional consequences impacting working people everywhere. Resistance to globalization, deregulation and resulting inequality may be understood in the context of these work- and workplace-related changes.

2.2 Insecurity Hypothesis has Policy Implications

Pervasive insecurity underscores the need for innovative policies to intervene in the labour market and reform the system of employment – policies, which include legal regulations of the terms and conditions of employment, reform of corporate governance and human resource policies of employers so as to build skills, employability and income security.[52] Evidence suggests that there is a strong and positive correlation between a country's openness to trade and how much it spends on active labour market policies as a percentage of GDP. Countries have to find a workable balance between the micro-level stability and macro-level employment or income security that a system affords. Workers' perception of their security also provides a basis for strong aggregate demand in the economy to sustain equitable economic growth.[53]

Both welfare state capitalism and state socialism of the twentieth century aimed at de-commoditification of labour. Both offered full employment and individual and collective security to a lesser or greater extent. Macro-economic policies were employed to maintain security. This era saw the introduction of all those above-mentioned multiple-dimensions of security, namely (1) labour market security – state-guaranteed employment or income; (2) employment security – protection from arbitrary dismissal, retrenchment and layoff or in cases of accident or sickness; (3) job security – protection of an occupation or skill; (4) skill reproduction security – improved access to training and apprenticeship; (5) representational security – protection of collective voice of labour.

There is a need to revisit these policies in new ways. Some of the best practices to deal with insecurity across the globe are discussed later in the study under the heading 'Active Labour Market Policies'.

2.2.1 *A Critique of IH*

A critique of IH has also emerged and has the following core arguments:

1. The first argument attacks the root proposition that the labour

market is changing in a fundamental way and that employment is becoming more insecure in an objective sense.[54] According to this, there is limited empirical support for growing job instability. Some modest changes may have occurred but there is a moral panic over insecurity, which will turn out to be temporary. Insecurity skeptics include Burgess and Rees (1996), Goddard Spencer (1996 and 1998), and Guest (1997).[55]

2. The second line of criticism is in defence of the government policies of deregulation and flexibilization of labour markets.[56] Essentially, it accepts that job insecurity is rising and imposes a cost on a portion of the workforce, but there are compensatory benefits to society that outweigh these costs.

   Allen Greenspan, former chairman of the US Federal Reserve Board is on record attributing America's prolonged non-inflationary upward swing during the 1990s to a growing sense of insecurity in the US workforce. Similar claims have been made in the UK where the death of inflation is judged to be a result of market reforms of the 1980s, which removed the protective shield of trade unionism from a large percentage of the labour force.[57] Consequently, macro-economic policy can be set within a looser framework with low interest rates and lower level NAIRU (Non-accelerating Inflation Rate of Unemployment). Insecurity serves to improve the rest of the economy. The rest of the economy here could well refer to corporate interests as against those of the working class.

3. A third line of criticism emphasizes the structural nature of changes induced by globalization in the economies of the developed countries as they shift away from labour-intensive manufacturing towards knowledge-based manufacturing and service sector growth. Calculations by the *Economist* indicate that manufacturing now accounts for less than 10 per cent of the jobs in America.[58] In 1820, agriculture accounted for 80 per cent of the jobs and today it accounts for less than 2 per cent. If all those workers had remained tilling the land, America would have been poorer. On the other hand, labour-intensive manufacturing continues to grow in all developing countries. In America, as well, manufacturing sector grew at 4 per cent

per year since 1991, although the growth there is oriented away from labour-intensive, low value-added industries like textiles or computer assembly, towards high value-added products like pharmaceuticals, aviation or computer design. America is the world's biggest manufacturer in value terms producing about twice as much as China, even if American markets are flooded with cheaper Chinese consumer products. Service sector employment continues to grow in DCs. Even in the case of the latter, the shift is towards knowledge-based high value-added services, which are not outsourced and have stayed at home, e.g. services like R&D, patenting of new designs, product marketing and financial services. Low rates of unemployment in America and UK today suggest that those who lost their jobs in manufacturing have got new ones over time. Developed countries will be forced to move towards higher skilled jobs, and countries that prevent this shift from taking place will be left behind. The low value-added manufacturing will shift to lower-cost countries like China. The current rate of growth of the Chinese economy suggests that it will outsize the American by 2050. Even as changes cause pain for some and are resisted, the government can facilitate change by providing assistance in the form of temporary unemployment benefits and retraining for those who lose their jobs. In the long run, economists like Bootle (2001) are optimistic about the prospects of the truly global economy, as the division of labour is made possible on a grand international scale.[59] Europe should not mourn the hollowing out of manufacturing jobs but specialize in knowledge-based high-technology industry.

4. In the developing countries, the same prescription of flexibility for economic health (albeit in very different circumstances) is being recommended. It is claimed that free trade will generate jobs in the medium to long term in labour-intensive sectors. The IH may be irrelevant in developing countries like India because 90 per cent of the workforce is in the informal sector, where even today, there is labour flexibility and there has never been any security. Poor implementation of labour laws has in any case made security in the organized sector a paper tiger.

> Regulatory attempts to protect employment security have so far restricted the overall growth of organized sector employment and succeeded only in creating islands of security. Flexibility will support growth, international trade, and investment. It will stimulate employment growth, which has been lagging, and benefit workers and firms in the long run. Examples of newly-industrialized economies of East Asia are given to endorse flexibility as a means of promoting employment, increasing productivity and real wages.

Critics either allege lack of convincing data to support a conclusion of increasing insecurity or else treat it as a transient but essential and inevitable phenomenon.

2.3 IH and Labour Market Flexibility

The inference that jobs for life are a thing of the past, and insecure workforce is on the rise has coincided with rapid growth in 'flexible' forms of work in the developed countries. While insecurity can be measured in terms of unemployment, redundancy, falling real income, etc., the term 'flexibility' is used in the context of growth in forms of non-standard employment, wage flexibility, and functional flexibility.[60] Non-standard forms of employment like part-time and temporary employees are perceived to be inherently inferior and less secure than full-time permanent jobs for employees.[61] Technically, it is important to note that growth in part-time work in the OECD countries was first linked to the feminization of the workforce and the growth of the service sector that took place after Second World War. New ways of working or new labour styles are not absolutely new. Home working, temporary work and shift working supported the early phases of the Industrial Revolution, while job sharing and flexi-time arrived as early as the 1950s. Team working and multi-skilling, teleworking, annual time, V-time, zero-hours, gain sharing, flexible benefits, virtual office, call centres have made their appearance in a formal way in the last 20 years in the OECD countries and now in the developing countries as well.[62]

Countries like the USA and UK with less regulated labour markets than France and Germany also have a higher category of flexible workers. The flexible American-style labour markets promoted in the name of increasing employment are based on a fragile theory that interventions to enhance job security or pay roll taxes to improve pension benefits would lead to inefficiency and increase in unemployment. The highly deregulated US economy is characterized by stagnant or falling real wages for a significant percentage of the low skilled workers. The high skilled workers have super-charged work schedules for out-competing others and meeting deadlines at all costs. They earn more but at the cost of more intensified work schedules, job security, individual stress, and social isolation. The flexible model of labour market is making sustained inroads into social Europe, and secure Japan under the guise of competitiveness, efficiency, and increased investments.[63]

The origins of flexible production and organization precede the current wave of globalization and also precede the rapid growth in flexible employment. Not all OECD-based firms, seeking to overcome the rigidities of Taylorism, turned to low-wage production sites offshore. Some of the firms succeeded in developing more flexible forms of production organizations at home. Toyota started in the late 1950s, and the clusters of small and medium firms in Italy, which developed during 1960-70, are probably the best-known early examples.[64] The late 1970s and early 1980s marked the watershed when the formidable dynamism and competitive strength of flexible producers led many Taylorist firms to start talking about the new rules of global competition. Above all, they were reacting to the much greater capacity of flexible producers to profitably exploit the flexible automation technologies that began emerging in late 1970s.[65] The first sign of crisis of Taylorism therefore predate the current wave of globalization and are more closely linked to events like slowing down of US productivity growth in the late 1960s, the spectacular growth of flexible Japanese automakers' share of the US auto market following the second oil-shock and the deregulation of global competition. Even though this may not be well appreciated by economists, the crisis of Taylorism is an important cause of the structural labour market problems in the OECD countries.[66]

There are broadly two types of flexible organizations. One is the large firm variety in terms of financial or marketing strength or what is called 'Intra-group approach to flexibility', i.e. like Japan's automobile and electronics producers, large firms in Germany and American firms like HP and Motorola. The second type is the district of industrial clusters, where a number of relatively small, independently-owned firms compete and cooperate with each other in close physical proximity.

Their principal differences from Taylorist firms are: (a) they claim to integrate thinking and do so at all levels of operations, (b) harness human capability of their workers, especially for anticipating and diagnosing problems, finding solutions and adapting to changing circumstances, (c) they organize work in teams that avoid excessive specialization and compartmentalization, (d) continuously innovate, which contrasts with Taylor's 'one best way', (e) higher degree of customization as against mass production, (f) higher productivity by exploiting economies of scope and quicker response to changes in market demands, (g) only a core group of relatively higher skilled workers, who are treated as long-term assets, and are trained continuously, and compensated as per the performance of their teams/groups, (h) lean middle level management, and (i) high dependence on infrastructure support.

In the automobile industry, which has been most extensively studied, the leading flexible producers in the mid-1980s (Toyota, for example) were found to have productivity levels twice those of leading European and US manufacturers. Equally, impressive differences in productivity and competitiveness have been reported by studies in other flexibly organized industries.[67]

Flexible production is no longer limited to assembly type manufacturing but also exists in processing industries like chemical, steel, ceramics, textile, high-fashion, modern services like insurance, banking, telecommunication and even in traditional public monopolies like power distribution and postal services. Implications of flexibility for developed countries are more serious for the workers used to the Taylorist organization, most significantly for unskilled workers because flexible organizations have little use for workers who lack strong basic literacy, numeric, social, and interpersonal social skills and general trainability. Other category of workers affected are: (a) highly skilled and too narrowly specialized, (b) middle management, and (c) low skilled. Their jobs are likely to disappear.

Developing countries like India already have a large number of small or tiny firms/unorganized sector and these tend to fall into the second type of flexibility offered in clusters albeit rudimentary type and here flexible organization offers considerably greater possibilities to adapt output levels and product features for relatively small markets with lower quality requirements. They also have a minimum efficient level (break-even level) of production, which is significantly lower than that of the Taylorist type. This is suited to smaller markets, where a number of medium-size producers can compete.[68] They also have greater employment potential.

It is not as if Taylorist firms are entirely redundant or irrelevant, and in fact, they account for one-third to half of all manufacturing in OECD countries. They also have considerable potential in developing countries because of their robustness in terms of economies of scale and scope, financial strength and their capacity to create transportation, communication, and power infrastructure to meet their own requirements. They can also absorb a fairly large number of unskilled, low-skilled workers. The successful use of this model over the past two decades in China is a testimony to its advantage.

It needs to be understood that increasing flexibility from the point of view of the organization of production of goods and services implies insecurity of employment from the point of view of the workforce.

2.4 Types of Labour Flexibilities

Many kinds of labour flexibility now find mention in the literature and are identified by Standing (1999) as below:[69]

2.4.1 *Organizational Flexibility*

Large firms have extended their division of labour by linking activities between firms and by outsourcing. By adopting flexible organizational structures that are decentralized (small firms are also building flexible specialization in turn) they are engaged in downloading risk and uncertainty to smaller firms. With the death of 'Fordism', as far as labour is concerned, decentralization, i.e. organizational flexibility has increased.[70] A defining characteristic of labour markets in the global era is smaller workplaces, fewer rules in the workplace, weaker unions, and wages tied to business cycles.[71] The United States has long used spatial dispersion and geographical isolation of employees as one of its prime but subtle mechanisms of labour control. But the recent transformation of the industrial organization, flexible location choices and deregulation have been turned into a totally obvious form of coercive exploitation and capitalistic control, which is pre- rather than post-Fordist in the organizational form.[72]

2.4.2 *Work Process or Functional Flexibility.*

Changes in the market or technology occur rapidly. The speed with which a firm can bring about internal changes in the organization of work is called functional flexibility. This is also referred to as vertical and horizontal flexibility so that workers carry out jobs above their level or below their level and accept lateral shifts. Here again, flexibility implies multi-skilling of workers, teamwork, work intensification, variable working hours, overtime, teamwork and shift work.

2.4.3 *Numerical Flexibility*

This refers to the ability of the firm to reduce or increase the workforce with minimum cost. Firms rely on flexible or contingent workers. In case of statutory regulations that make such flexibility difficult and costly, the firm has two sets of responses: (a) look for loopholes in regulations and create new labour categories, which are flexible, or (b) shift to capital-intensive technologies. The growing tribe of flexible categories include the casual, temporary, and permanently temporary workers. Casual workers are hired for fixed hours and paid on piece rates. Temporary workers have a fixed term contract, and the permanently temporary workers are long-term workers but lack the benefits and entitlements of the permanent workers. Then there are subcontractors, agency workers, home workers, tele-workers, part-time workers, consultants, associates, and concealed workers. The new systems that emphasize working flexibility have been introduced in an incremental way in three stages: first, they have been introduced to save money for the firms; second, they are associated with downsizing to deal with crisis; third, they have been expanded and retained as a business advantage leading to improvements in a firm's bottomline.

2.4.4 *Wage Flexibility*

Wage flexibility is critical to a flexible labour market. This wage flexibility is ensured by a decline of the fixed-wage component in the total income of an employee. Wide wage differentials separate the core from the peripheral, permanent from temporary, formal sector workers in core activities of the firm from informal set of workers in the non-core, outsourced work sites. Thus, workers fall into categories of increasing insecurity, the core being the most secure consisting of full-time, high wage-cum-benefit, permanent workers who are trained, multi-skilled and functionally flexible. They are followed by the first periphery, second periphery and external groups providing the numerical flexibility. This also results in total wage bill flexibility, wide wage differentials, and low labour cost as a proportion of the total cost. In neo-classical economics, mass unemployment is considered as a positive proof of the absence of downwards wage flexibility. Absence of wage flexibility consequently causes unemployment, inflation, stagnation in growth and lack of structural adjustment.

While the trend for greater flexibility continues and wage differentials widen, underpinned by performance related pay, the low wages and insecurity at the periphery are such that the Confederation of British Industry commissioned a report on flexible labour markets (CBI, 1996) asking the vital question, 'who pays for the training of atypical workers'.[73]

2.4.5 *Flexible Technologies*

As a popular concept, flexible specialization implies that the Fordist mass production is being replaced, in successful industrial economies, by decentralized production and less hierarchical management. Firms in the new industrial clusters innovate constantly using multipurpose machinery like CNC, CAD, CAM and workers are always learning new skills to supply fragmented and rapidly changing markets. Large firms are broken down into smaller decision-making units, while a network of small firms often but not always concentrated in industrial districts achieves collective efficiency by working together using complementary technologies, products, and skills.[74]

There is another way in which flexibility can be understood – as the converse of inflexibility. A labour market is inflexible for restructuring to bring about organizational flexibility of business firms if the level of unemployment insurance benefits is too high or their duration is too long, if there are many restrictions on the freedom of employers to fire and hire, if the permissible hours of work are too tightly regulated, if excessively generous compensation for overtime work is mandated or if trade unions have too much power to protect incumbent workers against competition and to control the flow of work at the site of production, or perhaps, if the statutory health and safety regulations are too stringent.[75] Hence, job security legislation refers to all the legal provisions that raise the cost of dismissing a worker and those that regulate the hiring of particular types of labour.

Flexibility is now so varied and widespread that the ILO has framed international conventions to deal with it.[76] The concept of flexibility has been widely applied to organizational-structure, workplace-functionality, size of the workforce, wage-benefit differentials, and flexible production or service technologies. It is a fundamental link between the pressures of global competition on firms on the one hand and insecurity of workers on the other.

2.5 Critique of Flexibility

There has been a strong defence of flexibility on the grounds that it is an imperative for survival in competitive conditions where demand is volatile and technologies change rapidly.[77] There have been a number of analyses of flexibility in the workplace of the developed countries under the theme 'Japanization of workplace'. Some of the studies come from the perspective of the management and look at 'Japanization' as a natural consequence of the salient position of Japanese manufacturing during the 1980s, which resulted in the Japanese methods acquiring a central place in most management studies and work organization practices. On the other hand, there are studies which have looked at flexibilities from labour's point of view, on effort-rate, skills, employee autonomy, shop floor empowerment, and social relations between the workforce, unions, and management. These studies understand flexibility as a continuum of capitalistic exploitation and subordination of labour accompanied by an inherent process of class struggle and resistance.

Japanization has been described as the application of the full repertoire of production practices like Total Quality Management, continuous improvement, statistical quality control, just-in-time production, labour flexibility, multi-skilling, job rotation, organization of labour into teams/groups and progressive substitution of labour union's influence by direct management control. In the first category, i.e. the management view, Womack, et al. (1990) presents lean production as a pre-eminent high-productivity manufacturing system dominant in Japan, which the West and the rest must emulate, because it removes all slack, human and material waste.[78] The dynamic work-team at the heart of the lean factory enriches the work environment, which compels workers to think and address challenges that arise at work. Kenny and Florida (1993) make similar arguments and argue that Japanization is an inevitable outcome of the capitalistic dynamics of technological and organizational progress.[79] They conceptualize the practices within a framework of innovation-mediated production, characterized by integration and harnessing of the intelligence and knowledge of the R&D staff, design engineers, and the shop-floor workers. Through the mechanism of mule-functional team, the shop floor is transformed into a continuously innovative production laboratory. On the basis of some case studies, Oliver and Wilkinson (1992), assert that the Japanization of the British industry is still in progress.[80] This system completely synchronizes production with the demands of the market by using human resource management practices such as long-term job security for a lean core of skilled workers, careful employee recruitment and selection techniques, performance-related pay, direct communication, and enterprise unionism. The implications of worker resistance to these far-reaching changes are however noted by the authors.

In the second category of studies (worker's point of view) Ackroyd et al. (1998) argue that fundamental differences between an integrated Japanese economy characterized by high level of coordination between banking, manufacturing and traditional capital and a highly-fragmented British economy imply a limit to Japanization of British industry and economy.[81] In their study of the Nissan car assembly transplant in Sunderland, Garrhan and Stewart (1992) provide an influential analysis of managerial endeavours to control and subordinate the workforce by mobilizing an ideology built on the appealing principle of consensus and participation.[82] According to the authors, despite the highly exploitative nature of the production system - labour intensification, low-skill job enlargement - the workers display corporate consciousness and identify with the objectives of their employers in the absence of independent trade unions. Ideology of consent works at two levels: through social forms such as teamwork and Kaizen, and second, through a wider organizational vision of a classless factory. But the authors convey a mixed picture of complete worker subordination and total management control instead of participation and consensus. Similar conclusions emerge from the study of Danford (1999). Operating within an economic environment of intensive global competitive pressure, managers of these firms were not interested in enriching the lives of their employees.[83] They regarded the notion that assembly line workers could enjoy meaningful empowerment and self-management as nonsensical. Their labour control priority reflected the timeless capitalistic exigencies of efficient surplus extraction and capital accumulation. Globalization of economy and its resulting intense competition is central to compulsions behind flexibility of labour and political consent for these changes.

From the point of view of the developing countries, evidence seems to be different. It indicates that the characteristics of the flexible specialization model, like multipurpose machines, broad skills, varied products, innovations, and local policy forces, which channel the competitive pressure towards permanent innovation, are based on the experiences of some developed countries like Italy and Japan. But due to labour surplus, lax labour regulations, and inadequate growth of trade unions, the competitive advantage frequently results from the sweating of labour rather than innovation. Schmitz (1989) gives examples from the hammock making industry in Brazil, knitting and clothing industry in Sao Paulo, and garment industry in India to show the dynamics towards low wage, low technology, and low quality. He raises doubts about the replicability of the model of advanced countries to the cluster of small firms in labour-surplus Third-World countries.[84]

Flexibility within the Japanese model works well in a cultural context that has strong elements of feudalism and patriarchy. It may not be possible to replicate the Japanese type of flexibility in another cultural context, e.g., Germany, without resistance form the workers, while in 'labour surplus' India it may impose a distinct penalty upon the workers.

2.6 Insecurity Hypothesis: Some Empirical Studies and Substantiation

The UK and USA are recognized as the leading deregulators of the labour markets. Flexible work practices (FWP) are common and some studies have evaluated the resulting insecurity. In India too there have been studies to examine flexibility of employment in the organized sector.

2.6.1 *UK*

Four seminal studies in England are noticeable for the methodology and empirical evidence they provide on the IH:

i. Picture of Job insecurity Facing British Men (2002).[85]
ii. Redundancy and the Paradox of Job Insecurity (2000).[86]
iii. Job Insecurity in the British Labour Market (2000).[87]
iv. Insecurity and the Flexible Workforce (2000).[88]

The first study 'Picture of Job Insecurity Facing the British Men' notes that job insecurity has significantly risen over the last two decades for the British men. It quotes chapter 5 of the 'OECD Employment Outlook 1997', which reports a significant rise in the proportion of both men and women who are not satisfied with the job security; as per the report dissatisfaction rose from 61.7 per cent in 1991 to 78.4 per cent in just five years (1995). It considers three aspects of job insecurity in the last two decades, i.e. 1980-2001. This period is particularly relevant as it coincides with major structural adjustments, privatization, and some deregulation of the labour market, which began with the Thatcher government after 1979. The study looks at: (a) the probability of becoming unemployed, (b) the cost of unemployment in terms of loss of real wages, and (c) probability that the continuously employed will experience substantial real wage losses.

It rejects job tenure as a sufficient measure of insecurity for two reasons. First, 'voluntary quits' which are strongly pro-cyclical, and, second, the job tenure exhibits no dramatic change in the period covered. The Labour Force Survey (LFS) found that the median elapsed job tenure for men had fallen slowly but steadily from 1975 to 1995 with the overall fall for the whole period being of the order of 20 per cent. But if this phenomenon is studied from 1960s the results could be more significant.

The sources of data for the study are (a) UK Labour Force Survey, (b) OECD Employment Outlook 1997, (c) British Household Panel Study, (d) Skill Survey 1997, (e) ESRC Social Change and Economic Life Initiative 1986, (f) UK New Earnings Survey,

(g) Joint Unemployment and Vacancy Operating System, and (h) National Insurance.

There was little or no evidence of any trend increase in the average chances of the men becoming unemployed over the last 20 years. However, lower-level non-manual workers do appear to face a secular rise in the average chance of becoming unemployed. Second, there has been a strong tendency for the cost of unemployment in terms of wage losses to increase for all men except those in the lowest skill groups. The losses in hourly earnings for the rest have risen by 40 per cent or more from the early 1980s to early 1990s with the largest losses affecting the two highest skilled groups. Third, the men who are continuously employed in the same job and for those who change jobs the chances of a substantial year-on-year decline (10 per cent or more) in real hourly pay has increased by 20-30 per cent from the early 1980s to early 1990s. Older workers and those in top skill groups have been the worst hit. A similar pattern holds for longer-term (three-year average) changes in real hourly wage. The overall change in the above three is not due to any increase in dispersion of wage changes. The median annual rise in real pay in the 1990s is smaller than in the 1980s.

The increase in earning insecurity is not concentrated in workers among the declining industries. Financial services have seen the largest increase in employment and earning insecurity.

The second study, 'Redundancy and the Paradox of Job Insecurity', notes that Industrial Relations Services/MORI index of insecurity rose steadily during the early 1990s and the Annual Survey of Employee Satisfaction conducted by the International Survey Research (1996: 15-17) found that by the mid-1990s, feeling of employment security was in a free fall. The paradox of insecurity in the 1990s was such that while the attitude surveys reported growing sense of insecurity among the workforce the academic research on job tenure and turnover indicated far lesser change. The study suggested a number of factors to explain this inconsistency; the demographic ageing of the workforce statistically has offset any fall in job tenure if any. (a) Age and tenure are positively correlated and marginal fall in the aggregate median job tenure disguises substantial fall among particular groups, i.e. among the less skilled groups. (b) Insecurity is influenced by other factors like cost of job loss, occupational downgrading and the risk of job loss. It quotes LFS that during the recession of 1991 the proportion of redundant men who experienced significant spells of unemployment was 62 per cent. This implies increasing cost of redundancy to the worker. During the spring of 1996, around 50 per cent of all the men who reported having been made redundant in the previous three months were unemployed at the time of their interviews. Over the period 1992-6, one in every three men of working age experienced at least one spell of unemployment. The cyclical and secular trend in the labour market over the past 20 years is examined and they illustrate a growing scale of redundancy. The data suggests a ratchet effect whereby redundancy never quite returns to its pre-recession level. Over the 20 years, the labour market has witnessed a secular increase in the number of involuntary job losses both in absolute terms and as a proportion of all job losses. Thus, even when the economy picked up, the workers were still insecure. The second reason why workers fear redundancy, which is well founded, is that both statutory and non-statutory redundancy arrangements in Britain do not any more favour the employee. Vulnerability to redundancy occurs not only during recessionary period but also as a consequence of downsizing. Reduction in employment is no longer accompanied by reduction in output. According to the study, redundancy as a managerial preoccupation of the recent years is the most corrosive factor to security. The study strongly recommends reorientation of managerial policies towards redundancy to improve security, morale, motivation, and productivity.

The third study, 'Job Insecurity in the British Labour Market', cites data from OECD's 1997 report, LFS, GHS, and BHPS to provide evidence on job stability, cost of job loss, involuntary job loss, and elements of job protection to examine the IH. It identifies different factors of IH like job tenure, cost of job loss, and concludes that there is some reason to think that the public perception of increased job insecurity is justified for some sections of the workforce. This is especially true of older and less educated workers. Findings confirm the first study. The data and factors used for analysis are the same.

The fourth study, 'Insecurity and the Flexible Workforce', covers the same grounds as earlier ones. It also uses the same data sources. However, it makes an additional comment on the role of changes in legislation and institutional framework after 1979. According to it, there is only one major change, which is the extension from 6 months to 2 years in the length of time an employee has to have been in continuous employment before gaining access to the right against unfair dismissal, and to qualify for redundancy payments. In the field of individual employment rights, there has been no net deregulation after 1979. But there are other institutional factors such as union membership and union power. International comparison reveals correlation between extent of coverage of collective bargaining and the degree of job insecurity. Wage councils were also abolished, which had earlier offered minimum wage protection to the lower end of the labour market in some sectors. The study does not however cover all the legislative and institutional changes that occurred in the labour market in 1980.

It makes special mention of flexibility and insecurity, and defines flexibility as growth in non-standard forms of employment, which are perceived to be inherently inferior and less secure than full-time permanent jobs. The pattern of growth, in the share of flexible non-standard forms of employment, suggests that the sharpest fall in the share of employment of full-time permanent employees took place in the early 1980s. Between 1979 and 1984, the share of full-time employees as a proportion of the total workforce fell by 7 per cent, and between 1990 and 1997, by another 3 per cent (LFS). Within the category of non-standard forms of employment, the study distinguishes between part-time, temporary, and self-employed. Part-time employment has been growing steadily since the 1960s and during the 1960s, it rose by 7 per cent. The growth in temporary employment in the UK is a very recent phenomenon. From 1964-90 there was no increase but during 1990-7 the proportion of workforce that were temporary employees rose from 4.5 to 6.5 per cent of the total workforce. Since 1991, the incidence of temporary employment has grown in all sectors except distribution. The highest incidence was in administration and public services. The other significant post-1999 factor in flexible employment was the growth in the share of self-employment. In the 1980s, this category too grew in all sectors except distribution. But in the 1990s, growth came to a halt. An observation by the study is that temporary employment grew more rapidly in the more regulated labour markets of the OECD countries. It is because the regulation of standard form of employment is relatively modest in countries like the UK and USA and always has been so. Thus, the employers have generally not had the incentive to switch to non-standard forms of employment. The study concludes that there is no direct and simple relationship between flexibility and insecurity. Flexibility is not the only or sufficient factor in explaining insecurity.

The above studies provide evidence to suggest that employment flexibility is increasing and insecurity has increased for some sections of the workers. These studies provide valuable insights into measurement and discussion of the problem.

2.6.2 *USA*

USA leads the world in making labour markets flexible. Studies by the Bureau of Labour make regular contributions to empirical evidence and methodology. There has been a sectoral shift in employment in the USA from manufacturing to service sector since the beginning of the 1970s. Initially, this growth was linked to expansion of the public sectors like health services and education, but by 1985 the US Bureau of Labour Statistics (BLS) estimated that the most rapidly growing jobs in the American economy till 1995 would be of janitors, fastfood workers, nurses, aides, and clerical workers. They expected a demand for only 120,000 computer programmers. In the category of business services, work increasingly consists of feeding data into computers on a piece-rate basis.[89]

Besides this sectoral shift in employment in America, the work itself has been restructured as part-time, home work, and temporary, and is replacing traditional employment in both services and manufacturing. In America, a worker is statistically employed if he or she works for three hours a day and for at least three days a week, or if the work is categorized as temporary. From 1980 to 1995, the number of part-time workers has grown 58 per cent, and they account for one-fourth of the total employed. Part-time work is especially prevalent in the new high-tech sunrise industries. In California's Silicon Valley, part-timers are 30 per cent of the total workers. The workers in this flexible work forms make up the bulk of what is called the working poor. The advantages of flexibility to the employers is obvious; there are no cost such as sickness pay, insurance, health cover, training or vacation. Wages are nearly one-half of full-time workers. This transient labour force is usually unorganized and exists because there is a large pool of the unemployed. The above-cited norms account for the faster expansion of employment in the US compared to other industrial countries because of the absence of so-called rigidity in the labour market.

2.6.3 *Flexibility and Insecurity Hypothesis in India*

Although the entire IH has been stated and tested in the developed countries where labour market conditions are vastly different, IH has relevance and applications in the context of developing countries.[90] IH directly impacts the modern, organized sector where a sizeable urban, educated, middle class is employed and where the informally employed aspire to be employed.

The first and the most obvious difference in the labour market of developed and the developing countries is in the percentage of labour employed in the formal and organized sectors of the economy. Ninety per cent of employment in the developed countries is in this sector. Organized sector here implies formally registered firms obliged to keep accounts and pay taxes. The opposite is true in India where the organized sector employment accounts for less than 10 per cent of the total employment.

The second important difference is the quality, extent, and efficiency of regulation of the labour market, which is far greater in the developed countries, for example, in the most basic aspect of implementation of the minimum wages, regulation against unfair dismissal, against discrimination at work place, and severance or redundancy payments.

The third difference, which is the cause and consequence of the first two, is in the trade union density in the labour markets of the developed countries where typical coverage is over 33 per cent as against less than 10 per cent for India. These differences notwithstanding, the flexibility and IH are becoming the debated terms in labour economics in India.[91] This is happening in the context of globalization and liberalization.

The World Bank, which has had influence in Indian economic policy formation through the liberalization period, has presented its views on rigidities in the labour market in its World Development Report 1995 titled 'Workers in an Integrating World'. The Bank says we are living in revolutionary times. Many developing and formerly centrally planned economies have embraced market-based development and integration into the world economy. All market-based strategies of development require the state to restrict its policies to help markets work more efficiently; they derive their justification in the general equilibrium analysis of neo-classical economics. As evidence to support its policy recommendations, it cites examples from flexible labour markets of East Asian economies. Workers have made great advances in these countries that embraced global trends of increasing international trade and investment and least state intervention. According to the World Bank, predictably, the state must do the following:

i. Pursue market-based growth path that generates rapid increase in demand for labour, and expansion in the skill of workforce, and raises productivity.
ii. Use new opportunities at the international levels by tracking capital and opening up to international trade, while managing the dislocation that this might bring about.
iii. Construct the framework for labour policy that takes into account informal and rural labour markets. Majority of the labour force in developing countries is not affected by labour policies since most work in the informal sector. Avoid the biases

that favour relatively well-off workers, provide safeguards for the vulnerable and support collective bargaining in the formal sectors.

iv. Try to design transition to market-based international integration so that it is rapid and smooth without excessive or permanent cost to labour.

v. Formal sector collective bargaining between firms and independent unions is an effective way to determine wages and working conditions. The governments do need to establish rules for labour-management negotiations, spell out the rights of the labour and the firm, establish dispute resolution mechanisms, and promulgate workplace health and safety regulations, which the unions can monitor. Decentralized bargaining under conditions of competitive markets produces the best results.

vi. Governments have to formulate policies for public employment. Quality of public service has suffered in some countries by a combination of weak governance, inadequate pay, and overstaffing. Reducing the number of public workers, combined with improvements in pay, recruitment, promotion and accountability is necessary.

The policy recommendation of the World Bank, IMF and WTO, which are referred to as the Washington Consensus have inspired policy shifts in India. The shifts have clearly been more pronounced since 1991, and the labour market in India yields some evidence of the effects of the policy changes towards market flexibility. Nagaraj (2004), Deshpande (1998), Fallon (1991) and Ramaswamy (1999) among others have analysed this evidence of the past 12-13 years.[92]

2.6.3 *Evidence of Flexibility from India*

This section uses published studies to indicate the true extent of flexibility and insecurity in the workforce. The case for deregulation of the labour market was orchestrated on the basis of the evidence that organized sector was growing slower than the

Table 2.1: Rate of Growth in Output, Organized Sector Employment, Labour Force, Workforce and Unemployment from 1977-8 to 1999-2000

Variable	*1977-8 to 1983*	*1983 to 1987-8*	-	*1993-4 to 1999-2000*
GDP at 1993-4 prices	3.8	4.1	5.6	6.5
Organized sector employment total	2.0	1.1	1.0	0.7
Public sector	2.6	1.5	1.0	0.1
Private sector	0.6	0.1	1.2	2.2
Population	2.0	2.4	2.1	1.8
Work Force (P+S)	2.1	1.8	2.1	0.8
Labour force (T+S)	2.0	2.0	2.2	0.9
Workforce (P)	2.6	2.0	2.3	1.3
Labour Force (P)	1.8	2.2	2.2	1.3
Unemployment (Live register)	10.3	6.1	3.3	1.9
Unemployment (Estimated from NSSO data)	-11.8	9.1	-2.7	1.2

Source: NSSO, data from 32nd, 38th, 43rd, 50th, and 55th rounds.

GDP, population, workforce and the labour force. The lag between the rate of employment and output was analysed from 1977-8 to 1999-2000, and it has been widening as evident from the Table 2.1.

The elasticity of employment with respect to output in manufacturing declined from 1.14 (1973-8) to 0.52 (1978-83), to 0.42 (1983-8), and to 0.33 (1988-94). Although the elasticity of employment in manufacturing was declining, the manufacturing employment grew faster at 3.3 per cent per annum compounded for the period 1991-2 to 1997-8 (according to the annual survey of industry) compared to 1.5 per cent per annum during 1985-6 to 1991-2.

Some economists have raised doubts regarding the role of labour market regulation in slowing down the growth of employment in the organized sector. Fallon and Lucas estimate that amendment in 1976 of the exit clause of the Industrial Dispute Act 1947, which prohibited the employers of 300 or more workers to retrench or close down without permission sought months in advance of closure or retrenchment actually reduced the demand for labour by 17.5 per cent. In 1984, another amendment lowered the employment limit to 100 workers. This reduced potential employment more drastically.[93] The wage increases and the amendments allegedly increased the real cost of employing workers to the employers. However, there is inadequate evidence to support the claimed rise in real cost or unit labour cost. Papola (1994) based on ASI data reports a decline in unit labour cost from 1971 to 1987-8. The labour productivity in manufacturing sector increased ahead of real wages. There is however a high correlation between productivity and wages. In the same period, the capital intensity with respect to labour did increase. This could have been in anticipation of increasing real cost of labour and as an argument to support the demand for deregulation of the labour market.

The debate on employment generation assumed intensity in view of the peculiar behaviour of job growth in the 1980s in India. Employment in the manufacturing sector grew rapidly during the 1970s while output grew at less than 5 per cent. During the 1980s, the output in the same sector grew by 7 per cent with an accompanying decline in employment. More importantly while employment grew in the unorganized sector it was negative in the organized sector from 1983-8. Employment grew in the organized sector in the first half of the 1990s, while deceleration in the other sectors continued. Some analysts have attributed this to increasing real wages and job security provisions, but Roy (1998), Nagraj (1994), and Papola (1994) have refuted this.[94] While analysing the ASI data for the period 1960-1 to 1993-4, Roy found that job security regulation (both 1976 and 1982 amendments) was not responsible for slowdown in employment growth. Nagraj found that higher wages were a result of increases in productivity or increase in person day work (longer hours). Goldar (2000) shows that, despite the presence of unaltered job security regulations, employment in organized manufacturing sector grew at 4.03 per cent per annum during the first half of the 1990s. Micro-level study supports the macro-level finding that employment growth had taken place during the early 1990s. Nagraj (2004) reported that 1.3 million employees lost their jobs during 1995-6 to 2001 in the organized sector, i.e. 13 per cent of the workforce.[95] So, either way through the 1990s, firms could increase or decrease their workforce despite the job security provisions.

Job security legislation is said to include all the legal provisions that raise the cost of hiring or dismissing a worker, for example, notification period, compensation cost (separation benefits, and legal cost of an appeal by the worker against allegedly unjust dismissal, cost arising out of court verdict). This is supposed to affect adversely the ability and willingness to create jobs and is therefore linked to lack of flexibility in the labour market and lower employment rates during expansion and higher employment rate during recession.[96]

A study by Deshpande et al. (1998), is also relevant to the IH and flexibility in India.[97] It was the first large-scale study of flexible labour practices adopted by employers in a local labour market, i.e. Mumbai, India. It was funded by the ILO, on the lines of the Malaysian Labour Flexibility Survey, and conducted in 1993. The study concluded that Mumbai, the industrial and financial capital of the country, experienced a decline of employment in the whole modern sector during the 1980s and not just in factory employment. Registered unemployment, informal employment and *badli*, contract labour and women employment increased. The study also concluded that although regulations are often blamed for unemployment, the employers in Mumbai enjoyed much greater flexibility as far as use of non-permanent labour is concerned than those in Malaysia.[98] Larger employers who are allegedly more regulated by law from retrenching their workers were in fact able to do so as freely as small employers. The growth in flexible labour category will represent much of the growth in employment in future and this portends ill for the maintenance of minimum labour standards in private factory employment as also for the union movement in the future.[99] The government policies and overall macro-conditions created by increasing liberalization and deregulation of the industrial sector were found to be closely related to the factors responsible for this state of affairs.

A pertinent study by Deshpande (2002), based on 1,300 firms belonging to 9 industries in 10 states and 8 different size groups of employment was undertaken to find out the determinant of levels and change in employment between 1991 and 1998.[100] The determinants were identified as (a) employment flexibility, (b) wage flexibility, (c) labour process flexibility, (d) impact of union on collective bargaining, (e) impact of state regulation, ideology and administrative action.

One of the findings of this study was that:

> total employment in the sampled firms belonging to the factory sector increased at 2.84 per cent per annum compounded during 1991-98. Non-manual employment increased at 5 per cent per annum, manual at 2.20 per cent per annum. Majority of the employers (60 per cent) increased total employment, while only 27 per cent decreased. Employers increased total employment by increasing the share of non-permanent employees and women workers. In the nine manufacturing industries investigated employment increased by 3 per cent per annum.

In the wage analysis confined to unskilled male manual workers, the study showed that four out of five firms paid a consolidated wage. Typically, wage has three components. The basic wage is a fixed component whereas DA and bonus are variable. The higher the component of the fixed wage the more secure is the worker. Basic wages are determined largely by the minimum wage law and to a smaller extent by collective bargaining. In the textile firms of the sample, other factors determined the basic wage in a majority of cases. These included experience, qualification, job evaluation, and adjudication. The textile industry was the most unionized. Proportionately more of the larger firms reported that the basic wages were determined by collective bargaining. Payment of separate DA was reported by only 12 per cent of the firms and that the larger firms were more likely to pay the DA. One-third of the employees were paid bonus at the minimum rate and the union presence was associated with higher bonus rates. In all 80 per cent of the firms paid consolidated wages and collective bargaining was associated with other allowances. By and large for manual labour, the compensation tends to be close to the minimum wage and not flexible.

The study found that over the seven-year liberalization period the share of permanent manual workers declined from close to 68 per cent in 1991 to 64 per cent in 1998. It increased only in three categories, non-metallic minerals, beverages, and tobacco. In the category of non-permanent employment casual workers increased the fastest making them the most insecure category. The big firms resorted to greater use of non-permanent workers - 33 per cent non-permanent and 8 per cent contract.

Relationship between location and share of non-permanent workers was not significant in the case of manual workers.

Another aspect, which could be used to indicate the increasing flexibilization and insecurity in employment in the Indian context is the quantitative growth of the informal/unorganized (IFS) sector. In manufacturing, it may be defined as not registered under the Factories Act, and in the service defined as employing less than seven persons. In this context the studies of Kundu (1993), Mitra, Nagamine (1993, 2004) and Mukherjee (2004) are important.[101] All these studies indicate the significance of the informal sector. The size and growth of the small-scale and the informal sectors have a relationship to the increasing organizational, numerical, wage and work flexibility sought by the organized manufacturing and service sectors in India. As per the NSSO and CSO surveys, the size of the IFS has not changed appreciably since 1984. Examining four successive NSSO surveys Mukherjee observes that in terms of enterprise numbers and employment, the sector experienced a marginal decline in 1984-9 but recovered after that and by 2000 there were 17 million enterprises and 37 million employees. The sector's heterogeneous growth pattern and recent revival and growth cannot be simply imputed to the distress factor of the unemployed, but there is a dynamic factor especially in the sub-segments of urban NDME and DME (Non-Directory Manufacturing Enterprises employing less than six workers including household workers and Directory Manufacturing Enterprises units employing 6 or more workers with at least one hired worker) which are linked to the growth of outsourcing and other linkages with the organized factory sector. Rural NDME and DME are linked to the growth of agricultural productivity and per capita income. In the post-reform period there was a strong revival of the IFS, and the number of enterprises and employment (grew at the rate of 2.85 per annum over 1994-2000) increased in all segments except rural NDMEs and DMEs. In fact, the share of OAMEs (Own Account Manufacturing Enterprise units operating with no hired labour) have increased during this period indicating that the distress factor of unemployment may also be working along with the retrenchment from, and, restructuring of large and small manufacturing enterprises.

Add to the above situation the fact that the small scale, as distinct from the IFS, has always been a large employer of insecure labour, the overall picture of insecurity is complete. The small scale accounts for an astounding 95 per cent of all industrial units in the economy and for 40 per cent of the value added, 34 per cent of the total exports, and 7 per cent of the gross domestic product. A study of SSI units based in MMR highlights the state of employees in the sector. Although the number of closures have increased after the reforms, mainly due to lockouts, the SSI are able to survive more easily when they are captive to the medium and large units through the system of putting-out and sub-contracting.[102] The study provides a graphic picture of the quality of employment as, according to the Bombay Small Scale Industries Association (BSSIA) data only 5.6 per cent workers were registered workers while the rest 94.5 per cent were daily voucher workers. In the sample of 446 workers, working in 109 SSIs, located in the 33 industrial estates surveyed, three-fifths of the workers had not found secure employment in the SSIs, in that they had been employed for less than five years. Only seven workers in the sample had a provident fund; the rest had regular weekly layoffs. All of them were multi-tasking in the units. Forty-five per cent of the workers had shifted job at least once in the last decade. Of this half used to be employed in the informal sector before they came into the SSI, while 37 per cent were (mainly temporary employees in the formal sector) from organized sector mills and factories and had come into the SSI due to closures, VRS, and retrenchments. This signifies that, perhaps as literature also suggests, restructuring in the formal manufacturing sector in Mumbai had begun more than a decade ago.

Three important studies therefore provide conclusive evidence on the high degree of flexibility of all types in India:

1. Sharma and Sasikumar's (1996) survey of firms in Ghaziabad 1991-5.[103]
2. Sudha Deshpande, et al. (1998) study of labour flexibility 1997-8.[104]
3. Lalit Deshpande's (2004) study of labour flexibility practices in ten states and nine industries in India during 1991-8.[105]

The main findings are as follows:[106]

Firms increased their total employment during the period (1987-2004) of all three studies. Lalit Deshpande found that total employment grew by 3 per cent, manual employment by 2.29 per cent and non-manual by over 5 per cent. Only 13 per cent firms surveyed did not change employment, 60 per cent increased employment and 27 per cent decreased the number of jobs.

All firms, small, medium, and large that increased employment did so by hiring primarily non-permanent workers. Firms employing 200-499 workers registered the largest employment increase. These were firms supposedly constrained by restrictive laws and trade unions. The percentage share of permanent manual employment decreased during 1991-8, while the percentage of non-casual labour belonging to the non-permanent category increased to more than one-third of manual employment. If contract labour is added then the share of non-regular, i.e. non-permanent plus contract was as high as 42 per cent. Large firms (100-plus workers) thus used more non-permanent labour.

Basic wages of unskilled male workers were based on the minimum wage law and not on the basis of collective bargaining. The law has many loopholes and is revised very infrequently with the result that the new minimum wage rates are lower in real terms than the pre-revision rates. In most cases, these minimum wages are below the poverty line as reported by the ILO.[107] Three-fourth of the firms in Lalit's survey paid a consolidated wage only and a mere 12 per cent, mostly large firms, paid a separate dearness allowance. Sudha notes that the Indian employers enjoy tremendous wage flexibility, and the labour institutions do not in practice enforce any rigidity.

Deshpande's study found that the unions were present in only a little over one-fourth of the surveyed firms, and this presence was not a deterrent to changing employment in either direction. She found that the unionized firms are more likely to introduce technological changes, alter the product range, and improve the quality of the product. Venkat Ratnam studying 204 collective agreements in 1990 found that unions were not a hindrance to introducing labour flexibility measures in the firm.[108] He cites several clauses of understanding reached between the unions and management, where flexibility, quality, and productivity yardsticks are spelled out. This is in tune with the international trend cited by researchers like Ozaki (1999) who noted that in recent years trade unions have toned down their resistance to flexibility in this age of intense competition.[109] The changing balance of power is evident in the fact that since the post-Mumbai textile strike (early 1980s) there has been more lockouts than strikes. The former is an important managerial strategy to weaken the union power and introduce flexibility.[110]

The studies underscore the fact that labour market flexibility in India is extensive and perhaps more than all the countries cited above.

2.7 Conclusion

The chapter developed the statement of the IH, its corollaries, the relationship between IH and flexibility and lastly the evidence on increasing flexibly in some OECD countries and India was summarized. In the OECD studies a wider variety of concepts and data are used to measure the phenomenon, like number of job losses, impact of job losses on future income, occupational downgrading, elements of job protection, loss of real wages and average tenure of employees in the organized sector. Flexibility is also viewed from the worker's perspective and related to the concept of insecurity. The Indian studies are at a more basic stage; they estimate the reduction in organized sector employment, numbers of non-permanent workers and the casualization of workers. In the vast informal sector on the other hand, non-permanent and atypical workers are the norm.

Despite the need to extend the empirical evidence and to generate more comprehensive data to support the hypothesis and its outcome over time, there seems to be adequate evidence to indicate a pervasive phenomenon of widening flexibility in even the erstwhile 'secure' sectors, and a deepening flexibility as the informal sector grows in India. In this study the relationship of flexibility to insecurity is explored in a survey based on the city of Greater Mumbai.

Chapter 3 will develop the array of correlates of the hypothesis that are important from the point of view of this study.

Notes

1. R.J. Burke and C.L. Cooper (2000): *The Organization in Crisis: Downsizing, Restructuring and Privatization*, Blackwell Publishers, Oxford.
   C.L. Cooper and R.J. Burke (2002): 'Introduction: The New World of Work', in Cooper and Burke (eds.), *The New World of Work*, Blackwell, Oxford.
2. Edmund Heery and John Salmon (2000): 'The Insecurity Thesis', in Edmund Heery and Salmon John (eds.), *The Insecurity Thesis*, Routledge, London.
3. K. Baker and K. Christensen (1998): *Contingent Work: American Employment Relations in Transition*, Cornell University Press, Ithaca.
   OECD (1997): *Employment Outlook*, Organization for Economic Cooperation and Development, OECD, Paris.
   Guy Standing (1997): 'Globalization, Labour Flexibility and Insecurity: The Era of Market Regulation', *European Journal of Industrial Relations*, 3, 1, pp. 7-37.

Suddha Deshpande, Guy Standing, and Lalit Deshpande (1998): *Labour Flexibility in a Third World Metropolis: A Case Study of Bombay,* Commonwealth Publishers, New Delhi.
G. Betcherman and R. Islam, eds. (2001): *East Asian Labour Markets and the Economic Crisis*, ILO, Geneva.

4. L. Elliot and D. Atkinson (1998): *The Age of Insecurity*, Verso, London.
U. Beck (1992): *Risk Society: Towards a New Modernity*, Sage, London.
5. Stephen Nickell, Patricia Jones and Leanda Quintini (2002): 'Picture of Job Insecurity Facing British Men', *The Economic Journal of Royal Economic Society*, vol. 112, no. 476, pp. 542-55.
6. P. Cappelli et al. (1997): *Change at Work*, Oxford University Press, New York.
7. OECD (1997): *Employment Outlook*, OECD, Paris.
8. H. Faber (1993): 'The Incidence and the Cost of Job Loss 1982-91, Bookings Papers on Economic Activity', *Microeconomics*, pp. 73-132.
9. Edmund Heery and Brian Abbott (2000): 'Trade Unions and the Insecure Workforce', in Heery Edmund and Salmon Jon (eds.), *The Insecure Workforce*, Routledge, London.
10. P. Cappelli (1995): 'Rethinking Employment', *British Journal of Industrial Relations*, 33, 34, pp. 563-602.
11. D.M. Rousseau (1996): 'Changing the Deal while Keeping the People', *Academy of Management Executive*, vol. 10, pp. 50-61.
12. Guy Standing (1997): 'Globalization, Labour Flexibility and Insecurity: The Era of Market Regulation', *European Journal of Industrial Relations*, 3, 1, pp. 7-37.
13. David Guest (2000): 'Management and the Insecure Workforce', in Edmund Heery and John Salmon (eds.), *The Insecure Workforce*, Routledge, London.
14. J. Wickham (1997): 'Part-time Work in Ireland and Europe', *Work, Employment and Society*, 11, 1, pp. 133-51.
15. Cappelli et al. (1997): *Change at Work.*
H. Beynon (1997): 'The Changing Practices of Work', in R.K. Brown (ed.), *The Changing Shape of Work*, Basingstoke: Macmillan.
R.K. Brown (1997): 'Flexibility and Security. Contradictions in the Contemporary Labour Market', in Brown (ed.), *The Changing Shape of Work*, Basingstoke: Macmillan.
16. Bernard Baumohl (1993): 'When Downsizing Becomes Dumb Sizing', *Time Magazine*, 15 March.

17. J. Broadbent et al. (1998): 'The End of Profession?', in J. Broadbent, M. Dietrich and J. Robert (eds.), *The End of Profession? The Restructuring of Professional Work*, Routledge, London.
P. Cappelli et al. (1997): *Change at Work*.
J. Kelly (1997): 'Industrial Relation: Looking to the Future', *British Journal of Industrial Relations*, 33, 3, pp. 393-8.
K. Legge (1998): 'Flexibility: The Gift-wrapping of Employment, Degradation', in P. Sparrow and M. Marchington (eds.), *Human Resource Management: The New Agenda*, Pitman Publishing, London.
18. C. Brown et al. (1993): 'Becoming a High Performance Work Organization: The Role of Security, Employee Involvement and Training', *International Journal of Human Resource Management*, 4, 2, pp. 247-75.
P. Edwards, M. Collinson and C. Reese (1998): *The Determinants of Employee Responses to Total Quality Management: Six Case Studies, Organization Studies*, Cochan and Osterman, pp. 449-75.
19. J. Bound and G. Johnson (1992): 'Changes in the Structure of Wages in the 1980s: An Evaluation of Alternative Explanation', *American Economic Review*, 82, pp. 371-92.
20. M.F. Mitchell (2005): 'Specialization and the Skill Premium in the 20th Century', *International Economic Review*, vol. 46, August, pp. 935-55.
21. C. Crouch (1997): 'Skill Based Full Employment: The Latest Philosopher's Stone', *The British Journal of Industrial Relations*, 35, 3, pp. 367-84.
C. Lane (1990): 'Vocational Training, Employment Training and New Production Concepts: Some Lessons for Britain', *International Review Journal*, 21, 4, pp. 247-59.
W. Streeck (1989): 'Skills and the Limits of Neo Liberalism: Enterprise of the Future as a Place of Learning', *Work Employment and Society* 3, 1, pp. 89-104.
Philip Brown, Andy Green and Hugh Lauder (2001): *High Skills*, Oxford University Press, Oxford.
22. Susan Christopherson (1987): 'Workforce Flexibility: Implications for Women Workers', *ISSR Working Paper* 3 (2).
23. *Monthly Review* (2004): April.
24. Michael H. Best (1990): *The New Competition: Institutions of Industrial Restructuring*, Cambrdige University Press, Cambridge, p. 160.

25. A. Kalhan (2004): 'Life Long Learning for What?', in *Teachers of the World*, July-September, vol. 5, no. 7.
26. K. Blanchard, J.P. Carlos and A. Randolph (1999): *The Three Keys to Empowerment*, Berret-Koehler, San Francisco.
27. Peter Jarvis (2000): 'The Age of Learning', in Peter Jarvis (ed.), *Continuing Education at the University of Surrey*, OUP, London.
28. P. Hargreaves and Peter Jarvis (1998): *The Human Resource Development Handbook*, Kogan Page, London.
29. ILO (2005): *World Employment Report 2004-05*, ILO, Geneva.
30. H. Beynon (1997): 'The Changing Practices of Work', in R.K. Brown (ed.), *The Changing Shape of Work*, Macmillan, Basingstoke.
    J. Gray (1995): 'The Undoing of Conservatism', in J. Gray (ed.), *Enlightenment Wake: Politics and Culture at the end of the Modern Age*, Routledge, London.
    E. Luttwak (1994): 'Why Fascism is the Wave of the Future', *London Review of Book*, April 7: 3, 6.
    W. Hutton (1995): *The State We're In*, Johnathan Cape, London.
31. Carnoy Martin (1999): 'The Family, Flexible Work and Social Cohesion at Risk', *International Labour Review*, vol. 138, no. 4, pp. 411-29.
32. Edmond Heery and Abbott Brian (2000): 'Trade Union and the Insecure Workforce', in Edmund Heery and Salomon John (eds.), *The Insecure Workforce*, Routledge, London.
    P. Leisink (1997): 'New Union Constituency Call for Differentiated Agenda and Democratic Participation', *Transfer*, 3, pp. 534-50.
    K. Wever (1998): 'International Labour Revitalization: Enlarging the Playing Field', *Industrial Relations*, 37, 3, pp. 388-407.
33. J. Gray (1995): 'The Undoing of Conservatism', in J. Gray (ed.), *Enlightenment Wake: Politics and Culture at the End of the Modern Age*, Routledge, London.
34. Jan Breman (1996): *Footloose Labour in India's Informal Economy*, Cambridge University Press, Cambridge.
35. Juned Shaikh (2005): 'Worker Politics, Trade Unions and the Shiv Sena's Rise in Central Bombay', *Economic and Political Weekly*, 30 April-6 May 2005, vol. 40, no. 18, pp. 1893-1900.
36. Ravi K. Srinivas (1992): 'Underclass, Hi-Technology and Los Angeles Uprising', *Economic and Political Weekly*, 24-31 October, p. 2388.
37. B.J. Silver (2003): *Forces of Labour: Cambridge Studies in Comparative Politics*, Cambridge University Press, New York.

38. S. Dex and McCulloch (1997): *Flexible Employment*, Macmillan, Basingstoke.
    E. Engberg (1993): 'Union Responses to the Contingent Workforce', in DS Cobble (ed.), *Women in Union: Forging a Partnership*, ILR Press, Ithaca, New York.
39. Thomas Frank (2004): *What's the Matter with Kansas?*, Metropolitan Owl, New York.
40. Jane P. Nolan et al. (1997): 'Job Insecurity, Psychological Well-Being and Family Life', in Edmund Heery and Salmon Jon (eds.), *Insecure Workforce*, Routledge.
    S. Dex and A. McCulloch (1997): *Flexible Employment*, Macmillan, Basingstoke.
    D. Gallie et al. (1998): *Restructuring the Employment Relationship*, Oxford Uinversity Press, Oxford.
41. J.P. Nolan, I.C. Wichert and B.J. Burchell (2000): 'Job Insecurity and Psychological Wellbeing and Family Life', in Edmund Heery and John Salmon (eds.), *The Insecure Workforce*,' Routledge, London and New York.
42. J.C. Latack and R.B. Dozier (1986): 'After the Axe Falls: Job Loss as a Career Transition', *Academy of Management Review*, 11, pp. 375-92.
43. T. Vuuren, B. Klandermans et al. (1991): 'Employee Reactions to Job Insecurity', in J. Hartley, Jacobson et al. (eds.), *Job Insecurity: Coping With Jobs At Risk*, Sage, London.
44. D. Collinson and M. Collinson (1995): 'Corporate Liposuction and the Re-Masculinisation of Management', Keynote address at *Gender and Life in Organizations Conference*, University of Portsmouth, Portsmouth.
45. W. Secombe (1986): 'Marxism and Demography, Family, Economy and State: The Social Reproduction Process under Capitalism', in J. Dickinson and Bob Russell (eds.), *Social Welfare*, Routledge, pp. 56-84.
46. Karl Polanyi (1957): *The Great Transformation*, Beacon Press, Boston.
47. Manuel Castells and Alejandro Portes (1989): 'World Underneath: The Origins, Dynamics and Effects of the Informal Economy', in Alejandro Portes, Manuel Castells et al. (eds.), *In the Informal Economy: Studies in Advanced and Less Developed Countries*, John Hopkins University Press, Baltimore.
48. James Dickinson (1986): *From Poor Law to Social Insurance: The Periodisation of State Intervention in the Reproduction Process*, Routledge, London.

49. N. Harris (1995): 'The Reproduction of Labour Force', in N. Harris (ed.), *The New Untouchables: Immigration and the new World Worker*, I.B. Tauris Publishers, London, pp. 157-85.
50. J. Wayne (1986): 'Function of Social Welfare in a Capitalist Economy', in Dickinson and Russell (eds.), *Social Welfare*, Routledge, pp. 56-84.
51. F. Tabak and M.A. Crichlow (2000): *Normalization: Process and Structure*, John Hopkins University Press, Baltimore and London, pp. 133-65.
52. Martyn Wright (1998): *Managing Competitive Crisis*, Cambridge University Press, Cambridge.
53. ILO (2005): *World Employment Report 2004-05*, ILO-Geneva.
54. E. Heery and J. Salmon, eds. (2000): 'Introduction', *Insecure Workforce*, Routledge Press, London, p. 11.
55. S. Burgess and H. Rees (1996): 'Job Tenure in Britain 1975-92', *The Economic Journal*, 106, pp. 334-44
    J. Goddard (1998): 'Review of Change at Work', *British Journal of Industrial Relations*, 36, 3: 501-3.
    D. Guest (1997): 'Towards Jobs and Justice in Europe: A Research Agenda', *Industrial Relations Journal*, 28, 4, pp. 344-52.
56. D. Smith (1997): *Job Insecurity versus Labour Market Flexibility*, Social Market Foundation, London.
57. R. Bootle (1996): *The Death of Inflation*, Nicholas Brealey, London.
58. *The Economist* (2005): 'The Great Job Switch', 1-7 October.
59. Roger Bootle (2001): *Money for Nothing*, Oxford University Press, London.
60. Peter Robinson (2000): 'Insecurity and the Flexible Workforce, Measuring the Ill Defined', in Heery and Solomon (eds.), *The Insecure Workforce*, Routledge, London.
61. A. Felstead et al. (1998): 'Insecurity at Work: Is Job Insecurity Really Much Worse than Before', *New Economy* 5, pp. 180-4.
62. J. Stredwick and Steve Ellis (1998): *Flexible Working Practices-Techniques and Innovations*, Institute of Personnel and Development London.
63. J.E. Stiglitz (2002): 'Employment, Social Justice and Societal Well-being', *International Labour Review*, vol. 141, nos. 1-2, pp. 9-29.
64. N. Piore and C. Sable (1984): *The Second Industrial Divide*, Basic Books, New York.
65. J. Womack et al. (1990): *The Machine that Changed the World – the Triumph of Lean Production*, Macmillan, New York.

66. M. Best (1990): *The New Competition*, Harvard University Press, Cambridge.
67. R. Cooper (1995): *When Lean Enterprises Collide*, Harvard Business School Press, Boston.
68. R. Caplinsky (1993): 'Is Flexible Production Relevant to Less Developed Countries', *OECD Development Center Working Paper*, OECD, Paris.
69. Guy Standing (1999): *Global Labour Flexibility: Thinking Distributive Justice*, MacMillan Press, London.
    Suddha Deshpande, Guy Standing and Lalit Deshpande (1998): *Labour Flexibility in Third world: A Case Study of Bombay*, Commonwealth Publications, New Delhi.
70. B.R. Holmstrom and J. Tirole (1989): 'The Theory of the Firm', in R. Schmalensee and R.D. Willig (eds.), *Handbook of Industrial Organization*, North Holland, Amsterdam.
71. Ronald Munck (2002): *Globalization and Labour*, Madhyam Books, Delhi, pp. 72-3.
72. David Harvey (1993): 'Class Relations, Social Justice and Politics of Difference', in Michael and Pile (eds.), *Place and Politics of Identity*, Routledge, London.
73. Confederation of British Industry (1996): *Flexible Labour Markets*, CBI, London.
74. Philippe Cadene and Mark Holmstrom (1998): *Decentralized Production in India*, Sage, New Delhi.
75. Robert M. Solow (2005): *What is Labour Market Flexibility?: What is it Good for?* Internet site www://Britac.uk/pubs/src/keynes97/text.html.
76. K.R. Shyam Sundar (2005): 'Labour Flexibility Debate in India', *Economic and Political Weekly*, vol. XL, no. 22, 23 May, nos. 23-8, June, pp. 4-10.
77. P. Forrester (1994): 'Flexibility, Politics and Strategy: In Defense of the Model of the Flexible Firm', *Work Employment and Society*, vol. 8, no. 2, pp. 221-42.
78. J.P. Womack, D.T. Jones and D. Roos (1990): *The Machine that Changed the World: The Triumph of Lean Production*, Macmillan, New York.
79. M. Kenny and R. Florida (1993): *Beyond Mass Production: The Japanese System and its Transfer to the USA*, Oxford University Press, New York.

80. N. Oliver and B. Wilkinson (1988): *The Japanization of British Industry*, Blackwell, Oxford.
81. S. Ackroyd et al. (1998): 'The Japanization of the British Industry', *Industrial Relations Journal*, 19, 1, p. 23.
82. P. Garrhan and T. Stewart (1992): *The Nissan Enigma: Flexibility at Work in Local Economy*, Mansell, London.
83. Andy Danford (1999): *Management Techniques and British Workers*, Mansell, London, New York.
84. H. Schmitz (1989): 'Flexible Specialization: A New Paradigm of Small-scale Industrialization', *Institute of Development Studies*, Paper no. 324, pp. 27-33.
85. Stephen Nickell, Patricia Jones and Glenda Quintini (2002): 'Picture of Job insecurity Facing British Men', *The Economic Journal*, 112, January, pp. 1-27.
86. Peter Turnbull and Victoria Wass (2000): 'Redundancy and the Paradox of Job Insecurity', in Heery Edmund and John Salmon (eds.), *Insecure Workforce*, Routledge Press, London, pp. 57-77.
87. Paul Greg and Genevieve Knight (2000): 'Job Insecurity in the British Labour Market', in Heery Edmund and John Salmon (eds.), *Insecure Workforce*, Routledge Press, London.

    Wadsworth Jonathan (2000): 'Insecurity at Work', in Heery Edmund and John Salmon (eds.), *Insecure Workforce*, Routledge Press, London, pp. 39-55.
88. Peter Robinson (2000): 'Insecurity and the Flexible Workforce', in Heery Edmund and John Salmon (eds.), *Insecure Workforce*, Routledge, London, pp. 25-38.
89. Joyce Kolko (2000): 'Restructuring the Working Classes', in Harry Dahms (ed.), *Transformations of Capitalism*, Macmillan Press, London.
90. K. Das and P. Panayiotopoulos (1996): 'Flexible Specialization: New Paradigm for Industrialization for Developing Countries', *Economic and Political Weekly*, vol. 31, no. 52, 28 December, pp. 57-61.

    K.V. Ramaswamy (1999): 'The Search for Flexibility in Indian Manufacturing', *Economic and Political Weekly*, vol. 34, no. 30, 6 February, pp. 363-8.
91. Sudha Deshpande, Guy Standing and Lalit Deshpande (1998): *Labour Flexibility in a Third World Metropolis: A Case Study of Bombay*, Commonwealth Publishers, New Delhi.
92. K.V. Ramaswamy (1999): 'The Search for Flexibility in Indian Manufacturing: New Evidence on Outsourcing Activities', *Economic and Political Weekly*, 6 February, pp. 363-9.

Sudha Deshpande, Guy Standing and Lalit Deshpande (1998): *Labour Flexibility in Third World: A Case Study of Bombay*, Commonwealth Publications, New Delhi.
T. Fallon and R. Lucas (1991): 'Impact of Changes in Job Security Regulation in India and Zimbabwe', *World Bank Economic Review* vol. 5, no. 3, pp. 121-34.
Sudha Deshpande and L.K. Deshpande (2002): 'Reform and Labour Market in India', Institute of Applied Manpower Research, *Reform and Employment*, Concept, New Delhi.

93. P. Fallon and R. Lucas (1991): 'Impact of Changes in Job Security Regulation in India and Zimbabwe', *World Bank Economic Review*, vol. 5, no. 3, pp. 121-34.
94. Sudita Roy (1998): 'Lags in Employment Adjustment and Inter-industry Differential ... An Analysis Using Dynamic Inter-related Factor Demand Function', Discussion Paper No. 199, IGIDR, Bombay.
R. Nagraj (1994): 'Employment and Wages in Manufacturing Industry...Trends, Hypothesis and Evidence', *Economic and Political Weekly*, vol. 29, no. 4, 22 January, pp. 177-86.
95. R. Nagraj (2004): 'Fall in the Organized Employment: A Brief Note', *Economic and Political Weekly*, 24 July, pp. 3387-90.
96. J. Heckman and C. Pages (2000): 'The Cost of Job Security Regulation. Evidence from Latin American Labour Market', Working Paper 7773, http: //www.nber.org/papers/w7773
97. Sudha Deshpande, Guy Standing and Lalit Deshpande (1998): *Labour Flexibility in Third World: A Case Study of Bombay*, Commonwealth Publishers, New Delhi.
98. Ibid., p. 83.
99. Ibid., pp. 46-9.
100. Sudha Deshpande and L.K. Deshpande (2002): 'Reform and Labour Market in India', Institute of Applied Manpower Research, *Reform and Employment*, Concept, New Delhi.
101. A. Kundu (1993): 'Urban Informal Sector: An Overview of Macro Dimensions, Socio-Economic Correlates and Policy Perspectives in India', in H. Nagamine (ed.), *Urban Informal Sector Employment: A Cross National Comparison Study*, Institute for Regional Planning and Development, Nagoya, Japan.
A. Kundu (1993): 'Trends and Patterns of Female Employment in India: A Case of Organized Informalization', *Indian Journal of Labour Economics*, vol. 40, no. 3, July-September, pp. 1785-93.

H. Nagamine (1993): *Urban Informal Sector Employment: A Cross-National Comparative Study*, Research Institute for Planning and Development, Nagoya.
H. Nagamine (2004): *Urban Informal Sector Employment: A Cross-National Comparative Study*, Research Institute for Regional Planning and Development, Nagoya.
Dipa Mukherjee (2004): 'Informal Manufacturing Sector in India: Pre- and Post-Reform Growth Dynamics', *Indian Journal of Labour Economics*, vol. 47, no. 2, pp. 293-310.

102. Ritu Diwan (2004): 'Captive Workers in Captive Small Scale Factories', *Indian Journal of Labour Economics*, vol. 47, no. 4, pp. 1039-52.
103. Alakh Sharma and S.K. Sasikumar (1996): *Structural Adjustments and Labour*, V.V. Giri National Labour Institute, Noida (mimeo).
104. Sudha Deshpande et al. (1998): *Labour Flexibility in Third world Metropolis*, Indian Society of Labour Economics, Commonwealth Publishers, New Delhi.
105. Lalit Deshpande et al. (2004): *Liberalization and Labour, Labour Flexibility in Manufacturing*, Institute for Human Development, New Delhi.
106. K.R. Shyam Sundar (2005): 'Labour Flexibility Debate in India', *Economic and Political Weekly*, vol. XL, nos. 22-3, 28 May-3 June, pp. 4-10.
107. ILO–FAAT (1996): *Indian Economic Reforms and Labour Policy*, ILO-FAAT, New Delhi.
108. C.S. Venkata Ratnam (2004): *Negotiated Change, Collective Bargaining, Liberalization and Restructuring in India*, Response Books, Sage, New Delhi/London.
109. Muneto Ozaki (1999): *Negotiating Flexibility the Role of the Social Partner and the State*, ILO, Geneva, p. 108.
110. K.R. Shyam Sundar (2003): 'Flexibility and Rigidity in Labour Market...Towards Balanced Prospective', *Journal of Indian School of Political Economy*, vol. 15, no. 3, pp. 679-88.

CHAPTER 3

The Survey and Analysis

Looking for Questions on the Field.

3.1 The Survey

The field survey in Mumbai, from 2005-7, overturned a few widely held views. For example the notion that had gained currency in the 1990s regarding the public sector – that the public sector was a sleepy, static working place where skill development ended, in contrast to the private sector; that the creamiest layer of workers in the organized sector are unthreatened by insecurity. Evidence from the survey also gainsays other commonly accepted ideas – that trade unions are pointless in the new global age; that the young inherited only opportunities for upward mobility in the post-liberalization period, that private institutions are most favoured for 'off the job' skill development; that insecure workers give up on acquiring new skills; and that the Indian labour markets are inflexible.

Most of these notions were boosted by the pro-liberalization task force for two decades, so much so that they became part of our collective perception. Time spent on the field in Mumbai threw up some fresh questions and different observations.

A survey of employees in the organized sector in Greater Mumbai was carried out during 2005-7 to provide estimates on the various dimensions and correlates of insecurity as experienced by the employees in the post-reform period, i.e. since 1991. In this chapter the process of generating survey data sets and estimates as well as the results are presented.

Section 3.1 recapitulates the background to the IH; the next section provides the survey perspective. Section 3.3 the scope of the survey, items of inquiry and a brief background of the region surveyed. Section 3.4 contains an account of the survey, method of data collection, period, design, and key concepts. The last section presents the survey results based on which the sampled population is described and key concepts like insecurity and its correlates are measured.

3.2 Background

Recapitulating briefly, the central premise of the Insecurity Hypothesis (IH) is that insecurity (transmitted through labour markets) is widening and deepening. Sectors (in this case the organized sector) and occupational categories (even white-collar) traditionally assumed to be secure are now facing insecurity. Further, employment security is assumed to be fundamental to income security, more so in the absence of adequate social security nets. Insecurity of course has an array of psychological, social, economic and political importations.

There has been an extensive ongoing debate on the anticipated consequences of globalization for the workforce at various levels. There has also been an scrutiny of its impact on prospects of long-term secure jobs, impediments to skill formation and upgradation in the absence of job and income security, required safety nets, and the infrastructure for supporting and encouraging equitable opportunity.

The process of globalization and restructuring started earlier in many countries and a number of studies have been conducted there to assess the resulting changes in the workplace.[1] The frequent concern seems to be the spread of digital technology, robotics, new HRM and flexible work practices, shift from long-term to short-term employment contracts, discriminatory terms of employment for core and peripheral workers, the diminished power of trade unions and the loss of secure employment. What is the likely future of work? Will liberalization and integration of global markets be resisted and cut short if insecurity swells? And how will that develop or play out in different countries in the absence of powerful trade unions, and political parties associated with trade unions? Several of these studies based in the OECD, and other countries have been reviewed and their findings summarized in earlier chapters.

In India, there are some studies to indicate the increasing flexibility of labour, but attempts to quantify and measure insecurity and its correlates that flexibility may cause have been meagre.[2] Broad concepts and possible quantification for this purpose have been defined here and an attempt made to outline and demonstrate an approach, which further investigations can follow and refine.

3.3 The Survey Perspective

Methods and approaches similar to ones employed in this survey have been used in other survey-based studies. In the USA, Osterman (1994) developed an analytic framework he used in 1992 in a survey to estimate the extent to which 'flexible work practices' composed of self-managed work teams, QC, TQM and job rotation were adopted in the United States.

Internationally competitive products and services have a higher technology content that requires high levels of skills. In addition, the choices that firms were making in following a highroad strategy that emphasizes quality, variety, and customer service requires HR practices like training and incentives for loyalty rather than short-term low-cost competitive strategy.[3]

Osterman's follow-up survey five years later indicated that that QC, TQM, and job rotation continued to diffuse at a rapid pace during the period.[4] Other researchers have reported similar conclusions about the use of new HR practices to induce increasing flexibility and worker productivity in the USA and UK.[5] In our study, a conceptually similar framework has been developed to estimate the quality of HRM practices.

In India, Hitoshi Ota (2005) used the Osterman-framework to study HRM practices in Bangalore in 2000. He planned for two data sets, the first for surveying the management and the second for (by) surveying the workers. He approached 300 firms and only 189 participated in the management survey (Establishment Survey).

For the second set involving workers, only 5 out of 189 firms consented to participate. Ota's work has been discussed earlier in detail. Similar management reluctance and non-response was expected and was experienced. The specifics are described later.

In India, NSSO conducts five-yearly surveys to estimate levels of employment and unemployment. Globalization, a comparatively recent phenomenon in India, has influenced the employment scenario both qualitatively as well as quantitatively. It has introduced novel patterns of job tenures, working conditions, compensation, and management practices and has influenced the role of the trade unions.

This study and survey was intended to estimate the level of insecurity actually experienced and perceived by the organized sector employees because of these changes. Second, the survey was to be used to investigate some correlates of insecurity.

3.4 Scope

This section details the items of inquiry of the survey, geographical coverage, brief history and trends in the region which have shaped the trends in the labour market. It gives special emphasis to the policies that induced structural changes in the economy.

3.4.1 *Items of Inquiry*

The primary objective of this survey was to measure:

1. The experience of insecurity since 1991.
2. The current experience of insecurity among the surveyed workers.
3. To relate the measured insecurity to its correlates.

There is tension in the literature between the objective and subjective notions of job insecurity. There is similar disagreement between the views of some social scientists that the world of work has changed fundamentally with respect to job security, which can be measured objectively, versus the view that these changes are minor and transient, and perceived mostly subjectively. It is assumed here that it is possible to measure insecurity objectively by a careful choice of factors constituting insecurity.

For example, as an objective measure, it is possible to identify the characteristics of insecurity experienced by an employee in terms of number of involuntary job separations and periods of unemployment experienced, the cost of separation in terms of wage loss, time spent in finding the next job, increased hours of work and so on. Such information is sought in Part 2 of the questionnaire. Thus, an at-risk segment of the population can be identified and its features can be learned. Perturbations, if any, are likely to arise from some subjective elements inherent in insecurity, which is likely to be heavily influenced simultaneously by employment trends outside an organization and management policies inside the organization.[6]

The questionnaire is framed on the foundation of work done in the 'Interrogation of the Insecurity Hypothesis' by British economists like Heery (2000), Robinson (2000), Turnbull (2000), and Nickell (2002). Ideas have also been incorporated from Arulampalam (2001). The guidelines on framing the questions were taken from a number of sources.[7] The four-part questionnaire broadly solicits the following facts:

- Part I of the questionnaire seeks personal information such as age, education, and gender.
- Part 2 seeks to measure the experience of insecurity since 1991. Various conceptual dimensions of insecurity are identified and operationalized. For example, it measures the scarring caused by unemployment in terms of the period and number of times a worker was rendered unemployed, wage loss, terms and conditions of the new jobs found, and time spent looking for jobs. It also separates the job mobility factor from the redundancy experience. The capability of the worker to improve his skills and qualifications in the context of his employment and wage insecurity experience is enquired.
- Part 3 seeks information about the present job and experience thereof. The terms and conditions of employment are sought.

The ranges of HRM policies as experienced by the individual worker are also obtained. His current state of job security is then scored.

- Part 4 of the questionnaire examines the state of the employee union. Information on the level of status of the union (centralization/federation) and the range of issues over which the union bargains with the management is obtained. Also covered are items like type of enterprises, their size, ownership, and changes in employment status, occupation, and industry. Lastly, the cause to which the worker subjectively attributes his job insecurity is sought.

The questionnaire is placed as an Appendix. The responses are either binary, i.e. Yes or No, or else on a scale 1 to 5, with 1 being most secure and 5 the least secure. Uniformity and gradation is achieved by consistently ensuring that the scale 1 always represents the least insecurity and 5 represents the most insecurity. For example, respondents were asked: How many jobs they had lost since 1991, due to the decision of the organization? A 'Nil' response is 1 (least insecurity) and a response of 'more than 6 jobs lost' is 5 (the most insecure). This principle is observed while creating a consistent five-point rating scale.

To interrogate the hypothesis of insecurity, non-parametric correlations were obtained between the state of insecurity and its causative/associative variables like presence of an employees union, strength of the union and state of HRM policies. Insecurity by age, gender, education, and industry were also measured.

All questions were close-ended, unambiguously worded using conventional language, which was necessary bearing in mind that some of the respondents might not even be matriculates. English, Hindi, and Marathi versions were prepared. The respondents were required only to tick the appropriate answer, and, no written sentences or even words were required, to avoid possible sources of ambiguity or non-response.[8]

Response options involved simple objective comparisons made by the employees about their experience in the labour market, both in the past and current employment. Since the period over which the worker had to make the comparison was the recent past (14 years) it was assumed that the respondents would remember major events like job losses and make an objective comparison. The vague and troublesome questions were refined more than once after two pilot studies covering over 50 employees. Help was taken from labour lawyers, trade unionists, and professional translators to avoid confusion in language and interpretation.

The target population was workers below the managerial cadre in the organized manufacturing and service sectors. In terms of the national classification, occupations covered are Division 3, Group 30-9, i.e. clerical and related workers; Division 4, Group 42, 43, 44, and 49, i.e. sale workers; Division 5, Group 50, 51, 52, 54, i.e. service workers; Division 7-8-9 which is broadly production and related workers, transport equipment operators and labour.

Information on several correlates pertaining to IH was therefore gathered. Questions were put to the workers in order to understand their voluntary-mobility, skill upgradation activity level, and to what factors the workers subjectively attribute their insecurity. An effort was also made to collect information on the qualitative aspects of employment, like experience of HRM practices. As stated earlier items like type of enterprises, their size, ownership, and changes in employment status, occupation, industry, and availability of trade unions, were also sought.

Data allowed calculation of frequencies, composite frequencies, and intensity of parameters associated with an item of inquiry.

3.4.2 *Geographical Coverage*

According to the draft regional plan for Mumbai Metropolitan Region, 1996-2011, Greater Mumbai makes a very significant contribution towards the national economy, and it has been assigned a major role in facilitating integration of the country's economy with the rest of the world.[9] In the context of liberalization of economic policy, Greater Mumbai has a very significant role to play not only in contribution to the national economy but also in facilitating integration of the country's economy with the rest of the world. With its premium position as the country's financial capital, its leadership in country's international trade and industrialization, its strategic location with respect to global market centres, and its ability to provide a wide range of technical, professional and business services, Greater Mumbai has the potential to emerge as an international city, fostering hi-tech export-oriented financial and business services. MMR is economically the most dynamic region in the country. Mumbai itself has 23.5 per cent of Maharashtra`s and 3.2 per cent of India's total registered working factories It has 30.6 per cent of Maharashtra's and 3.2 per cent of India's total workers in factories, and 4.5 per cent of India's and 31.7 per cent of Maharashtra's NDP. Mumbai's per capita alone is three times that of India's according to the Economic Survey of Maharashtra 1998-9. Within MMR Greater Mumbai alone contributes the highest proportion of corporate taxes amounting to 35 per cent of the total corporate tax collected in India, and 16 per cent of the income tax collections. It has one of the oldest, largest, and most well diversified ranges of economic activities in the organized sector. Greater Mumbai has witnessed the full spectrum of changes from being an international port and trading centre in the colonial era, to becoming a textile-manufacturing sector, then a major industrial sector in the post-Independence period and now a financial and service centre in the post-liberalization period.

AREA OF STUDY

The area of the study covers factories and establishments in Greater Mumbai, Mumbai suburbs and Thane-Belapur area, i.e. Zone 1 and 2 under the 1991 Industrial Location Policy. Some judgement was exercised to include mainly, establishments employing more than 10 workers and workers in the age group of 32-50 years.

The Factory Act defines the term 'factory', and establishments are entities recorded as such in the BMC records. Factories and establishments with a workforce of more than 100 workers were chosen to get a reasonable sample size within the organization and to avoid the very small establishments that may not have a coherent Human Resource Policy.

The purpose of the following section is to suggest that MMR is a more suitable location to study the IH, as compared to other cities where the force of policies – economic liberalization, relocation, and restructuring – may have manifested itself more gradually over the last decade or two. Above all, it is the home of a large proportion of organized labour working in the manufacturing and service sectors; it is pertinently suited to a study based on the organized sector workers.

BRIEF HISTORY AND TRENDS IN THE REGION'S ECONOMY

In the mid-seventeenth century, Mumbai Island, lying on the Konkan coast, was just one of the several small coastal ports but within half a century, from 1650 to 1707 it became one of the principal trading stations of the British East India Company on the west coast of India. The next phase to follow from 1707 to 1850 brought about a major growth in its trading activities, transforming this trading station to a major western seaport. The third phase from 1815 to 1850 changed this chief western seaport to a political power centre. In this period, British political power expanded far beyond the political boundaries of the tiny island of Mumbai to most of western India. Thereafter, it was organized into a province called Mumbai Presidency. The fourth phase from 1851 to 1931 is the period in which Mumbai entered the industrial era, becoming the cotton mill centre of India and an important node in the new railway network.[10] By the 1930s, three-quarters of the city's labour force was employed in the textile mills, and the city remained an industrial metropolis over the next 50 years, and manufacturing remained a major economic activity.[11] After the 1960s, there was a sustained and rapid increase in the city's population.

Between 1981 and 1987, factory employment in MMR declined at the rate of 3.89 per cent per annum as against India's decline of only 0.96 per cent. By 1990-1, rubber, plastics and chemical industries had the largest share of the employment (21 per cent) among major industries in MMR, followed by cotton textiles at 13 per cent. While the first three industries improved their share of employment between 1981 and 1991 cotton textiles lost their leading position of 1976-7 with their share dropping from 28 to 17 per cent by 1981 and 13 per cent a decade later. This was because of a loss of about 1.33 lakh jobs in the cotton textile industry. However, even in 1991, 29 per cent of the Mumbai workforce was employed in manufacturing. The entire manufacturing workforce was distributed in such a manner that, 4 per cent in food processing, 13 per cent was employed in cotton textile, 10 per cent in wool, rubber, and chemicals, 21 per cent in transport equipment 5 per cent, and others account for 47 per cent.[12]

The decline of the cotton textile mills began in the late 1970s and accelerated after liberalization. After reaching its peak in 1978-9, in terms of employment share (28 per cent), and value addition (17 per cent) it declined rapidly and reached its lowest level in 1982-3; and although it recovered partially thereafter, widespread obsolescence and sickness affected its performance. Its share of value added fell to 10 per cent in 1986-7. During this period, the wool and synthetic textile industry made good progress and improved its share of value added, thereby partly compensating for the decline in the cotton textile industry.

The decline in manufacturing employment and textile employment in particular in Mumbai has been researched extensively.[13] It is important to consider the policy and causes behind the phenomenon in order to understand the structural shifts in employment in Mumbai.[14] They have been linked to a host of factors like the post-1980 phase of liberalization, changes in the National Industrial Policy, changes in land use and industrial location policy in Mumbai, the national textile policy; and the policy of encouraging the development of small and decentralized textile industry. Other factors associated with decline in manufacturing employment are the organization of labour and rising wages, excise taxes in Mumbai, the growth of the power looms in Bhiwandi, Surat, competition from other states in offering a wider and liberal range of incentives to industries and finally to the astronomical land and real estate prices in Mumbai which act as a strong incentive to liquidate and relocate manufacturing plants.[15]

Economic Survey of Maharashtra (2001-2, p. 123 and 2002-3, p. 168) has drawn attention to the decline in formal sector employment, particularly in the manufacturing sector in the state. The Government of Maharashtra has itself identified macro-economic policies of globalization for the trend. The city of Greater Mumbai remains the worst hit in relation to work stoppage (severity rate) which rose from 3 per cent in 1990-1 to 4 per cent in 2000-1 (Office of the Labour Commissioner, Government of Maharashtra, Mumbai).

For reasons mentioned below the employment patterns in Greater Mumbai have shifted and changed rapidly in the period after 1981 (figures are given in the Appendix), engendering flexible labour markets even before the official date line for economic liberalization used in this study. That process of structural change accelerated after 1991, as economic policy shifts became more pronounced and announcements about converting the city into a global financial centre became recurrent.

The process that occurred in Mumbai may indicate the future directions in other regional labour markets. The resulting level of insecurity may also offer, out of the ordinary, data for interrogating the IJ.

3.5 Main Factors Influencing Employment Patterns in MMR

This section highlights the salient policies which have influenced the structure of the region's economy and the labour market in turn.

3.5.1 *Industrial Policy in India and Maharashtra*

Industrial policies that influenced growth of manufacturing industry in Mumbai and the rest of MMR were devised and implemented at three different levels, i.e. national, state, and regional. At the national level the policy is implemented by the Government of India under the provisions of the Industrial Development and Regulation Act 1951 (IDRA), which allows licensing and regulation of industry. The IPR adopted by the Government of India in 1956 was the first comprehensive industrial policy that defined the government's approach towards the country's industrial development. This approach remained valid largely despite successive changes in 1970, 1973, 1977, and 1980. The main thrust was rapid industrialization, diversification, import substitution, reducing regional imbalances in industrial growth, and promotion of small-scale industries. The thrust of the 1980 industrial policy was to establish a more dynamic industrial economy. The steps taken were (a) streamlining licensing procedure, (b) automatic growth beyond licensed capacity, (c) fixing licensing capacity taking into account minimum economic scale, (d) flexibility in product-mix by broad banding, (e) encouraging modernization, (f) raising investment limits of SSI from 20 to 35 lakhs.

In June 1998, all except 26 categories of industries were delicensed up to an investment of Rs. 50 crore if located in backward areas, and Rs. 15 crore in other areas.

In July 1991, radical changes in industrial policy were announced. The new policy sought to dismantle the regulatory system and its aspects like licensing, location, monopolies and restricted practices, foreign investment and protective measures for small-sector. A very significant change was that the entire issue of industrial location and approval for industries in cities with a population of up to 1 million was delegated to the states and subject only to conformance with environmental legislation.

Maharashtra was the first state to adopt policies complementary to the national industrial policy. It developed land and infrastructure through MIDC (Maharashtra Industrial Development Corporation), and made special promotional effort for project identification, investment guidance, loan advice, and equity participation through State Investment Corporation of Maharashtra (SICOM). Financial assistance to small and medium units was provided through the Maharashtra State Finance Corporation (MSFC). MSSIDC (Maharashtra Small Scale Industries Development Corporation) was set up to assist SSI units in procuring of raw materials and marketing. It offered a package of fiscal and other incentives such as exemption from sales tax, octroi and water royalty.

3.5.2 *Industrial Location Policy*

The origin of Industrial Location policy lies in the regional plan for BMR, 1973. Historically, Mumbai has been a densely populated manufacturing and trading island city where the issues of congestion in the central business district, the island-city pressure on urban infrastructure, and housing have been debated long before they became important in other Indian urban centres. The major guidelines of the 1973 regional plan were:

1. BMR was divided into four distinct zones in 1974. Zone one was the island city; zone two suburbs of Greater Mumbai, Thane, Meera Bhayandar; zone 3 New Mumbai, and zone 4 rest of BMR.
2. Incentive and inducement for decentralizing of industries and moving out of Mumbai.
3. Zones for industry in Greater Mumbai were to be curtailed by 800 ha.
4. For relocation of industries and for future growth, new industrial zones were to be created in the region, i.e. 1500 ha in Nava Sheva for port-based industries, 200 ha in Bhiwandi *tehsil*, 200 ha in Bassin and 200 ha in Apte-Turade near Rasini.
5. Consumer industries, ancillaries of existing industries should be allowed in Greater Mumbai. Chemical and allied industries may be allowed in the authorized zones.
6. No further industrial units in Thane-Kalyan belt.
7. Small-scale and resource-based industries (sugar, etc.) may be set up freely beyond an 8 km distance from major industrial zones.
8. Since 1974, the industrial location policy has been amended several times. Between February 1984 and May 1992, the policy in zones 1 and 2 prohibited any new small, medium, or large-scale industrial unit. It however allowed modernization of existing units provided it did not result in increased capacity and replacement of the older small-scale units or expansion of existing small-scale unit up to an investment of Rs. 20 lakh.

9. Post-1991 liberalization, the four zones of BMR were reduced to three zones by merging the earlier zones. Zone one now comprised the Mumbai island city, Thane and Meera-Bhayandar. Zone 2 had Kalyan, Navi Mumbai, Ulhas Nagar, Ambernath, Kulgon, Badlapur, Bhiwandi, Uran, Vasai-Virar and zone 3 is the rest of BMR.
10. Industries were also divided into three schedules – schedule one, non-polluting high-value added; schedule two, polluting or hazardous; and schedule three, others. In zone 1, schedule 1, industries could be established or expanded but the expansion of schedule 2 was prohibited. In zone 2, schedule 2 industries were allowed only in MIDC areas and the other schedules were allowed freely. In zone 3, all industries were allowed without any location clearance.

The industrial location policy for BMR had the intended effect, which was reinforced by the national licensing policy, and the state-location policy.

3.5.3 *Backward Areas Policy*

In the early 1970s, the industrially backward states and districts were identified and a scheme of fiscal and financial incentives was introduced. This included grant of central subsidy up to 15 per cent of its capital, transport subsidy, income tax concessions, and preference for import of machinery and raw materials, and concessional finance from financial institutions. By the policy of 1977, the central government decided that no more licenses would be granted to industrial units in and around the metropolitan cities, and urban areas with population of five lakh and above. The units not requiring licenses were to be denied financial assistance if they were already located within these areas. It was also decided to provide assistance to large industries to shift out of congested metropolitan cities to backward areas. In June 1998, except 26 categories, all industries were delicensed up to an investment of Rs. 50 crore in backward areas. However, licensing was required for industries within 50 km of cities with a population of 25 lakh,

30 km for population of 15-25 lakh, and 15 km for population between 7.2 to 15 lakh. Policy adjustment in 1990 sought to relax these restrictions by delicensing new units with up to Rs. 25 crore investment in non-backward areas and allowing non-polluting industries like IT, electronics, and printing anywhere.

Although there are divergent views regarding success in reduction of regional disparity, a measure of its achievement is the increase in the number of industrial concentrations in the country from about half a dozen in the 1950s to 40-50 today. Industrially advanced states have also lost ground in their share of industry, and a few among the backward districts, located near metropolitan cities, secured a major share of investments.

Maharashtra had a very proactive industrial policy for backward areas. (Critics contrast this with the relative neglect of agricultural infrastructure like irrigation. In their opinion this has led to a continuous supply of cheap labour from the hinterland.) The state was divided into four groups in order of increasing degree of backwardness. Group one comprised the Mumbai-Pune belt where no incentives were available and restrictions were placed on setting up new industries in the Greater Mumbai-Kalyan belt. In contrast, in other areas MIDC subsidized industrial plots, water, power, and removed disparities in tariff between developed and backward areas.

According to a 1978 study of the effects of the industrial location policy, investments were redirected to new growth centres like Nasik, Nagpur, and Aurangabad and this is evident from the number of factories registered there, and their greater share in industrial employment and consumption of electricity. Another study by BCCI confirmed this though it also noted the lack of social facilities there.

3.6 Changing Structure of Employment

Policies aimed at industrial dispersal had an impact on the employment pattern within BMR. Jobs moved away from factories to the service sector, and to unorganized sectors and non-unionized regions as factories relocated. Information about the trend is available from the census reports of 1961, 1971, 1981, 1991, and 2001, though for 2001 the employment pattern. Informal sector employment grew by 33 per cent from 1961-71, by 49 per cent from 1971-81, and by 41 per cent from 1981-91. Quite the opposite was true for the formal sector where employment grew by 28 per cent from 1961-71, by only 13 per cent from 1971-91, and fell by 7.5 per cent from 1981-91. The total employment (primary census) in BMR grew by 30 per cent from 1961 to 1971, by 30 per cent from 1971-81 and 20 per cent from 1981-91 (Table 3.1). The share of industrial employment other than household industries had continuously remained dominant, but its share began to decline, while the share of trade and commerce began increasing. The establishment (service sector) employment was 15.28 lakh in 1971, 21.99 lakh in 1981 (a growth of 43 per cent), and 24.6 lakh by 1991 (growth of 11.87 per cent). Along with the sector shift, there was a spatial shift to suburbs and other zones.

3.6.1 *Employment Analysis*

Tables 3.2-3.6 summarize the trends.

Within MMR Greater Mumbai has the highest density of population and economic activity. According to the Census 2001, it has a population of 18.7 million (classified as a mega city second only to Tokyo in population) and represents nearly 2 per cent of India's population. Mumbai's per capita at Rs. 48,954 (at current prices) is twice that of Maharashtra and three times that of India. Of the 3.43 lakh main workers employed in the city, 68 per cent were already employed in the service sector in 2001. The service sector generates 64 per cent of the income in Mumbai. Job opportunities in the organized manufacturing sector had been declining for a decade. Thirty-three per cent of the state's income comes from Mumbai's registered manufacturing, and as high as 28 per cent from unregistered manufacturing units. The changes in the structure of economic activity are caused by many factors – geographical location as an island port, historical developments in the colonial period, concentration of economic activity in the island city, rising prices of real estate, congestion, rising cost of

Table 3.1: Employment Analysis Background

(figures in '000s)

	Employment in Greater Mumbai							
			Formal Sector			*Informal Sector*		
Year	*Primary Census*	*Economic Census*	*Public*	*Private*	*Total*	*Primary Census Total*	*Economic Census Total*	
	2	3	4	5	6	(2-6)	(3-6)	(2-3)
1961	1,687	NA	330	552	882	805	NA	NA
1871	2,198	1,528	492	638	1,130	1,068	398	670
1981	2,864	2,199	652	624	1,276	1,588	923	665
1991	3,434	2,426	711	469	1,180	2,254	1,246	1,008

Source: MMRDA Draft Regional Plan for Mumbai Metropolitan Region 1996-2011, October 1995, p. 112.

Notes: 1. If total employment as reported in the primary census is taken, then the share of informal employment is 49 per cent, 65.6 per cent in 1971, 1991; an increasing trend in greater Mumbai.

2. Informal sector employment increased by 33 per cent from 1961-71, by 49 per cent from 1971-81, and by 41 per cent from 1981-91. Formal sector employment rose by 28 per cent from 1961-71, by only 13 per cent from 1971-91, and fell by 7.5 per cent from 1981-91.

Table 3.2: Regional Domestic Product

At constant prices for districts of Greater Mumbai, Thane and Raigadh

	1980		*1990*
Primary	9	Primary	5
Secondary	50	Secondary	50
Tertiary	41	Tertiary	45

Source: MMRDA Draft Regional Plan for Mumbai Metropolitan Region 1996-2011, October 1995, p. 145.

Notes:
1. There is a gradual change in the share of secondary and tertiary sector in the total domestic product of greater Mumbai.
2. Growth rate of the secondary sector at 3.93 per cent was slower than that of the tertiary sector at 6.05 per cent.
3. Growth of unorganized manufacturing sector within the manufacturing sector was 9.42 per cent p.a. compared to the registered manufacturing sector at 2.82 per cent p.a.
4. In Thane district also, the growth of secondary sector was high @ 7.6 per cent; however the tertiary grew at a faster rate of 11.7 per cent.
5. Only in Raigadh, did the secondary sector perform better than the tertiary sector. Here growth in registered manufacturing sector was more than in the unorganized sector.
6. The total regional domestic product of BMR increased @ 5.89 per cent p.a. and per capita @ 3.18 per cent, while the corresponding rates for Maharashtra were higher, i.e. 6.28 per cent and 4.06 per cent respectively. This indicates a shifting of manufacturing out of BMR.

living, growing external diseconomies of scale for manufacturing activity and so on. Changes in the economy of the region have accelerated after the 1980s because of multiple policy shifts, like location-policy shifts after 1970s that started showing results in the period after 1980s, and economic policy changes after 1991.

Investigations here are therefore likely to reveal multiple reasons for the shift in the structure of the economy and labour markets - some reasons predating globalization. The factors that

Table 3.3: Employment Changes in Greater Mumbai 1971-90

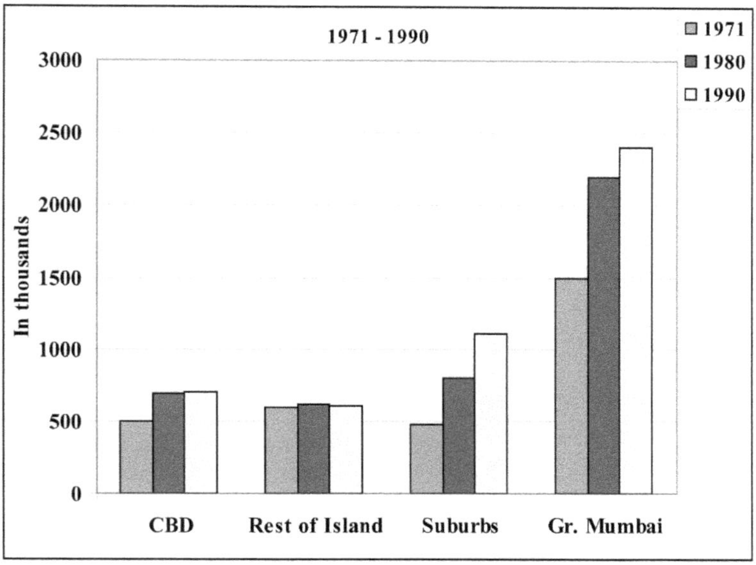

(in thousands)

	1971	*1980*	*1990*
CBD	500	690	700
Rest of Island	600	620	610
Suburbs	480	800	1,100
Gr. Mumbai	1,500	2,200	2,400

Source: MMRDA Draft Regional Plan for Mumbai Metropolitan Region 1996-2011, October 1995, p. 104.

Notes: 1. Comparative picture of spatial distribution of employment in 1971, 1981, and 1990 shows a marginal decline of 4 per cent in the share of employment in CBD in Greater Mumbai.

2. More than 10 per cent reduction in employment share in the remaining part of the island city has taken place.

3. Employment in suburbs has more than doubled, with the manufacturing sector dominating.

Table 3.4: Employment in Registered Factories 1961-91

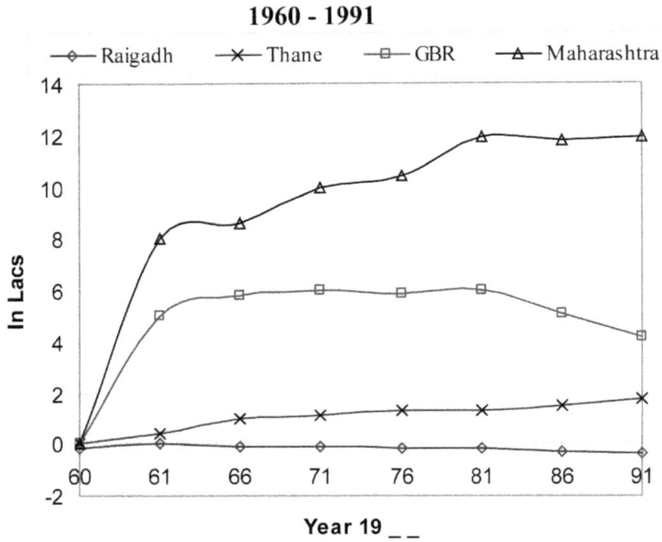

(in lakhs)

	Raigadh	*Thane*	*GBR*	*Maharashtra*
1960	-0.2	0	0	0
1961	0	0.4	5	8
1966	-0.1	1	5.8	8.6
1971	-0.1	1.1	6	10
1976	-0.2	1.3	5.9	10.4
1981	-0.2	1.3	6	11.9
1986	-0.3	1.5	5.1	11.8
1991	-0.4	1.8	4.2	11.9

Source: MMRDA Draft Regional Plan for Mumbai Metropolitan Region 1996-2011, October 1995, p. 110.

Notes: 1. The data on the number of factories and workers in Greater Mumbai, Thane and Raigadh in BMR shows a growth in employment from 1961-81 and a marked decline from 1981-91.

2. Number of factories has increased over all this period but the increase in the decade 1981-91 did not add to employment.

Table 3.5: Industrial Employment in Bombay and BMR
1980-1 to 1990-1

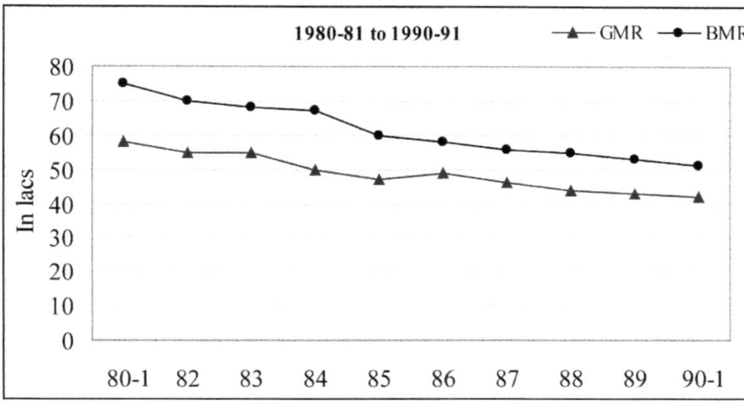

Year	*GMR*	*BMR*
1980-1	58	75
1981-2	55	70
1982-3	55	68
1983-4	50	67
1984-5	47	60
1985-6	49	58
1986-7	46	56
1988-9	44	55
1989-90	43	53
1990-1	42	51

Source: MMRDA Draft Regional Plan for Mumbai Metropolitan Region 1996-2011, October 1995, p. 109.

Note: 1. The data about employment in manufacturing industries in BMR and GMR show that employment in traditional industries like cotton textile, wood, paper, alloys and manufacturing declined. In the other industries like, e.g., wool, silk, synthetics it showed growth. Decline in employment in textile & chemical industries was not compensated.

2. The employment in service industries followed a similar trend.

Table 3.6: Formal Sector Employment in Greater Mumbai 1979-91

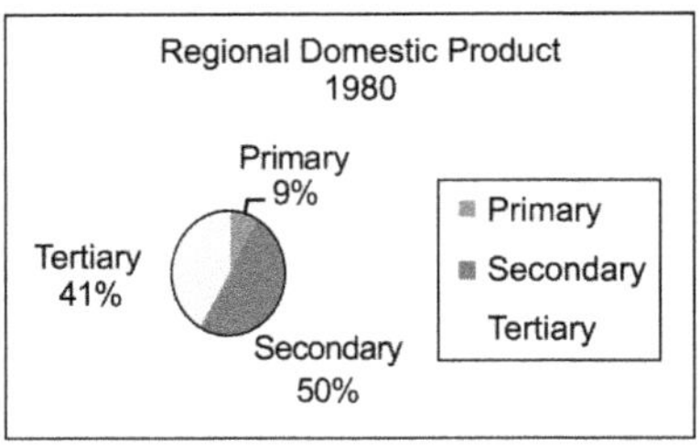

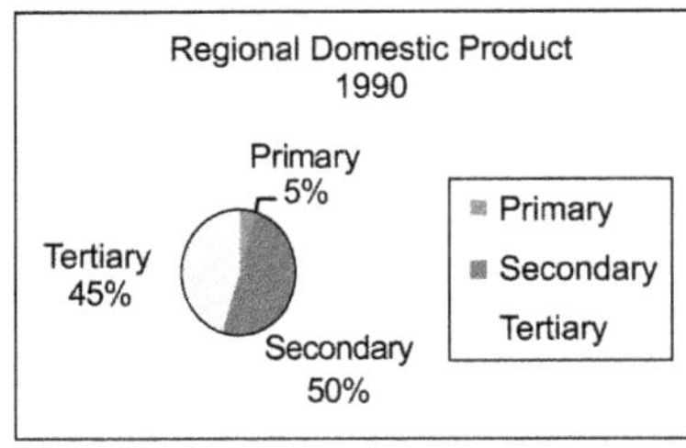

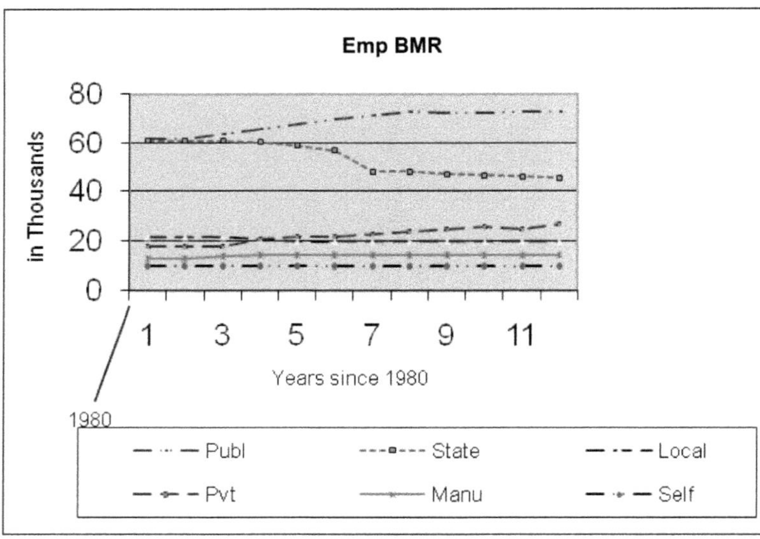

(in tens of thousands)

Year	*Public*	*State*	*Local*	*Private*	*Centre*	*Self-Quasi-government*
1979	62	61	22	57	13	10
1980	639	61	22	63	13	10
1981	64	61	22	62.5	14	10
1982	66	60.5	21	59.4	14.50	10
1983	68	59	20	56.7	14.50	10
1984	70	57	20	55.2	14.50	10

1985	71.5	48	20	54	14.50	10
1986	73	48	20	50.5	14.50	10
1987	72.5	47	20	51	14.50	10
1988	72.5	46.5	20	48	14.50	10
1989	73	46	20	49	14.50	10
1990	71.1	45.5	20	46.9	14.50	10

Source: MMRDA Draft Regional Plan for Mumbai Metropolitan Region 1996-2011, October 1995, p. 107.

Notes:
1. Category-wise data on employment variation in Greater Mumbai shows that public sector employment grew from 6.39 lakh in 1980 to 7.11 lakhs in 1990.
2. The private sector showed a marked decline from 6.22 lakh to 4.69 lakh. Employment is governed by many factors like demand shifts and decline of some industries.
3. Central government employment also showed decline due to recruitment restrictions. The same is true for state and quasi-state employment. However, the quasi-central government employment and the number of establishments have shown an increase in Mumbai because of expansion of branches of nationalized banks, and ONGC, JNPT and Mazagaon docks.
4. Tables show no growth in factory employment in BMR during 1971-81, and thereafter there was a rapid decline. In term of value-addition, BMR industries show a modest growth. The process was accentuated by the closure of a large number of textile mills in BMR following the 1982-3 textile strike, the largest and longest strike in the history of industrial disputes.
5. Though factory employment has fallen, employment in unorganized sectors has grown rapidly, 14 per cent per year from 1971-80 and at 2.4 per cent per annum thereafter. By 1990, 45 per cent of the industrial employment was in the unorganized sector, i.e. units employing less than 10 employees and outside the purview of the Factories Act. This indicates a very vigorous growth of the tiny and unorganized sector.

may be recognized are accelerating pace of change in its economy, the emerging employment patterns after 1981, and even more so after 1991. These periods coincide with internal and external liberalization of the economy respectively.

The survey covers both manufacturing and service sectors, in private and public domains, and in old and the new economic activities. Within manufacturing, it covers machinery and equipment, transport equipment and parts, metal products and parts, basic chemical products like rubber, plastic, and petroleum. Within the service sector, the survey includes financial institutions, hotels and restaurants, and BPOs, services like HR, event management, courier, software, retail, transport, health, and educational establishments.

3.7 The Survey in Brief

This section explains the method and period of study, the evolution and adaptation of sample design in view of the issues encountered on the field, the key concepts and how they were operationalized.

3.7.1 *Method of Data Collection*

A field survey based on interview method was designed and conducted in Greater Mumbai, in various sub-segments of the manufacturing and service sectors including both private and public-sector establishments. A sample of factories and establishments in Greater Mumbai was selected based on municipal corporation records. Detailed ward-wise break-up of employment is also available in the reports of the MMRDA (1995): Draft Regional Plan for Mumbai Metropolitan Region 1996-2011. Within the Mumbai Municipal Corporation, the office of the Inspector, Shops and Establishments, maintains ward-wise listings. The office of the Inspector of Factories also maintains ward-wise listings. Due to non-response of many factories in the original sample, alternate factories and establishments distributed over selected wards (chosen in terms of employment-density and industry-type) were selected for survey of employees on the basis of personal contacts. Twenty-nine such factories and establishments responded. Within these establishments, 1,000 employees below the managerial rank were given questionnaires. Only 779 employees responded adequately. Their responses are analysed. The sample thus mainly represents employees of large and very large establishments in Mumbai employing more than 100 and 1,000 people, respectively.

The term worker is used here as in the NSSO surveys on employment and unemployment and so is the term establishment. The basis of sample design and selection are discussed later.

It needs to be restated at the outset that in most cases, our survey requests made to managements were delayed interminably or politely refused. It became increasingly impossible to access workers in the organized sector inside their workplace, as mentioned earlier. The managements (except in the case of a cooperative retail outlet) were not willing to entertain a survey, especially because the survey needed the participation of workers to gauge the working experience of the employee, their perception of HRM practices and the state of the employee union within the firm. Managements were a lot more forthcoming if only their views were sought. Once managements officially refuse permission it is not possible to access the firm or obtain worker cooperation even informally in the survey. During the study, it was observable that this managerial non-cooperation could create a non-sample bias. Hence, a method of approaching the firm via unions or informal networks was used, and, most of the factory-level surveys were possible with some help of unions within the unit or by informally contacting the workers where no unions existed. There is a need for the managements to be more open and cooperative in research-exercises conducted by academic researchers. The management's participation could enhance the quality and size of sample, range of parameters and the quality of the results. In this context, earlier in Chapter 3, other sample-based studies were recorded (e.g. Hitoshi Ota in Bangalore) which faced similar problems.[16] Surprisingly even the government's own agencies like the Labour Bureau face similar problems.[17]

3.7.2 *Period of Survey and Work Programme*

The fieldwork started from 1 July 2005 and continued until 30 June 2006. The survey process was divided into two phases. First, the employees filled the data independently or with the help of a trained surveyor. The filled questionnaire was checked for errors and ambiguity, and if required, the employee was revisited for confirmation. The data was entered in computer-readable format and a 100 per cent check was made of conformity with the questionnaire. However, some employees could not be contacted for confirmation or clarification, and about a score of such cases with more than one missing responses were rejected.

3.7.3 *Sample Design*

AN OUTLINE OF THE SAMPLE DESIGN AND SAMPLE FRAME

Annual survey of Industry Times Series data in different manufacturing industries is available in the Reports of the MMRDA (1995): Draft Regional Plan for Mumbai Metropolitan Region 1996-2011. It provides a fairly detailed and comprehensive picture about employment. The Municipal Corporation of Greater Mumbai maintains records pertaining to shops, commercial establishments, residential hotels, restaurants, eating houses and theatres. The Inspectorate of Factories also maintains ward-wise data on factories, and workers. It has data regarding the geographic distribution of factories and the Average Daily Employment by major groups and wards. From the above sources 70 factories and establishments were selected to reflect the overall employment categories in the manufacturing, trade and other principal sectors.

At first, 70 firms were selected based on systematic random samplings and approached. More than twice the planned sample size was approached expecting poor management response. The management response was indeed so poor that eventually a more workable strategy for accessing factories and establishments, and contacting workers via personal contacts and trade unions had to be adopted. In the study the term 'factory' is as defined by the Annual Survey of Industries (ASI), 'establishment' as registered by the Mumbai Municipal Corporation, 'banks' as scheduled by RBI, and 'registered companies', which are registered with the Registrar of Companies.

SAMPLE SIZE

Eventually 779 employees in 29 factories and establishment were surveyed. While attempting to represent the diversity and geographical clusters in which factories and establishments are found in Greater Mumbai, some judgement was also exercised to give preference to mature workers with a longer work experience, in the age group 32-50 years.

3.7.4 *Key Concepts and Their Operationalization*

As stated earlier, the study deals with estimates of insecurity in the organized sector in Greater Mumbai (GM), along with its correlates as obtained from tables generated on data collected on applicable items. As such, the focus is limited to such items and concepts, and the estimates have been generated based on these. All the concepts have been developed based on the theory discussed in Chapters 2 to 5. To analyse the data generated from the survey the following few concepts and definitions were developed, defined, and measured:

PAST EXPERIENCE OF INSECURITY (PEI)

This is defined by the scaled response on two questions: The years of unemployment experienced (question 2.1) and jobs lost (question 2.3). If since 1991, the respondent has not spent a single year unemployed the response is scaled 1. On the other hand, if he has spent more than six unemployed years it is scaled 5. Similarly on question 2.3 'jobs lost due to management action since 1991' a nil is scaled 1 and more than six job losses is scaled 5. Rounded average of 2.1 and 2.3 is therefore an estimate of the PEI. The intensity of PEI in turn is scaled as nil = 1, low = 2, high = 3 or 4, severe = 5.

COMPREHENSIVE PAST EXPERIENCE OF INSECURITY (CPEI)

This is a more exhaustive measure of the past-experience of insecurity because it includes not just 2.1 but also 2.2, 2.3, 2.4,

2.5, 2.7 and 2.8. The responses on questions regarding past jobs and compensation changes experienced, working hour changes, work day, time spent in current job are similarly scaled from one to five. To estimate CPEI the responses are averaged and the mean is rounded to the closest integer. The intensity score is then scaled as for the PEI above: nil = 1, low = 2, high = 3 or 4, severe = 5.

EXPERIENCE OF INFORMALIZATION (EOIf)

Is a measurement based on question 2.6, where the respondent is asked if they experienced any or all of the following changes in the past 14 years – shift from unionized jobs to non-unionized ones, from full-time jobs to part-time, temporary or casual jobs, and from regular wages to self-employment. The scores are on three, where a score of one indicates an experience of informalization, two indicates a high level and three a severe level of EOIf.

CURRENT EXPERIENCE OF INSECURITY (CEI)

CEI is a simple yes or no response to question 3.4 regarding whether the respondent thinks he could lose the current job and this is a subjective perception.

HIGH ROAD HUMAN RESOURCE MANAGEMENT CHANGES (HRHRM)

These are estimated as a score out of 10 on question 3.6, which has ten subparts. Score 0-3 represents low range of changes in the HRHRM practices at the workplace, 4-6 medium range, and 7-10 represents high range of changes. The highroad practices were distinguished based on literature survey of HRM where some practices are associated with high productivity and 'high quality'-based competition as a strategy for long-term competitive advantage. These include introduction of new technologies/machines, training, quality circles, teams, worker participation in management, performance appraisals, etc.

LOW ROAD HUMAN RESOURCE MANAGEMENT CHANGES (LRHRM)

These are also estimated on a scale of ten in question 3.7, which also has ten sub-parts and questions aimed to get worker response regarding such HRM changes as may be associated with cost-saving competitive strategies like reducing staff strength, outsourcing work, increasing use of non-permanent staff, work intensification, redundancy, and VRS schemes. These are referred to as Low Road Policies perhaps because they engender high levels of insecurity in the employees, and are also mainly associated with and directed at the 'low-end-of-the-value-chain' type of competitiveness, and are generally considered to be short-term manoeuvres to deal with rising competition by reducing costs of labour.

COMPOSITE EXPERIENCE OF HUMAN RESOURCE MANAGEMENT CHANGES (CEHRM)

Sum of questions 3.6 and 3.7 (10 sub-parts each) is an absolute measure of HRM changes experienced by employees. Their mean score is computed and scaled. A score of 0-3 represents low range of changes in HRM practices at the workplace, 4-6 as medium range and 7-10 representing high range of changes.

FLEXIBLE WORK PRACTICES (FWP)

These are work practices which promote job flexibility within the organization. They are commonly associated with new HRM policies that arise out of restructuring organizations, such as reduction in job grades, work intensification with workers being required to do multiple tasks, or additional tasks, and worker participation in teams and quality circles. Hence, sub-parts of questions 3.6 and 3.7 such as 3.6.8 + 3.7.4 + 3.7.5 were selected and summed up on a score of three. Low levels of FWP = 1, medium = 2, high = 3.

MOBILITY AND JOB CHANGES

Question 2.2 elicits job changes for any reason whatsoever and the number of sampled employees affected. Question 2.3 asks for the number of job changes resulting from management decisions, and the difference (2.2 minus 2.3) reflects voluntary mobility, which is defined and measured as changes arising out of the employees' own initiative since 1991. The mobility scale ranges from zero to five. Nil mobility = 0, low = 1, high = 2-3, very high = 4-5. High mobility is usually taken as an indication of an increasing demand for labour.

TRADE UNIONS: RANGE OF BARGAINING INFLUENCE

Question 4.3, with ten sub-parts, solicits information regarding the range of the union's influence. Score out of ten is the measure of participatory influence; scaled as nominal 0-1, low 2-3, medium 4-6, and high 7-10. Besides the usual bargaining about compensation and hours of work, information is sought about emerging issues like new technology, training, and participation in management.

SKILL BASE

Using the standard criteria for measuring skill base, the questionnaire sought information regarding the basic school- or college-level education or vocational skills. The skill base is scaled on five, with the lowest scale equal to 1 for less than matriculates and the highest scale of 5 for graduates and above. The subsequent skill upgradation activity of any kind, including one on the job is also considered.

3.7.5 *Brief Description of the Sampled Population and Correlations*

During the survey a total of 779 employees in the organized sector in MMR were sampled. The primary categories were:

1. 180 (23 per cent) from manufacturing, 583 (75 per cent) from service sector and 16 responses which could not be classified into these categories.
2. 176 (22.6 per cent) employees were from the public sector, 591 (76 per cent) from private sector, and 12 responses could not classified into these categories.
3. 612 (78.6 per cent) were unionized, and 167 (21.4 per cent) were not. Of the unionized, 472 belonged to federated unions and 140 to non-federated types.
4. Females were 188 (24 per cent) and males 591 (76 per cent).

Note: All additional and relevant tables are placed in the Appendix 'Survey Data Tables' and referred to as, for example, Table 1A.

AGE

The mean age is 35.6 years and the age distribution of the sample, as expected, is skewed to the left. The median age is 35 while the modal is 40 years. Since some amount of judgement was exercised to capture workers above 32 and below 50 years, 62 per cent of the employees surveyed were between the age group of 32 and 50 years. In addition, 35 per cent of them were between 19 and 32 years of age (Table 1A).

This segment, between 32 and 50 years of age, is most likely to have been employed or seeking employment since 1991, or likely to be employed over some part of that period. They are also likely to constitute a relatively more experienced segment of the employees, if they have been employed in the organized sector over the period. Assuming that seniority in service implies security in the organized sector under the prevailing norms, this age group is also likely to be more secure. They are also likely to have a more extensive past experience of insecurity if any. The age group less than 32 years, is likely either to have just entered the workforce in 1991 or have a shorter work experience. Their past-experiences of insecurity are likely to be different and could reveal a different pattern among younger workers (Table 2B).

PAST AND COMPREHENSIVE PAST EXPERIENCE OF INSECURITY (PEI AND CPEI)

As far as Past Experience of Insecurity (PEI) is concerned, 53 per cent experienced some and 47 per cent experienced none. Within the lot who did experience some insecurity (numbering 412), 55.1 per cent experienced low-level, 43.4 per cent high-level and 1.5 per cent severe-level of insecurity. At the sample level 29 per cent experienced low, 23 per cent experienced high, and 0.8 per cent experienced severe PEI. So, even inside the bastion of the organized sector there is a sizeable proportion, nearing one-fourth of the sample that had experienced high and severe levels of insecurity (Table 2A) by the first decade of the twenty-first century.

When the more inclusive CPEI was estimated, 49 per cent experienced no insecurity, and 51 per cent experienced some insecurity. Among the latter, 39 per cent had experienced low levels of insecurity and a higher proportion of 61 per cent experienced high levels of insecurity.

These figures do not represent a movement out of the insecure unorganized sector employment into the organized sector, because in the latter the employment has been shrinking, as suggested by macro-level data on the city. In that case, it is possible to suggest that insecurity has permeated 51 per cent of the organized sector sample (Table 2E).

In the cross tables of age and PEI, the differences in experience are evident. The age group of less than 32 years have a higher PEI compared to the age group 32-50 years. While 54 per cent in the older age group had experienced no insecurity since 1991, only 30 per cent in the younger age group had no past experience of insecurity. Whereas 22 per cent in the older age group experienced low levels of insecurity in the past, 44 per cent experienced low levels in the younger age group. When one considers the experience of high to severe insecurity the differences however narrow down; 26 per cent of the young sample experienced high to severe insecurity, while 24 per cent of the older age group also experienced high to severe insecurity. There seem to be a segment of the workforce that is vulnerable to high PEI due to factors other than age, such as skill base or location in sectors and firms that have conditions detrimental to security (Table 3.2).

The Pearson chi-square for the age groups and PEI groups cross tables is also high at 82.63. With six degrees of freedom (df) the null hypothesis that age and insecurity are not related can be rejected at both levels of significance 0.1 and 0.01.

CURRENT EXPERIENCE OF INSECURITY

Forty-nine per cent of the sampled employees thought that they could lose their present job. Although 73 per cent of the sampled employees have described themselves as full-time and permanent workers, 78 per cent got PPF. Seventy-nine per cent were members of some trade union (Table 6A), yet a surprising 49 per cent of them thought that they could lose their present job. Moreover, 46 per cent felt that they could lose their job within the next ten years, and 23.5 per cent within five years (Tables 3.7-3.10).

CEI (current experience of insecurity) is influenced by comprehensive experience of HRM changes. Of all the employees who thought that they could lose their current job, 80 per cent reported medium to high levels of HRM changes in their workplace (Table 3.12).

If one looks at the nature of HRM changes, then 81 per cent of those who feared job loss also reported medium to high levels of negative, low-road HRM practices at the workplace. Further, majority of employees cited management policies as the most important threat to their job security. However, there is some evidence to suggest that employees can overcome CEI (fear of job loss) through their own solidarity and support of their trade unions, since a smaller percentage of members of trade unions seem to fear current job loss compared to non-members (Table 3.6).

When asked what they perceived as the most important threat to their job, 30 per cent of the sampled employees thought that the single most important threat to their job security was the labour policies of their management, and 27 per cent thought that labour policies of the government were to blame. In the case of public sector employees, the government is often perceived as a surrogate management. If so, 'managements policies' emerge as the central focus of attribution. About 25 per cent felt that increasing domestic competition was threatening. Only 12 per cent were of the opinion that imported substitutes were the most-important factor threatening their jobs (Table 3.11).

When asked what they perceived as the second most important threat to jobs, again, most blamed the management and government policies in that order. However, increased awareness of threats from competition, both domestic and imports, assumed almost equal importance at 20 and 19 per cent respectively. This offers a significant insight into the employee's perception of the sources and causes of their insecurity. Employees do not normally look beyond their firm or organization for national or global causations. This perception and consciousness of insecurity is created by many factors occurring simultaneously – the background of sectoral shift in the employment pattern in the region, slow growth of employment opportunities in the organized sector, changing policies of the management and the government, their own and their co-workers' shared past-experiences of insecurity. These issues, of perception of insecurity (caused by news) vs. objective facts regarding insecurity, have been raised in the literature as well[18] (Table 3.12).

HUMAN RESOURCE MANAGEMENT POLICIES

The methodology for measuring High-Road HRM (HRHRM) has been described above, where a low score between 0-3 has been taken as representing poor experience of HRHRM management strategy while scales 4-6 represented medium, and 7-10 represented high scores. The HRHRM practices are about increasing productivity and developing human resources simultaneously, to position the firm for global competition while moving up the value chain. Hence, employees were asked whether new machines/technologies have been introduced; if they had received sufficient training on the new machines; if training was linked to promotion; if performance appraisals were done; payments were linked to performance;

workers participated in teams and quality circles, and if they increasingly communicated directly with managements. These are the characteristic textbook indicators of HRHRM practices.

The second sets of questions were aimed at determining/measuring (ranking) the employees' experience of 'low-road HRM' policies aimed at squeezing wage costs and other costs to position the firm for competition. The employees were asked whether VRS had been offered, work intensification had taken place via reduction of job grades, decreasing staff strength, relocation of plant, employment against individual contracts was offered and so on. The scores were out of ten and scaled, as in the previous question on HRHRM policies. The endeavour was to correlate these policy types with the current experience of insecurity of workers.

It was found that 75 per cent of the workers reported use of new machines/technology in the workplace. Only 54 per cent said they received training on those new machine/technologies, 67 per cent said that performance appraisals were introduced, 47 per cent reported promotions being linked to performance. Only 41 per cent thought that they received sufficient safety training. Among the workers, 40 per cent held that worker participation in management had increased. Only 36 per cent believed that direct communication between management and employee had increased. Even fewer, 35 per cent, felt that worker participation in quality circles, and team programmes had increased (Table 5A).

On the other hand, 79 per cent of the workers in the service sector and 52 per cent in the manufacturing sector held that work intensification had occurred and workers were required to do additional duties. And, 67 per cent reported that staff strength had been reduced. This was more in manufacturing than service; 66 per cent said job grades had been compacted; 61 per cent reported that use of non-permanent workers was greater than before, and 57 per cent held that outsourcing had increased. VRS was offered to 45 per cent, and 30 per cent felt that idleness was forced upon workers. Thirty-two per cent of them felt that frequency of legal proceedings between employees and firms had increased. Over one-fourth (27 per cent) said that office and plant relocation had occurred. The experience of workers largely suggested that flexible work practices were very common across sectors and low-road HRM policies were more common and familiar to the employee (Tables 5B, E, G, Q).

In other items studied under HRM experiences of employees it was found that the manufacturing sector employees as a whole experienced more staff reduction, employment of contingent workforce and outsourcing than their counterparts in the service sector. This seems to corroborate the shift away from manufacturing. However, over all, the changes in HRM practices were greater in the service sector.

Firms and establishments seem to be employing a mixture of HRM policies of both categories to cope with pressures of increased competition. That is why 80.5 per cent respondents reported medium to high scale of comprehensive (low + high road) HRM changes. Therefore, while many employees (59 per cent) have reported medium to high levels of HRHRM changes, equally high number (74 per cent) reported medium to high level of low-road HRM changes (Tables 5C, D, E, N).

Employees' experience, of comprehensive HRM changes shows that 20 per cent experienced low levels of changes, but 64 per cent fell into the category of medium levels of HRM changes, and 17 per cent experienced high level of HRM changes. Therefore, 81 per cent of the employees are reporting that HRM policies have been changing significantly at the firm level. If breakdown of the types of HRM changes is considered then 41 per cent report 'low' incidence of positive high road changes in their HRM policies, and as the sample indicates, most employees (74 per cent) are reporting medium to high levels of low road HRM changes (negative type) (Tables 5C, D, E, H).

Sector-wise patterns reveal that the 89 per cent of public sector employees have experienced medium to high levels of HRM changes, while 78 per cent of the private and cooperative sector experienced the same against the sample average of 81 per cent. The public sector also fared better in the quality of HRM experience for the workforce. Of the public sector employees, 64 per cent reported medium to high levels of positive HRHRM practices while a lower 57 per cent of private and cooperative sector experienced the same (Tables 5F, H).

The highest reported incidence of HRM practices is requirement to do additional duties (79 per cent), introduction of new machinery (75 per cent), performance appraisal (67 per cent), reduction is staff strength (66 per cent), reduction of job-grades (66 per cent) and use of non-permanent staff (61 per cent) (Table 5N). Two of these items relate to high-road and others to low-road practices. The organizations employ both type and hence analysis by type of HRM practices does not show significant difference in current experience of insecurity.

FLEXIBLE WORK PRACTICES (FWP)

As far as flexible work practices are concerned, 67 per cent of the surveyed employees are reporting medium to high incidence of such practices in their workplace. Only 9 per cent reported no incidence of FWP and 24 per cent reported low incidence of FWP. Here there is substantial indication of work intensification within the organized sector (Table 5P).

EXPERIENCE OF INFORMALIZATION

In the sample, 61 per cent experienced no informalization and 39 per cent did. In addition, among the latter a high 51 per cent experienced change from unionized to not-unionized establishments, and an even higher, 64 per cent from regular to temporary status. In addition, about 37 per cent had been transferred to the self-employed category at some point over the past 14 years. These changes may have been transient or otherwise. Among those who experienced informalization during the 14 years since 1991, 33 per cent experienced two of the three types of informalization estimated here, 10 per cent experienced all three types, and 57 per cent experienced only one type of informalization (Table 2M).

Among the surveyed workers, 89 per cent in the manufacturing sector and 53 per cent in the service sector experienced no informalization. Therefore, only 11 per cent of the manufacturing sector employees experienced informalization compared to a much higher 47 per cent in the service sector where 20 per cent experienced high to severe levels of EoIf. It is worth pointing out that the manufacturing sector in the survey region had experienced large-scale downsizing, retrenchment, relocation, and outsourcing over two decades prior to the period of survey as pointed out earlier, and the survey covered workers who continued to be employed in the organized sector in 2005 (Table 2N).

Of the public sector employees, 74 per cent had no EoIf, 9 per cent had a low experience, and 17 per cent had high to severe EoIf. In the private sector, only 58 per cent of the employees had no EOI, 26 per cent had a low experience and 16 per cent had a high to severe EoIf (Table 2O).

For instance, among all age groups, the groups 26-30 and 30-5 years had both, the lowest percentage (41 per cent) of people not experiencing any informalization, and the highest percentage that had experienced high or severe informalization. The young therefore seem to have higher levels of both PEI and EoIf when compared to the older workers. This could indicate a difference in the experiences of the younger vs. the older workers in the organized sector in India, due to post-liberalization changes in the labour markets (Table 2P).

MOBILITY AND JOB CHANGES

Only 16.7 per cent of the sample had changed jobs voluntarily and 83.3 per cent of the sample had not experienced any voluntary-mobility as defined, implying that they had not changed jobs of their own volition since 1991. This shows a significant preference for secure employment in the sample, similar to the NSSO findings (although differently defined to include any kind of job changes) in 1999-2000 where the all-India urban employment status and establishment mobility was only 5-8 per cent. Greater Mumbai is likely to offer more opportunities for mobility.

Levels of experienced voluntary-mobility were at low levels for 74 per cent of the sample and 26 per cent exercised high to very high mobility. Mobility is likely to be closely associated with basic skill levels, skill upgradation experienced, and industry type (Table 2T).

Mobility refers to the phenomenon in the labour market where job changes occur as workers search for better wages, working conditions or both. This is distinct from redundancy, which forces workers to search for other jobs. High voluntary-mobility is generally indicative of a tightening labour market and the possibility of upward movement in wages. Some other measures of the state of the market are the time taken to find the next job, compensation therein, working hours and so on.

Of the sample, 51 per cent had changed jobs in the course of their employed years since 1991 (voluntary and non-voluntary job changes). Among these 67 per cent changed due to management decisions, i.e. 34 per cent of all employees in the sample.

Of those who had changed jobs for any reason, 62 per cent had changed one or two jobs, 25 per cent had changed three to four jobs, and the remaining 12 per cent experienced more than four changes (Table 2R, S).

Further 33 per cent of those who did change jobs claim that they did not do so because of management decisions, i.e. this segment of the sample (16.7 per cent of all surveyed) experienced voluntary-mobility in 14 years. They moved perhaps in search of better wages and prospects (Table 2T).

A little more than half, i.e. 52 per cent of those who changed jobs due to management decisions lost between one and two jobs, and another 9 per cent lost three to four jobs during their working years. This indicates a high intensity of experienced-redundancy in the organized sector due to restructuring since 34 per cent of all the sampled employees changed jobs due to management decisions. All evidence from earlier macro-level studies (presented here) confirms the trend towards flexibilization and even of movement out of the organized into the unorganized sector (Table 2S).

In all, 398 employees (51 per cent) changed jobs. The transition experience is varied, with the highest proportion (37 per cent) claiming that the time taken to find the next job remained the same. For another 37 per cent of the sample, it seems to have declined while for 26 per cent it has increased. Therefore, the time spent finding the next job seems to have either remained the same or decreased for about 74 per cent of the population. In addition, the diminishing time to find the next job experienced by 37 per cent may be indicative of an expanding labour market for trained/skilled/experienced workers within the organized sector but on poorer terms of employment (Table 2Y).

Almost 48 per cent also claim that their nominal compensation has increased compared to their earlier jobs, and of these 9 per cent report substantial increase. On the other hand, 47 per cent of those who shifted jobs claim that their compensation has remained the same and for 5 per cent it decreased. These experiences are expected to be sector and skill related. The organized sector overall seems to have maintained its nominal wages. It is important to add that this survey however does not capture those who lost their organized sector jobs altogether and are now either self-employed or working in the informal sector (Table 2W).

Of those who changed jobs 31 per cent said that their working hours have increased, and among these 7 per cent experienced substantial increase in working hours. A majority of 57 per cent felt their working hours remained nearly the same even after job-changes. The hours decreased for only 12 per cent. Almost a third had longer working hours after shifting jobs. It is informally reported that for much of the private sector the workday had increased throughout the period to upwards of 10 hours. If travel time is factored in than it would cover all the daylight hours (Table 2X).

GENDER

Seventy-six per cent of the sampled population of organized sector employees is male. This is indicative of the low representation of females in the organized sector (Table 1B). Only 68 per cent of the women were union members, against 82 per cent of the men. In all categories, a higher proportion of women faced insecurity. Thirty-one per cent of the women endured high or severe PEI, while only 21 per cent of the men were in that category. Also, a much lower percentage of women (26 per cent) than men (54 per cent) had no experience of insecurity. Forty-three per cent of the women had a low PEI while only 25 per cent of men were in that category. There is an indication of a gendered experience of insecurity (Table 6C, 2D).

Females have higher skill hunger; a high 78 per cent of females upgraded their skills, while only 48 per cent of males did so. Majority of them had upgraded their skills, and many may have done so over their working life, as 76 per cent of the older women (over 35 years) did upgrade. The skill upgradation experience was somewhat higher among younger (less than 35 year old) women, 80 per cent of them had improved their skills compared to 76 per cent of the older (above 35 years of age) group. Similar pattern is true for the males where the younger are more likely to upgrade skills over their working life. Skill-desire is higher among females and 65 per cent of the females wanted to continue to upgrade their skills further compared to men (44 per cent). (Table 4F and Table 6.5 A, B below).

Across the spectrum women were also more mobile than men. Some mobility was experienced by 34 per cent females against 23 per cent males. Comparisons in sub-categories were: very high mobility (2.1 per cent females vs. 0.2 per cent males), high mobility (8 per cent vs. 5.6 per cent), low mobility (24 per cent vs. 17 per cent) respectively. The reasons could be varied, e.g., result of relocation due to marriage, expansion of service-sector jobs for women (Table 2V).

SKILLS

Of the sample, 25 per cent of the employees answered to the job description of professional, technical and related, 19 per cent described themselves as service workers, 18 per cent as production workers, 15 per cent as clerical and related, 8 per cent as transport, equipment operators and labourers, 7 per cent as sales workers, and 8 per cent others. Some workers fell into more than one category (Table 7G).

At the time of the survey, 68 per cent of them were in the wage

Table 3.5A: Skill Upgradation by Gender

	Female Upgraded		*Male Upgraded*	
	Yes	No	Yes	No
	147	41	286	305
Per cent in gender	78.0	22.0	48.0	52.0

Source: Survey data.

Table 3.5B: Skill Upgradation by Age and Gender

Age	*Female Upgraded*				*Male Upgraded*			
	Yes	*No*	*Total*	*Per cent Yes*	*Yes*	*No*	*Total*	*Per cent Yes*
18-35	94	24	118	80.0	174	117	291	45.0
36-60	53	17	70	76.0	112	188	300	37.0

Source: Survey data.
Note: Younger age groups of both genders upgrade skills more frequently than the corresponding older groups, but the percentage of females is far ahead of their male counterparts.

category of Rs. 5,000-20,000 per month, and within this group, 45 per cent were in the Rs. 5,000-10,000 per month category (Table 7K).

The sampled population is almost entirely literate; 34 per cent of the sample is at graduate level or more (post-graduates or doctoral); 25 per cent have passed class X and 20 per cent have passed the XII grade. About 9 per cent have vocational degrees. Only 11 per cent of them have not passed the X grade. This suggests the higher skill base of the organized sector (more so organized service sector employees) compared to the employees in the unorganized sector. Thus, the observations and estimates characterize the insecurity status of such a workforce. It may be logical to suggest that lower the skill higher the insecurity other things remaining constant. On an average, illiteracy level is about 40 per cent in the general Indian workforce (Table 1C).

Of the sampled employees, 56 per cent had upgraded their skills since 1991 and 44 per cent had not upgraded. Of the employees, 66 per cent who did upgrade after 1991 in the sample were 30 years old or above at the time of the survey and could have been employed over the period. This is important to factor in an overlap because those who did upgrade skills might also include workers in the less than 30-year-old category, who may not have been seeking employment or employed since 1991 and might have been in high school, college or vocational training institutes in that period (Table 3.5C below).

WHO PAID FOR SKILL UPGRADATION?

Sixty-one per cent of those who had improved their skills and qualifications had done so using their own savings. Employer had paid for 48 per cent, and 21 per cent had used bank loans. The percentages add to more than 100 because many had used a combination of sources to fund their skill upgradation, and acquired multiple skill upgrades. More pertinent perhaps to the policy aspect was the revelation that of those who upgraded, 89 per cent (50 per cent of all) had used public funded institutions

Table 3.5C: Skill Upgradation by Age

Age in years	*Yes*	*No*	*Total*	*Per cent upgraded*
18-24	35	13	48	73
25-29	111	56	167	66
30-34	100	51	151	66
35-39	92	66	158	58
40 +	95	160	255	37
Total	433	346	779	

Source: Survey data.

Notes: 1. Yes below 30: 146 = 33.7 per cent. Below 35: 246 = 56.8 per cent. Age 30 or more: 297 = 68.6 per cent. Age 35 or more: 187 = 43.1 per cent.

2. This grouping also confirms that the younger age groups are more active in upgrading their skills.

for their upskilling, and 72 per cent had also been trained and skilled within their employing organization. Only 25 per cent had used private training institutions for improving their skills. Thus ability to save from own income for own skill upgradation and company-level initiatives are crucial for developing skill edge. Hence, income security seems to be more critical to skill upgradation than job security (Table 3B, C).

SKILL UPGRADATION IN CURRENT JOB

Of the sample, 54 per cent said that they received sufficient training on the job or new machines in their current employing organization. Therefore, 46 per cent did not get any training and could not upgrade their skills in their current jobs. This is likely to be associated with the preliminary entry-point skill level (education) since skill upgradation overall is also associated with entry-level education, terms of employment (permanent/temporary/contract), industry type, and sector and management policy. For example, the higher entry-level skilled worker is more likely to receive further training and undertake skill upgradation opportunities, just as a permanent is more likely to receive it (Table 3D, 5A).

Forty-nine per cent of the sampled employees wanted to upgrade their skills further for continued employability and 19 per cent of them wanted to change over to a new profession or skill type. These percentages indicate a high skill-hunger in the employees and recognition of the salience of new or improved skills and qualifications for continued employability (Table 3E, F).

SOME SKILL UPGRADATION FACTORS

For an employee there is a link between basic education and the likelihood of skill upgradation after joining the workforce. Only 25 per cent of those who were less than matriculates and 36 per cent of those who were matriculates could upgrade their skills, while 56 per cent of those who were high school graduates, 74 per cent of the vocational graduates, and 75 per cent of the graduates were able to upgrade their skills (Table 3D).

Basic education has a consistent and progressive influence on skill upgradation. Looking at the correlation from that point of view 433 employees in the sample upgraded their skills – of these 75 per cent were graduates, 73.6 per cent had basic vocational qualification, 56 per cent were high schoolers, 36 per cent were matriculates, and 25 per cent were less than matriculates. Percentages do not add up because those who upgraded skills on average did 1.63 upgrades.

Pearson's chi square for education and skill upgradation is high at 116. At four degrees of freedom (df) the null hypothesis that basic education and skill upgradation are not related can be rejected at 0.1 and 0.01 levels of significance.

Further, there seems to be some sort of virtuous cycle at work for those who had higher basic education; not only were their chances of skill upgradation higher but their skill hunger was higher as well. Graduates (34 per cent wanted to upgrade further) had the highest skill hunger followed by matriculates (25 per cent) and high schoolers (20.4 per cent). There seems to be a satiation level associated with vocational diploma or a lack of feasibility of further upgradation, as only 9.2 per cent wanted to further upgrade their skills. This is surprisingly the lowest in all categories of education. There is a need to probe this and re-examine the quality and delivery of vocational education.

Among those who had previously upgraded their skills, 69 per cent were sure that they wanted to upgrade their skills further. These constituted 78 per cent (more than three-fourths) of all who want to upgrade their skills. Against this, only 22 per cent (less than one-fourth) of those who had not previously upgraded wanted to do so (Table 4A).

Those wanting to upgrade their skills now (at the time of the survey) constitute 49 per cent of the sample. The desire to continue upgradation was not dependent on age groups; it was almost evenly distributed over age groups 26-30, 31-35, 36-40 and above 40 years. Of all those who wished to upgrade further, the smallest number lay in the age group 18-25, who are fresh entries into the labour force, and the highest number lay in the more mature age group of 31-5 years. Graphs reinforce the premise of virtuous circle that early education enhances earning capacity, and prompts further upgradation (Table 4B).

The correlation between PEI and skill upgradation is interesting. It appears that as experience of insecurity increases so does the likelihood of skill upgradation. If one looks at the data, then 47 per cent of those who had no past experience of insecurity (PEI) upgraded, 55 per cent who had low experience upgraded, and 73 per cent of those who experienced high insecurity in the past (PEI) upgraded their skills (Table 2C). The possible explanation of this direct relationship between PEI and skill upgradation could be as follows. The sampled population was in the organized sector and a substantial section (47 per cent) had experienced an increase in nominal incomes (only 5 per cent reported a loss of nominal income). Hence, a higher PEI for workers within the organized sector could be linked to a higher need, priority, and ability to upgrade skills. Given some probability of retaining one's job or acquiring a better one, insecurity seems to induce a fight-back reaction from employees who react by acquiring skills. Fight-back effort in the sector rises with PEI, but at severe PEI-level, people seem to give up. Further, since the most preferred source of finance is personal savings and organizational support, skill upgradation is likely to be sensitive to income security. Ninety-six per cent of the employees whose income increased substantially have upgraded their skills. Fifty-eight per cent of those whose income had increased somewhat upgraded their skills. And, 42 per cent of those whose income remained the same had improved their skills (Table 7J, L).

Another fact also indicates the same directional link between insecurity and upskilling. The lowest proportion of upskilling seems to be occurring in the category of the most secure workers (Table 6.5E). However, part-time permanents have the highest proportion of up-skilled employees, followed by the full-time but temporary employees.

There also seems to be an important link between basic education, PEI, and response to insecurity. When they experienced a high PEI, 95 per cent of graduates and vocational diploma holders, 88 per cent of high schoolers (XII), but only 33 per cent with lesser education upgraded their skills. This is a trend across all levels of insecurity.

In the service sector, 57 per cent of the employees wanted to improve their skills further compared to only 19 per cent in the manufacturing sector (Table 4G). This inclination was also more in the public sector, where 67 per cent of the employees wanted to upgrade their skills compared to the private and cooperative sectors, where only 43 per cent wanted to upgrade (Table 4H). It is possible that this skill appetite is related to the rate of introduction of organizational support for skill improvement, introduction of new technologies and the management policies in the sector. In the public sector, 89 per cent reported introduction of new technology and 68 per cent received some training, however, in the private sector 68 per cent reported new technologies and 48 per cent received training.

In the service sector, 79 per cent reported of new technology and 59 per cent received some training, while in manufacturing 51 per cent reported new technology but only 31 per cent received training (Table 6.5D below).

UNEMPLOYMENT

Half of those currently employed have claimed to experience some period of unemployment, and, the other half had not experienced any since 1991. Thirty-eight per cent of the sampled employees

Table 3.5D: Technology and Training by Manufacturing, Service, Public, Private Sectors

Sector (Total)	*New Technology*	*Percentage of Sector*	*Trained*	*Percentage of Sector*
Service (599)	473	79	353	59
Manufacture (180)	93	51	54	30
Public (178)	158	89	121	68
Private (601)	408	68	286	48

Source: Survey data.

had experienced 1-4 years of unemployment, while 12 per cent had experienced 5 years or more of unemployment (Table 2BB).

Fifty-three per cent of employees have been in the current job for more than eight years. This segment can be assumed to be more secure in their current employment in the organized sector. Another 12 per cent had spent 6-8 years in their current job and this segment also can be considered relatively mature and secure in their current job (Table 7F).

Of the sampled population, 35 per cent is less than 32 years of age, and in the age group 19-31 years. This segment represents the young employees and they are likely to be more insecure. This group, however, is also likely to be strongly dependent on its past and current experiences with regard to unemployment, contingent employment, and other issues like training, up-skilling, and management policies. Their experiences when compared to the older age group are likely to reflect the changes in the labour market over the last decade.

EMPLOYEE UNIONS

Of the sample, 79 per cent was unionized. In addition to union density, 61 per cent of employees were members of a federated union, and the questionnaire sought to determine the range of issues that unions bargained for (Table 6A, B).

Ninety per cent of the members said that their union bargained over wages, 77 per cent over bonus issues, 66 per cent over the length of the working day, 60 per cent over training on the job. Fifty-four per cent reported that their union bargained over issues related to reduction in staff, 51 per cent over relating promotion to length of service, and 50 per cent over issues of training in new technology. Only 42 per cent held that their unions bargained over issues related to the nature of new technology and machines to be introduced. In addition, 41 per cent of the members said that their unions bargained about issues related to work and performance measurement (Table 6D).

Range of bargaining influence of the unions seems to be spread more or less evenly. While 33 per cent of the employees rated their union's range of bargaining influence as nominal or low, 37 per cent rated it as medium, and about 31 per cent rated it as high (Table 6E).

Unions do seem to influence the current experience of insecurity. Fifty-six per cent of the employees who were not unionized feared a job loss; while a lower 47 per cent of those who were unionized feared job loss (Table 6F).

To recapitulate the organized form of employment in the sample, 73 per cent described themselves as full-time and permanent employees, the remaining 27 per cent fell into various categories of contingent employment like part-time, contract, casual, *badli* (6.5E below). Of them, 78 per cent had provident fund. Seventy-two per cent were employed in the organized private sector and 23 per cent in the public sector, while 5 per cent were employed in the cooperative sector. Thirty-five per cent of them were employed in factories and establishments where the size of the employees was between 100-999 workers; 19 per cent between 1,000-4,999 workers, and 21 per cent in above 5,000-worker category. The remaining 25 per cent were employed in smaller-sized units (Table 7B, C).

It is therefore apparent that the sample represents the cream: the most secure and privileged section of the employees. It is in this context that their experience regarding real incidence of insecurity and perceived insecurity, skill and training, human resource

Table 3.5E: Current Terms of Service by Skill Upgradation Undertaken

Term of service	*Yes*	*No*	*Total*	*Per cent of who upgraded*
1 - Full-time and Permanent	281	284	565	50
2 -Part-time and permanent	34	4	38	89
3 - Full-time and temporary	97	42	139	70
4, 5 - Part-time and Temporary, Contract, casual, *Badli*	21	16	37	57

Source: Survey data.

policies of managements have to be understood. For example, it became evident that 44 per cent of this creamiest layer of the employees had not upgraded their skills since 1991 and 46 per cent said that they had not received sufficient training on the job or on new machines. However, the majority who remained within the organized sector seems to have maintained their nominal wages at least, even though their work has been intensified.

Notes

1. Joan Greenbaum (2004): *Windows on the Work Place*, Cornerstone Publications, New Delhi.
   Daniel Bell (1976): *The Coming of Post-Industrial Society*, Basic Books, New York.
   J.A. Fraser (2001): *White-collar Sweat Shops: The Deterioration of Work and its Rewards in Corporate America*, WW Norton, New York.
   M.D. Yates (2003): 'Naming the System: Inequality and Work in the Global Economy', *Monthly Review Press*, New York.
2. L. Deshpande et al. (2004): *Liberalization and Labour: Labour Flexibility in Indian Manufacturing*, Institute for Human Development, New Delhi.
3. Paul Osterman (1994): 'How Common is Workplace Transformation and Who Adopts it', *Industrial and Labour Relations Review*, vol. 47, no. 2, January, pp. 173-88.
4. Paul Osterman (2000): 'Work Reorganization in an Era of Restructuring: Trends in Diffusion and Effects on Employee Welfare', *Industrial and Labour Relations Review*, vol. 53, no. 2, January, pp. 179-96.
5. Ota Hitoshi (2004): 'Flexible Work Organization, Human Resource Practices', *5th Asian Regional Congress of the International Industrial Relations Association (IIRA)*, held from 23-6 June 2004, at Seoul, South Korea
6. David Guest (2000): 'Management and the Insecure Workforce', in Edmund Heery and John Salmon (eds.), *The Insecure Workforce*, Routledge, London and New York.
7. C.A. Moser and G. Kaltron (1971): *Survey Methods in Social Investigation*, Heinemann, London, Chapters 11 and 13.

Judith Bell (1993): *Doing Your Research Project*, Open University Press, Buckingham, Philadelphia.

8. J. Kirk and M.L. Miller (1985): *Reliability and Validity in Qualitative Research*, Sage, California.
9. BMR Development Authority (1995): *Draft Regional Plan for BMR: 1996-2011.*
10. Pankaj Joshi (2002): 'An Introduction to Urban Regeneration of the Harbour of Mumbai', Unpublished Dissertation at the University of York, in Darryl D'Monte (ed.), *Ripping the Fabric: The Decline of Mumbai and its Mills*, Oxford University Press, New York.
11. Rajnarayan Chandavarkar (1994): *The Origins of Industrial Capitalism in India: Business Strategies and the Working Classes in Bombay, 1900-1940*, Cambridge University Press, New Delhi.
12. MMRDA (1995): *Draft Regional Plan for Mumbai Metropolitan Region 1996-2011*, October, p. 10.
13. S.R.B. Leadbeater (1993): *The Politics of Textiles: The Indian Cotton Mill Industry and the Legacy of Swadeshi*, Sage, New Delhi.
14. H. Joshi and Vijay Joshi (1976): *Surplus Labour and the City: A Case Study of Bombay*, Oxford University Press, Mumbai.
15. Lokshahi Hakk Sanghatana (1996): *Murder of the Mills: An Enquiry into Bombay's Cotton Textile Industry and its Workers*, Mumbai, p. 6.
16. Hitoshi Ota (2005): 'Flexible Work Organization, Human Resource Practices and Worker Perception in India: A Case Study of Bangalore City', *Indian Journal of Labour Economics*, vol. 48, January-March, pp. 115-29.
17 Labour Bureau (2009): Report on the Effect of the Economic Slowdown on Employment in India', For Ministry of Labour and Employment, Government of India. Chandigarh, India. The most revealing statements in the report are numbers # 1.10 on page 8, #1.15 on page 10, # 2.2, 2.3, 2.4 on page 11, #2.13 on page 14. All of these are methodological declarations and indicate the lack labour data in India, the reluctance of employers' associations to participate in quantification processes, the unavailability of employment rolls for contract labour even though required by law, specially in the construction sector, the inability to track employment in enterprises that employ less than 10 workers and so on.
18. Heery and Salmon (2000): *The Insecure Workforce*, Routledge, London and New York.

CHAPTER 4

Correlates of Insecurity: Human Resource Management

> Most of what we call management consists of making it difficult for people to get their work done.
>
> PETER DRUCKER

Examination of the insecurity hypothesis would be quite inadequate without studying the role played by the new HRM rhetoric and practice at the firm level. In Section 4.1, the evolution of HRM is traced and in 4.2 the principles and principal tools of HRM are elaborated and its critique and the relationship with industrial relations (IR) and personnel management are presented in Section 4.3. Section 4.4 details the HRM scenario in India and the changes in the legislative framework for labour. In Section 4.5 the report of the Second Nation Labour Commission is summarized to draw attention to the trends. Section 4.6 concludes the discussion.

4.1 Evolution of Human Resource Management

The new HRM is described as a strategic and coherent approach to the management of a firm's most valued resource, i.e. the people working in the firm who individually and collectively contribute to the achievement of its goal. HRM has emerged as the new approach to people management since economic restructuring began in America and the UK. This approach has pushed the conventional theory and practice of personnel management and industrial relations into the background.[1]

Kochan (1986) advances a link between the external environment of the firm and the institutional structure of the firm-level IR.[2] A destabilizing incident such as increased competition sets in process business and industrial relation decisions. These decisions are mediated by history, current structure, and values of the main actors. There is no one common set of responses. Writers have argued that the IR policy is essentially contingent upon business policies and external economic context. Schuler and Jackson (1987) derive a set of human resource policies that is consistent with Porter's alternative competitive strategies available to firms, such as low cost strategy, high quality strategy or differentiation strategy.[3] For instance, firms competing on the basis of low cost will logically adopt an anti-collective bargaining stand to drive down wages. On the other hand, high quality strategy may opt for collective bargaining, skill formation and responsible autonomy strategies. Other studies have criticized such rational planning assumptions in which management is attributed with adequate power and sufficient information to align its human resource policy with the external environment.[4] The room for manoeuvre in management policy depends upon product market power such as degree of competitive pressures from other competitors, barriers to entry, level and stability of consumer demand and so on.[5] The management could convey the pressure from the global market to its industrial relation practices.

Martyn Wright (2000) compared 50 highly unionized companies in 1979 and then again in 1991 in the UK, and he derived a set of conclusions which are important, even though these need to be validated again, since 15 additional years of neo-liberal policies and competitive pressures have intensified changes at the firm level. Wright's findings are summarized below[6]:

According to Wright, few countries, experienced the economic crisis as severe or the reframing of employment laws as marked as Britain, yet there was little evidence to suggest widespread work restructuring, fundamental redesigning of jobs, advanced team working systems, or a large-scale abandoning of trade unions and collective bargaining. The diversity and the quality of IR experiences suggest that major actors like the government, union, and management do display a degree of choice and control over their preference. Management exercises its choices at three levels: (a) long-term strategic business policy, (b) issues such as investment, plant location, new technology, personnel policy and collective bargaining and, (c) workplace relations at levels such as supervisory style, worker participation, and work organization.

Wright's research on these 50 firms in the UK showed that most firms experienced severe economic crisis in the early 1980s, which took the form of collapse in corporate profit, threat of stock market takeover, other capital market pressures or threat of privatization of the public sector. These changes often resulted in change of management policies, a shift away from collective bargaining policies and a decline in management support for union organization. Managers also reported an increase in their perceived bargaining power, perhaps as a result of legislative changes. Union security, judged by the level of union density, presence of collective bargaining, and informal closed shop remain largely intact for manual and craft workers, but was more prone to the erosion of white-collar workers among whom the ethic of union organization is less well entrenched. Widespread changes in substantive working rules were reported, but the extent of change varied widely. Firms differed in the degree to which the crisis situation was translated into a change or the changes themselves were routed through collective bargaining procedures.

Collective bargaining seems to have largely survived in Wright's sample of UK firms during 1979-91. Bargaining institutions were adhered to partly due to management fear of more aggressive unions stepping in. Joint negotiations were known to have no negative effect and in some case a positive effect on performance. Where the firm had withdrawn from bargaining rights they had done so deliberately as a part of a generic shift in personnel policy. The pay determination has become more widely decentralized down to the plant-level managers. Only a degree of control, formal or informal, existed at the establishment level for pay bargaining. The sample also showed that the most common changes in work organization were increased job flexibility, changes to working time, staffing levels, and reduction in the number of job grades, followed by production system redesign and the introduction of new technology. Categories least often changed were employee communication and union job controls. (These factors have been taken into consideration in the Mumbai-level survey done as part of this study, for example, questions 3.6 and 3.7 in the questionnaire in the appendix focus on the nature of HRM changes at the firm level in the region.)

But firms diverged widely in the extent to which they changed work organization, even within the same industrial sector and under similar unionization. By 1991, sampled UK firms came to operate in the markets which were marginally more competitive in terms of the number of competitors or their market share, and in which there were strong pressures to reduce costs. Although the experience of recession of the early 1980s was evident, the responses were diverse depending on the market environment in which the firm operated. For the larger group of firms, once the demand conditions had recovered by 1990, there was little evidence of renewed intensification of market competition. But circumstances in which there is intensification of competition could produce different outcomes.

HRM has its origins in the USA where the transformation of the American industrial relations began in the 1980s as a direct response to external pressures.[7] The economic supremacy of the USA, built on demand management, mass-production, economies of scale, and Taylorian division of labour, which counted on close supervision of low-skilled workforce, had begun to crumble. The pressures first came from Japanese exports and eventually from the other Asia Tigers. In the USA, with the maturation of systems of mass production and IR, the personal incomes had risen for two decades, as also did income inequalities. As both income levels and inequalities of income grew the tastes and preferences of consumers changed. The spread of consumerism meant increase in quantities and eventually variety of goods consumed. The continuous need for new variety and models was a demand that the standardized goods from the assembly-line systems could no longer satisfy, specially for high-end consumers. Those at the lower and middle ends now had access to quantities of imported goods at cheaper prices. Most economists regard this reality as the root cause of the restructuring of business organizations and the resulting 'flexibilization' discussed extensively in Chapter 2.

This has forced the firms to direct their human resource policies towards innovative techniques of flexible working practices.[8]

The technological revolution of microelectronics and automation made it possible to alter design and produce products rapidly at affordable prices. Time to market a new TV, for example, has shrunk from two years to six months. Economies of scope rather than scale became viable. The recession of the 1980s, which was the worst since the depression of the 1930s, forced the American industry to respond with a range of strategies. The new understanding was that the key to Japanese dominance of the world market did not lie in its command over natural resources and superior technology, but in the calibre and performance of its human resource.

The new HRM has a close connection to the flexibility that organizations seek today. As markets become fragmented, product cycles become short, and competition intensifies along with the rate of innovation, flexibility becomes the key concept and tool. But in practice, flexibility is quite an ambiguous term. It can take the form of proactive versatility (High Road) to exploit market niches, quickly respond to orders, and new technology on the basis of skills and polyvalent workforce. Examples of this come from Sweden, Japan, Germany, Italy (Emilia-Romaegna model) or it can mean passive pliability (Low Road), i.e. submitting to outside pressure by resorting to wage cuts, numerically flexible and contingent employment. Developing countries and especially their small firms tend to indulge in the second form of flexibility as they are often exempt from protective labour regulation, have no formalized industrial relations and no unions. In case of India, for example, flexibility has come to mean little more than docile, unprotected, and disposable workforce – in short the Low Road to global competition.[9]

The New HRM, according to its advocates, however, is unique; it seeks to achieve competitive advantage through the strategic deployment of highly committed and capable workforce, using an integrated array of cultural, structural and personnel techniques.[10] The basic assumption/belief of HRM practitioners is that it is the human resource among all the factors of production which really makes the difference. Human capabilities and commitment in the final analysis distinguish successful organizations from the rest. It follows from this premise that human capital ought to be treated carefully, nurtured as a valued asset, and not as a cost alone. At a broader level, HRM involves a cultural reorientation of senior management in an organization towards an attitude of investing in people.

Typical characteristics of various versions of HRM can be identified as follows:

1. Its emphasis on the need for a strategic fit between the goals of the business and its HR policies.
2. Its stress on gaining the commitment of its workforce to the organization's mission and values – it is commitment oriented.
3. Its accent on building a culture and value system in the organization within which highly committed teams can be made to deliver.
4. Its emphasis on the need to treat people as assets to be invested in, i.e. as human capital and not as variable cost.
5. Its prominence in identifying best practices and creating a bundle or configuration of mutually supporting policies.
6. It is top-management driven.
7. Employee relations are unitarist rather than collective, individual rather than collective.
8. Its organizing principal is organic, flexible and decentralized.
9. HRM contributes in a measurable way to building competitive advantage.
10. It is focused on delivering high levels of customer satisfaction and shareholder value.

Many of these ideas have permeated management jargon over the last two decades even in developing countries like India. Ultimately the drive to adopt HRM is based on the case of a need to respond to threats from increasing business competition. But it appeals to managements who strive to increase competitive advantage through investing in new technology and human resources.[11]

But the rhetoric is fashionable among all kinds of managements and there are different versions of HRM. These policies have by now displayed some recognizable trends and consequences across the globe as indicated in Chapters 1 and 2. National institutions and policies also induce firm-level policies and these policies have direct repercussions on the insecurity of workers. But the firms sometimes are capable of adopting clearly different variations of human management policies in the same national institutional set-up, and, hence different levels of insecurity may be experienced by workers in different firms within the same industry and national institutional framework. However, there is some reason to believe that with mounting competitive pressures firm-level strategic HRM options may eventually diminish. The New Economy ushered in by globalization leaves no part of the business firm unaffected. Although few leading business thinkers would deny that new management models should revolve around people, the practice would become very different. The distinctive advantage/edge of firms in a highly competitive global economy today should be the composition of the workforce itself, the quality of its motivation, commitment, and their participation in decision-making and implementation. Despite the enthusiasm with which this new 'Peoplism' model of HRM is discussed in management journals and books, the evidence of practice is not so encouraging. And the practice of HRM has found many detractors, especially among trade unions.

4.2 Principles of Human Resource Management

Managing people is unfamiliar territory and difficult to measure. In a classical management dilemma 'whatever gets measured gets managed', hence even though the new management models claim to be people-centred, the HR department plays a marginal role in most companies with no representation on the board of directors or any strategic significance in business planning.[12]

The evidence for HRM comes from its two leading practitioners, i.e. the USA and Britain. In some cases HRM has supplanted the traditional IR of trade union power, collective bargaining and proceduralism. In other green-field cases firms have moved to new regions to avoid union opposition and installed HRM systems right from the time of the firm's inception. There are some basic HRM strategies that are commonly practiced, such as communication, participation, flexibility, just-in-time, and cultural context. While the traditional business firm avoids communicating with individuals because it subverts union authority or incurs the risk of non-compliance with direct instructions, the HRM keeps the individual informed about a wide range of issues through direct communication, house journals, employee reports, team briefing, video shows – family days are common ways to win the hearts and minds of employees. From both sides of the Atlantic, academics have published ground breaking reports to show that certain high-commitment, high-involvement practices around recruitment, employment security, team working, communication and decentralization are associated with better productivity and profits. These are better predictors of success than technology, marketing strategy and R&D.

4.2.1 *Team Briefing*

A survey of large British companies found that 86 per cent had installed a system of team briefing in which workers, supervisors and first-line managers participated. Fifty-nine per cent of the firms claimed that it reached beyond supervisory grades to all of the staff.[13] Opinion surveys and suggestion schemes are important techniques used by HRM.

4.2.2 *Participation*

Participation is a synonym for involving employees in management specified activities. There is no statutory basis to the involvement, the type or the level and frequency of involvement being very much at the discretion of the management.[14] The most common form of participation in HRM is the quality circle (QC). In HRM jargon 'quality' is defined as conformance to customer expectation and a general pursuit of excellence. The term 'customer', includes internal downstream recipients of goods and services and the conventional external recipients. The QC consists of a voluntary group of 6-8 people from the same department who meet every week in order to solve work-related problems that they experience. They select the problem to be solved, collect the necessary data, apply problem-solving techniques, present the solution to the management, implement the solution where feasible, and monitor the outcomes.[15] While QC taps into the workers' knowledge by getting them to look for better ways of doing things, it is also a threat to organizational hierarchy and a move towards flatter organizational structure. Therefore, QC cannot function as a freestanding institution; it has to be firmly integrated into a total quality management programme that is part of company-wide culture.[16]

4.2.3 *Flexibility*

To fully utilize the human resource, HRM seeks numerical and functional flexibility. Creating a class of privileged core workers with guaranteed employment, training or skill formation and career opportunities, and a subordinate class of peripheral and seasonal workers achieve numerical flexibility. Subordinate class is used to cope with shifts in demand and they do not have the benefits of the core class. This is typical of the Japanese model. Functional flexibility is multi-skilling of the core group. Jobs are assigned to semi-autonomous work groups called teams, which are free to rotate the members. The objective is to break the monotony, enrich worker's experience, and improve his versatility. Job rotation is generally a horizontal process between similar jobs at a particular level of production and not between different levels of skill. For job enrichment to take place, workers must be cross-trained in multiple skills. Japanese organizations make investments of time and resources to do that, but it is not common in America or the UK. Flexibility also requires flatter organizations with levels of designations kept to the minimum. It leads to work intensification as job grades are reduced.

Quality circles along with labour flexibility are known to step up the tempo of work, which in HRM jargon is euphemistically called 'smart work'.[17] Annual hours instead of work week, continuous shifts, part-time work, teleworking, virtual teams, outsourcing, call centres, flexible rewards, individual contracts, and flexible benefits are some of the more common examples of flexible HRM work practices.[18]

4.2.4 *Just in Time*

The aim is to produce and deliver finished goods just in time to be sold; sub-assembly just in time to be plugged into finished goods; fabricated parts just in time to go into the sub-assembly; and purchased material just in time to be transformed into fabricated parts.[19]. It implies minimizing inventories and waste. Waste may be anything – too many employees, too much space, idle time, too many breakdowns or too many products. In principle, everything that does not add value to the product in a direct sense is a waste. This is the foundation of what is also known as 'Lean Production'. Just in time, in contrast to the older 'just in case' is a system which counts on efficient supply chain management information system, transportation system, flexible labour system, and shifting variable demand for products.

4.2.5 *Training and Development*

There is widespread consensus that training has a desirable effect on productivity at the firm level and cumulative effect on national economic competitiveness and performance. In England, the evidence comes from study conducted by the National Institute for Economic and Social Research and is widely quoted in policy-making circles.[20] There are differences in the methods of training, e.g., the formal training programme vs. on-the-job training in internal labour markets where the emphasis is on demonstration and learning by doing. These differences embrace the labour market regimes and make comparisons between firms complicated. According to experts the level of commitment a firm shows towards investing in the skills of its workers is the litmus test of HRM, i.e. of whether or not firms are changing the way they manage labour. A number of international firms like IBM, Marks and Spencer, Nissan, ICL, Jaguar Cars, Lucas Industries and British Steel are acknowledged to be at the forefront of the HRM movement. HRM requires institutional support, internal labour markets, and quality rather than price competition, all of which are lacking in a rapidly globalizing economy.[21] Since there is no guarantee that HRM pays off in financial terms, therefore, when production for profit is the goal of capital there are alternate routes to accumulate capital. Many will be tempted to take recourse to low-skill, labour-intensive forms of production. This point can be highlighted by comparing the USA and UK with Singapore, Japan, and Germany as many researchers have done.[22]

4.2.6 *Cultural Context*

HRM is more than sum of its parts, and the subject has attracted much attention. The quest to replicate Japan's success in promoting employees' commitment to organization's objectives has not been easy in different cultural milieus. The Japanese culture is supposed to breed commitment to hard work, group and team spirit suitable for implementing HRM policies. Critics say that this is achieved through subtle and not so subtle coercion, feudalistic relations, and antipathy to democratic norms or independent trade union movements. Workers who cannot articulate their interests to an independent trade union have no real option but to comply with the management objective. First-hand accounts of work in Japanese factories are rare. A rare exception is Satoshi Kamata's narration of his life as a seasonal worker at Toyota in *Japan in the Passing Lane – 1983*, which discounts claims that Japanese workers willingly cooperate with management objectives and are different from workers elsewhere. Morris and Wilkinson studied Toyota and Toshiba in Japan and provide some evidence:

> In both cases there is an extremely powerful management, largely unchallenged by enterprise union, which exerts detailed control over employee behavior.[23] At Toshiba, Yomomoto documents the training of the supervisors in the technique of identifying and dealing with 'trouble

makers and problematic workers', including tailing suspects outside the workplace. Problematic workers include those who take all paid holidays, work only for the stipulated hours, or insist on exercise of their rights. They are dealt with through preventive approaches or surgical direct treatment.

As a Canadian trade unionist put it:

> It is easy for management to fill up the time we save with our improvement. This continuous redistribution of work costs us jobs and eventually puts such a burden on us that we risk injury from trying to work too quickly, forgetting about safety ... if you can figure out a way to do something in less time keep your secret within the team. That is your time and you have earned it.[24]

In a study conducted in American and European firms implementing the just-in-time and other Japanese practices, it was found that workers reacted adversely to attempts to intensify work. The most successful cases of resistance are from Wales, which witnessed much investment by Japanese in the electronics industry. Wilkinson says: after a bottleneck usually a person, but occasionally a machine or robot had been identified, targeted and cured, then either the line feed would be increased, or an individual would be taken out of the team, and the line rebalanced (the individual's task would be shared by others). The engineers would then seek out the next bottleneck in a never-ending process of continuous improvement.[25]

4.3 HRM and Insecurity

There is research evidence based on random samples of workers in the UK to show that there is a direct link between the type of HRM policies and the sense of security and satisfaction from the job.[26] This evidence has been duly incorporated in the questionnaire.

4.4 HRM and Skill Development

It is often assumed that the nature and quality of skills in an industry are determined by the system of education and vocational training. This view ignores the role of on-the-job training, skill utilization patterns in the workplace, teamwork, job rotation, multi-tasking, average length of employment in the firm, security of employment, communication between functional departments like design, development, production and marketing, and horizontal coordination in skill development. In other words it ignores the role of work organization and human resource policies of the enterprise in the development of skills. Studies demonstrate how the actual skill content and task responsibilities at work enhance skill levels of workers and often lead to increased innovation in the firms.[27]

One finds a variety of organizational patterns within every society; international comparisons also show socially significant organizational variations. Comparisons of British, American and Japanese firms are common. These studies, for example, illustrate that the British pattern of organization tends to be characterized by mechanistic features such as functional segmentation between functional departments like production, engineering and management leading to a high degree of specialization of roles and professional careerism. In contrast, the Japanese style of organizing work is less rigid, moving people across departmental boundaries as a routine, leads to the formation of teams and generalists who are organization based and enterprise driven. A study that draws evidence from a detailed investigation of work-roles careers and on-the-job training experience of 60 Japanese and 55 British R&D engineers in large electronic firms is important.[28] The analysis looked at the management and organization of product development activities and explored the extent to which the work roles of engineers enables fuller utilization of their capacities and provides opportunities for skill development. It shows that even for a highly qualified category of the workforce such as engineers, who acquire their general conceptual knowledge through a formal training system, substantial part of their skills such as capacity for processing information, organizational knowledge, contextual skills can only be acquired and honed by learning at the workplace.

According to Inoki and Polanyi (1958), such specific knowledge is distinct from general conceptual knowledge and is concerned with particular conditions of time and place, and it is also difficult to codify and conceptualize.[29] Inoki argues that the essence of skills in work is based on the second type of knowledge, which is shaped by the workplace organization. It is obvious that a significant part of human capital formation is linked to the HRM policies of the firm that make the workers less or more secure and induce specific skill development.

4.5 A Critique of HRM

One of the main criticisms is that HRM promises much more than it delivers. It claims to view employees as valued assets but it sacrifices them frequently in pursuit of the shareholder's value. Second, it identifies almost completely with the management interests and is viewed as a management activity.

In its soft seminar-room version, HRM policies focus on delivering resourceful humans to the organization. It emphasizes the importance of developing capabilities of employees for their career development and individual growth along with the organization's growth. Soft HRM is reflected in investments in skill training, safety measures, training-linked promotions, design of career paths, quality circles, suggestion schemes, and worker participation. In its hard factory-floor version HRM exercises planning, monitoring and control exclusively for competitive and strategic interests of the firm and nearly ignores the employees. In hard-HRM there is greater emphasis on numerical and functional flexibility, work intensification, lean production and low wage costs.

Commenting on the relationship between Industrial Relations and Personnel Management (IR&PM), scholars have said that this was the old name for HRM. However, there are different positions on that. One group of management scholars endorse the similarities between the two approaches that emphasize the virtue of treating people as key resources.[30] The other group agrees that HRM is no revolution but an evolution of personnel management; it is different in its emphasis on including managerial and non-managerial staff in an exercise to create a friction-free (nonconfrontational) organization focused on maximizing its goal in a competitive market.[31] HRM is becoming more popular in the post-restructuring and globalization period as an adaptation and a management strategy to deal with the rapidly changing business environment.

4.6 HRM in India

Unlike Latin American and South-East Asian countries, industrial relations in India had an early legislative framework that guaranteed to labour the right to employment and collective representation. India was a relative latecomer to integrating in the global economy and old IR has morphed into HRM. Popular in the post-economic restructuring phase, HRM in India is in a state of infancy, and requires labour support; but labour must have some reason to support a vastly more exacting production system. Indian industry is more familiar with the practice of human resource development that focuses on improving the skill, knowledge and attitude of management and supervisory classes but that practice often does not cover the workers.[32] By and large relations in the Indian manufacturing industry where the blue-collar workforce is large, are not marked by trust, cooperation, participation and involvement.

Early evidence of flexible labour practices provided in Chapter 2 of this study comes from various sources and provides ample evidence of flexibility. India's large reserve army of unemployed and the equally large unorganized sector has shored up such practices.[33]

Now there is increasing evidence from the Indian corporate sector that an ever more number of companies face global competition, and forced to upgrade the quality of their products and services have introduced new HRM policies like 5S, Kaizan, supply chain management, etc.[34] These companies are trying to align their HR function to business strategy.[35] Some companies have been adopting group-based work systems that may enhance flexibility in manpower allocation.

A study based in India and founded on an Osterman (1994)

study in America highlights the point made above. Osterman had developed an analytic framework and used it in 1992 in a USA survey to establish the extent to which flexible work practices composed of self-managed work teams, QC, TQM and job rotation was adopted in the United States.[36] Some factors associated with the adoption of these practices were internationally competitive product markets, technology contents that require high levels of skills, a firm's choice in following the high-road strategy that emphasizes quality, variety and service, and HR practices like training and incentives rather than low-cost competitive strategy.[37] His follow-up survey five years later indicated that that QC, TQM and job rotation continued to diffuse at a rapid pace during the period in USA.[38] Other researchers have reported similar conclusions about changing human resource practices to induce increasing flexibility and worker productivity in the USA and UK.

Hitoshi Ota (2005) used this framework to establish the HR practices in India. He generated two data sets from two surveys conducted in Bangalore in 2000. The first data set was from a questionnaire survey of HR practices and labour management relations covering 189 establishments referred to as the Establishment Survey and the other regarding worker perception and satisfaction in five manufacturing companies referred to as the Workers Survey. Hitoshi Ota examined various issues like (1) the extent to which Flexible Work Practises (FWPs) were adopted in India – Bangalore; (2) rheir diffusion in relation to related HR practices, i.e. whether they were adopted in bundles; (3) worker perception regarding FWP.[39] The Establishment Survey questionnaire asked about HR and organizational practices adopted among core workers at the establishment and not at the company level. Ota uses Osterman definition of core employees as the largest group of non-supervisory, non-managerial workers in the establishment who are directly involved with making the product, or providing service at the establishment, and core jobs are defined as 'jobs that are executed by core employees'.

For the Establishment Survey, firms employing 50 or more employees, in Bangalore city were used. A firm could be in secondary and tertiary industrial categories as listed in four different directories in 2000. Bangalore has a wide spectrum of industry ranging from textile, food processing, engineering, bio-chemical, IT and BPO, to automobile, electronics, aerospace and military, and is widely regarded as the showcase of liberalization since 1991. After identifying 301 establishments that agreed to cooperate with the survey, the questionnaires were posted out to them. The questionnaires were in three sections to be answered by managers and above, i.e. persons who were familiar with practical issues on the shop floor and in the best position to answer the questions. The total number of establishments that actually responded was 189, i.e. a response rate of 62.8 per cent. These 189 companies constituted the sample size.

The second data set was from the questionnaire survey of workers. Ota developed the questionnaire based on studies of Denison (1990), Cappelli and Rogovsky (1998). Questions seeking other than personal information were designed to secure response in terms of a five-point scale showing the degree of fit for each statement question. The questionnaire was prepared in both English and Kannada. The sample here could cover only five manufacturing firms and this limitation was realized only after having completed the Establishment Survey. The total number of workers in the sample was 173. The sampling method was not random due to the reluctance of the companies in cooperating with the worker survey and those that agreed to cooperate were reluctant to provide the researcher with the list of their employees. The researcher therefore had to depend on the contact person inside the establishment, usually the GM in the HR department, to select about 30 respondents randomly. The workers were to fill the forms and hand them over to the researcher in the premises. A point to be noted about Ota's work is that all of the establishments responding in the worker survey had a trade union, were establishments more than 20 years old, were Indian firms with the exception of one JV with an MNC. The conclusion of Ota's study indicates that it is not only large-scale companies, but also medium and smaller scale establishments in Bangalore that have seen diffusion of flexible work practices such as work teams, QC and TQM as defined by Osterman. The extent of diffusion was less than in the United States. But other factors like FWP were being adopted in a bundle of HR practices, FWP being associated with high levels of skills.

Skill associated with core jobs was true for Bangalore as well, in accordance with the hypothesis of Osterman's study. In the USA, younger establishments were more likely to adopt flexible work practices while larger establishments with 55-999 workforces were less likely to adopt FWP. In Bangalore, no significant relation was found between ownership pattern (public, private, MNC) and FWP adoption. Trade unionism was not found to be an impediment in the adoption of FWP.

As regards workers' perception and satisfaction, workers in FWP felt that their seniors listened to them, took their suggestions, and also gave them adequate feedback compared to their counterparts in firms where FWP was not in vogue. Neither job satisfaction nor quality of work-life was found to be related to adoption of FWP among the sampled workers of the five establishments.

Consequently in the questionnaire committed to workers in this study HR policies were clubbed into two broad categories: those most commonly associated with efforts to raise productivity and security-enhancing practices, also referred to earlier as the High Road. These include the introduction of new technology, training, performance appraisals, quality circles, teams, direct communication with employees, and worker participation in management. The other set includes those associated with rising insecurity and the Low Road such as redundancy, VRS policy, outsourcing, relocation, work intensification, use of non-permanent workers, litigation against workers, and so on.

4.7 Legislative Framework for Industrial Relations in India and Recent Changes

The following explanation puts the subtle but sustained changes in the legislative and implementation framework in the post-liberalization period in their historical context. The post-colonial governments had demonstrated a will to intervene to protect the rights of the working class; a will that has lately been undermined considerably and changes have resulted in increasing flexibilization of the workforce and insecurity.

Labour-management relations are subject to state regulations in all parts of the world. But, the state domination of industrial relation is deeply rooted in India's colonial past.[40] With the exit of the British, planned economic development became the paramount goal of the country and industrial conflict came to be viewed as a dampner to that effort. Social justice, it was argued, could be ensured without recourse to conflict because the country now had a democratically elected government. The tripartite system inherited from the British operated without change for half a century thereafter. In this system, the state is charged with the responsibility of containing conflict and negotiating order in labour management relations. The state is armed with the power to take note of industrial dispute, receive notice of a strike or lock-out, conciliate to resolve differences, decide whether the dispute should be referred to judicial decision, set up courts for adjudication, provide interim solutions pending court verdict, ban strikes or lock-outs if required or even compel labour to get back to work.

4.7.1 *The Framework*

Three pieces of legislation have played a role in shaping Indian industrial relations: (a) Indian Trade Unions Act 1926 (TUA), (b) Industrial Employment Act 1946 (IEA) (Standing Orders), and (c) Industrial Disputes Acts 1947 (IDA).

The TUA confers on the union the basic minimum legality, which protects them from civil or criminal liability arising out of the conduct of industrial disputes, and enables them to function as lawful associations. Any seven workers can register a union and take advantage of this legal cover. But there is nothing in this law to compel the management or employer to recognize this union or to deal with it in any manner. Since labour is a concurrent subject, the states may also legislate and some have provided for statutory recognition.

Under the IEA, every establishment employing 100 or more workers is required to have a set of certified Standing-Orders defining conditions of employment such as hours of work, attendance, proper conduct, punishment for misconduct, and means available for redress of unfair treatment. The purpose of this law is to ensure certain minimum standards of employment even if there is no union to fight for then workers.

The IDA aims to resolve conflicts through conciliation, arbitration and adjudication. The labour department sets into motion conciliation procedures when it receives intimation of an industrial dispute. But it can also do so when it apprehends imminence of a dispute. Conciliation consists in bringing the two sides together to resolve their difference through persuasion. If it fails, the two sides are encouraged to voluntarily submit the dispute for arbitration by a third party. If they are not willing to seek arbitration, the law provides for an adjudication system composed of courts and tribunals to which the government may refer the dispute for judgement.

Industrial relations have so far assumed a limited connotation of maintaining working relations between employers and the unions.[41] Although India has a long history of state intervention in labour management, according to some observers, this interventionist approach has paid no dividend. Instead, it has led to lack of voluntarism and strong unions, delays in settlement of disputes, politicization of dispute settlement mechanisms, and increasing incidence of industrial disputes and antagonism. And there is pressure for roll-back of the state and promotion of bipartisanism. This may appear convenient from labour-management relation point of view, however, it may not satisfy distributive justice issues, which require responsive legislation by the state, more so in the absence of strong federated institutions of labour or management with commitment to broad-based economic progress.

In India, in the period up to 1991, there was evidence of increasing trend for industrial action and lost man-days, and in these, India was ahead of Korea, Japan, Malaysia, and USA, UK, and Germany. The case for changing the industrial relation legislation must be seen in the background of structural changes occurring in the economy and the deeply antagonistic positions taken by the management and labour. In the context of structural changes, which are still afoot, the industrial relation policy, particularly issues relating to employment, industrial disputes, and bargaining must be reviewed. The major instrument of Industrial Relation

Policy (IRP) in the country is IDA 1947 as it exists today, after several amendments, and attempts at its major refurbishing. Its legislation framework is aimed at industrial sector and workmen as defined by it.

The concept of industry has undergone substantial changes primarily with the landmark judgement in 1978 wherein the attempt to segregate hospitals, educational and charitable institutes under a separate bill did not materialize. As such, the Act came to cover all organized activity except a few which were specifically excluded. Industry means a systematic activity carried out cooperatively by an employer and employees, whether such employees are employed by the employer directly or through an agency or a contractor, for the production, supply, distribution of goods and services with a view to satisfying human wants and wishes, whether or not (1) any capital has been invested or (2) such activity is carried out with a view to make any profit. This definition included any activity relating to promotion of sales or business or both and has come to include: (a) any agricultural operation, (b) hospitals, dispensaries, (c) educational training institutions, (d) charitable, philanthropic organizations, (e) Khadi and village industries, (f) domestic services, (g) professional practices, (h) cooperatives, clubs, etc. Activities not covered by the IDA are covered by a separate legislation. The definition of workman reflects the nature of work being done by him and not his economic status. It excludes from its purview managerial staff and special categories of government employees, e.g. defence.

The amendment of 1984 made it compulsory to constitute grievance redress machinery in organizations employing more than 49 workers with a suggestion that every establishment should have a panel of grievance arbitrators to arbitrate cases unresolved at the appellate level. However, this has not been implemented.

In respect of collective demands, the recognition of the majority union by the management is considered to be logical and natural. However, in practice it has assumed a voluntary nature after the signing of the code of discipline in 1950. The experience of collective bargaining across the country has been varied depending upon practices and procedures in different states. A major controversy here concerns the necessity for recognition of majority union by secret ballot.

Another issue in IR has been the advocacy of participative forums to displace the traditional conflict-based collective bargaining. The first forum for participation of workers in management was the 'works committee', which was required to be formed under the IDA in every enterprise employing 100 or more workers. The committees were to consist of equal number of representatives from management and workers and its task was to promote measures for securing and preserving good relationship and to communicate on matters of common interest or concern. Since these committees had no clear agenda, or support from either the management or the unions they languished. A tripartite study group, after studying participative management in several European countries, gave shape to new policies prescribed by the Second Five-Year Plan and the Industrial Policy Resolution 1965. It recommended the formation of joint management councils (JMC). Worker participation was considered a prerequisite of increased productivity, cooperation, and commitment. It was to be the basis of industrial democracy and socialist society. The JMC was to consist of a maximum of 12 members drawn equally from labour and management with the choice of chairman and vice-chairman left to the council. All decisions of the JMC were required to be unanimous. The councils were assigned some decision-making powers. But eventually, the council-powers ranged from non-controversial to inconsequential, examples being safety, training programmes, holidays, changes in the standing orders, reorganization of work, retrenchment, closure, etc. Regarding larger issues like production, sales programmes, balance sheet and profit and loss statements the council could only seek information. As there was no legislation to mandate creation of JMCs, there was no proliferation and their numbers dwindled from 99 in the 1960s to 80 by 1970.

Bill for worker participation in management was introduced in the Rajya Sabha in 1990. The newly elected National Front government called a conference of trade unions, employers and academicians to discuss the issue of participation. The Bill recommended a three-tier system. At the lowest level were the shop-councils and establishment-councils. Workers had 13 per cent representation on the board of directors. Employee representatives on the board were either nominated or elected by the union, and discharged all the functions of a board member including the right to vote. At the highest level was the government proposal for labour participation in equity capital.

The employers vehemently opposed the last two items. The sponsoring government fell and the Bill was never passed. According to scholars, the Bill was too revolutionary for Indian employers. In the decade after 1991, economic restructuring put a different set of demands on the industrial relations system. Employer interests came to dominate IR agenda in the form of exit policies, labour flexibility, and the need to minimize industrial disputes. The National Front government's Bill had represented the first bold/rash attempt to mandate worker-participation.

The dispute resolution machinery centres on labour courts or tribunals. Voluntary arbitration has played little role, and although it is an extension of bipartisanism and the negotiation process, it has found few takers. The first National Commission of Labour 1969 had recommended the selling up of Industrial Relation Commissions (IRC). IRCs were central to trade unions and Industrial Disputes Bill 1988. IRCs were to adjudicate any dispute that could not be resolved by the bipartite committee. The Bill empowered labour courts to act rapidly for speedy disposal of issues.

Although the 1988 Bill did not state any process by which strike decisions are validated to be democratic, the Industrial Relations Bill of 1978 and committees after that have recommended a secret ballot and also that a strike must be supported by at least two-thirds of the workers. Trade unions have contended this on the ground that similar condition does not apply for a lock-out, or for recognition of the major collective bargaining agent.

The ESMA of 1981 (Essential Services Maintenance Act) had assumed tremendous power to prohibit industrial action in a list of chosen industries or part thereof on the premise that they directly affected community welfare. The provisions empower the government to produce the striking workmen before the nearest magistrate for summary trial of the case without recourse to appeal.

Labour redundancy has been a source of contention between management and unions; while the presidents of various federations of Indian chambers of industry or commerce want easier hire-and-fire policies, the trade unions want stricter enforcement of rules for exit, social security, and compensation. In addition they want major initiatives for training and retraining of workers.

4.7.2 *Changes in Framework*

When the new economic policies were introduced in 1991, an adverse impact on IR and labour markets was expected. The Government of India's statement on New Industrial Policy (NIP) stated that the government would fully protect the interests of the labour, enhance their welfare and equip them in all respects for dealing with technological changes – it was the belief of the government that no small section of the society can corner the gains of growth, leaving the workers to bear its pains. Labour would be made an equal partner in progress and prosperity.[42]

However, efforts to get rid of surplus labour have been the most noticeable feature of industrial relation practices since 1991. It has taken various forms in the context of IDA, the most common being VRS. The *Economic Times* reported that 23 manufacturing companies had cut their workforce by 43,000, i.e. 16 per cent in years between 1998-2001 and these companies accounted for 17 per cent of the total sales in the private manufacturing sector in 2000-1. These workforce reductions were affected through VRS, and so the bottom lines have zoomed reflecting this restructuring. Similar large reductions in the workforce of the banking sector were also reported.

In 1992, the Supreme Court had ruled that section 25 of the IDA 1947 (prescribing the conditions precedent to retrenchment of workmen) was constitutional. As per this section, an employer is required to take prior permission of the government for retrenchment of workers where the number of employees are 300 or more, and for closure of the plant where employees are 100 or more. To overcome this, managements have taken recourse to VRS, citing reasons of technological upgradation, falling market shares and profits, industrial sickness, and so on.[43] This is true for public and private sectors.

Chapter 5B of the IDA has aroused an intense debate between trade unions and employer associations. It relates to retrenchments and closures. The employer lobby seeks to dilute Chapter 5B of the IDA and Section X of the Contract Labour Regulation and Abolition Act, so that companies can hire and sack workers at will and use the contract labour unhindered. Contract labour in practice are not able to organize because their services are terminated as soon as they form a union. The macro thrust of the employer-side of the debate is that low wages and unprotected labour will improve export competitiveness on the one hand and also encourage MNCs to invest in India. Both these factors will eventually increase employment. The trade union view is that implementation of labour laws is lax and rejuvenating the enforcement machinery along with suitable amendments to the law for social security and stringent punishment for violation are necessary before making further changes in the IDA.

The second national commission notes that it will be good if there can be prior scrutiny of grounds on which the closure is sought. It was for this reason that the provision of prior permission was incorporated. However, the permissions for closure are kept pending for months and years and therefore managements try various subterfuges to close the enterprise and disappear instead of waiting. Most disputes take more than one year to settle and 20 years are not too rare. Management disappears without paying wages, dues or compensation to the workers. Hence, the commission on labour says that: in the new circumstances of global competition, it may not be possible for increasing number of enterprises to meet the economic consequence of competition. In such cases, one cannot compel non-viable enterprises to continue.[44] They should have the option to close down, provided that all the dues and compensation to workers are paid. This is also the case for retrenchment – all worker dues have to be paid. The commission also recommended increased rates of compensation and obligatory insurance cover for employee-dues by the employer. The commission also noted that those who demand the right to hire and fire want to bring about a fundamental change in the nature and perception of employment. They want all employment to be on contractual basis for a stipulated period, hence, there will be no permanent jobs. This transformation needs social and economic institutions that can take care of the consequences, such as: (a) a system of social security that includes employment insurance and provision for health care, (b) the evolution of a system of skill development for upgrading employability, and (c) a system of dual contracts, one with the individual and second with the collective bargaining agency or union. The commission made the significant comment that the centrality of the state in ensuring security has to be acknowledged, and, unless backed by an adequate compensation and security system, suffering and starvation can become the causes of acute and explosive social unrest. In the circumstances the better course will be to allow closure and provide for adequate compensation to workers and in the event of an appeal, leave it to the labour commission to find a way to arbitrate or adjudicate. Prior permission is not necessary for retrenchment or lay-off for establishment of any size. Workers will be entitled to two months' pay or notice pay in lieu of notice in case of retrenchment. However, in case of establishments employing 300 or more workers, where lay-off exceed a period of one month, the establishment should be required to obtain *post facto* approval of the appropriate government authority. The provisions of Chapter 5B pertaining to permission for closure should be made applicable to all establishments irrespective of size. Every employer will have to ensure before closure that all dues of the workers are paid as a precondition to closure.

A notification issued in 2003 added a new classification for workmen – 'fixed term employment workmen' with the implication that a fixed-term employee need not be made into a permanent employee as required by the IDA till that time. While this provides far greater flexibility in the labour markets, it has the potential of wiping out permanency of all jobs even in the organized sector.

Amendments in 2006 have made it possible to employ contract labour on a permanent basis in EPZs.

Commentators on IR have made following observations about the impact of labour legislation on the labour market and on the economy:

First, there are 45 labour laws in operation, enforced by the central and state governments, without reference to a common framework. India's labour laws have introduced uncertainty and ambiguity about key concepts, thus increasing the scope for conflicting interpretation.[45] The term 'wage' itself is defined in 11 different ways. The meaning of worker, employee, and employed-person also changes depending upon the piece of legislation and so on.

Second, it has encouraged the small and informal sector because reporting requirements are waived for firms using power but employing less than 10 workers, and less than 20 otherwise. The requirement to establish pension funds too is waived for such firms. Mandatory health insurance under Employee State Insurance Act 1948 is waived for firms with less than 50 employees. The requirements of physical amenities, rest room, canteen, medical dispensary, para-medical staff, and crèches increase with a firm's size. In addition small firms get additional benefits, like excise concession, cheaper credit, and reservation, i.e. exclusive rights of the SSIs to produce a list of goods. As a result, employment in firms with more than a 100 employees has been virtually stagnant for 10 years since 1984 (Table 4.1).[46]

It is not possible to conclude from Table 4.1 that job security regulations (applicable to firms with more than 100 workers after 1984) were responsible for decline in employment growth in large firms. There are too many other factors at work. For instance, in the case of large firms the capital intensity has increased; second, small firms (less than 100 workers) have received policy support for generating employment. Third, the labour laws have made the government a central party to the labour market and for providing mandated benefits to the employees. The state runs the Employee State Insurance (ESI) network of hospitals and

Table 4.1: Growth in the Number of Firms and Employment

(Average annual compounded)

Firms employing	*Employment*		*Number of firms*	
	1973-84	*1984-93*	*1973-84*	*1984-93*
> 100 employees as per cent of units	2.6	0.4	2.6	3.7
< 100 employees, as per cent of units	3.4	3.6	4.0	2.5
Total as per cent of units	2.8	1.3	3.8	2.7

Source: NSSO and Annual Survey of Industry.

dispensaries throughout the country, administers pension funds, and employment exchanges to which firms employing more than 25 persons must notify existing vacancies and from which they must solicit applications.

Fourth, it has encouraged the substitution of capital for labour. A study by Fallon and Lucas (1991) is based on the annual survey of industry data which covers the factory sector and covers enterprises with more than 100 employees or 50 if using power for the period 1973-82.[47] It therefore covers the period after 1976 when government permission for dismissal in firms with more than 300 employees was required. The study explains employment as a function of real wages and output in 35 industries before and after 1976. It concludes that the 1976 changes in legislation reduced long-run employment by 17.5 per cent on the average. Sectoral variations were found to be considerable and could be explained by the share of small enterprises in each sector, importance of the union, and the importance of public enterprise in the sector. But the study also found that the fall of employment in the factory sector was not offset by increase in employment in smaller enterprises.

Fifth, the law made it costly for firms to adjust to changes in market conditions and technology and this factor became a serious hurdle for the industry after 1991. Sixth, the law encouraged employers to make greater use of casual labour, sub-contracts, VRS, and to resort to lock-outs.

Evidence on new HRM practices, and the best or worst amongst them remains sketchy and public policy initiative to promote best practices has been meagre. This study is an attempt to gain some insights into the HR practices inside Indian firms located in MMR. The questionnaire seeks information from the workers/ employees about the type of HRM that they experience in their current employment.

4.8 National Commission on Labour and Review of Labour Laws

In November 1999, the Government of India decided to set up a commission on labour to do the following: (a) suggest rationalization of existing laws relating to labour in the organized sector. The dictionary meaning of rationalize implies 'to act to make business more efficient by reorganizing it to eliminate or reduce waste of material, labour, time'; (b) to suggest an umbrella legislation to ensure a minimum level of protection to the workers in the unorganized sector. The resolution of the government stated that the commission should take into account the new environment generated as a result of globalization of the economy and liberalization of trade and industry. In other words the commission had a mandate to examine and to bring the existing labour laws in tune with the ground reality.

The recommendations of this second National Commission on Labour give an indication of the fundamental shifts taking place towards the flexible labour market systems in the ideological and institutional framework, for example, the recommendation that no prior permissions should be needed to carry out retrenchment and lay-offs in any establishment of any size, workers are entitled to two months' notice or notice pay in lieu of notice. For establishments with more than 300 workers, *post facto* permission should be acquired from the appropriate authority if lay-off periods exceed one month. The commission therefore suggests appropriate changes in chapters VA and VB of the IDA pertaining to retrenchment and closures. Similarly, the commission notes that in a rapidly changing economic situation on the one hand and changes in technology and management on the other, there cannot be a fixed number of posts in an organization for all times. Organizations need flexibility to respond to changing environments. Hence, it recommended that although contract labour should not be engaged for perennial non-core services, employers might engage temporary labour for core production/service activities for seasonal and sporadic demand. This also alters the spirit of the Contract Labour (Abolition) Act.

None of these recommendations of the SNLC have been implemented to date. However, a number of judgements by the Supreme Court have gone against the interests of organized sector workers including the right of government employees to strike, and other contract-worker rights. These adverse rulings must be understood in the context of lax implementation of labour laws, as they exist.[48] Thereafter, several rulings have been given against contract and temporary workers.

4.9 Conclusion

In conclusion, while the new HRM claims to achieve competitive advantage through the strategic deployment of highly committed and skilled workforce using an array of cultural, structural and personnel techniques, there is a growing gap between the jargon and practice of HRM. This gap is most evident for lower skill workers. In most cases HRM is disposed towards low-wage, high-insecurity model. Changes are occurring at the workplace globally.

These changes are supported by changes in the legislative framework and by the state both overtly and covertly. In India too, over the last 15 years there is ample proof of these changes. The direction and speed are varied across enterprises and sectors. However, the flexibilization of the workforce is evident across industries. The long-term implications of these changes are not however known and most specifically its impact on skill formation needs to be explored. This study attempts to fill the gap by looking for correlations between different types of HRM practices, skill formation and insecurity at the workplace.

Notes

1. E.A. Ramaswamy (2000): *Managing Human Resources*, Oxford University Press, New York.
2. T. Kochan et al. (1986): *The Transformation of American Industrial Relations*, Basic Books, New York.
3. R.S. Schuler and S. Jackson (1987): 'Linking Competitive Strategy with Human Resource Management Practices', *Academy of Management Executive* 1, 3, pp. 209-13.
   M.E. Porter (1980): *Competitive Strategy: Technique for Analyzing Industry and Competitors*, New York, Free Press.
4. J. Storey and K. Sisson (1993): *Managing Human Resources and Industrial Relations*, Open University Press, Milton Keynes.
5. M. Marchington and P. Parker (1990): *Changing Patterns of Employee Relations*, Harvester Wheatsheaf, Hemel Hempfteadt.
6. Martin Wright (2000): *Managing Competitive Crisis*, Cambridge University Press.
7. J. Storey (1995): *Human Resource Management: A Critical Text*, Routledge, London.
8. John Stredwick and Steve Ellis (1998): *Flexible Working Practices: Techniques and Innovations*, Institute of Personnel and Development, London.
9. P. Cadene and Mark Holmstrom (1998): *Decentralized Production in India*, French Institute of Pondicherry and Sage, New Delhi and London.
10. J. Storey (1995): 'Development in the Management of Human Resources', in John Storey (ed.), *Human Resource: a Critical Text*, Routledge, London.
    J. Storey et al. (1993): 'The New Agenda and Human Resource Management: Round Table Discussion with John Edmondson', *Human Resource Management Journal*, vol. 4, no. 1, pp. 63-70.
11. M. Armstrong and Angela Baron (2002): *Strategic HRM*, Chartered Institute of Personnel and Development, CIPD House, London.
12. A. Reed (2001): *Innovations in Human Resource Management*, Chartered Institute of Personnel and Development, CIPD House, London.

13. J. Storey (1992): *Developments in the Management of Human Resources*, Blackwell, Oxford.
14. M. Marchington (2007): 'Involvement and Participation', in J. Storey (ed.), *Human Resource Management: A Critical Text*, Thompson Learning, London.
15. K. Legge (1995): *Human Resource Management: Rhetoric and Reality*, MacMillan.
16. S. Hill (1991): 'Why Quality Circles Fail and Total Quality Management Might Succeed', *British Journal of Industrial Relations*, vol. 29, no. 4, pp. 541-68.
17. P. Forrester (1994): 'Flexibility, Politics and Strategy: In Defense of the Model of the Flexible Firm', *Work, Employment and Society*, vol. 8, no. 2, pp. 221-42.
18. M. Beatson (1995): *Labour Market Flexibility*, Employment Development, London.
    Confederation of British Industry (1996): *Flexible Labour Markets*, CBI, London.
19. R. Schoenberger (1982): *Japanese Manufacturing Techniques*, The Free Press, New York.
20. H. Steedman and K. Wagner (1987): 'A Second Look at Productivity, Machinery and Skill in Britain and Germany', *National Institute Economic Review* 122, no. V, pp. 84-95.
    H. Steedman (1987): 'Vocational Training in France and Britain: Mechanical and Electrical Craftsmen', *National Institute Economic Review*, 126, December, pp. 57-71.
    A. Daly, D. Hitchins and K. Wagner (1988): 'Productivity Machinery and Skills in a Sample of British and German Manufacturing Plants', *National Institute Economic Review* 111, February, pp. 48-61.
21. T. Cutler (1992): 'Vocational Training and British Economic Performance: A Further Installment of the British Labour Problem', *Work Employment and Society* 6(2) June, pp. 161-83.
    F. Green (1992): 'On the Political Economy of Skill in Advanced Industrial Nations', *Review of Political Economy* 4(4), pp. 413-35.
22. S. Glynn and H. Gospel (1993): 'Britain's Low Skill Equilibrium: A Problem of Demand?' *Industrial Relations Journal* 24(2), June, pp. 112-25.
23. J. Morris and B. Wilkinson (1995): 'The Transfer of Japanese Management to Alien Institutional Environments', *Journal of Management Studies*, vol. 32, no. 6, pp. 719-30.
24. J. Rhinehart et al. (1994): 'Reunifying Conception and Execution

of Work Under Japanese Production Management?: A Case Study', in Tony Elger and Chris Smith (eds.), *Global Japanization? The Transnational Transformation of the Labour Process*, Routledge, London, pp. 152-74.

25. B. Wilkinson et al. (1995): 'The Iron Fist in a Velvet Glove: Management and Organization in Japanese Manufacturing Transplants in Wales', *Journal of Management Studies*, vol. 32, no. 5, pp. 819-30.
26. D.E. Guest and N. Conway (1997): *Employee Motivation and the Psychological Contract*, Institute of Personnel and Development, London.
    D.E. Guest (1999): 'Human Resource Management: the Workers Verdict', *Human Resource Management Journal*, vol. 9, no. 2, pp. 5-25.
27. Marc Maurice, A. Sorge and W. Malcolm (1980): 'Societal Differences in Organizing Manufacturing Units', *Organization Studies* 1, pp. 59-86.
28. Alice Lam (1996): 'Work Organisation & Skill Development and Utilisation of Engineers', in R. Crompton, D. Gallie and K. Purcell (eds.), *Changing Forms of Employment*, Routledge, London, New York.
29. T. Inoki (1987): 'Skill Transfer and Economic Organization', in K. Koike and T. Inoki (eds.), *Skill formation in Japan and South East Asia*, Tokyo: University of Tokyo Press.
30. D.E. Guest (1989): 'Personnel and HRM, Can you Tell the Difference?', *Personnel Management*, January, pp. 48-51.
31. D.P. Torrington (1989):'Human Resource Management and the Personnel Function', in J. Storey (ed.), *New Perspectives on Human Resource Management*, Routledge, London.
32. K. D'Souza et al. (1997): *Empowering Workers Through Human Resource Development*, Allied Publishers, New Delhi.
33. B. Harris-White (2003): *India Working: Essays on Society and Economy*, Cambridge University Press, London.
34. J.S. Sodi (1997): *Industrial Relations and Human Resources Management in Transition*, Sri Ram Centre for Industrial Relations and Human Resource, New Delhi.
    C.S. Venkatratnam (1997): 'Collective Bargaining and Flexibility in India' – Paper presented for *Labour Law and Labour Relations Branch*, ILO, Geneva 1997.
35. Sarosh Kuruvilla (1999): 'Impact of Globalization on Economies and IR/HR Systems: Theory and Evidence', in A. Sivananthiran and C.S. Venkata Ratnam (eds.), *Globalization and Labour Management*

Relations in South East Asia, pp. 11-64, ILO–SAAT, New Delhi.
Mahrukh Engineer (1999): *Liberalization and Human Resource Management: Challenges for the Corporation of Tomorrow*, Response Books, New Delhi.

36. Ota Hitoshi (2004): 'Flexible Work Organization, Human Resource Practices', *5th Asian Regional Congress of The International Industrial Relations Association (IIRA)* held from 23-6 June 2004, at Seoul, South Korea.
37. Paul Osterman (1994): 'How Common is Workplace Transformation and Who Adopts it', *Industrial and Labour Relations Review*, vol. 47, no. 2, January, pp. 173-88.
38. Paul Osterman (2000): 'Work Reorganization in an Era of Restructuring: Trends in Diffusion and Effects on Employee Welfare', *Industrial and Labour Relations Review*, vol. 53, no. 2, January, pp. 179-96.
39. Hitoshi Ota (2005): 'Flexible Work Organization, Human Resource Practices and Worker Perception in India: A Case Study of Bangalore City', *Indian Journal of Labour Economics*, vol. 48, January–March, pp. 115-29.
40. E.A. Ramaswamy (2000): *Managing Human Resources*, Oxford University Press, New York.
41. V.R.K. Reddy (1991): *Labour Policy 2000: Proceeding of the Seminar 3-4 October 1991*, Friedrich Ebbert, Stiftung, New Delhi.
42. P.A. Sangma (1991): *A Statement*, Union Minister of State for Labour, GOI.
43. P. Sinha et al. (1994): *Voluntary Retirement Schemes and Workers Response*, Maniben Kara Institute, Friedrich Ebert Stiftung, New Delhi.
44. GOI, Ministry of Labour (2002): *Report of the Second Commission on Labour*, vol. II, pp. 34, 43-4.
45. M.G. Gopal (1994): 'India: Economic Liberalization and the Legal System', *World Bank Working Paper*, Washington.
46. R. Zagha (1999): 'Labour and India's Economic Reforms', in J. Sachs, A. Varshney and N. Bajpai (eds.), *India in the Era of Economic Reforms*, Oxford University Press, New Delhi.
47. P.R. Fallon and R. Lucas (1991): 'The Impact of Changes in Job Security Regulations in India and Zimbabwe', *The World Bank Economic Review*, vol. 5, no. 3, pp. 395-413.
48. K.R. Shyam Sunder (2005): 'State in Industrial Relations System in India: From Corporatist to Neo Liberal', *Indian Journal of Labour Economics*, vol. 48, no. 4, December, pp. 917-37.

CHAPTER 5

Correlates of Insecurity: Skill Formation

> History is progress through the transmission of acquired skills from one generation to another.
>
> E.H. CARR

This chapter and the following two are an appraisal of the correlates of the insecurity hypothesis. They examine various factors that influence and are influenced by insecurity, for example, skill formation, their periodic upgradation and reproduction. It is important to do so in the context of human resource policies and practices adopted by firms to deal with the impact of global competition. The role of trade unions and the pressures on them to resist the adverse changes in the labour markets cannot be ignored in the analysis. This and the next two chapters also discuss the linkage between the principal correlates of insecurity. The survey, carried out as a concluding part of this study, among workers and employees in Mumbai, also seeks data regarding these issues and their relationship to insecurity.

Section 5.1 introduces the debate about the nature of competitive advantage, insecurity and skill formation, 5.2 builds upon the economic rationale for the High Skill Society starting with the human capital and the human capability approach. Ideas of employability, decent work and political economy of high skills are also developed. In Section 5.3 some alternative measures of the benefits of education and training are examined, while a diversion is introduced in Section 5.4 to present evidence with reference to the impact of restructuring and the resulting insecurity on skill formation. Studies from the UK, USA, OECD, and UNDP are reviewed. Reverting to the conceptual framework, Section 5.5

presents a critique of the conventional human capital approach. Section 5.6 dwells on the political economy emerging from these changes, and Section 5.7 presents different models of skill formation from some of the success stories in Germany, Singapore, Korea and Ireland. Section 5.8 is devoted to the Indian scene with an appraisal of the skill development system, status of skills and some empirical evidence in terms of skill data and case studies from India to show the deprived condition of skill formation and demand for skills. Section 5.9 concludes the conceptual debate by providing a review of the political aspects of the high skill economy.

5.1 Insecurity Hypothesis and Issues Regarding Skill Formation

Liberalization and globalization have brought to the centre stage debates about the nature of competitive advantage and issues of employment. As far as competitiveness is concerned different economies have to develop their own strategies on the basis of their resources, institutions and history, but there is increasing evidence published in the research publications of international agencies like the ILO, UN, and World Bank that education and skill levels of the population are now important determinants of success or failure in global competition. The ILO reports go a step forward to suggest an 'activist' human-resource-led development strategy to meet the challenges that globalization poses to developing countries.[1] The focal point of this debate in the developed countries is the question of national routes to a high-skills/knowledge economy. Education and skill development have become central to competitive strategies as well as for social policies. The view that human capabilities are more central than ever, is now common political rhetoric.[2] Politicians have reasoned that skills-strategy is central to the political platform in an era where the financial structure of the global economy has limited the economic policy options. Nations have used different strategies for skill formation, compulsory free primary education, public-funded higher education, apprenticeship system, firm-specific training incentives and individual motivation.

The second debate relates to issues of employment. It argues that changes in the nature of work and the workplace in the post-industrial economy due to technology, management innovations and competition in the global market are transforming the kinds of knowledge, skills, and attitude needed for successful work performance and employment. Here a change has occurred in political discourse away from promises of full employment to full employability. Full employability is a shift away from demand-side policy to promote employment towards supply-side policy that emphasizes individual education and skills.

This shift must also be understood in the context of structural transformations in the economy as employment in agricultural and industrial sectors has been completely overtaken by the service/tertiary sector. Technological change, especially, in the industrial sector has raised the minimum schooling required. It has rapidly reduced the demand for unskilled and low skilled labour, while the demand for professional work has risen simultaneously.

A third debate, as yet immature, explores the relationship between the pressures of global competition on the firms and their response in terms of chosen competitive strategy with special reference to human resource development. Different combinations of technology, labour market institutions, management practices and state interventions do influence the process both of skill formation and skill degradation. The drive, towards flexible methods of production in the last 25 years has resulted in a very rapid and simultaneous process of deskilling, reskilling and multiple skilling.[3] The availability of manual skills which require apprenticeship/training have diminished due to reduced skills training since the 1970s and poor demand for the same among workers. Frequent recessions and redundancies have also led to the exodus of skilled people from their jobs, never to return to their former trade.[4] Has there been a slow whittling away of many types of skilled workforce due to frequent redundancies and relocations? The net effect of the process of flexibilization, especially numerical flexibility, on skills is yet to be examined. The survey conducted in this study makes an attempt to relate insecurity with ability and willingness, i.e. effective skill enhancement and improvement of workers.

In the new global economy labour markets have changed and become more competitive. Many factors that had protected employment and wages in the OECD countries, such as different forms of state social insurance and trade union power have waned. Whether the removal of workers' protection is a cause or effect of global movement of capital, the more progressive politicians have seized upon the development of skills as the working class primary and perhaps only recourse in present times. A highly skilled workforce is now seen to bring many benefits. The economic benefits have already been well analysed by the proponents of human capital and international trade theory. The social benefits of a highly skilled workforce in sustaining social capital and democratic norms are now receiving attention. As liberalization and globalization widen income disparities within society and threaten social cohesion, the upgradation of workforce skill is intended to reduce the income gap to recreate a middle class, reduce unemployment and poverty. Since work in the twenty-first century is likely to be unstable and insecure, providing worker with skill is now perceived as the only insurance and bargaining power.[5]

5.2 Economic Rationale for High Skill Society and the Concept of Human Capital

The Human Capital (HC) Theory assesses the impact of investment in education and training to the individual, to the firm, and to the economy. Human capital theorists argue that much of the unexplained increase in productivity, wages, and economic growth recognized by economists could be explained by investment in human capital, and therefore, by investing in self through education and training, the individuals are able to increase their lifetime earnings. Equally, the governments could use such investments deliberately as way of enhancing economic growth.[6]

In the USA for instance the output per production worker has virtually tripled between 1930 and 2000 from a value of $ 22,000 to $ 60,000, and over the same period the proportion of the workforce directly engaged in production has declined from 27 to 15 per cent. Moreover, for every production worker there are another 21 non-production workers employed in sales, marketing, clerical, technical and managerial and professional activities, and most of these non-production workers have received some form of tertiary education.[7] Indeed, the expansion of higher education from elite to a mass provider is explained in terms of being both the cause and consequence of exponential increase in scientific and technical knowledge, which has led to greater investment in human capital to supply the required technical, professional and managerial workers, in the shift to post-industrial societies.[8] Other commentators have suggested that human capital has increased in economic significance where it has become as important to contemporary society as land was to feudal society and financial capital was to the Industrial Revolution. Between 1948 and 1953, almost one-fifth of the increase in GNP was attributed to the expansion in the American education system. Subsequently, when productivity growth began to falter in America between 1973 and 1981, the contribution of education to productivity rose from 20 per cent to more than 30 per cent.

In Britain it has been estimated that in 1867 the returns to skilled labour accounted for between 5 and 25 per cent of the national income, whereas by 1967 they amounted to between 46 and 58 per cent of pre-tax household income. By the 1990s, the figures would have increased significantly as the differentials between educated and unskilled workers have dramatically polarized, specially in the USA.[9] Based on Occupational Employment and Wages report of the US Bureau of Labour Statistics (2008) given interindustry differences wage differences are explained by skill levels. Mean wages of manual labour like waitresses, loaders, janitors, etc., are at the lowest end of the scale even today.

It is notoriously difficult to measure the contribution of human capital to productivity and economic growth, as one could argue, but various attempts have been made to take such measurements. Theodore Schultz (1961) focused the attention of economists on the methods of evaluating the returns on investment in education and the concept of human capital that generates a stream of future returns similar to physical or financial capital.[10] Contributions were made to the theory by Becker (1964), Bowen (1964) and Bowmen (1965). The concept acquired greater significance in the 1980s and

1990s and there was a shift in contemporary economic analysis, from seeing capital accumulation in tangible physical terms towards viewing it as a process in which the productive quality of human beings is integrally involved.[11] The growth theories emphasized that via education, learning and skill formation people can become much more productive and this contributes significantly to the process of economic growth.[12] Acquisition of human capital has become central to development and growth.[13] Studies of economic growth, which re-examined the experiences of America, Japan and NICs, thereafter, emphasized the role of human capital to a greater extent than earlier studies.[14] This was followed by some education-sector analysis by international financial institutions.[15]

There are three main components of HC: early ability, innate or acquired; qualifications and knowledge acquired through education; skills, competencies and expertise acquired through training on job.[16] The concept of HC arose from the recognition that an individual or firm's decision to invest in education or training is similar to other types of investment undertaken by them. The HC investment involves initial cost, tuition and training fees, foregone earning while at school or reduced wages and productivity during the training period. On this cost, an individual or a firm hopes to gain, in future, through increased production or higher firm productivity. Like an investment in physical capital, the HC investment will only be undertaken by the rational wealth-maximizing individual or firm if the expected return from investment is greater than the market rate of interest.

At the beginning of the 1990s there was another major contribution to development theory, viz., the work of Amartya Sen and others on human capabilities.[17] This, over two decades, emerged into the human development approach partly manifested in the Human Development Report of the UNDP, and the technique of composite index of human development (HDI). This can be used to rank countries on the basis of their human development measured in terms of not just per capita income but also the education and health indicators of the population. Thus human capital has merged with human development ideas to become a dominant discourse in development theories even as the vital differences between the two approaches are significant.[18] These discourses have dovetailed into the high-skill paradigm, which states that in the post-industrial economy, a more flexible system of work organization is the most outstanding feature of the workplace.[19] It provides customized or new products, and new models at an ever more rapid rate. This requires a workforce which is multi-skilled and high-skilled.[20] Raising the skills of the national workforce through education and training has become a primary objective of the economic policy for promoting the national competitiveness.[21] The acquisition of skills not only makes people more productive, but also, in an era of rapidly changing technology makes them more adaptable to technological progress.[22]

In the developing world too, the salience of human capital is becoming a central theme in the literature on labour markets. The argument is based not only on the premises of increased globalization and the possibilities of attracting FDI on the basis of a better skilled and educated workforce or on the premise of moving up the value chain in exports, but also on the basis of the concept of 'decent work' evolved by the ILO. The concept aims at creating conditions of work and service which do not fall below certain accepted norms. Decent work, particularly in the large informal sector, can be achieved as a cause and consequence of improvements in productivity and incomes of the workers in the sector. This can occur largely through upgrading formal and informal skills, introducing technology, products and raw materials, and by multi-skilling the workforce. The organized sector may have the capacity to train and upgrade its workers within the organization, but the vast, tiny small-scale sector that employs a majority will not be able to do so without considerable support from public funding, incentive systems and public-private partnerships.[23]

5.3 Measuring the Impact of Education and Training

The inadequacy of the popular methods like cost-benefit analysis used to measure the benefit of education and training tend to ignore the social and political benefits of education. They also fail to grasp the integrated nature of primary, secondary and tertiary education in creating a high-skill economy. This causes policy distortion in developing countries particularly, which adopt such methods.

5.3.1 *Impact of Education*

Two approaches to the cost-benefit analysis – rate of return and discounted lifetime earning – have been used most often to measure the net benefits of education. Human capital acquired through education, training, apprenticeship and mobility involve expenses and earnings forgone. The benefits in the form of increased lifetime income after tax as a result of increased education accrue in the future and are assumed to be durable. The costs result from tuition fees, forgone earnings, costs of books and materials, transport expenses and other incidental expenses incurred for higher education. There are social and private rates of return. While the private rates include all those costs and benefits directly borne and obtained by the individual, the social rates include the externalities, e.g. costs to society at large not borne by the individual. For example, aid and public funding of education, institutional costs, and scholarships, etc. The social benefits are harder to capture but do include increased tax contributions from their higher income, and their increased capacity to participate in civil society and democratic processes. The rate of return is the discount rate, which equates the discounted value of future benefits to the cost incurred.

There are several problems that arise (specifically relating to indistinct social costs and benefits) in trying to estimate the true causal effect of education and training on individual, firm or economic performance. Estimates of return on education in line with theoretical literature on HC suggest that education confers on an individual a significant wage advantage. The evidence for UK and the developed Western countries suggests that the average estimate of gross rate of return for one year's education ranges between 5 and 10 per cent. Individuals in the UK who complete schooling with some sort of formal qualification have significantly larger return than individuals who have the same years of schooling but no formal qualification. There are significant differences in the rates of return for different types of qualifications and the subjects taken, and interestingly some subjects favour a particular gender more. Looking at the historic evidence, it appears that the rate of return on education in UK was higher than ever before prior to the Second World War. It declined temporarily in the 1970s and rose again in the 1980s.

Since the 1980s the rate-of-return method of estimation of the impact of education has been used extensively to determine which sub-sector of education, the state should invest resources in – primary, secondary or tertiary education.[24] The evidence from less developed countries shows the rate of return to education tends to be higher in low-income countries and the returns are the largest for investment in primary education. The argument has been used to cut public funding to higher education in developed and developing countries. Empirical research has also highlighted the importance of other variables in the cost-benefit analysis, like individual's ability measured in early childhood, families' socio-economic background, cultural factors, parental education, and the number of siblings.[25] But, the rate-of-return method is unable to account for the heterogeneity of social backgrounds of students and it underestimates the social and political benefits of education. Its conceptual framework has also been questioned.[26]

5.3.2 *Impact of Training*

Training is distinguished from school and post-school qualifications, which are viewed as education. Training is defined in terms of courses taken to help individuals develop skills that might be of use in their jobs. The returns to individual from employer-provided vocational training in terms of real earnings have been consistently found to be significant. Individuals taking employer-provided training earned on average just above 5 per cent higher real earnings. The returns were between 5 to 10 per cent if the training also resulted in middle or higher vocational qualification. In particular, employer-provided training has higher return than off-the-job training from other sources. Employer-provided training not only has the largest impact but its effects are also the longest lasting.

A number of studies found that employer-provided training is portable. Parts of the benefits from training investment in the firm derive from their positive influence on subsequent occupational status and likelihood of promotion. Trained workers are much less likely to change or quit their jobs or to be made redundant. Trained workers are much less likely to experience spells of unemployment.

All the studies looking at the determinants of training found that individuals with higher aptitude score higher educational attainment, higher previous training, or higher professional or skill status, and are more likely to participate in training. Thus, there is a strong complementarity between the three main components of HC, i.e. earlier ability, formal education or competence, and expertise acquired through training on the job. It also highlights the self-sustaining nature of HC growth. On the other hand, it also highlights the widening skill gap that results in a vicious cycle of low skills. Temporary part-time workers, older workers, and women with children are less likely to receive training than full-time workers. Union members are found to participate more in training than non-union workers. Public sector firms, large firms, and industries experiencing rapid technological change are also more likely to provide for training on the job.

5.3.3 *Impact of Training on Firm's Productivity*

According to a 2001 report 'Making Technologies Work for Human Development', formal education is only a part of the skill creation system.[27] Vocational and on-the-job training are just as important. When technology is changing, the enterprises have to invest in worker training to remain competitive. They are more likely to do so when their workers are better educated to start with, since that lowers the cost of upgrading skills.

There is a paucity of micro-level studies that have directly assessed the effect of employer-provided education and training. Although there is a direct link between skill composition of the workforce and productivity, the relationship between training, skill and profitability is not direct. Some studies have found a strong positive relationship between the bundle of human resource practices including training and firm-productivity. However, firms are likely to under-invest in training unless there are strong institutional forces at work, because it presents a contracting problem for the employee and the firm.[28] The firm that shares the cost of developing human capital of an employee loses the return on its investment if the latter switches to another firm. On the other hand, the effort and training to acquire some firm-specific skill are difficult to measure. The employee cannot enforce the contract that requires the firm to pay for the effort. In such a transaction continuity between firm and worker is valued as some sort of safeguard for this investment.[29] Williamson mentions severance pay and job security as mechanisms for protecting workers' investment in firm-specific skills, and pensions as a mechanism that discourages workers from quitting. When the employing organization and the employment relationship can exist over a longer term the use of mechanisms like assured career path and severance pay are incentives to make investment in skills that have more value for the firm.

Several macro-level studies in Columbia, Indonesia, Malaysia and Mexico have shown a high impact of enterprise training on firm-productivity. Such training can be an effective and an economic way to develop the skills of the workforce, particularly where the employers are well informed about skill needs, e.g. in Columbia in 1992, 75 per cent of enterprises provided informal training while 50 per cent provided formal training. In Indonesia the same year, 19 per cent provided informal and 19 per cent provided formal training. In Malaysia in 1994, 83 per cent provided informal and 35 per cent provided formal training. In Mexico in 1992, 11 per cent each of informal and formal training was provided. The cost of enterprise training tends to be lower than that of formal training though employers lose part of the benefits if employees leave. Studies also suggest that enterprise-based training yields higher private returns (means higher productivity as well as wage) than other post-school training, both in the developed and developing countries. Enterprise training is an essential complement to new investments in technology, plant and equipment. Many studies in industrial countries suggest that shortage of appropriate worker skills is a major constraint to the adoption of new technologies. Well-trained workers accelerate their adoption.

Despite the demonstrated gains in productivity from training, not all employers provide it. Training involves costs in terms of materials, time, and forgone production. The provision of training is strongly related to the strength of the management and the size of the enterprise; smaller enterprises paying less attention to this aspect. On the other hand, weak management, high training cost, inability to exploit scale economy in training, absence of competitive pressure and poor awareness about the benefits of training, inability to capture the private gains of the firm, low levels of technology used in production are some of the more common reasons why firms provide too little training.

Most common market failures include:

1. Lack of information about skill needs in the industry.
2. Inadequate incentives for trainers.
3. Low basic skill and educational attainment among managers and employers and inability to form efficient training programmes in line with changing skill and technology needs.
4. Poorly educated workers and therefore poor absorption capacity.
5. Concentration of training in urban industrial and service sectors and neglect of the same in agriculture and allied activities.

Skill development therefore requires policy intervention in many forms. For example:

1. Training centres involving industry associations.
2. Incentives to industry associations to establish and manage their own centres, a common practice among the 'Asian Tigers'.
3. Generous tax allowances to smaller firms for sponsoring their employees for training, e.g. Malaysia and Thailand give up to 200 per cent tax reduction.
4. Comprehensive strategy for skill creation needs to address the

entire range of market failures through a mix of institutional and other policies.

In providing incentives for high-quality training, Singapore has made a remarkable effort. The Skill Development Fund established in 1979 collected a levy of 1 per cent of payroll from employers to subsidize training for low-paid workers. Its four polytechnics worked closely with business in designing courses and imparting technical training. In addition, with government assistance for industry-based training programmes, employers conduct training matched to their needs. The Economic Development Board continuously assesses emerging skill needs in collaboration with leading enterprises and mounts new courses. The total national investment in training reached 3.6 per cent of the annual payroll in 1995, double of the 1.85 per cent in the UK. The government plans to raise it further and include medium and small-scale industries. As a result the workforce has shifted towards more highly skilled job with the share of professional and technical workers rising from 15.7 per cent in 1980 to 23.1 per cent in 1995.[30] The April 2014 World Economic Outlook, published by the International Monetary Fund, reports that global activity is strengthening and predicts it to improve further in 2014-15. The data reported in the World Economic Outlook support the conclusion that organizations' investment in training and development is at healthy level compared with years past. With low inflation rates and a stabilizing economy, organizations are maintaining their investment in talent development.

5.4 Impact of Restructuring on Skill Development

Many studies have tried to analyse how the process of economic restructuring has impacted the skill levels and the task/work experience of those in employment. In contrast to the expectation of labour process theorists, the most comprehensive studies on skill trends in Britain in the mid-1980s concluded that by far the most general and strong tendency was for a rise in the skill requirement of jobs.[31] The trend changed in the latter half of the

1980s.[32] Whereas in the early 1980s, employers were restructuring in the context of strong union presence in the workplace, in the late 1980s there was a marked retreat in the union power in the workplace. Besides, the public sector, which had provided strong institutional safeguards, was also whittled down in the later period. This was a period which would have allowed greater workplace manoeuvring space for the employer referred to as flexibilization/flexible firms and promote a move greater polarization of employees, with its distinction between a core of relatively skilled and secure employees and a periphery of low-skilled workers that can be easily dispensed with, in case of adverse demand/recession. One section of the supposedly flexible workforce, i.e. part-time female workers, has been expanding through the 1980s, with particular disadvantages in skill upgradation, weak unionization and employment protection.[33] A comprehensive study was based on data generated from three nationwide surveys in Britain. These surveys were:[34]

- Class in Modern Britain survey 1984, sample of 1,770 mainly aged, working people.
- Social Change and Economic Life Initiative (SCELI) 1986, covering 6,111 people.
- The Employment in Britain survey 1992 covering 3,477 employees aged 20-60 years.

Their conclusions were as follows. The general trend from the mid-1980s up to the early 1990s was towards an expansion of high-level jobs, especially those in management and the professions; of course this could be a result of change in the use of titles for describing jobs. And this is not enough to gauge the change in skills within occupational categories. Arguments for up-skilling have been linked to the view that there has been a long-term shift in the nature of skill because of the nature of technological changes that have led to the replacement of traditional manual/craft skills by conceptual and decision-making skills that require primarily higher levels of general education. So, one measure of skill change is the change in level of educational qualification needed to carry out a job, besides the conventional measurement of frequency and duration of vocational/on-the-job training that an employee has received. On both measures, there was a clear indication that there was an increase in the overall qualification levels required for a job in the period 1986-92. There was an increase in the training and experience required to do a job. It was not clear whether the training was imparted on the job or had to be acquired by the employee at his/her expense or via past experience. Majority of employees (63 per cent) reported that the level of skill that they used for their job has increased over the previous five years; this was true for upward mobile workers as well as those who remained in the same job. In contrast, only 9 per cent said that the skill they used at work had decreased. They were mainly semi- and non-skilled manual workers.

The index of task discretion varies from 0.21 among those who have increased their skill to 0.29 for those who have not, indicating that the quality of job experience, control over the job, responsibility, variety of work, and opportunities for self-development levels rise with the skill level.

It was also clear that the rise in skill levels was associated with an improvement in the quality of work-task, and, it lead to a marked increase in the effort required at work. While the rigidity of traditional skill lines breaks up, there is a growth of multi-skilling or polyvalence, increasing the work demands, i.e. intensification of work.

The issue of skill trends is of course linked to spread of new microprocessor-based advanced automation and computerization. By 1992, 56 per cent of the workforce already worked with computerized or automated equipment, up from 39 per cent in 1986 and its use was most prevalent in the white-collar sector. In the professional manager category 76 per cent, 80 per cent of lower non-manual employees, and 54 per cent of technicians and supervisors were working with it. The gender gap in the use of technology was also reducing over the period. The rate of diffusion of these technologies was associated with higher skill levels, higher training levels, and higher responsibility levels according to the Human Development Report (2001).[35]

Sustaining the argument made by the UNDP and others about the salience of knowledge and skills of the workforce at the turn of the twentieth century, Silver (2003) says that a prerequisite for the mass expansion of this information-based workforce has been the expansion of mass education, and, one might even argue that the education industry has become the central capital-goods producing industry of the late twentieth and early twenty-first century.[36] In attempting to capture the overall nature of the post-Fordist transformation, diverse analyses have emphasized the new centrality of information or the emergence of knowledge-based economy. David Harvey (1986) saw capitalism as depending more and more on 'mobilizing the powers of intellectual labour as a vehicle for further accumulation'. For Peter Drucker (1993) and others the basic economic resource is no longer capital, land or labour; rather it is and will be knowledge.[37] Manuel Castells and Yukio Aoyama (1997) have conceptualized what they refer to as the 'Informational Economy'.[38] Moreover, as Hardt and Negri (2000) emphasized, knowledge itself has to be produced and the production of knowledge requires new kinds of production and labour.[39] Mass education therefore appears to be the key capital goods industry of the twenty-first century in producing knowledge and producing the workers who have the necessary skills for the new knowledge-intensive forms of capital accumulation. Like textile workers in the nineteenth century, autoworkers in the twentieth century, education workers are central to the process of capital accumulation in the twenty-first century.

Empirical support for deteriorating economic position of the less skilled members of the workforce in the USA and western Europe over the last 20 years has come from many sources; one such is Dreze and Sneessens (1997).[40] In Europe, the deterioration manifests itself mainly in higher unemployment, and in the USA it manifests itself in lower real and relative wages. The phenomenon has a cyclical aspect, associated with slow growth and recession. There is also evidence of a structural trend associated with technological development and competition from low-wage countries; a trend that is increasing over time, causing a concern for equity and efficiency aspects of unemployment policy. Using the simplest and the most objective measure of skill, i.e. educational attainment, authors reviewed unemployment rates for five levels of education in the OECD countries in 1989. In every single country there was a marked decline in unemployment as education spread (in India, for reasons of statistical methodology, structure of the economy, and the nature of unemployment and employment, the reverse is true, i.e. open unemployment rates rise as educational attainment rises). In India, in the age group 25-60 years, it seems that while, on the average, 11 per cent of the pre-primary and primary educated were unemployed, 34 per cent of the higher education and university graduates were unemployed. In Britain, the unemployment rates by skill were the highest for manual (15.5 per cent), personal (15.5 per cent), skilled manual (12.6 per cent), other non-manual (12.2 per cent), clerical (8 per cent) and lowest for professional and managerial (5.3 per cent) levels. In the USA, the same trend of polarizing market value of labour held true in 1987.

International trade theory offers a direct argument in support of the fact that the increased competition from low-wage countries should negatively affect the market position of low-skill workers resulting in lower employment or lower wage. The argument comes from the factor price equalization theorems associated with the Heckscher-Ohlin model of trade. These theorems state that under certain conditions free trade in final goods brings about international parity of factor prices (wages). Although there are real and significant differences in the practice of international trade in comparison with the assumptions of the model there are some overall long-run trends towards factor price equalization. The policy dilemma/implications of this trend are huge and the fragility of our knowledge on all these counts is both a cause of embarrassment and an invitation to prudence. The crux of the dilemma is how to reconcile labour costs low enough to promote employment of low-skill workers at reasonable income levels, and, proper incentives towards economic efficiency, i.e. incentives to work and acquire skills. The social reproduction of labour would require public intervention, as there is no private incentive here. This observation has implications for India as well. If the free trade policy trajectory focuses mainly on cheap Indian labour advantage, then the low and flexible wages can in fact set off cumulative causations towards low skill and low educational attainment of the labour force over time.

The debate surrounding the long-term trajectory of skills – downwards or upwards – has gone on for decades. On the one hand, there are those who argue that technological change has raised the complexity of work tasks and skills required to carry them out. Failure to up-skill, to encourage employee initiative and discretion could put an organization at a competitive disadvantage. On the other hand, there are authors for whom technological change is used by employers to remove employee discretion from work, to render most jobs as routine, to make it easier to substitute one employee for another, so as to tighten the grip on the work process and raise productivity and profits.[41] The de-skilling scenario emphasizes the cost of labour approach as against the up-skilling one that looks at labour as a resource. Between the two approaches is a third position, which recognizes that each of these tendencies may exist simultaneously, e.g. within different departments of the same firm. This argument also uses the core and periphery groupings within the flexible firm, in different sectors of the same economy, or in the product market positions of different firms, or in the institutional settings of different economies within the global trading systems at large. The third position develops into a polarization thesis. In this approach there are two trends, up-skilling at one end in the primary labour market and down-skilling at the other in the secondary labour market.[42] British surveys from 1986 to 1992, called Social Life and Economic Change Initiative (SCELI) assessing the nature and extent of skill change in Britain provide evidence of both up-skilling and polarization where the more skilled are more likely to receive training.[43] This occurred in the period after 1987 and more vigorously in the post-1992 period. This overlaps with same period that Britain was liberalizing and structurally adjusting its economy to the pressures of globalization.

There has been a policy response to that evidence. The skill and training system has since been extended, made more coherent and tuned to the market so that it has come to involve the Confederation of British Industry (CBI), Training and Enterprise Councils (TEC), Regional Development Agencies (RDA) and the

Trade Union Congress in Lifelong Learning and National Targets for Education and Training. One of these targets, the employer target, requires 70 per cent of the organizations employing 200 or more and 35 per cent of those employing 50 or more to achieve the 'Investors in People Standard' and according to Margaret Murray, Training Manager, CBI, this is likely to be met. The Investors in People Standard was developed in 1990 in collaboration with business organizations. The standard provides for a framework of HRM practices; much of this framework is related to reviewing the continuous training and development of employees, and by 1999, 31,000 organizations had obtained recognition.[44] The policy is based on the principle that the primary purpose of an education and training system is to provide individuals with skills necessary for them to get work, keep the job and progress at work. Focusing on the post-compulsory education levels, it explains the need for a highly skilled, flexible workforce. Over the last 15 years, it has built up a national qualification framework of National Vocational Qualifications (NVQ) based on the rigorous competency needs of industry. And two million certificates were awarded by 1998, and 43 per cent of the workforce had at least NQV Level 3 and equivalent qualification. There has been a substantial increase in public expenditure on adult education and guidance, which is a top-down policy for skill development but there is an increasing trend of rising individual expenditure on one's own learning; it constituted 12 per cent of total expenditure on learning in 1995.

5.5 Critique of Human Capital Theory

There is no doubt that the HC theory's policy appeal for investment in HC will remain central to the debate about globalization and competitiveness. It seems to offer a win-win scenario for the company and the individual, but many have challenged this win-win scenario.[45] Brown (2001) shows that a national economy can remain competitive without upgrading the skills of a large section of the workforce. HC theory only looks at the supply side of the skills, and without effective economic planning and policy the demand for high skills may not bring adequate returns on investment in HC. Nations have to coordinate both the supply and the demand.

5.5.1 *Supply Side Bias*

The HC theory reduces people into a bundle of technical skills that are fed into an economy, while it successfully challenges the limited understanding of capital in classical economics. In treating investment in human being as no different from investment in land or machine it tends to analyse labour in isolation from social relations in which the human factor is embedded. It is not actually human beings who are input into the production process but their capacity to work. Individual capacity to work is socially created, nourished and sustained. The weakness of the HC theory, like other neo-classic theories, is its tendency to maintain tight disciplinary boundaries between economics and other social sciences to create a very mechanistic view of labour. The issue of motivation for instance is a question of striking a right balance between incentives and punishments (items like status, promotion, pay). This is based on a model of economic rationality used by the HC theory.[46] But this model of economic rationality, based on the assumption that human beings are self-interested optimizers has received sustained criticism not just from other streams of social science but also from practitioners of HRM. Also the motivation to learn and acquire skills is only partially explained by economic incentives. Research on working class youth in Britain shows the influence of ethnic, gender, parental education, income and other class factors on attitudes and approaches to learning. These influences can lead young people to restrict their commitment to education and training irrespective of cost benefit analysis in favour of their self-interest.[47] As the economy becomes more knowledge based, social and cultural issues of identity, motivation, and high trust assume centrality in the related issues of skill, productivity and economic competitiveness. The failure to understand the social and political context of motivation has other dimensions of creating commitment to quality consciousness, teamwork, and learning.

5.5.2 *Demand Side Problems*

The HC theory assumes that investment in HC will create its own demand as employers upgrade worker's skill base and well-qualified labour is available. But the evidence is not that clear.[48] Japanese practice was to fund training and subsidize its employment in new, sunrise industries.

The centrality of capitalism as a driving force of liberalization and globalization has shown that tools of technology can be appropriated in different ways in the pursuit of profits and financial returns to shareholders, for instance, by importing skill or outsourcing to the detriment of the local skill pool. Information technology and microelectronics offer greater flexibility and discretion to senior managers in how to organize production or to deliver services.

Emergence of these global markets for education and skilled labour on the one hand and fiscal pressures to privatize local education and training on the other can have serious impact on national educational and training systems.

There is ample evidence, presented previously, on the revival and expansion of sweatshops, working-out-of-home other and informal labour practices, de-skilling and MacJobs (any low-end service job poorly paid and excluded from basic job security and occupational welfare entitlements) both within the OECD countries and across the developing world to draw attention to the issues of skill formation, market failures, inequality of opportunity and the need for public policies that intervene to counter low skill equilibrium traps.

5.5.3 *Measurement and Rewarding of Skills*

Besides the problems of measurement of rate of returns to human capital investments mentioned in Sections 3.3.1, there are other questions of definition and measurement. The HC theorists also cannot define and measure skill. Skill is variously defined as the expertise, ability, or competence to undertake any activity, acquired through formal instruction or work experience. The practical problems related to its measurement are significant. This is solved by assuming that in competitive labour markets, wages reflect skill and productivity of labour. This view completely ignores the power of individuals, occupational groups and trade unions to hike up their income or for employers to pay women, immigrants and other socially disadvantaged groups less for the same work. A clear example is of American CEOs whose average pay packet in 1965 was 44 times that of the factory worker and rose to be 419 times within 33 years.[49] The wages of CEOs in US corporations are 106 per cent higher than in France, 155 per cent than in Japan, 159 per cent higher than in Germany, and 44 per cent higher than in Britain.

5.6 Political Economy of High Skills

The neo-liberal analysis of globalization and liberalization is based on the premise of general equilibrium analysis. A corollary to this is that global labour markets will emerge, and the rewards to skill will converge in the long run, but initially the competitive labour market will generate rewards that are not commensurate with skill. The less developed countries will attract flow of capital, and generate low-skill, labour-intensive employment because of the competitive advantage offered by cheaper labour. Twenty-five years of hindsight have shown that (a) there are no genuine global labour markets and nationality restricts competition for jobs, even more so, at the low skill end. These restrictions are sometimes loosened in response to national shortages and demand and policy shifts in the developed countries, (b) large-scale mass employment of low-skill workforce has occurred only in some countries that have favourable conditions like infrastructure, entrepreneurial abilities or state initiatives. Even here it is not the demand for raw low-skill labour that grows most rapidly but for semi-skilled workforce with some industrial experience and high-skill or professional workforce. So, increasing investments in education and training are becoming imperative. But aspects of global competitiveness like high capital productivity may work against high skill formation because return on capital can be increased through mergers, acquisitions, cost reductions, and flexible employment practices.[50] In the flexible labour market the employers can simply tolerate lower productivity and reward it with lower wages and thus create low skill equilibrium.[51]

Therefore there is a strong case for government involvement in economic planning and policies for skill development. This is especially true of developing countries, where there are no examples of competitive success and economic growth without the visible hand of the state.[52]

The most cited examples are Japan and Asian Tiger economies in the 1970s and 1980s.[53] Singapore has the highest proportion of any workforce in the world working for foreign multinational companies but has a major government involvement in planning. Contrary to proclamation of the end of the nation state, globalization has made it more important to have a democratic political voice that serves national interests rather than the interests of a few. There is no other institution as yet to balance the interests of the individuals and various social groups.

In the USA a committee consisting of representatives of the National Academy of Science, the National Academy of Engineering and the Institute of Medicine produced a report in October 2005, on how America can enhance its technological base to stay ahead in the global race. The report makes the following observations:

> Because of Globalization workers in virtually every sector must face competitors who live just a mouse click away in Ireland, India, Finland or dozens of other countries whose economies are growing. Having reviewed the trends in United States and abroad the committee is deeply concerned that the scientific and technological building blocks of our economic leadership are eroding when many other nations are gathering strength.

That was followed by recommendations to strengthen science and mathematics teaching at schools, recruit more teachers and encourage students with scholarships, increase federal funding for fundamental research by 10 per cent a year for seven years.[54]

The political economy of high skills is reflected in the fact that at least half the expenditure of modern states is concerned with redistribution in the forms of taxation for universal education, health care and other social programmes. Such internal transfers are 50 times larger than international transfers and take the form of economic, technological or other aid programmes.[55] The organization of political economy for emphasis on education and training will shape the future direction of skill formation and global competitiveness.

This is why the idea of global convergence of national economy based on free market principles is rejected by Brown (2000). Instead, what is proposed is an alternative New Political Economy (NPE) of skill formation. The approach has its roots in economic sociology and new institutionalism.[56] The NPE proposes that high skill societies exist by design, not by market or by evolution. The issues of skill formation and economic performance are socially constructed and experienced within social institutions such as school, offices, or factories that can be organized in different ways. Therefore, skill upgrading is as much a political agenda as an economic goal. Concerns about economic inequality, poverty, opportunity, and democratic participation are also central to NPE of skill. It is a way of reuniting principles of social justice and economic efficiency.

Building societal capacity for high skills depends upon the creation of a number of complementary conditions. Brown, et al. outline the ideal set of complementary conditions called the 7Cs: Consensus, Competitive Capacity, Capability, Coordination, Circulation, Cooperation and Closure.

5.6.1 *Consensus*

The extent to which the competing groups coalesce around the idea of high skills will determine policy commitment and implementation. The consensus depends on binding together major stakeholders, i.e. employee trade unions, employers and the government, on the basis of mutual trust and commitment to progressive improvement in education and training system, industrial relations and corporate governance.

5.6.2 *Competitive Capacity*

Without a viable strategy for creating value-added products based on quality, a company will find it difficult to increase investment in education, training, research and development. Zero sum variety of rivalry between companies that leads to cost cutting, and downsizing results in de-skilling and no increase in demand for skilled labour. Advancing knowledge is essentially a coordinated process where the blue sky research and big scientific breakthroughs are public funded while incremental improvements in product innovation, design, production technique, delivery system, reliability, and standardization, where, the cost benefit can be handled by the firm can happen with private funding. The coordination of public and private is typical in the USA. Synergy between basic research and market applications needs supply of experienced and trained people. Eventually, discoveries have to be diffused through specialized technology clusters and finally to the national economy. But this cannot be achieved when employers adopt a plug-in-and-play HRM model.[57]

A flat-pack model of skill training where the skills of employees are built up and supplemented within a work context is what is needed. The importance of on-job training is heightened because research shows that vocational training can never be a substitute for on-job training.[58]

5.6.3 *Capability Building for Skill*

The dominant arguments of human capability assume that only a minority is capable of high-skill work and that the education system must be organized to identify and cultivate the limited pool of talent. The alternative model of human capability is based on the belief that all have the potential to benefit from learning and skill upgradation. It recommends an inclusive system of education and training that achieves comparatively high standards for all social groups by teaching new basic skills to all. An example of this would be very high-quality primary and secondary education for all and essential exposure to information technology and communications for all.

5.6.4 *Circulation of Skills*

Circulation refers to diffusion of high skills throughout the economy. This depends on removing information bottlenecks and social rigidities, and to prevent any closures of the diffusion effect. That is, there ought to be opportunities for any person to upgrade his educational status or skill level without any arbitrary entry bars. There must also be active programmes for documenting and disseminating best practices in various sectors.

5.6.5 *Closure Prevention*

In high-skill societies more than 50 per cent of occupations will be categorized as technical, managerial or professional. The rest of the population should be in the process of upgrading its skills to next higher levels. Hence, the culture of learning has to be promoted and made inclusive of all social and ethnic groups.

5.6.6 *Coordination*

Coordination refers to the need to bring together the supply and demand sides of the human capital. This would require integrated policy involving government departments, local governments, employers' organizations, trade unions, and local communities. This would also entail systems of indigenous inward investment, small and medium enterprise policy, institutions that support enterprises to engage in new technology, information gathering, building international and national markets, and investment capital.

5.6.7 *Cooperation*

Capitalist economies are typically characterized by economic conflict between competing economic classes or in terms of competing rational self-seeking individuals. But in practice, the virtue in this view appears to be exaggerated. Cooperation refers to trust relationships. High-skill societies need to be based on models of cooperation, communication and shared goals. Cooperation is willingness to give and receive help and due recognition of the other's contribution.

Some of the case studies described below illustrate some of the 7Cs of a high-skill society model.

5.7 Some Models of Skill Development

Four successful models of successful skill development are presented below for the unique insight they provide into the possibility of using public policy to effect large-scale high-quality skill transformation.

5.7.1 *Germany's Model of Skill Development*

It is relevant here to recall a prominent model of a high-skill country. Germany is often taken as a model case of a high-skill society. High-skill economy is defined as an economy with a wide distribution of workforce skills where these are optimally utilized to achieve high productivity across a wide range of sectors and at the same time producing a high wage rate and relative income equality. A high level of workforce cooperation supported by social capital and civic trust is seen as an important part of the model.[59] In contrast with economies characterized by high-skill elite, Germany has a relatively even distribution of skills. Though the labour market is highly segmented, labour is accorded equality of status and pay backed by the drive towards equality of productive capacity.

Productivity is a useful measure of skill. It is also a measure of national competitiveness. Total factor productivity (TFP) includes both capital and labour productivity. Labour productivity can be measured in three ways – output per worker, output per hour of work, output per head of population. The most common is hourly output, which is a function of technology, organizational efficiency, knowledge, and skill but it cannot be separated from the capital invested in plant and equipment, with which the labour sets to work. This problem is overcome by using the TFP method. USA has the highest TFP because its capital productivity is high. Germany has relatively low capital productivity because its financial sector is under-developed but labour productivity is high in the manufacturing sector, which is the driving force of the economy. The output per head of population and output per worker have remained high despite recent high levels of unemployment as a result of reunification, and shorter working hours.[60]

Historically the German society has dense associational networks, apprenticeship or training system, neo-corporatist form of interest group bargaining, societal respect for knowledge, professional autonomy, and technical skills. These are institutionalized in the dual system of occupational training, which prepares two-thirds of German youth for working life and serves to transform the majority of paid jobs into skilled occupations. Its institutional features are:

1. Federal form of government; mandatory power distribution between different tiers of government, independent agencies, and associations all of whom have constitutional status.
2. Distinctive form of capitalism – called social market.
3. State intervenes and strictly regulates the market.
4. Protection of the participating interest groups.
5. Large and powerful trade associations.
6. Regulated labour-management relations.
7. Federal government constitutes and regulates an extensive apprenticeship training system. It invests in research and development through intermediate technology transfer organizations like Max Planck, Fraun Hofer.
8. Sectoral agreements on skill standards and wages.
9. At the local levels there are chambers of commerce covering most sectors. They play an important role in policy forming and overseeing the dual system of apprentice training.
10. At the firm level co-determination laws give employees representative rights along with managers, shareholders and other stakeholders. As per Work Council Laws 1972 all firms employing more than five employees must have work councils

who approve all hiring, dismissal, transfer, work allocation, and alterations in scale and speed of production.

11. Two-tier system of control over corporation, i.e. supervisory boards on which workers are represented alongside management, creditors, and shareholders and managerial executive. By 1976, workers were given equal representation on supervisory boards in companies with over 2,000 workers.
12. Company law in Germany encourages long-term investment. Banks hold major part of equity of firms on their own behalf and their investors' behalf. They also follow a practice of non-voting shares. As a result private shareholder influence is limited.
13. By law a takeover requires a 75 per cent shareholder majority to go through, thus promoting long-termism or patient capital.

Germany has evolved a unique system of education and training in which the government, firms, chambers of commerce, and workers partner each other, called the Dual System. Two-thirds of the youth pass through this system, and 90 per cent of them qualify as skilled workers with solid grounding in occupational theory, skill and general education, and 20 per cent of these apprentices go on to qualify as MEISTERF, i.e. as technical supervisors-cum-teachers or other higher skill levels.[61] The Dual System involves a three-and-half-year contract according to rules and regulations determined by the BIBB. Apprentices train for three days in a week in the firm receiving a structured and formally approved programme of training under a technically qualified teacher (MEISTERF), and two days in a week in an academic institution studying general education and theoretical foundation of their profession. Employers support the system because of legal reasons and the various incentives. Laws require firms employing young people in classified occupation to provide training according to the regulation. Major incentives for the firm are (a) reduced cost of future employee selection, induction and training, (b) reasonably low trainee wages, (c) savings from trainee productivity, and (d) flexibility in employment. The young people are motivated because the apprentice qualification gives access to skilled jobs from which they would otherwise be excluded by federal law, which credentialize access to jobs by laying down minimum qualifications. Laws also oblige school leavers to continue part-time education any way. But the most important factor that induces students and firms to stay in the system is the high quality of training, tight specifications and quality standards decided by the tripartite BIBB, and its monitoring at the local levels by the chambers of commerce and the work councils. The assessment system similarly rests on the joint partnership with training committees and apprenticeship jurors at the chambers of commerce. Having undergone such occupational training, students can opt for work, for further training or university courses for higher education.

An early exposure to practical technical work encourages students to take up further specialization and 19 per cent of all degrees awarded in Germany are in engineering. Proportion of research scientists and engineers is high and next only to Japan and the USA. Also the rate of patenting is second only to the USA.

5.7.2 *Singapore: An Asian City-State Model*

Singapore is a small island with 4 million population and no natural resources, which became self-governing only in 1959. It is a multi-racial society. It had to create capital advantage through its human resource. The state has been proactive in raising the supply of skills as also the demand for such skills.[62] As a result of these strategic policies it experienced three decades of growth averaging 9 per cent per annum, which was above the average of Asian Tiger economies. Singapore is the third richest country in the world in terms of per capita GDP. It also was ranked number one in the World Economic Forum's Global Competitiveness Report 1997. The human resource policies play a critical role in forging social cohesion and nation building through rapid expansion of primary and secondary education in English media and shift toward export-oriented industries in 1965, which created demand for higher skills. Some successful initiatives, both governmental and institutional that helped the growth are:

1. Banning of ghettos – i.e. exclusive racial residential colonies.
2. Education in English medium and very high quality of instructions. Every child is trained to be computer literate.
3. Technical Education Department within the Ministry of Education (MOE) started numerous joint training schemes with foreign MNCs.
4. By the mid-1970s the MOE had developed strategy for more technical and skill-intensive industries in the face of increasing competition from areas of low-wage, low cost manufacturing.
5. Generous tax incentives to MNCs for high-tech investment.
6. Introduction of skill development fund, funded by 1 per cent levy of payroll for each worker receiving S$750 or less per month.
7. New wage policy in 1979 by the National Wage Council, which recommended substantial increase in minimum wages: employers are required to pay 4 per cent in national insurance contribution over and above their contribution to central provident fund. Result was a 41 per cent increase in wage cost during 1979-81.
8. Rapid increase in funding for R&D and expansion of science park industrial districts. New institutes of technology in collaboration with other countries, e.g. Germany, France, and Japan in disciplines like electrical, software, and other engineering disciplines.
9. Thrust for enrolment in universities, polytechnics, institutes of technical education and skill centres. There was a 50 per cent increase in enrolment.

New Economic Policy 1986 placed greater emphasis on service industries to make Singapore a business hub of the Asia-Pacific.

5.7.3 *South Korea: Another Asian Model*

The South Korean economy was shattered by the three years of war (1950-3) against North Korea, and starting in the mid-1960s made rapid progress for three decades resulting in its manufacturing base becoming the second best in Asia. Being a non-industrial society, the government support for vocational, technical education and training was important in developing skills that helped fuel Korea's rapid growth.[63]

1. In 1967 the government set up a national training system following the enactment of vocational training law.
2. The national technical qualification law put in place a skill certification system.
3. Later in 1976 the law induced and formalized mandatory in-plant vocational training and established a vocational training promotion fund, financed by a training fee levied on firms that did not have an in-plant training programme.
4. In 1982 the Ministry of Labour formed the Korean Manpower Agency (KOMA) as the training arm.
5. In 1989 the Korean Institute of Technology and Education was established to provide teacher training programme for the vocational sector.
6. Ten years later about 500 vocational training institutes were providing various levels of training. Of these, 40 were run by KOMA, 53 by other government agencies, 237 were in-plant training centres, and 170 authorized training centres in the private sector.
7. By 1998 a total of 3.3 million people had received training in these centres.

In 1997, at the start of Asian Crisis the government passed an act reinforcing vocational training. Under this legislation the Ministry of Labour can offer financial support to employers implementing the vocational competency development programme. It can also support employees seeking vocational training. Subsequently, a quarter of all unemployed received government-sponsored vocational training. This scheme along with the employment insurance scheme helped the jobless during the downturn (1997-9). Since then further initiatives to strengthen, expand, and diversify vocational training, involve the private sector, and introduce IT systems for job matching have been undertaken.

5.7.4 *The Case of Ireland*

Taking a cue for the UK, Ireland moved faster and quicker in the late 1960s. Government made secondary education free, making it possible for many more working-class people to get a high school or technical degree, and as a result when it joined the EU Ireland was able to draw on a more educated workforce. By 1996, when the opposite was happening under neo-liberal pressures in the UK, Ireland made college education free and implemented a combination of policies like low corporate taxation and low wages as part of the macroeconomic policy settlement between unions and government; good transport system; and moved up the value chain, while aggressively courting of FDI. These resulted in the setting up of pharmaceutical and electronic companies at the high value end in Ireland. While it integrated with Europe and the world Ireland has grown rapidly so that it had the second highest per capita income in Europe by 2005.[64]

5.8 Skill Development in India

Against in the background of the debate about relationship between globalization and skill formation the following section reviews the existing state of human capital in India. The skill formation systems are also described and placed in the context of high-skill models of Germany and Singapore discussed above. This offers valuable insight into the inadequacy of the Indian systems.

5.8.1 *Skill Status of Indian Workforce*

The skill status of the workforce can be analysed both at the macro and sectoral levels. A number of significant studies are discussed below.

MACRO- AND SECTOR-LEVEL STUDIES

Evaluating the pace and pattern of qualitative improvement in human capital index during the 1980s and 1990s G.K. Chaddha

(2004) uses education as the central parameter of this index.[65] Although, the investment in human capital can take many forms such as informal education, on-the-job training, health improvement and learning by doing, formal education is taken as the central parameter because it is regarded as making a fundamental contribution, which can be complemented but not substituted by other forms of human capital investments. Also data on formal education is the only readily available data in three levels or stages of education, i.e. primary, secondary and tertiary. Production-relevant skills are assumed to be embodied to a greater extent in individuals who have acquired greater quantity and quality of education.[66] Therefore, secondary or higher secondary level of schooling is taken as the dividing line between educated and not-educated workers. Thus, the primary- or middle-level schooling is categorized as semi-educated, and below that level as illiterate or uneducated. Then, the NSSO data from 1983-2000 showing the distribution of principal-status workers by the level of their education based on national industrial classification of CSO, shows up the following features:

- All sectors of Indian economy have seen a gradual decline in the proportion of illiterate workers. The decline was more rapid in the 1983-93 periods than in 1993-2000. Agriculture and construction had the highest percentage of illiterate workers. For the total workforce the proportion of educated workers started from 9 per cent in 1983 and increased to 19 per cent in 2000.
- The degree of improvement is varied among sectors. For example, in the 1999-2000 period, 44 per cent of all workers were illiterate but in finance, insurance and real-estate only 2 per cent were illiterate, in utilities only 7 per cent were illiterate, in community, social and personal services only 20 per cent were illiterate.
- Third, in manufacturing, trade, transport, storage and communication there was a varying mixture of illiterate, semi- and educated workers. In non-metallic mineral workers 53 per cent were illiterate, in machine tools and electrical machinery only

7.2 per cent were illiterate. The data highlights the extremely sharp segmentation of the Indian labour market on the basis of quality of the workforce.

- Medium-quality workers with middle and primary level schooling have increased in each sector of the Indian economy. In 1999-2000, such workers constituted one half of total workers in manufacturing, construction, trade, transport, storage and communication; one-third in agriculture, mining, quarrying, utility, community, social and personal services; one-fifth in insurance, finance and real-estate. For the economy as a whole, this medium-quality constituted no less than 37 per cent of the total workforce.
- Fifth, sectors which are big from the point of employment, like agriculture, mining, quarrying, trade, transport and manufacturing have enormous problems regarding the quality of the workforce.
- In 2000, 44 per cent of the workforce was illiterate and only 18.6 per cent was secondary-educated or above. This contrasts with Sri Lanka, which has only 3.6 per cent illiterate workforce. The rural-urban gap is also very wide across all sectors; the rural workforce is of poorer quality, e.g. not more than 12 per cent are educated. The male-female gap in education is also wide, the latter being of poorer quality. Three-fourths of the female workers were illiterate compared to one-fourth of the male workers. Only 7 per cent of the females were educated compared to 23 per cent of the males.
- State-wise scenario is also varied although in every state the proportion of illiterate workforce has declined.

Another comprehensive study by Mathur and Mamgain (2004) uses household level data from the 1999-2000 NSSO statistics to estimate the HC content of the total population as well as the workforce in terms of 17 categories of human capital.[67] It includes every category except illiterates in the gross stock of human capital. It also examines the impact of these HC categories on state-level growth rates, per capita income, incidence of poverty, and the extent of disparities. The study also examines the utilization of the 17 categories of human capital in terms of education-specific workforce participation and unemployment rates.

The study finds a strong positive influence of HC on state-level per capita income. Education-specific work participation rates rise with the level of education. But interestingly, unemployment rates tend to rise in case of a higher-order HC. This indicates either a mismatch between demand and supply in specific segments or an overall low skill growth trajectory in the post-1991 period. Moreover, under-utilization of human capital is highest in the technical diploma holder category.

Looking at another aspect of skill development in India at the macro level, Unni and Rani (2004) use NSSO, employment and unemployment survey 1993-4 and 1999-2000 to examine whether there was skill-based growth in the workforce in India in the later part of 1990 and if this was a result of skill-biased technical change.[68] They conclude that there is clear evidence of movement towards skill-based workforce in the latter part of the 1990s. This is true for one-digit industry groups, and also when data is disaggregated to urban/rural, regular/casual, and male/female. Defining high skill (H) as all those in the age group of 15-64 years, with higher secondary and above education, and low skill (L) as others with lesser than higher secondary education they found that the H/L ratio increased from 0.67 to 0.78 per cent between 1993-4 and 1999-2000 in urban areas. The wage premium defined as Wh/Wl (wages of high-skill workers/wages of low-skill workers) also increased from 2.38 to 2.56 over the same period in urban areas. In rural areas the ratios increased marginally from 0.10 to 0.13 while wage premiums actually fell from 2.68 to 2.40 over the same period. The skill ratio of the workforce and the wage premium both moved positively in the manufacturing and service sectors, proving that in some sectors at least the elasticity of substitution between skilled and unskilled was less than one. An observation in this context is that rising wage disparity is inevitable in the early stages of development when skill ratios of workforce are low. And interestingly, if at this juncture technological change and growth are not strong enough to increase productivity of the skilled with rising skill premiums then the demand for skill workers will not grow, and eventually incentive to invest in education and skill development will decline.[69]

The experience of OECD countries in this complex issue is also worth nothing.[70] The trend increase in the net relative demand for skills has the potential to lead to higher overall levels of unemployment in higher wage regions. The size of transfers to offset the relatively widening wage inequalities will be too large to be politically feasible within the existing paradigm. A positive supply effect to offset the increase in demand cannot be assumed. Hence, offsetting local finance effects of increasing income inequality on primary and secondary education will have to occur. The induced increase in skill is good for growth but there is no conclusive evidence to indicate that rate of technological change itself will accelerate as the proportion of skilled workers in the workforce increases. So, the rapid growth of labour productivity cannot be assumed.

SECTOR STUDIES

The IT sector, and this is often held up as an example of advantages of globalization, has strong export orientation and large potential for high-skilled employment, but Datar (2004) points to the possible neglect of up-skilling, low skill equilibrium and shortages of high-skill manpower in the near future.[71] The point has been highlighted by many NASSCOM seminars thereafter. Broadly comprising software, information technology enabled services (ITES), and business process outsourcing (BPO) the exports of this sector have soared from 29 per cent of all exports in 1993-4 to 64 per cent in 2003-4. Employment too increased from 6,800 in 1986-7 to a little over a million by 2006. Today (2016) it employs over 2.5 million directly. The fastest growing sub-sector here is the BPO sector. According to NSSO (55th round) data, indications are that out of the total employees only 8.2 per cent were system analysts and programmers but the bulk of the employees were stenographers, typists, card/tape punch operators and computer operators. Only 4 per cent had degrees in engineering, or technology, 65 per cent were general graduates, 27 per cent had secondary- or higher-secondary certificates. Datar concludes that the advantages of the Indian industry, mainly low wages – one-third of wages in Singapore and half of these in Russia – would remain effective till a relatively lower-cost country enters the sector.

Some further indications/explanations for this under-utilization of skills may be found in the study of auto component factories in NOIDA district.[72] In a sample of 30 firms, of which 90 per cent were registered firms, only 37 per cent of the workers were technical diploma holders, 43 per cent were graduates, 12 per cent post-graduates, and 7 per cent had studied further than 12th standard. Further, if one looks at the terms and conditions of their employment one can see a link to on-the-job formation of HC both in quantity and quality. Only 37 per cent of the workers had ESI and 27 per cent of the workers had provident fund (which can serve as a proxy for security of service). Thirty-eight per cent of workers were contract and daily wage in 1995 and by 2004, 49 per cent were on contract or daily wage. Only two firms employing more than 100 workers had unions. Even though 57 per cent of the firms had ISO 9000/2000, only 27 per cent gave regular training to workers so as to upgrade their skills over time. Although 87 per cent of the firms had provided some or the other form of training, it was not regular or systematic like their Japanese counterparts. The authors felt that the low levels of unionization had a significant indirect effect on wage inequality causing the wages of skilled workers to fall. As the workers became skilled and experienced over time, their wages were not increased but to stem disaffection the firms had adopted the strategy of offering workers an opportunity to set up their own firm (sub-contracting) for profit. Another interesting feature was that the demand for skilled workers did not increase with the introduction of new machinery and technology like CNC and PLC machines. The skilled workers were employed on a part-time basis, while some semi-skilled were trained to handle remaining less skilled part of the job. This was another popular cost-cutting strategy. The result of all of these methods was that there was no net step-up in human capital drawn into the auto component factories in the region.

Sustaining the conclusions of this investigation is another one based on a sample of 600 workers in the enterprises set up within the export promoting zones (EPZ) in the NOIDA area.[73] This investigation looked at NEPZ that was set up in 1985 and had 146 units in the production of a wide range of products like electronic hardware and software, engineering products, plastics and rubber, garments, gems and jewellery. It found that the quality of employment was very poor in the firms and so was the skill and training of workers. The situating was worse in the small firms employing less than 50 workers, which formed 65 per cent of the units. Their proportion of total employment and value of exports was low. In the large units, 76 per cent of the workers were permanent and in the small units only 52 per cent. Of the workers, 55 per cent, in the large firms were skilled while 45 per cent were unskilled. In the small firms, 67 per cent were unskilled. The tendency of short-run labour contracts is a response to the uncertainty of conditions in the international market, and the ability of the firms to pass on the risks of international business to workers. Bargaining position of labour was weak in the EPZs. The consequence was high degree of worker dissatisfaction, low wages, high turnover, low levels of investment in on-the-job training and low productivity eventually. Training was found to be a neglected issue in almost all the firms in the zone.

5.8.2 *Vocational Training Systems in India*

A comparison with high-skill models like Singapore, South Korea and Germany described above is valuable. The draft youth policy lays emphasis on education, employment and training.[74] According to it, education above the secondary level should have career counselling and a high degree of vocationalization to enable the youth to acquire such skills as would open up increasing employment opportunities for them and also to upgrade their existing skills. It stresses the need for developing a sound basic educational base, closer links between the educational system and prospective employers to prevent a mismatch between skill requirements and availability and to monitor shifts in employment patterns. An analysis of live registers of employment exchanges revealed that even as the number of job seekers in the live registers of employment exchanges were increasing, an increasing percentage of vacancies in the category of professional, technical, production and related workers remained unfulfilled in the 1990s. On the other hand, there was evidence of decreasing unemployment among the technical degree and diploma holders during the reform period and a considerable decrease in the waiting period to get the first job, especially in the states, which had sustained a higher growth rate.[75]

The vocational training system in India has come to include vocational training at the secondary level, polytechnics, and ITI. And all of these exist both in the public and private sectors. At the plus-two secondary level, it is regulated by the NCERT and SCERTs, and the polytechnics and ITI are regulated by Vocational Board of AICTE/DGET and the Central Apprenticeship Council formed under Apprenticeship Act 1961.[76]

The system has grown considerably. Starting from 54 ITI institutions in 1953 catering to 10,000 students, it has gone up to 4,274 in 2001 for a student population of 6,28,000 students. Private sector's participation can be gauged from the fact that 2,620 institutions out of 4,274 are in the private sector and receive little government aid. By March 2001, 17,800 public and private establishments were covered under the Apprenticeship Act 1961 and allocated 2,20,000 trainee seats of which 1,58,000 were utilized.

ORIGIN AND GROWTH

The recommendations of the D.C. Kothari Commission formed the basis of the 1968 National Policy on Education. The commission felt that it would be possible to divert at least 50 per cent of the students completing class ten to the vocational stream, reducing the pressure on universities and better preparing students for employment. The vocational education scheme at the ten-plus-two stage came into existence in the late 1970s. The national working group on vocational education (V.C. Kulandaiswamy Committee, 1985) reviewed the VEP extensively and developed guidelines for the expansion of the programme. Till then, only a handful of states and union territories had taken some initiative in imparting vocational training. Based on the recommendations of the 1985 committee, a centrally sponsored scheme on vocational training at secondary level began in 1988 and is being implemented through the state governments/union territories. The funding is shared by the centre and the states, with the centre bearing most of the burden. Pundit Sunderlal Sharma Central Institute of Vocational Education (PSSCIVE), Bhopal, under the NCERT provides research, development and training to the teachers and also draws up the curriculum for most of the courses for adoption by the state councils of education research and training. The main objectives of the scheme are: (a) provide an alternative for those pursuing higher education, (b) enhance employability, (c) reduce the mismatch between the demand and supply for skilled manpower, and (d) involve the non-government organizations in vocational training for the non-formal sector. During the Ninth Plan, an outlay of Rs. 100 crore was provided for the scheme. In the formal sector the state governments implemented the scheme at plus-two stage through approximately 6,700 schools. More than 150 courses were offered in six major disciplines like agriculture, business and commerce, engineering and technology, health and paramedical services, home sciences and humanities. The Ministry of HRD had involved the Department of Economic Affairs, in the Ministry of Finance with the purpose of persuading nationalized banks and financial institutions to offer soft loans. In the non-formal sector, the scheme provides assistance to NGOs, which help rural unemployed youth and school drop-outs. Eighteen NGOs were assisted and funded.

The scheme was evaluated by the ORG and NCERT in 1988 and 1996 respectively. It was found that vocational training at the plus-two level was not popular among students who preferred traditional general courses. Such students constitute the bulk of 50 million educated unemployed in India. The states were also according lower priority to the scheme and were reluctant to provide full-time teachers. The NCERT observed that full-time teachers must be appointed as in the general education scheme. Vocational training must be covered under the Apprenticeship Act 1961. That students passing out should have access to tertiary education in a related discipline. Active partnership of industries should be secured and block-level vocational institutions should be set up. Infrastructure in vocational secondary schools, polytechnics, and NGOs should be reviewed.

Vocational Training of the Directorate General of Employment and Training (DGET), Ministry of Labour, is the key government body responsible for the administration of vocational training in the country. The VT programme comprises:

The Craftsmen Training Scheme (CTS) that imparts skills in 42 engineering and 18 non-engineering vocational trades through a network of ITIs administered by state governments. The period of training varies from 1 to 3 years and entry qualifications vary from 8th to 12th standard. There are 4,172 such institutions (of which 458 were exclusively for women) with an enrollment capacity of 36,000 students in the year 2000. The CTS has expanded rapidly but its financing has not kept pace with the levels needed for quality and relevance of technological training being imparted.

Apprenticeship Training Scheme (ATS): A statutory tripartite body, the Central Apprenticeship Council (CAC) advises the government on aspects of the Apprenticeship Act 1961. Under this Act, it is obligatory for employers to engage a predetermined number of trade apprentices. They undergo on-the-job training of between 6 months and 4 years. On completion of the period they take an all-India trade test conducted by NCVT. In 2000, there were 2,35,000 seats available for training in central and state-sector establishments combined. Of these, 725 seats had been utilized.

Graduate Technician and Technician Apprenticeship (GTTA): The Apprenticeship Act 1961 was amended to include graduation and diploma in engineering and technology. Regional boards of apprenticeship training under the Department of Education, HRD ministry, administer the training of this category. The programme is centralized and standardized at the central level and lacks flexibility to absorb local and dynamic and multi-skill categories. It is also limited to the organized manufacturing sector and does not cater to the expanding service sector.

There are a number of other schemes administered by different bodies like the Shramik Vidyapeeths for non-formal, continuing adult education in urban communities. Fifty-eight such institutions in 2000 offered 225 different VT programmes ranging from candle making to computer literacy. A scheme Community Polytechnics (CP) scheme was started by the DOE in 1978-9 and aims at providing non-formal, skill-oriented, short-term trade-courses open to all. By 2000, 442 CPs were imparting training in 120 vocational and technical trades. They had trained 0.62 million youths and out of these, 50 per cent secured self or wage employment. There are also a number of schemes administered by Ministry of Rural Development, like the Programme for Development of Women and Children, Training for Rural Youth for Self-Employment (TRYSEM): (a) Training under Khadi and Village Industries Commission (KVIC) set up to promote self-employment by production of marketable commodities. Training is an important activity of KVIC and it has 51 training centres comprising 21 Khadi Gramodyog Vidyalayas run by societies and NGOs. (b) The Ministry of Industry also runs some training programmes. The National Institute of Design (NID) too runs courses for school and graduate level in designing products, furniture, ceramics, textiles, apparel, graphics, video, film animation, exhibitions, etc. (c) the Prime Minister's Rozgar Yojna is aimed at promoting self-employment among educated youth. It stipulates a period of training in industry and service sectors against a start-up loan sanctioned by the district industries centre.

5.8.3 *The Main Shortcomings of the Vocational Training System*

Although there are multiple agencies providing VT like the Ministry of Labour, Ministry of Education and Human Development, Ministry of Rural Development, Ministry of Industry, when compared to the high skill models discussed above there is need to create an information base on the demand and supply aspects of skills (1) for horizontal coordination among them to prevent duplication while maximizing access and variety; (2) horizontal links with industry and service sectors to upgrade training; (3) create a national/international-level acceptable testing, and benchmarking system for all types of trades and skills; (4) avoid the practice of targeting only the poor in VT programmes because the quality and sustainability of such targeted schemes is doubtful. Instead inclusive universal access is a better assurance of quality and robustness.[77]

A working group on vocational training education was constituted in the Tenth Plan, in 2000. It recommended the recasting of the centrally-sponsored scheme, and increase in the outlay to Rs. 350 crore. All vocational training at secondary schools and polytechnics should come under one department of the state government for better networking. The 'All India Council for Technical Education Vocational Board' needs to be reactivated to provide technical support to the school system and linkages with technical institutions. The courses should be made modular to enable transfer of credits and thus make the scheme a 'multi-point entry-exist' system.

At the national level the Directorate General of Employment and Training (DGET) is the nodal agency for formulating policies, certification, testing, and standards for vocational training. The responsibility is shared by the centre and the states. Every year, 5.5 million students complete class X, of which 3.3 million go to class XI, leaving 2.2 million out of the general education system. Besides this, there are 19 million who drop out after class VIII. There is a need to expand this programme manifold and customize it for about 21 million youth, the current formal training capacity being only 2.3 million students.

The skills of the teaching staff need to be continually upgraded. Against this need, only 40 per cent of the 55,000 instructors have undergone full instructor training courses. Catering to the school drop-outs will be a special challenge requiring participation from KVIC, Ministry of Rural Development, Ministry of Women and Child Development, NGOs, etc. The scope of the Apprenticeship Act should be reviewed to facilitate and expand training in the service sector in a vast variety of services at different levels of skills. Ranging from highly professional and organized (insurance, health, legal) services to semi-formal (tourism, cosmetic, food) to informal and unorganized service opportunities.

5.8.4 *Relation between Skill, Training and Quality of Employment in India*

The possible correlation between insecurity of employment and human capital/skill formation on the job are indicated by some empirical studies. Studies that are revelatory in this context are detailed here. The first study surveys 600 workers working in the NEPZ. The zone was set up in 1985 and has the highest number of units next to SEEPZ, Mumbai. There were 146 units as against valid approval of 252 units. The main items of export from NEPZ are electronic hardware and software, gems and jewellery, garments, engineering products, plastics and rubber. The EPZs are based on the assumption that the growth of the Southeast Asian Tigers has been led by a focus on export and facilitated by labour flexibility.[78] Research has also found association between productivity, quality, exports and investment in skill and training.

The survey found the formal educational qualification of the workers very low. Around 78 per cent of the workers had an educational background of below secondary or secondary level, only 4 per cent were graduates and post-graduates. Further, only 13 out of 600 workers had technical qualifications. And the units in most cases had no facility to train new workers. Only 43 workers reported the existence of a human resource development or training centre in their unit and all of them belonged to two large companies. The system of apprenticeship was the main way of skilling in the zone and 53.8 per cent of them reported their apprenticeship is under a system of helpers. Since workers, mainly drawn from rural/non-farming unskilled category are employed as helpers, on-the-job training is rare, wages are low, probability of separation is high and neither the worker nor the employees are willing to invest in more general or specific training. Unskilled or low-skilled workers constitute a large proportion of workforce in all the sectors of EPZs. Many other studies have pointed out that the employment created in the EPZs are low-paying assembly-line work, which provides little scope for mobility and upgrading.[79]

In the NEPZ, total employment increased by 80 per cent between 1995 and 2000. Exports from EPZs and NEPZs showed a rapid increasing trend in absolute terms in the early 1990s but the share of NEPZs in that export showed a decline after a peak of 15.36 per cent in 1995-6. The declining share is across the sectors within the NEPZ. Electronic software accounted for the largest share in the exports from EPZs at 57.8 per cent in 1998-9, and it declined to 10.7 per cent in 1999-2000. At the national level, the performance of the zones in terms of contribution to the total exports, output and employment is being debated now. The low share of foreign investments in the EPZs at 16 per cent of total investment in 2001 is despite all the incentives and implicitly flexible labour laws in EPZs.

Industrial sickness and closures is a regular feature in the NEP zones. In the last 10 years up to 2004, 78 units had closed down compared to 146 functional ones. Volatile export markets in gems, jewellery, garments, electronics, and in 2001-2 the software slump were responsible for this, but the inability to compete is also relevant. The employment practices in these zones are typically focused on increasing cheap casual labour, which constitutes one-fourth of the total workforce. The second category is of short-term contract workers. The contracts are often unwritten; only 18 per cent of the workers had written contracts. The rest of the workers were long-term casual or short-term daily basis workers. The zone does not have a history of more than 20 years. Long-term workers with poor education and skill would mean higher wage costs for little additional productivity, since wages rise with seniority and skill requirements are low. The uncertainty in the export market for low value-added products is such that there is a high risk of separation and turnover. This makes on-the-job training cost high for the employer. Workers, on the other hand, respond to insecurity, low pay, low levels of job-specific training, and poor incentives for long-term service by high rates of mobility across industry and firms. Although the average years of service are high, 5 to 10 years, this is because of the dual category of workers, one of the permanently casual, higher skilled workers for whom work is almost certain, and the other casual workers for whom work is highly uncertain. High overall degree of insecurity is maintained through casual dismissal of workers, threats of dismissal, retrenchments of entire departments citing competitive pressures, employment of outsiders and the experience of closures in the zone. The workers respond by high degrees of opportunism and mobility.

So a vicious cycle sets in keeping the EPZs focused on low value addition exports, and low-skilled cheap workers. This is the reverse of the virtuous cycle linking long-term growth in exports, quality augmentation, moving up the value chain and investment in human capital as experienced by the Asian Tigers. The ILO reports of increasing evidence to support the link between education level of the workforce, productivity performance and economic growth.[80] This is also supported by UNDP and the ADB.[81] Pigato, et al. show that Southeast Asian economies were able to develop supporting skills, which enabled them to move up the value chain and produce technologically advanced products.[82] The share of technically advanced goods manufactured in exports is used as a measure of technological upgrading. South Korea, for example, had only 8.8 per cent of its manufactured products in the technologically advanced category (TAC) in 1970 and this rose to 42.6 per cent in 1995. Corresponding figures for Singapore were 9.4 per cent and 68.5 per cent and for Taiwan 14.6 per cent and 42.4 per cent. Figures for India were 1.7 and 2 per cent for the same period. Interestingly the share of TAC in manufactured exports of India was higher at 2.6 per cent in 1985 compared to 2 per cent in 1995. Even Brazil had moved up from 3.7 to 42.4 per cent over the period. This takes into account the value added per unit of output and the intensive use of capital and skills.

Another study relevant to the issue of poor demand-pull augmentation of skill levels in India's Industrial sector in this context is by Vikram Chadha (2004).[83] Here, the S&T manpower refers to the sum of diploma holders, degree-holding graduates, and postgraduates in science and technology. It concludes that the overall growth of all types of science and technology personnel employed in the public sector has declined over the study period 1990-7 based on data of the Ministry of Science & Technology, Government of India. Their employment has however registered a high rate of growth in the private sector industry, but the growth of S&T personnel employed in auxiliary services and administration has exceeded that in primary R&D activities, which indicates a trend in under-employment of the educated. This trend in the private sector was mainly due to the presence of MNCs in some sectors of industry. But now, the same is true of the aggregate S&T employment in the industry as a whole where primary R&D employment of S&T workers is slowing down.

Research has found strong correlations between the size of an enterprise, its industrial diversification and employment of scientific manpower.[84] The nature and extent of employment of R&D personnel in industry is an important determinant of an industry's capacity to develop and exploit innovation potential. Moreover, technical skills are required to absorb technological change and scale up and down the existing technological possibilities.

5.8.5 *Second National Commission on Labour and Skill Development in India (SNLC)*

The report of the Second National Commission on Labour (2003) identified seven key challenges of globalization for Indian labour in relation to skill development.[85] Unfortunately, it does not make any analytical connections between the evidence on the deteriorating quality of employment and its likely impact on human capital formation in India. It does however make fashionable comments on the salience of skill development for continuous employability of labour, need for enlarging and utilizing the infrastructure for education and training; and absorption of new technologies by labour using education and training. A study group on skill development has examined the different training systems prevalent abroad, and made the following recommendations:

1. Setting up of a competency base by a continuing training system covering all sectors of the economy.
2. Modular approach and well-defined certification system for the competencies acquired during the programme.
3. Desired academic flexibility to allow for training, and periodic retraining of learners.
4. Continual and flexible assessment and accreditation opportunities.
5. Evaluation tests for certification and recognition of the competence, and such competencies may be acquired formally, informally, through distance learning, self-learning, or workplace training.
6. Independent regulatory authority to set standards for modular programmes, evaluations, certification, and for accreditation of institutions.
7. Labour market intelligence system to forecast the demand for marketable skills at the international, national and local levels. To strengthen intelligence about the informal sector.
8. Increase training capacity from the present 4,274 industrial training institutes, and upgrade the infrastructure in them.
9. Revise the courses and teacher training.
10. Increase industry-institution interactions from merely advisory nature at present to joint management.
11. Fiscal incentives to industry and other providers of training. Expense on industry training to be treated as revenue expense, and capital expenditure on training infrastructure to be eligible for depreciation.
12. Setting up a Skill Development Fund with contribution from organizations which are eligible to contribute for provident fund. The fund would consist of 2 per cent of the employers' contribution towards PF and employees to contribute 1 per cent of their contributions. Government would contribute every month two times the amount collected from the employers and employees. Collections would be routed and administered by regional provident fund offices. All organizations and individuals making contribution would receive tax concession. Twenty-five per cent of the SDF would be invested in a corpus.

The collection and its utilization would be jointly monitored by industry associations, government and trade unions. The SDF will also initiate special programmes for training of the rendered unemployed due to voluntary or non-voluntary reasons such as retrenchment, VRS and temporary lay-offs.

13. Government would create a coordination mechanism between ministries of HRD, labour, rural development and industries, which are already providing vocational training in India.
14. The Central Board of Workers Education set up in 1958 has been active and would be strengthened and integrated with the skill development programme.

5.9 Conclusion

According to an ILO study the main obstacles to the process of upgrading human resources, training and education are the widespread tendency of the market to fail to provide training and reluctance of enterprises to embrace technical change and innovation.[86] Contrasting the case of India with that of East Asian and Pacific economies, the ILO says that starting in the 1960s when these East Asian Pacific countries had less than three years of average schooling they improved their human resource base rapidly. By 1990s, they had the highest average level of educational attainment in the developing world, had rapidly improved female educational attainment and the teacher-student ratio. They achieved this through planning, control and coordination of their education system with the ministries of trade and Industry. They used this base to move up the value chain in production and export. On the other hand, India and Pakistan remained mired in a low-skill low-competency trap. The problem begins with a low enrolment ratio, high drop-out ratio and continues into the skewed distribution of higher education and skills across socio-economic groups.

The situation in India is illustrated with the examples of two leading export industries – leather and software. Leather is the fourth largest export earner employing 1.65 million workers (90 per cent in the informal sector) but with a declining share in the world market. In a vicious cycle brought on by the manner in which this industry is organized only 635 candidates underwent formal training in leatherwork out of a total capacity of 420,000 seats in the Indian training institutes, while the apprenticeship programmes attracted only 355 students out of a total capacity of 144,000. Most companies do not invest in training, R&D, product design or teaching infrastructure. There is no system by which companies can retain the workers they train in the informal structure of the industry. On the other hand, is the case of rising software exports made possible by the large supplies of educated and skilled manpower supplied both by educational institutes and in-house training within large companies. All of these IT companies function in the organized sector and have industry associations which are increasingly involved in coordinating training requirement with supply, e.g. in August 2005, NASSCOM initiated a move for competency tests for the BPO workforce to bring in fresh supply and standards.

Income and social disparities within which the industry functions become a strong bottleneck to human resource development, and the ILO report concluded that current trends indicate that the developing world risks encouraging new technologies appropriate to a small fraction of the workforce with high skills and in contrast it also undertakes large-scale export activity requiring low- to semi-skilled labour in the rest of the economy, leading to a widening divergence of the workforce and hence society. The skill pool needs to be widened and there is a strong correlation between skill/training levels and state and institutional support from trade unions and employer associations for coordination of industry-level skill needs. Similarly, training and institutional norms that encourage long-term commitment between employer and employee and internal career paths, e.g. higher severance pays and longer processes like notice periods, fiscal incentives for training expenditure of firms, and the incentive system for skill acquisition must be to the advantage of both firms and employees. Further, there is a strong correlation between the availability of nationally and internationally recognized flexible certification systems and the acquisition of skills.

The next chapter will review human resource management issues and develop their relationship to the insecurity hypothesis while maintaining a link to skill formation and trade union issues.

Notes

1. ILO (1998): *Employability in the Global Economy and How Training Matters*, World Employment Report 1998, Bureau of Public Information, September, ILO, Geneva.
2. Philip Brown, Andy Green and Hugh Lauder (2001): *High Skill*, Oxford University Press, Oxford.
3. V.K. Seth (2002): 'Primitive Flexible to Modern Flexible Manufacturing and the Process of Skilling and Deskilling of Labour', *Indian Journal OF Labour Economics*, vol. 45, no. 4, pp.. 1175-93.
4. H. Catt and Patricia Scudammore (1997): *Solving Skills Shortages*, Kogan Page, London.
5. Charles B. Handy (1984): The Future of Work, Basil Blackwell, Oxford.
6. G. Psacharopoulous (1981): 'Returns to Education', *Comparative Education*, vol. 17, pp. 321-41.
7. OECD (1998): *Human Capital Investment: An International Comparison*, OECD, Paris.
8. D. Neef (1998): *The Knowledge Economy*, Butterworth-Heinemann, Oxford.
9. Department of Commerce (1999): *21st Century Skills for 21st Century Jobs*, US Government Printing Office, Washington.
10. T.W. Schultz (1961): 'Investment in Human Capital', *American Economic Review*, vol. 51, pp. 1-17.
11. M.J. Bowman (1966): 'The Human Investment Revolution in Economic Thought', *Sociology of Education*, 39(2), Spring, pp. 111-37.
    G.S. Becker (1964): *Human Capital: A Theoretical Analysis with Special Reference to Education*, Columbia University Press.
    W.G. Bowen (1964): *Economic Aspects of Education: Three Essays*, Princeton University Press, Princeton.
12. J.R. Barro and Salai-Martin (1995): *Economic Growth*, McGraw-Hill, New York.
13. G. Psacharopoulous and M. Woodhall (1985): *Education for Development*, Oxford University Press, New York.

14. A. Amsden (1989): *Asia's Next Giant: South Korea and Late Industrialisation*, Oxford University Press, New York.
    R. Wade (1990): *Governing the Market: Economic Theory and the Role of the Government in East Asian Industrialization*, Princeton University Press, Princeton,
    World Bank (1993): *The East Asian Miracle*, World Bank, Washington D.C.
15. World Bank, (1999): *Knowledge for Development*, World Bank Report, World Bank, Washington DC.
16. R. Blundell, L. Dearden, C. Meghir and B. Sianesi (1999): 'Human Capital Investment', *Fiscal Studies*, vol. 20, no. 1, pp. 1-23.
17. Amartya Sen (1985): *Commodities and Capabilities*, Oxford University Press, Oxford.
18. Santosh Mehrotra (2005): 'Human Capital or Human Development?', *Economic and Political Weekly*, vol. 40, no. 4, January 22, pp. 300-405.
19. M. Piore and C. Sabel (1984): *The Second Industrial Divide: Possibilities of Prosperity*, Basic Books, New York.
20. Peter Cappelli (1999) (ed.), *Introduction in Employment Practices and Business Strategy*, Oxford University Press, New York.
21. Surjit Singh (2002): 'Education Skills and Training Some Perception', *Indian Journal of Labour Economics*, vol. 45, no. 4, pp. 1079-90.
22. D. Acemogul (1998): 'Why do New Technologies Complement Skills? Directed Technical Change and Wage Inequality', *Quarterly Journal of Economics*, vol. 113, pp. 1055-89.
23. P.K. Ray (2002): 'Decent Work in the Informal Sector: Training Issues', *Indian Journal of Labour Economics,* vol. 45, no. 4, pp. 1163-73.
    GOI (2001): *Report of the Working Group on Skill Development and Training*, New Delhi, Government of India.
    ILO (2000): 'Income Security and Social Protection in a Changing World', *World Labour Report,* 2000, ILO, Geneva.
24. G. Psacharopoulous and H.A. Patrinos (2002): 'Returns to Investment in Education: A Further Update', *Policy Research Paper 2881*, Washington DC, World Bank.
25. L. Deardel (1998): 'Ability, Family, Education and Earning in Britain', *Institute for Fiscal Studies - Working Paper,* no. 98/14.
    J.B.S. Tilak (2002): 'Education in Unequal World', in Monees Raza (ed.), *Educational Planning: A Long Term Perspective*, Concept Publishing Company, New Delhi.

26. J.S. Hammer (1996): 'The Public Economics of Education', *Draft for Comments, Public Economics Division*, Policy Research Department, World Bank, Washington.
27. UNDP (2001): Human Development Report 2001, Oxford University Press, Oxford.
28. Errol D'Souza (2002): 'Firm Nation and Training', *Indian Journal of Labour Economics*, vol. 45, no. 4, pp. 2134-43.
29. O.E. Williamson (1985): *The Economic Institution of Capitalism: Firms Markets and Relational Contracting*, Free Press New York, pp. 242-7.
30. Philip Brown, Andy Green and Hugh Lauder (2001): *High Skill*, Oxford University Press, Oxford.
31. W.W. Daniel (1987): *Workplace Industrial Relation and Technological Change*, Frances Printer and Policy Study Institute, London.
    R. Penn, M. Rose and J. Rubery (1994): *Skill and Occupational Change*, Oxford University Press, Oxford.
32. N. Millward (1994): *The New Industrial Relations*, Policy Studies Institute, London.
    N. Millward et al. (1992): *Workplace Industrial Relations in Transition*, Aldershot, Dartmouth.
33. D. Gallie and M. White (1993): *Employee Commitment and the Skill Revolution*, London: Policy Studies Institute.
    Duncan Gallie (1991): 'Patterns of Skill Change: Upskilling, Deskilling or the Polarization of Skills', *Work Employment and Society* 5 (3), pp. 319-51.
34. Duncan Gallie (2004): 'Skill Gender and the Quality of Employment, in the Recomposition of Skills and Employment', *Work Employment and Society* 4 (2), pp. 211-21.
35. UNDP (2001): *Making Technology Work for Human Development*, Oxford University Press, Oxford.
36. B.J. Silver (2003): *Forces of Labour*, Cambridge University Press, Cambridge.
37. Peter Drucker (1993): *Post Capitalist Society*, Harper, New York.
    David Harvey (1989): *The Conditions of Post Modernity: An Enquiry into the Origins of Cultural Change*, Basil Blackwell, Oxford, p. 186.
38. Manuel Castells and Yukio Aoyama (1997): 'Paths Towards the Informational Society: Employment Structure in G-7 Countries, 1920-1990', *International Labour Review* 133 (1), pp. 325-30.
39. Michael Hardt and Negri Antonio (2000): *The Empire*, Harvard University Press, Cambridge, MA, pp. 461-2.

40. J.H. Dreze and Henri Sneessens (1997): 'Technological Development, Competition from Low Wage Economies and Low Skilled Unemployment', in D.J. Snower and G. Dehesa (eds.), *Unemployment Policy*, Cambridge University Press, Cambridge.
41. H. Braveman (1974): *Labour and Monopoly Capital*, Monthly Review Press, New York.
    J. Zeitlin (1979): 'Craft Control and the Division of Labour: Engineers and Compositors in (1998): Britain 1890-1930', *Cambridge Journal of Economics* 3(3), September, pp. 263-74.
    B. Elbaum et al. (1979): 'The Labour Process, Market Structure and Marxist Theory', *Cambridge Journal of Economics* 3(3), September: pp. 227-30.
42. P. Doeringer and M.J. Piore (1971): *Internal Labour Markets and Manpower Analysis*, Heath and Co., Lexington, MA.
43. J. Storey (1995): *Human Resource Management: A Critical Text*, Routledge, London.
44. Stephen Hoare and A. Jolly (1999): *Skills and Training Handbook*, Directory Publishers Association.
45. Ibid.
46. G.S. Becker (1964): *Human Capital*, Chicago University Press, Chicago.
    G.S. Becker (1996): 'The Economic Way of Looking at Life', Nobel Lecture.
47. Paul Brown (1987): *Schooling Ordinary Kids: Inequality Unemployment and the New Vocationalism*, Routledge, London.
    G. Rees et al. (1997): 'History, Place and the Learning Society: Towards a Sociology of Life time Learning', *Journal of Education Policy*, 12/6, pp. 485-97.
48. R. Kuttner (2000): 'The Role of Government in Global Economy', in W. Hutton and A. Gidden (eds.), *On the Edge: Living with Global Capitalism*, Johnathan Cape, London.
49. W. Lazonick and M. O'Sullivan (2000): 'Maximizing Shareholder Value: The New Ideology for Corporate Governance', *Economy and Society Journal*, vol. 29, no. 1, pp. 13-35.
50. M. Albert (1993): *Capitalism against Capitalism*, Whurr Publishers, London.
51. D. FineGold and S. Soskice (1998): 'The Failure of Training in Britain: Analysis and Prescription', *Oxford Review of Economic Policy*, vol. 4, no. 3, pp. 21-53.
52. ILO (1998): 'Employability in the Global Economy and How

Training Matters', *World Employment Report 1998*, Bureau of Public Information, September, ILO, Geneva.
53. C. Johnson (1982): *MITI and the Japanese Miracle: Growth of Industrial Policy 1925-1982*, Stanford University Press, Stanford.
C. Johnson (1995): *Japan – Who Governs?: The Rise of Developmental Stage*, WW Norton, New York.
(1998): 'Economic Crisis in East Asia: the Clash of Capitalism', *Cambridge Journal of Economic*, 22, pp. 653-61.
54. www. nationalacademies. org
55. P. Kennedy (1993): *Preparing for the Twenty-first Century*, Random House, New York.
56. M. Granovetter and R. Swedberg (1994): *The Sociology of Economic Life*, Westview, Boulder, Colorado.
M. Best (1990): *The New Competition: Institutions of Industrial Restructuring*, Cambridge University Press, Cambridge.
57. H. Lauder (1999): 'Competitiveness and Low Skill Equilibrium: A Comparative Analysis', *Journal of Education and Work*, 12/3, pp. 281-94.
58. D. Ashton et al. (1996): *Work Skills in Britain*, Warwick University, Skope.
59. Wolfgang Streeck (1997): 'German Capitalism: Does Information Technology Exist, Can Information Technology Survive', *New Political Economy*, 2/2, pp. 237-53.
60. R. Dore (2000): *Stock Market Capitalism: Welfare Capitalism, Japan and Germany Versus the Anglo Saxon*, Oxford University Press, Oxford.
61. W. Streeck (1992): *Social Institutions and Economic Performance*, Sage, London.
62. D. Ashton and J. Sung (1994): *The State, Economic Development and Skill Formation: A New East Asian Model*, Centre for Labour Market Studies, University of Leicester.
63. Soon-Hie Kang et al. (2001): 'World Bank and ILO', in G. Betcherman and Rizwanul Islam (eds.), *East Asian Labour Markets*, pp. 126-37.
64. Thomas Friedman in *The Hindu*, 30 June 2005.
65. G.K. Chaddha (2004): 'Human Capital Base of the Indian Labour Market, Identifying Worry Spots', *Indian Journal of Labour Economics* vol. 47, no. 1, pp. 3-38.
66. Norman Gemmell (1996): 'Evaluating the Impacts of Human Capital Stock and Accumulation on Economic Growth: Some New Evidence', *Oxford Bulletin of Economics and Statistics*, Special Issue on Human Capital in Economic Development, vol. 58, no. 1, February.

67. A. Mathur and R.P. Mamgain (2004): 'Human Capital Stocks, their Levels of Utilization and Economic Development in India', *Indian Journal of Labour Economics,* vol. 47, no. 4, pp. 655-76.
68. Unni Jeemol and U. Rani (2004): 'Technical Change and Workforce in India: Skill Based Growth', *Indian Journal of Labour Economics* vol. 47, no. 4, pp. 683-92.
69. E. D'Souza (2004): 'Wage Disparity and Human Capital Accumulation', *Indian Journal of Labour Economics,* vol. 47, no. 4, pp. 677-82.
70. O.J. Blanchard (2004): 'Macroeconomic and Policy Implications of Shifts in Relative Demand for Skills', in D.J. Snower and G. Dehesa (eds.), *Globaliztion and Skills,* Cambridge University Press, Cambridge.
71. M.K. Datar (2004): 'Human Capital Approach and Indian Labour Market: The Case of Information Technology Industry', *Indian Journal of Labour Economics,* vol. 47, no. 4, pp. 825-32.
72. U. Rani (2004): 'Technology and Skill Transfer in Auto Component Firms of the National Capital Region', *Indian Journal of Labour Economics,* vol. 47, no. 4, pp. 1067-82.
73. N. Neetha (2004): 'Employment Conditions and Quality: A Study of Small Enterprises in NOIDA Export Promoting Zone', *Indian Journal of Labour Economics,* vol. 47, no. 4, pp. 1083-91.
74. GOI (1999): *Report: Ministry of Human Resource Development,* Dept. of Youth Affairs.
75. National Technical Manpower Information System (1998): *Annual Technical Manpower Reviews,* Institute of Applied Manpower Research, New Delhi.
76. GOI (2002-7): *Tenth Five Year Plan,* Government of India, chapter 2.4.
77. Rajendra Mamgain and Vandana Parashar (2000): 'Enhancing Employability of Youth Through Education and Training', *Indian Journal of Labour Economics,* vol. 43, no. 4, pp. 757-80
78. N. Neetha (2004): 'Education and Skill Development of Workforce in NOIDA Export Processing Zone', *Indian Journal of Labour Economics,* vol. 47, no. 2, pp. 269-80.
79. Eddy Lee (2001): *Export Promoting Zones and Industrial Employment in Asia,* ILO-ARTEP, Bangkok.
    Ashok Kundra (2000): *The Performance of India's Export Promoting Zones: A Comparison with the Chinese Approach,* Sage, New Delhi.
    Chanda P. Korgaonkar (1995): *Workers and Working Conditions in EPZs in India: A Case Study of SEEPZ,* INTUC, New Delhi.

80. ILO (1998): 'Employability in the Global Economy: How Training Matters', *World Employment Report 1998-99*, ILO, Geneva.
81. UNDP (1996): *Human Development Report 1996*, Oxford University Press, New York.
    ADB (1997): *Emerging Asia: Changes and Challenges*, ADB, Manila.
82. M. Pigato et al. (1997): *South Asia's Integration into the World Economy*, World Bank, Washington DC.
83. Vikram Chadha (2004): 'Changing Structure of Scientific and Technical Workforce in India's Industrial Sector', *Indian Journal of Labour Economics*, vol. 47, no. 3, pp. 281-92.
84. L.R. Amy (1964): 'Diversified Manufacturing Business', *Journal of Royal Statistical Society*, Series A, vol. 127.
85. GOI (2003): *Report of the Second National Commission on Labour*, Ministry of Labour.
86. ILO (1998): 'Employability in the Global Economy and How Training Matters' in *World Employment Report 1998-99*, Bureau of Public Information, ILO-Geneva.

CHAPTER 6

Correlates of Insecurity: Trade Unions

> The history of all countries shows that the working class exclusively by its own effort is able to develop only trade-union consciousness.
>
> V. LENIN

> Men don't and can't live by exchanging articles, but by producing them. They don't live by trade, but by work. Give up that foolish and vain title of Trades Unions; and take that of laborers Unions.
>
> JOHN RUSKIN

This chapter will explore the role of labour unions in the context of the insecurity hypothesis. It presumes that there is a correlation between the two. The weakening and erosion of trade unions is associated with rising insecurity. An indication of the nature of this correlation was made in the previous chapters. The survey undertaken in Chapter 3 sought information from employees about the state of the union and the range of its bargaining influence.

Section 6.1 describes the association between trade unions and insecurity (and reviews their evolution) in the context of restructuring in the developed countries. It puts forth records on falling trade union density in the OECD countries; and evaluates the theories that explain the role, relevance and the reinvention of trade unions respectively. Some discussion is devoted to the situation in the developing countries, and the strategies that trade unions have to consider for survival and expansion. Section 6.2 focuses on the trade union movement in India in the post-liberalization period while the next section, reviews the official thinking on the issue as evident in the report of the Second National Commission on Labour. Section 6.4 gives examples of how trade unions have been incorporated in social dialogues in Southeast Asian countries like Malaysia, Korea, and Thailand as a part of the strategy to recover from macro-economic crisis of 1997. This gives us some indication of the additional role that trade unions are capable of playing in the context of increasing insecurity and continual restructuring amidst globalization. Section 6.5 sums up the discussion.

6.1 Trade Unions, Insecurity and Restructuring

The effectiveness of worker trade unions is related directly to the worker-security it can nurture, as the unions influence both income and employment security. Insecure workforce needs organized protection that a formal union can provide, but periods of greater worker insecurity usually coincide with weakening of the trade unions. While union membership and coverage by collective bargaining have fallen in Britain, Australia, New Zealand, the USA, Germany and other countries, simultaneously, workers' vulnerability to assertive action by employers and exposure to hostile market forces increased. In Britain, available evidence indicates that episodes of employer de-recognition of trade unions have been followed by a decline in relative wages, greater use of contingent contracts and the imposition of managerial regime characterized by tighter surveillance, work intensification and closer scrutiny of individual employee performance.[1] While union decline may hasten the birth of an insecure workforce, the reverse may also be true and a shift towards more precarious and insecure employment may pose a serious threat to unions as insecure workers in categories like temporary contracts, part-time workers, self-employed are more difficult to organize and represent.[2]

The post-Second World War trend has been that unions are concentrated in large workplaces. Flexible work practices imply that workers get detached from a fixed workplace and workplaces become geographically fragmented. Besides, there are social and cultural issues since the divisions between secure and flexible workers are often based on social differences of race, sex and age, making the workforce more diverse and fragmented. On the other hand, this offers a new opportunity and challenge to the unions who historically have built their strength by struggles to regulate casual and piecework. This eventually made earnings and employment insecure in mines, docks and automobile industry in the UK and USA. Unions historically do have the successful experience of organizing the unorganized and giving them a voice and influence. The organized sector is so because of the momentous historical efforts of trade unions to regulate wages and benefits.

6.2 Trade Unions and Restructuring

With the restructuring of economies across the integrating globe have come major changes in labour organization in the industrial countries. In December 1985, the OECD reported that labour power as measured by union membership and strike activity had fallen to Second World War low in most countries.[3] In the developed countries, this reflected restructuring of employment, which most significantly started in the highly unionized heavy-industry sector. Rising unemployment accompanied this phase in all OECD countries.

Changes in the labour organization or trade unions were also a response to a considerable effort by conservative and liberal governments to weaken legislative and institutional support and to turn the public opinion against the prevalent trade union powers and roles. This also changed subjective perceptions of the workers about the changing circumstances like (a) factors like external competition, the pressure of falling profits triggered by globalization, slow economic growth and inflation were real and too strong to be resisted or accommodated without adjustments on their part, and (b) the trade unions would not be able to protect their interests or even maintain status quo.

The situation perhaps has changed a lot as far as the strength of trade unions to protect real income and job security of their members is concerned. According to the annual report of the Bank of International Settlements 2005, the correlation between core inflation (which excludes oil and food) and the growth in unit labour costs in the USA was nearly 0.8 per cent in 1965-79, and it had fallen to 0.3 per cent in 1991-2004.[4] The link between inflation and unit labour costs declined in other developed countries as well, most sharply in France from 0.78 to 0.1 per cent; in Japan from 0.98 to 0.5 and so on. This reflects two things: first, the integration into the world economy of China, India and other emerging economies with vast supplies of cheap labour has curbed the bargaining power of workers in the developed economies. These workers therefore find it harder to secure wage hikes when inflation picks up. Second, fierce competition has made it difficult for firms to pass on increases in wages through to consumers. Even increases in raw material costs are not easy to pass on but are more likely to show up in profit margin swings.

Such results have been corroborated by extensive empirical studies comparing NICs and OECD countries, which find a significant negative impact of internationalization on union bargaining power that influences the distribution of profits between workers and employers to the detriment of workers.[5]

During 25 years preceding 1985, the union strength had grown; wage and benefits were secured regularly. In several cases, bargaining was elevated from enterprise to industry level and this rationalized the system of collective bargaining. This was especially true in oligopolistic industries where price administration was possible. However, all this changed in the 1980s in the US and UK who were leading the economic restructuring. These changes eventually spread to the rest of Europe and the developing world within the next two decades. Industry-wide wage bargaining collapsed in the US and UK and reverted to company or plant level in the restructuring of the 1980s.[6] All the gains of the previous decades began to crumble as unions stood confused.[7] New approaches to industrial relations invented in the USA and called Human Resource Management, discussed in the previous chapter, were introduced and to the workers the change was presented as the new ideal of social partnership for growth and national competitiveness.

The unions made concessions to prevent threatened bankruptcy or to gain the promise of job security for the core of the workforce. The companies secured two-tier wage scales, one for core workers, and the other for the rest, i.e. contingent workers and subcontracts. New work rules enlarged the jobs by adding duties, restricting seniority considerations, and the new wage agreements endorsed wage cut, wage freeze or marginal rise. The unions remained useful to the industry for negotiating and implementing these concessions. By the end of the 1990s, it became evident to the workers that concession bargaining had become a pattern, but it did not assure job or income security.[8] In the 1980s, the management was demanding changes in most work rules from the duration of washroom breaks to bypassing of seniority. Most of the strikes, by the mid-1980s, were over changes in the work rules and against union-negotiated contracts. As the union membership fell through the two decades, the unions began to raid other union territories to sustain their status and income. The level of services provided by the national unions to local unions declined, protests and representations to government regulatory agencies diminished, and eventually the unions began their own staff layoff.

From 1980-4, USA, where restructuring originated, saw union membership among formally employed workers fall by 2.7 million. Only one-fifth of the labour force was unionized, down from a peak of 36 per cent in 1945. By 1994, the union density stood at 16 per cent; there had been a marked shift in American worker's attitude towards the unions.[9] In 1950, unions had won 73 per cent of the elections to organize new unions. By 1970, the figure had dropped to 58 per cent and by 1982 only 48 per cent agreed to unionize.

This phenomena was becoming continental as well, is evident in the observations of Trade Union Institute of Brussels (1984):[10] Somehow governments in western Europe, of whatever political hue and orientation, had now begun to feel that they ought to be tougher. Many of the problems would exist even if there were socialist governments in every capital because the economic crisis cannot be escaped. In the end, the critical consequence of the entire restructuring process in the developed world (and eventually in the developing world) has been, to reverse the position that the labour had attained over the preceding decades and call into question the

Table 6.1: Union Membership Density by Country 1960-99

(Members in thousands, Density as percentage)

	USA		*UK*		*Canada*		*Australia*		*New Zealand*	
	Member	*Density*	*Member*	*Density*	*Member*	*Density*	*Member*	*Density*	*Member*	*Density*
1960	18,117.0	31.4	9,437	44.0	1,459	32.3	1,912.4	58.0	332.4	38.0
1970	20,751.0	27.2	10,672	48.5	2,173	33.6	2,314.6	50.0	378.5	34.7
1980	20,095.3	23.0	12,239	54.5	3,397	37.6	2,952.1	55.0	516.3	39.4
1890	16,739.8	16.1	8,835	38.1	4,031	34.5	2,660.0	40.5	611.3	41.5
1999	16,477.0	13.9	7,257	29.5	3,600	30.0	1,878.2	25.7	302.4	17.0

Source: US Department of Labour, Bureau of Labour Statistics, Employment and Earning, Washington DC.

Notes:
1. The US union density data refers to all full/part-time workers who are members of a labour union or employee association as a percentage of all, full or part-time workers excluding self-employed workers.
2. By 1994, British unions represented only one-third of the work force. France was worse off at 10 per cent and other countries where unions faced depleting membership included Japan, Italy, Netherlands, etc.[11] Germany was better off.
3. Interestingly and broadly, but with poorer statistical support, economists have observed the same trends in India.

relevance of the trade unions. Table 6.1 sums this decline in Union membership in the last four decades of the twentieth century.

6.3 Are Trade Unions Still Relevant?

In a classic essay titled 'What are Trade Unions For' Flanders (1970) enlarged the role of trade union from its economistic definition as given by scholars like John Dunlop.[12] The purely economistic view, also known as the 'system approach' to the study of industrial relations, argued that just as the business sought to maximize the profit, so did the trade unions seek to maximize wages earned by its members. Flanders essayed that 'the unions, first and foremost, have to defend and if possible improve their members' terms and conditions of employment'. The overriding responsibility of all trade unions is the welfare of their own members and not just wages. That is their primary commitment.

A union collects members' contributions and demands their loyalty, especially for the purpose of protecting their interest, 'not their allegedly true or best interest as defined by others'. They have to defend and if possible improve their members' terms and conditions of employment. Rule-making and enforcement were as important to the worker's interests as were the pursuit of wages and better benefits. One of their principal purposes is regulation or control of work. It is to limit the power and authority of the employer, lessen the arbitrary will of the management and reduce the impact of market fluctuations on the employees. The effect of rules made by collective bargaining is to establish and clarify rights with their corresponding obligations. The unionism has to expand and promote industrial/economic democracy. Trade unionism for Clegg (1960, 1979) was a system of opposition. One of the central principles of modern democracy is that concentration of power is to be feared so much that opposition must be positively encouraged.[13] In this task of promoting economic-industrial democracy, Clegg found the union's customary role to be far from satisfactory.

Unions are a mixture of a movement and organization. They came in to existence because of a sense of common purpose and a need to move towards that common interest. In order to survive and realize their goal the unions had to find expression through an organization without which the working class could not be held together to work consistently. Contradictions emerge once a hierarchical organization is established. It becomes homeostatic, somewhat forgetful of the purpose of the movement that imparted the seminal impetus to organize, and by now unable to adapt rapidly to circumstances. Unlike business organizations, trade unions cannot purchase the compliance of its members through monetary rewards, but only by renewing the movement. Quoting Flanders, 'Trade unions need organization for their power and movement for their vitality, but they need both power and vitality to advance their social purpose.' The issues that could have provided impetus to the movement were issues of furthering industrial democracy, participation of workers in management, and the terms and conditions of employment for all types of employees. However, the trade unions historically have been found to be too preoccupied in negotiating wage increases to be able to focus on the movement or even the organization of the unorganized sectors of the economy. This is true in developed and developing countries.

For the Marxist-Leninists, organization of the workers into trade unions is also a matter of ideology besides movement and organization. The movement is to explore and ultimately find the common interest of the entire working class in the overthrow of capitalism. Marx urged in a resolution passed in the International Workingmen Association,

> in addition to their original task, the trade unions must learn how to act consciously as focal points for organizing the working classes in the greater interest of their complete emancipation. They must support every social and political movement directed towards this aim... [By doing so] the trade unions succeed in rallying around themselves, all workers still outside their rank. They must convince the whole world that their efforts are far from narrow or egoistic....

For the purposes of organization the trade unions have to carry out their daily battle, enroll members, create organizational resources, build formal structures, communication system, and fight for better working conditions and better wages. Sectionalism and economism were the underlying features of trade union consciousness and even Lenin recognized this. Elaborating his views in a pamphlet, 'What is to be Done' he says that: history of all countries shows that the working class exclusively by its own efforts is able to develop only trade union consciousness, i.e. the necessity for combining as unions, in order to fight or restrain the employer and to try to persuade the government to pass necessary legislation.

In the post-globalization period, the answer by some influential industrial relation scholars, to the question 'what the trade unions are for', has been opposite; they call the unions 'social partners'.[14] In practice, this forms the basis of HRM and this represents a shift from opposition to accommodation as a pragmatic response to pressure. Here a distinction must be made between the traditions of social partnership in the social market of Sweden and Germany and the new Anglo-Saxon variety. In the former countries, it is a partnership embedded in the all the institutions of social market economy, but on the other hand Anglo-Saxon experience of social partnership at best has been very mixed. There has been a growing reaction to the gap between the promises and practices of HRM; where job enrichment becomes job enlargement, multi-skilling becomes multi-tasking, lean production becomes mean production, teamwork becomes peer control, and creativity becomes sophisticated standardization. Social scientists have documented these aspects well.[15]

A second post-globalization view of the role of trade union takes its cue from the developments in countries like Brazil, South Africa, Philippines and is known as social movement unionism. In this view trade union must imbibe the spirit of the movement and connect with it through building social alliances with other movements for human rights, social justice, environment, and democracy. Social movement unionism is autonomous from capital, state and political parties; setting its own agenda from its own perspective, yet willing to consider modifying its perspective on the basis of negotiations with its allied social movements.[16] As the experience of countries, particularly Latin American countries, unfolded in the 1990s, it became clear that social movement unionism brings renewed strength and energy to unions. It also encounters realities of strong interdependence between social, economic and political ideologies – a reality that is often missed by academics. It encounters the need to negotiate new political equations and equilibrium. The facts of class interest and class struggle reinvent themselves; the political agenda of the worker class is executed within the framework of and as a constituent of successful social movement unionism.

To summarize three social contributions of the trade unions emerge:

1. They play economic role of facilitating production and ensuring equitable distribution of the value added. This is achieved mainly through collective bargaining and negotiations at various levels of enterprise, industry and nation. They also provide special services to members of the union, e.g. representing workers in the grievance procedures and embracing broader agendas like mutual aid to members, skill training, credit, insurance, social security, housing, health care, leisure and recreation, retirement and other non-wage benefits of employment. A remarkable case is that of the trade union 'Histadrut' of Israel, which provides health care that covers almost the entire population.[17]
2. They play the democratic and representative role of providing a voice and identity to labour at the workplace and society at large, achieved mainly through representing workers at all levels of enterprise, industry, economy and giving voice to the labour view.[18] The experience of the developed countries suggests that union-capacity for mobilization has a synergetic effect on the development of democracy.[19] Unions have consolidated their political space and in the process shaped institutions that govern the labour market and even the political system.[20] Particularly notable has been the role of Korean trade unions in forging political democracy; their social role of nurturing social cohesion by involving workers in democratic processes, and in shaping institutions which promote solidarity among workers and cooperation with employers.[21]

3. They use their political space to build a social contract, which sets the terms of compromise between the capital, state and the labour in sharing the national product.[22] They also serve as an anchor for broad-based social movements, which give voice to societal concerns about democratic and human rights.

6.4 Decline and Reinvention of Trade Unions

According to some commentators, the late twetieth-century workforce was in the throes of drastic transformation, which represented a fundamental shift in social consciousness away from traditional, class-conscious collectivism of the industrial workers towards the self-interested individualism of the skilled, mobile, career-centred white-collar worker.[23] For the new workforce, traditional trade unions, their structures and practices must be abandoned. Refuting these premises based on inadequate understanding of theory of collectivism, John Kelly (1998) developed an alternative theory about the future of trade unions.[24] His theoretical framework is an adaptation of the work of Charles Tilly and Douglas Macadam's mobilization theory. The mobilization theory allows an analysis of the processes by which workers acquire a collective definition of their interests in response to employer-generated injustice.

The perception of injustice leads to the defining of interest. This involves a cognitive transfer from a belief in the legitimacy of the status quo to a sense of injustice and a conviction that an event or action of the situation is illegitimate or wrong. A sense of injustice causes a social group to coalesce with a collective interest. It encounters the need to negotiate new political equations and equilibriums. The facts of class interest and class struggle reinvent themselves; the political agenda of the worker class is executed within the framework of and as a constituent of successful social movement unionism. There are three critical processes in this: attribution, social identification, and leadership.

It is of essence that an aggrieved individual blames an agency for his/her problem, rather than attribute them to unknown or uncontrollable forces or events. Social identification is a process by which people develop a sense of a group with shared interests and values. Attribution is an explanation for an action or an event in terms of causes, reasons, etc. It imposes structure on the world and our experiences. At the same time, it satisfies a basic human need for cognitive parsimony.[25] Leadership plays a catalytic role in the processes of attribution and social identity. Tilly goes on to develop the concept of mobilization further into five components – interest definition, organization, mobilization, opportunity, and action. Mobilization, then, depends upon the sharpness of interest definition, the degree of organization, and the costs and benefits of taking action. Organization is a quantitative as well as a qualitative phenomenon. For example, the total size of the trade union movement is measured in terms of membership and density and the number of structural properties like number of workplace organizations, number of stewards, steward member ratio, etc., but all this tells you very little about the willingness of the organized workers to act collectively. Opportunity is the next component of Tilly's framework. The policies and actions of the employers and the state create the opportunity for collective action. Industrial research is full of evidence on how the authoritarianism of the employer in different forms, e.g. unfair dismissal, imposition of new work practices, curtailment of pay and entitlements, unilateral change in collective bargains, shifts in balance of power between employer and employee have provided opportunities to mobilize for collective action. Collective action takes many forms besides strike, such as overtime ban, non-cooperation, go slow, work to rule, petitions, collective appeals, lobbying, etc.

Kelly's prediction, based on mobilization and theory of long wave, is that trade unions will survive and reinvent themselves as long as the objective conditions exist. He sees no evidence of diminishing rate of exploitation of the working class, or lessening conflict of class interests in the process of globalization. He draws on the long-wave-theory to construct a historical account of alternating periods of worker mobilization and employer counter-mobilization linked to Kondratieff's (1999) long waves or upswings and downswings in the economy.[26] The transition period between the upswings and the downswings are marked by unusually intense and wide-ranging class struggle, resulting in rupture of existing institutions. Restructuring of productive forces, class relations and the recomposition of the working class characterize long downswings. This is quantified as decline in worker collectivism or trade unionism.

Kelly may be right for there is increasing evidence of revival of trade unions and their successful adaptations. There are two aspects of revival of trade unions, (a) the renewed organizational drive of the old unions, and (b) the emergence of new structures in the informal sectors of the economy. Globalization has induced a convergence in the circumstances of organized labour across the globe. Many unions and national labour movements are experiencing similar situations. With improved communications and travel, the last decade has witnessed growing linkages and consultations, especially amongst the OECD and Anglo-Saxon unions, sharing experiences, ideas and strategies across borders. There have been mergers of unions to consolidate and expand services offered to the union members. Amongst the most popular ideas is the mission of intensive membership-recruitment drive. Members are encouraged and trained to take responsibility for solving their own problems at the local level and to take an active role in extending union membership. The training for self-sufficiency, creativity, and workplace activism is imparted to every member.

This is the bottom-up union building strategy, which is distinct from the older service model, where paid union staff and full-time officials solved problems for the workers. They would channel union management problems through formal and legalistic processes. The service model was top-down and needed a lot of union resources. The new organization model has generated intense interest over the future strategies of the unions.[27] Many are allocating resources into organization. Observers of the labour movement find evidence of resurgence in Australia, New Zealand, and the USA.

In 1998, for the first time in decades, the American unions enrolled as many new members as were lost from lay-offs, plant closures, contracting out, and de-certifications. Service Employees International Union (SEIU) in California unionized 74,000 homecare workers. Hotel and restaurant employee unions in Los Vegas organized 10,000 workers. The Communication Workers of America organized 26,000 airline reservations agents. The above are recent examples from America. The American labour movement at the turn of the century offers some examples in renewal.[28] American unions have recently won major victories on issues such as minimum wages and restrictions on company unions. This was the result of grassroot education, mobilization of members, and community allies. Then, there were a series of bargaining victories against powerful corporations like Verizon, Boeing, UPS, Continental Tyres, and Kaiser Aluminium. A new wave of activism in the interest of labour is focusing on anti-sweat shop campaigns and other labour issues, and this has spread to university campuses. The media has noticed it and given it prominent coverage for the first time in decades.

Job loss and employment insecurity was a major political issue in the US presidential campaign in 2004. In 2006, immigrant workers, supposedly illegal but employed across the economy brought the country to a halt on May Day as they protested and stayed away from work for a day. These are signs that globalization is creating new opportunities for trade unionism. Trade Unions played a supportive and enabling role in the American chapter of the Occupy Wall Street Movement in 2011, just as they have been supporting the rise of left formations in Greece and Spain.

In another important observation made on trade union role in the twenty-first century, the authors maintain that membership and density are not the only measures of union strength.[29] As they say in the political arena, an organized minority can become a majority. Union presence and influence can go beyond its numerical size. It depends on many factors like what unions do in addition to pure wage bargaining, coverage of collective bargaining in terms of issues, extent of coordinated bargaining across various sectors of the economy, the extension of coverage of collective agreements to non-unionized firms and members, the involvement of unions in policy making, and implementation of welfare schemes, its interaction with the welfare state, the institutional framework within which unions function. All these can make a qualitative difference to the power of unions as can be seen even today while comparing Europe with USA.

The union's role in insecure work environment will be greater not lesser, but, their methods of organization, their concerns, issues and demands raised by them will have to develop. A new agenda being proposed is the one related to training and investment in workforce to build competency and productivity. Some evidence of that comes from the TUC in Britain.

6.5 The Situation in Developing Countries after Globalization

In the formative years of trade unionism, similar earlier movements in the developed countries inspired movements in the developing countries, and were strongly influenced by the ideological currents which dominated the political debate in the twentieth century. Eventually the movements had to deal with the objective conditions in their own countries. They adapted and sometimes invented new organizational structures and practices.

Globalization has made an impact on the workers and their organization in the developing countries. The earliest manifestations of this were in the newly industrialized countries of East and Southeast Asia. The state had assumed a developmental role and built paternalistic industrial relations. In Korea, Malaysia and Singapore policy measures were designed to insulate export-led economic-growth strategy from wage pressures. Legislation and executive mechanisms were preferred to collective bargaining by independent unions. Enterprise unionism model was copied from developed countries as an appropriate form of representation of workers' interest.

The build-up of competitive pressures both in the domestic and international markets led to the adoption of neo-liberal economic policies. The break from paternalistic relations and the social pact of the state with the trade union led to increased labour militancy as a reaction against breach of trust. On the other hand, business leaders in the private sector made repeated calls for flexible labour market and removal of legislation protecting labour.

Elsewhere in the developing world, for instance India, the recent decades have witnessed a shift away from an inward looking economic strategy and a break from the socialistic pattern of economic development where the state had occupied the commanding-heights of the economy. New economic policies made their appearance in the mid-1980s and the transition continued through the 1990s. These policies had disturbing consequences for growth of employment and the labour markets, posing immense challenges for the trade union movement.

The challenges faced by the unions in India and other developing countries had some common features: (a) changing labour-management relations, with enterprise managers turning to HRM policies which subvert the unions. HRM being a distinctive approach to employment management seeks to achieve competitive advantage through the strategic employment of highly committed and capable workforce using an integrated array of cultural, structural and personnel techniques, (b) decentralized production carried out in geographically-dispersed small- or medium-sized facilities.[30] Decentralization of production crosses national boundaries, as also the margins between unorganized and organized sectors, in search of lower labour costs and higher profits. The global mobility of capital makes unionization difficult, (c) rising wage disparity based on skill levels and location has fragmented worker solidarity, (d) changing levels of state commitment to protecting the interests of labour, under the influence of neo-liberal policies, and global institutions like the World Bank, the IMF and WTO, (e) Trade union strength weakened across the spectrum as evident in their declining membership, resources, ability to service their members and influence their employers or the state.

The union movements in the developing countries are, despite the setback in the recent decades, reinventing themselves to survive. Their strategies are broadly similar to their counterparts in the developed world; they hinge on building their membership base, changing the union structures to reach out to geographically dispersed member base, organizing the informal sector in more suitable new structures, building broad alliances with other unions, and progressive social movements to resist attacks on their democratic and representative rights.

The response of TUs to the new objective conditions is summed up in three sets of issues.

6.5.1 *Building Membership Base*

Webster and Adler (2001) observe that all over the world unions are surrounded by greater liberalization of economic and political regimes, and these two developments offer opportunities for new rules of the game and new roles for key social actors – organized labour, community organizations, governments and business.[31] The ability of unions to emerge as key players, however, depends on their mobilization and organizational ability. To include the middle class more comprehensively where a divergence of interests has taken place due to changes in technology and conspicuous individualism, i.e. highly-skilled professionals, white-collared workers, women workers and informal-sector workers. In adverse circumstances, special strategies for traditional constituents like protection of social security, decent working conditions, legal and advisory assistance, credit support, and most significantly, involvement in skill and career development of traditional constituents is important.

On the other hand, casual workers fall into two categories: high skill and high education who choose to take up part-time work, and, the low-skill, low-income category which has a large component of immigrants, women and service-sector workers. Though this group is too heterogeneous in its occupations and interests, it lives in and around the same neighbourhood. Hence, community-based action for civic or other needs led by unions are suitable here. Latin America has had much experience in this form of organizing union activity.

6.5.2 *Changing Union Structures*

Bargaining is shifting out to decentralized production units. There is an inverse relationship between the cost of unionizing and collective action on the one hand and the size of the enterprise on the other. Small unions are weak and highly vulnerable.[32] The possibilities of organizing on an industry-wide or occupational basis have to be explored continuously. It is also important not to allow the separation of the bargaining and voice functions of the trade unions. The voice function is their political role and connection without which they will eventually be unable to influence policies or intervene in the democratic process.

6.5.3 *Initiating Collective Action for Institutional Benefit*

Union ability to deliver outcomes favourable to the working class depends a good deal upon the legal and regulatory institutions of the labour market. To build institutional capacity the unions have to work towards the objectives of creating legislative provisions for minimum wages, social security, job security, unemployment insurance, severance package, health care, pension and provident fund schemes, multi-employer agreements on hours of work, holidays, wages, non-wage benefits, and so on.

Building democratic institutions, enforcing human rights, enforcing redistributive justice, and correcting inequalities by building broad social coalitions are the critical democratic role of TUs. The voice of the trade unions in social and political affairs will be strengthened by these coalitions. This can be seen in the impact of the Asian, European, and World Social Forums on the media, masses and social consciousness. The organizing backbones of these events in Latin America, India, and Europe have been such broad coalitions of trade unions and civil society special interest groups.

Contentions about the state of world labour are based on assumptions about the impact of contemporary globalization on workers' bargaining power. Silver (2003) makes a powerful case about the possibilities for revival of labour power in the twenty-first century albeit in different geographical locations, among new classes and new industries across the globe.[33] The basis of the prognosis is the evidence based on 135 years of recorded labour unrest and capitalist resistance that have followed a cyclical pattern in history. According to Silver, a useful starting point for differentiating types of workers' bargain power is Erik Olin Wright's distinction between associational and structural power. Associational power consists of the various forms of power that result from the collective organization of workers, most importantly trade unions and political parties. Structural power consists of the power that accrues to workers simply from their location in the production system. Structural power is of two types: market bargaining power that results directly from tight labour markets, and workplace bargaining power that results directly from the strategic location of particular group of workers within a key industrial sector. Marketplace bargaining power can take several forms: (1) the possession of scarce skills that are needed by the employers, (2) low levels of general unemployment, and (3) the ability of workers to pull out of the labour market entirely and survive on non-wage sources of income. Workplace bargaining power on the other hand accrues to workers who are enmeshed in tightly integrated production processes where localized work stoppage in a key node can cause stoppage on a wide scale.

Those who see globalization as bringing about a terminal crisis of labour movement perceive the weakening of all forms of workers' power to bargain. On the one hand labour marketplace bargaining has been undermined by the mobilization of a world-scale reserve army creating a global glut, and the spread of capitalist agriculture and manufacture which has reduced the scope of non-wage sources of income and increased the size of the proletariat. By weakening the sovereignty of the state, globalization has led to the reduction in the associational bargaining power of labour. Historically, associational bargaining power has been embedded in the state's legal framework that guarantees rights to form trade unions and bargain collectively, enjoy institutional social security nets, and regulated labour markets. Labour's workplace bargaining power has been weakened by post-Fordist transformations in the organization of production and labour processes. Vertical disintegration/fragmentation of production, subcontracting, etc., are all indications of reversals of workplace bargaining power.

However, Silver provides a historical perspective when she examines labour forces over 130 years, both associational and structural, in leading industries. How labour's associational and structural power rose as industry grew, waned when it relocated and grew again as the trade unions followed by organizing themselves in different industries and different geographical locations. Hence, the déjà vu story in the textile industry in the second half of the nineteenth century, the automobile industry in the first half of the twentieth, followed by the microprocessor industry, the education industry and the vast personal services industry in the late twentieth century.[34] The tendency of capital to innovate and concentrate in the first world was followed by the creation and strengthening of a new working class. Its tendency to resist forces of labour, domestic competition, and declining rates of profit attracts it to the Second and Third World, where again new working classes are created and strengthened. The relocation of capital or spatial fix from existing sites of production tends to weaken established working classes. With the new entrants, the industrial labour unrest reappears and capital is forced into new product, technological and organizational fixes. Labour has shown an ability to gradually respond to these fixes by new strategies where weakened associational or workplace bargaining is dealt with by changing forms of association, i.e. from workplace unions to community unions or associations with other unions, social forces of resistance, political parties and so on. New opportunities of workplace bargaining can be exploited, for example, in the JIT inventory organization, fragmentation of production, and in search for new economies of scale by producers of products and services, centrality of transport, information and communication systems in the new methods of organization and so on. Silver finds some evidence for a trend towards overall strengthening of labour's workplace bargaining power. Also, there is evidence of increasing general strike actions from across the globe during 2004-5.[35] Some of these were: Italy on 30 November 2004 by three trade union confederations to protest against the government's neo-liberal economic and financial policies; South Korea, 1 April 2005, in which 16,800 workers participated in a four-hour warning strike protesting the use of temporary workers and in support of their rights; South Africa 27 June 2005, by the main trade union confederation COSATU to protest high rate of unemployment and job losses; 26 January 2005 by the Greek trade union confederation, GSEE, in which a million workers took part against flexible working hours and changes in payment for overtime work; India, 29 September 2005, general strike by the public-sector employees and other TU confederations who struck against proposed privatization of pensions, use of contract workers, and lack of pay revision. Again, a general strike was called against anti-worker policies of the government on 14 December 2006. France 4 October 2005, against privatization and changes in labour laws to allow small firms to hire and fire workers at will, and Belgium 7 October 2005, against anti-working-class policies. After a gap of over three decades, the United Auto Workers Union served notice on General Motors to strike work at all its 80 plants in December 2007, if its demands for wage settlement were not met.

Francis Piven and Richard Cloward blame the transformation of the discursive environment for the losses of the labour movement. The idea of power itself has been an important source of worker power.[36]

Mobilization over the past century has been fuelled by the belief that workers do indeed have power and their power can be used effectively to transform their working conditions and life for better. What globalization has done is to puncture this century-old belief in worker power, deflate popular political morale and the willingness to struggle for change. Such shifts in workers' beliefs at one level mirror the shifts in the real bargaining power of workers, but at another, they are a psychological response to the changing world, which can and will be overcome with new experiences of resistance.

6.6 The Situation in India

The New Economic Policy (NEP) announced by the government in 1991 consolidated and reinforced the process of restructuring which began in the 1980s. The repercussions brought about by the process had already rendered thousands of workers jobless, expanded the enclaves of unprotected labour, and weakened the trade unions.[37]

Using data from the NSSO surveys, 50th and 55th rounds, economists have indicated that there is a weakening of the spread of unions and a decline in their membership during the period of globalization. The state has been party to the process of disempowerment of labour. Across the globe, essentially similar processes have been ascendant although at varying speeds in different regions. The pace of change reflects the diverse institutional structures in different regions that mediate the process of globalization.[38]

The economic reforms had freed industry from bureaucratic control, but it also pushed up the level of competition, put an end to protected assured markets, captive customers and easy profits. Employers reacted by demanding an exit policy which would give them freedom to hire and fire. They claimed that the Indian laws on employment security were among the most stringent in the world. They alleged that the Industrial Dispute Act 1948 put many hurdles in closing down loss-making enterprises and unprofitable operations. Government permission to close down was seldom given; even conditions of service were difficult to alter, since the employers were required to serve a three-week notice of change; employment in permanent category could not be terminated as being unnecessary or redundant and permission for retrenchment of workers rendered surplus by new technology, plant relocation, and declining demand for product and services was seldom given. These restrictions generated so-called rigidities in the labour market, which management had to circumvent by hiring only temporary or contract workers, sub-contracting, offering VRS and in some unscrupulous cases, the employers abandoned the plants after stripping them bare.[39] These manoeuvres of management had become very common in the late 1980s and through 1990s. So, while it is true that governments have failed to bring about necessary labour laws, which would allow flexible use of labour in the face of international competition, the fact is that it allowed the employers to get away with many changes, which Bardhan calls 'reforms by stealth'.[40] As he says, Indian labour laws especially regarding job security are amongst the most stringent in the world on paper, and several attempts to change the laws have been met with enormous opposition. Yet, in practice, employers have got away with many changes, e.g. many workers have been pushed out under the so-called VRS with or without legal compensation. There has been widespread use of contract or casual labour, substitution of regular labour via task redefinition, many units have been closed and relocated in backward areas through subterfuge without compensation, and large-scale outsourcing and subcontracting to small units and in backward areas. Other researchers, discussed earlier in detail, have given evidence of de facto 'flexibility' in India; have also pointed to the same trend for increasing use of atypical employment even within the premises of the firm, which is reflected in the employment statistics of the NSSO, etc.[41]

Hence while mainstream economists have concentrated on the strength of organized labour and rigidity of labour markets, using selective aggregate statistics, other sociological and inter-disciplinary studies based on desegregations and fieldwork have dwelt on the ineffectiveness of labour laws in India due to poor implementation and the inability of workers to get justice in courts and labour departments. These problems only become more acute in the absence of strong trade unions.[42]

So, in spite of the clamour of the associations of industry, the Narasimha Rao government, which initiated the economic reform, did not come up with an exit policy. It would have been a social and political disaster to put at risk the employment of millions without a safety net. Instead, the government created a National Renewal Fund to be used to rehabilitate surplus labour by imparting useful skills. But in effect, the money was used to finance voluntary retirement in the public sector. The organized labour had the political clout to stall changes in public policy regarding labour, but since the public policy had not changed overtly, organized labour response was at best defencive or confused. Even though all the trade unions irrespective of their political affiliation expressed opposition to the NEP-1991 as being anti-working class, the NEP was indeed implemented.[43] Some weaknesses of the organized labour movement in this period became evident.[44] In this phase employer actions reduced the permanent workforce, shifted the bulk of production to ancillary units, and employed casual, contract or other forms of unprotected labour. Union membership declined, and an atmosphere of job insecurity among workers curtailed militant trade union action as indicated in Table 6.2.

An analysis of the incidence and duration of strikes from 1961 onwards reveals that the total number of strikes doubled from 1,240 in 1961 to a total of 2,478 in 1971, and then peaked in 1973. The trend thereafter was downward. The yearly average is high by international standards.[45] The reasons for this according to the authors are multiple. First, lack of stringent definition of legal strike and due notice to employers; second, multiplicity of unions in the organized sector and inter-union rivalries; third, lack of a well-developed arbitration mechanism and discretionary involvement of the government. Overall, the 1960s was marked by the concepts of socialism, egalitarianism and the respect for collective bargaining, and these were conducive to the growth of union power. By the 1970s, the industrial landscape changed. The emergence of large business houses, tilt of the state in favour of higher growth and away from cumbersome regulations led to the intensification of

Table 6.2: Industrial Disputes in the Organized Sector

(Man-days lost in thousands)

Year	*Strikes*	*Lock-outs*	*Total*
1985	11,487	17,753	29,240
1986	18,824	13,925	32,746
1987	14,026	21,332	35,358
1988	12,530	21,417	33,947
1989	10,700	21,960	32,660
1990	10,640	13,450	24,090
1991	3,540	6,200	9,740

Source: R. Nagraj (2004): 'Fall in Organized Manufacture Sector Employment', *EPW*, 24 July.

struggle between capital and labour. In this period, the durations of strikes became longer with a quarter of the strikes lasting three weeks or more, and nearly half of the strikes lasting more than five days. Only 30 per cent of the strikes lasted for less than one day in the 1960s. As the trend towards deregulation was carried forward in the mid-1980s, the face of industrial disputes changed, longer strikes became the norm and shorter strikes became sparse. This has been analysed as rising employer militancy. In 1995, 68.67 per cent of the industrial disputes resulted in strikes and 31.33 per cent in lock-outs. By 2000, strikes caused 55.25 per cent of the disputes and lock-outs resulted from 44.75 per cent of the disputes. In the period after 1991, the frequency of strikes declined, the long-duration strikes fell marginally, and the short-duration strikes increased. The number of lock-outs on the other hand increased. Trade unions found themselves in a new situation of rising rates of unemployment, employee militancy, decline of the old industries and growth of new ones, growing use of contract labour, and rising international competition. The man-days lost due to strikes also fell steadily, while those from lock-outs increased.

There is, however, a controversy about the loss of union membership in India. One group of researchers has used data on union density from 1980-97 to argue that there has been a decline in union density in all countries.[46] In India, China, and Philippines union decline has occurred even when the percentage employment in industry has increased. Bhattacharjee endorses this estimation and uses the decline in number of unions submitting returns to the central government, the level and coverage of bargaining and state-level data to declare union decline.[47] On the other hand, Sengupta (2003) quotes claimed union membership and verified membership of central trade unions to assert that there is no evidence of declining membership. Registered unions showed an increasing trend throughout the period 1961 to 1996, though the rate of growth had slowed down compared to the period 1980-9.[48] So, the weakness of the unions in the 1990s cannot be ascribed to loss of membership.

The second weakness in the trade union movement came from its deeply fragmented nature and division along political lines, with each having a number of factions within. To compound the fragmentation was the growth of caste welfare associations and factions within the unions due to the reservation policies and the dynamics of caste politics. The fragmentation was a result of many factors including the small size of the average enterprise in India and the competition among political parties to capture the loyalties of workers. One of the consequences of these small-sized unions was their poor financial health. Since the subscriptions to unions is low compared to wages drawn by the workers and international standards, the finances of unions often do not permit long-term research, planning and mobilizations. That often results in high mortality rates.[49] The working class was fragmented through the introduction of new technologies into high and low skill segments, where the high-skill equated itself with the middle class in terms of aspirations. Feminization of the workforce also took place. In the organized sector, the urban, educated middle-class women joined public and private sector employment with a distinctive indifference to union activities. This could be a result of family pressures as a wife, mother, housekeeper or the double income status of the family.[50]

Third, the enterprise-level unions that grew in the 1980s were atomized and narrow in their vision, relied on professional collective bargainers who had no long-term commitment to the union-causes, and efforts to bring them under one umbrella had not been successful because of their lack of a common ideology. While the political unions were more interested in larger issues of ideology, growth of employment, and influence by national and political issues, and bureaucratic behaviour, the enterprise-level unions were non-affiliated and viewed trade unions in terms of benefits, i.e. purely in instrumental terms. This growth of militant unions or selfish unions, as Bhattacharjee (1987) calls them, lost public support for the union movement for a while.[51]

Holmstorm (1978) attributes this phenomenon to basic socio-economic circumstances in India such as the deeply fragmented working-class easily divisible on caste and religious lines, slow rate of growth of the economy, and even slower growth rate of organized-sector employment compared to the growth of workforce in the context of widening inequalities and conspicuous consumption, which made the new generation of workers, particularly service sector employees, more focused on their own security, benefits and middle-class aspirations.[52]

Fourth, the central trade union organizations had been slow to respond to the changing economic environment and relied excessively on protest and agitation in a situation where political support was not available. The rapid growth of foreign investment in India, especially the entry of MNCs, and their ability to hold more than 50 per cent equity in their Indian subsidiaries introduced a new and more aggressive management style for which the trade unions were unprepared.

Effectiveness of the MNC strategy is demonstrated by the case of Hindustan Lever, which during the 1980s completely relocated two major production centres from Mumbai and Kolkata to industrially backward regions where no trade unions existed. In the new plants they employed a small permanent force and a large number of temporary and contract workers, adopted flexible work practices, paid lower wages closely tied to performance and worked a seven-day week with a staggered holiday for everyone. They built up a vast network of sub-contractors. Once these strategies were in place, Hindustan Lever decided to undermine the federation of Lever union in Mumbai and Kolkata with ruthless tactics and eventually managed to reduce the labour force in the Mumbai plant from 4,000 in 1970 to 1,700 by the mid-1990s, and their drive to reduce labour force is continuing. In October 2005, the company was in the courts defending the process of relocation for its last soap-making factory from Mumbai. It offered a golden handshake to its employees who accepted it, and paid nothing to the members of the trade union who had resisted closure in the same factory – an all-out attempt to deal a death blow to the union.

Fifth, the central organizations neglected training of rank and file, membership drives, and bringing the vast unorganized sector into their fold (which employed 290 million workers, i.e. 91.5 per cent of the employed).

Lastly, the central organizations had stagnated in their measures to promote internal democracy, information gathering, processing, and research, which are critical arsenal in changing times. As Ramaswamy and Schiphorst (2000) argued, 'Adversity, low levels of membership participation in the union, low standards of internal democracy, seem not only to go well together but actually reinforce each other'.[53]

Research would have revealed that the NEP portended serious long-term consequences for the growth of employment in organized sector and serious consequences for the health of trade unions. While some of the post-1991 changes have increased labour market flexibility, they have not increased labour demand, and, if anything there seems to be a distinct increase in unemployment rates in the 1990s, as discussed in Chapter 1. Some macro-indications of union strength can also be imputed from the fact that over the period 1980-97 registered manufacturing earnings per man hour for which firm-level data is available had grown at 1.5 per cent per annum, while gross value added grew at a much faster rate and labour productivity grew at a rate in multiple of wage increase. The unions were unable to secure favourable redistribution beyond a point. Unit wage costs have been going down since the mid-1970s. A steady decline in centralized, industry-wise and region-wise collective bargaining has become evident. A steady shift has occurred in manufacturing employment towards smaller-size factories within the organized sector, which employ less than 100 workers and where unions do not have a significant presence or bargaining power. Declines in the registered manufacturing sector, along with a rise in informal-sector employment, all have significant portent for union survival. Nagraj (1994) has referred to a decline in strength of trade unions using various standards.[54] It should have prompted an urgent need for adopting new strategies to regain relevance and effectiveness. To do so, unions need to innovate on both the organizational front and methods of protest to be able to draw more public-attention and attract into their folds unorganized sections of the workforce.[55] Had evidence from Latin American countries, which had undergone structural adjustment programmes, been interpreted by Indian unions, it would have presented trends and strategies. All the Latin American countries experienced growth in unemployment in the post-liberalization period. From 1980-4, average rates of unemployment went up from 7 to 11 per cent. In Chile, Columbia, Peru and Venezuela there was a 50-100 per cent increase in unemployment. In India, according to projections made by the economist Sudipto Mundle (1991-2), the official NSSO unemployment rate was likely to jump from 4 per cent in 1991-2, to 5 per cent 1992-3, to 6.3 per cent in 1993-4, and 7.3 per cent by 2000. According to predictions by Indian researchers, the additional unemployment due to the structural adjustment programme would put out of employment 4 million under high-growth scenario, and 10 million in a low-growth scenario. Similarly, research on the impact of technology and structural adjustments available from the rest of the world, along with social security and employment policy options should have forearmed the unions in 1991. According to the Ministry of Labour and Employment the unemployment rates for 2009 was an all time high of 9.4 per cent. These numbers do not convey the gravity of the problem of unemployment because of the manner in which unemployment is defined in India or the number of working poor.

Many revival strategies are being tried out across the world and in India, which include social movement unionism, service unionism, union participation in skill development, consumer cooperatives, providing health services, acceleration in the mobilization of atypical workers and the unorganized participation in management to lobby more actively for long-term worker interests. The decade after 1991 did witness increased worker resistance across the globe and in India.[56] There has been an increasing trend towards joint trade union action and general strikes since 1991. Between 1992 and 2005, there were 10 general strikes in India and these were in addition to industry-wise and sector-wise agitations. Besides this, there was a clear and consistent attempt to make alliances with other social groups to forge a social movement towards increasing social sector spending by the state, and uphold the rights and benefits of the working class.[57] Hence, though the frequencies of work stoppages declined, the mobilization for anti-privatization and anti-globalization was significant.

But it is clear that the public policy on labour relations is in deep coma in India. It is hardly possible to ignore the stagnation in Indian human relation practices. Adversarial stances and distrust continue to be the foundations of labour management relations today as they were 50 years ago. Human resources management, empowerment, etc., are superficial and restricted to a few core workers and some quality-oriented firms and sectors. Meanwhile, even as the union movement is in the process of reinventing itself, the state has gone from regulation to lip service to indifference.[58] Now there is mounting evidence of hostility, the latest being the report that the state is creating huge territories within the country called Special Economic Zones, where labour laws/institutions will not be relevant. These zones will however offer all types of tax/tariff waivers and infrastructure facilities to business firms earning foreign exchange.[59]

6.6.1 *The Second National Commission on Labour and Trade Unions*

The prescriptions of the report of the SNLC can be taken to reflect the contemporary official policy perspective on labour (GOI, 2002). The commission was appointed by the Government of India in December 1998, and it had several mandates; however, the two express objectives were (a) to suggest rationalization of existing laws relating to labour in the organized sector, (b) to suggest umbrella legislation for ensuring a minimum level of protection to the workers in the unorganized sector. This report released on 29 June 2002 identifies correctly the important problems confronting most of the workers. For instance, with respect to the patterns and trends of employment, it highlighted several disturbing features, which are well known. The pressing problems identified by SNCL include the following:

1. Compared to the 1980s, there was a marked deterioration in employment generation in the subsequent decade; for the former, the annual growth was 1.55 per cent whereas in the latter

it came down to 1.01 per cent per annum. The problem of open unemployment became even more serious in the latter period even as disguised unemployment continued to be significant.

2. Casualization of the workforce has continued and the proportion of such workers went up from 27 per cent in 1977-8, to more than 33 per cent in 1999-2000.
3. Employment growth in the organized sector in the 1990s almost came to a standstill. In fact, towards the end of the 1990s, the number of openly unemployed in the economy, going by the more conservative estimate, was higher than the number employed in the organized sector.
4. The proportion of workforce without any protection was close to 93 per cent whereas only a minuscule percentage comprising organized labour had any protective coverage. In terms of absolute numbers, as per the 1999-2000 count, out of a total of 397 million working people in India 369 million were in the unorganized sector of which 237 million were in the agricultural sector, 17 million in construction, 41 million in manufacturing, 37 million in trade and transport, and another 37 million in communication and services. It is this huge bulk of labouring humanity that is especially vulnerable with no economic protection.
5. Forty-four per cent of the workforce in 1991-2000 was illiterate; barely 5 per cent of it was estimated to have the required vocational skills; hence, the issue of quality deficit was a huge one.
6. The report also acknowledges that the pressures of global competition had resulted in the loss of jobs in the organized sector due to VRS, outsourcing, sub-contraction and so on.

Further, based on the review of industrial relations on the 1981-90 (pre-reform), and post-reform 1991-2000 decades, labour seemingly receives a pat from the SNCL, as it notes that the number of person days lost during the latter decade was almost half of that in the former, and lock-outs accounted for a higher proportion of losses compared to strikes. The report also noted with concern a large number of complaints on the VRS schemes, including elements of indirect coercive pressure tactics, innovative forms of mental harassment compelling employees to resign by threatening to terminate their service, and in some cases physical torture and threats of violence against themselves or dependents. It also made a few general observations about industrial relations which are worth quoting: (1) it is increasingly noticed that trade unions do not normally give a call for strike because they are afraid that a strike may lead to the closure of the unit, (2) service sector workers feel that they have become outsiders and are becomingly increasingly disinterested in trade union activities, (3) there is a trend to resolve major disputes through negotiations at bipartite level. The nature of disputes or demands is changing, (4) the attitude of the government, especially of the central government towards workers and employers seems to have undergone a considerable change. Now the permission for closure and retrenchment are more easily granted, (5) the conciliation machinery is more eager to consider problem of employers and considers issues like increasing productivity, cost reduction, financial difficulties of employer, competition, and market fluctuations, (6) recovery proceedings against employers who could not pay heavy dues of workers are not being seriously perused by the industrial relations machinery if the financial position of the employer is very bad. The labour adjudication machinery is more willing to entertain the concerns of industry.

On the other hand, recommendations made by the SNCL to deal with the vulnerability of the worker even in small organized organizations, are ironic. Its recommendations are:

1. Unfettered rights to close without prior permission establishments that employ up to 300. Currently, as per Chapter VB of the IDA, establishments employing up to 100 workers are required to secure prior permission from the government concerned.
2. In the case of closure of establishments employing more than 300 workers, the recommendation is that the employer shall apply for permission to the appropriate government 90 days before the closure and also serve a copy of the application

to the recognized negotiating agent. If the government does not respond within 60 days of receipt of such application permission will be deemed to have been granted.

3. Employers may be granted unfettered right of retrenchment and layoff in all establishments of any size without prior permission. The only suggested requirement in such cases is that the worker be entitled to two months' notice, or notice pay in lieu of notice.
4. The commission makes a distinction, quite arbitrary on the face of it, between 'core' and 'non-core' and recommends that contract labour shall not be engaged in the former; however, even in such activities it is suggested that to meet sporadic seasonal demand they may engage contract labour. In essence use of temporary and contract labour is recommended across the board.
5. Employer may be given the right to effect changes unilaterally in the service/working conditions of the workers just by giving 21 days' notice.
6. It recommends the rationalization and judicious consolidation of all labour laws and Industrial Disputes Act 1947, the Trade Unions Act 1926 and all other acts pertaining to industrial relations into a single law which may be called a labour management relations law. Further, it sees a minimum role for government involvement.
7. It is proposed that legal provision be made to have negotiating agents particularly on behalf of workers to adjudicate disputes, etc., and such agents may take the shape of labour courts and labour relations commission to be set up at different levels. The idea seems to be to delegitimize trade unions. A trade union can be a negotiating agent but only if 66 per cent of the workforce endorses its authority.
8. It is proposed that the registered trade unions ought not to be allowed to represent or act on any issue of collective or policy nature unless they are recognized by the management. It also proposed that the recognition be decided through a check-off system and not through secret ballot.
9. There is an attempt to impose a virtual ban on strikes in case

of essential services through stipulation of formalities like strike ballots. Only the recognized negotiating agent can call strikes as per the recommendations, and that too only with the consent of 51 per cent of the workers in a strike ballot. It is proposed to have a complete ban on strike in establishment sectors considered socially essential.

10. Establishments employing less than 20 workers need to be taken out of the purview of general labour laws.

All in all, the report highlights the impact of liberalization on prospects for the trade union movement, the unfavourable direction of policy changes in the backdrop of negligent minimum labour standard enforcement. The direction of change has becoming evident since the Supreme Court has made a number of judgements against the interest of worker's employment security.[60]

In India, there is a perception among policy makers that legal framework, very tough on paper and very effete in practice, must be rectified to enable even more flexible employment. The issues of general decline into 'low skill, low quality trap' and of providing adequate safety nets for the workers are ignored. However, the Maruti workers unrest over three years that caught international attention, 15 major all-India strikes jointly by national trade unions since 1991 with increasing participation of the unorganized sectors, organization of young, skilled and unskilled workers in the SEZ and in the new industrial zones does indicate that the labour movement is alive and resisting. There is no reason to believe that this drive will ebb as better-educated, more skilled, trained workers join it.

6.7 Trade Unions, Social Dialogue and Insecurity Hypothesis

Trade unions in many countries have played a constructive role in economic development and management of crisis. An appreciation of the synergetic and complementary role that the unions can play is decisive to long-term strategic advantage.

6.7.1 *The Imperatives of Growth: Effective Participation*

For competitive advantage in the global markets, an enterprise requires flexibility to adjust to externally-induced economic changes, and to regularly offer new products and services. Ability to respond adequately to economic changes, to quote Roderick (1999), depends on social dialogue and macroeconomic performance of a country:

> the ability to maintain macroeconomic stability in the face of turbulent external conditions is the single most important factor accounting for post-1975 economic performance of countries.[61] Inability to adjust economic policies resulted in rapid loss of productivity. Generally, the failed states had inadequate social and political institutions to effect bargains required for macro adjustments, to mediate between social groups for timely action without policy paralysis. Evidence shows that participatory political institutions, civil and political liberties, high-skilled bureaucracy, and protection measures like unemployment insurance can bridge these cleavages.

A classic case being cited of a country's ability to intervene effectively for restoring the macroeconomic balance is that of the USA, which since the 9/11 upheavals has kept the interest rates at historic low levels, and simultaneously expanded and extended the unemployment benefits.

Even though the East Asian 'miracle economies' worked without significant democratic participation, and the long-term basis of economic performance was unstable, they understood that social dialogue could avoid serious disruption, 'jarring the long-term basis of economic performance'. The economic crisis of 1997 was severe and resulted in some far-reaching measures (with labour participation) to redress basic deficiencies. It was recognition of the fact that the economic cost of non-participation can be high indeed.

In Korea, the political opposition grew as a backlash of economic recession, the ruling party lost the next presidential election and a highly respected opposition leader got elected to the post. The conservative party, which had the parliamentary majority, tried to upturn the popular verdict and passed a resolution for his impeachment. The popular resentment was even higher, and the conservatives lost the next parliamentary elections. The party ended up losing both the presidency and the parliament. The supreme court overturned the impeachment vote of the parliament. In contrast with the above, during the recession, an effective tripartite mechanism was introduced to minimize industrial disputes and industrial action. This was successful and the economy bounced back during 2000 with a 7 per cent growth rate, and unemployment fell from 8.7 to 6.61 per cent.[62]

In Thailand popular demand resulted in constitutional reforms, which aimed at greater openness, participation and consolidation of democracy. Legal reforms to back this were initiated. The Eighth Plan objective was to undertake 'people centered development'.[63] In Philippines membership of trade unions grew through the recession, and the unions gained power in the national decision-making process. Indonesia ratified the core standards of the ILO. Malaysia incorporated its largest trade union Malaysian Trade Union Congress (MTUC) in the National Action Council, headed by the PM. The head of the MTUC was appointed to the senate. In cooperation with the MTUC, several key measures were initiated and successfully implemented.

Another impressive model of responsible social dialogue and participation is Sweden, where 90 per cent of the workforce is covered by collective bargaining (for several decades), and since 1999, when the Euro was launched, its GDP growth rate has been significantly more than that of the EU, except for one year.[64]

6.7.2 *Rationale of Social Dialogue: Quality Decisions Need Information*

No one group or individual has all the relevant information for making an optimal decision. It is known that the interests of the labour, government or management do not fully converge and they tend to withhold relevant information, for fear of it being interpreted differently or used in an unintended manner. Yet, such behaviour can only result in less than optimal decisions. More importantly, once the decision is taken its implementation can suffer from non-compliance, resistance to change, reduced effort, motivation and commitment. Even though various groups have different interests, they also hold different but relevant information and exercise influence in their respective spheres. This points to the necessity of involving important players in the change and adjustment processes in a cooperative, consensual mode.

A firm, in an age of rapid changes in technology, products and services, is highly dependent on the skills, and decision-making ability of the employees. The attendant corollary is that the employee must be equipped with innovative skills, knowledge, and information. That is the subtler flexibility required by the firm, which it must support with open communications, and information exchange. Labour and management cooperation requires effective participative mechanisms for maximum utilization of assets, ensuring quality of products and services, to anticipate markets and to innovate. Unions can be made channels for the flow of relevant facts and ideas. The role of industrial relations function is to enable flow of information and to secure commitment. To internalize the concerns of all affected via an effective 'voice mechanism'. The attempts at participative processes as they evolved in Malaysia during the economic crisis of 1997-9 are briefly discussed. The Malaysian example is an interesting case of effective social dialogue. By 1998, the Malaysian GDP had declined by 13 per cent. Government data suggest that only about 80,000 workers were retrenched and an overwhelming number of these were placed in new jobs, although at lower wages. Tripartite National Economic Action Council was constituted, headed by the PM, and included 12 ministers, representatives of Malaysian Trade Union Congress (MTUC), and Union of Employers to implement the National Economic Recovery Plan.

The MTUC took part in all decisions including those affecting the macroeconomics, exchange rate adjustments, etc. Some of the measures it implemented were:

1. Initially the government imposed a wage freeze and banned collective bargaining. However, on the intervention of MTUC,

this was withdrawn, collective bargaining was restored with a new basis for negotiations, i.e. 'the ability to pay'.

2. Severance payment laws or unemployment insurance did not cover a large number of workers. The MTUC proposed a fund for such unemployed workers, which was raised by levying a contribution of one Ringet per employed worker to be paid by the employee and the employer. This enhanced the prestige of the union and enabled it to implement major adjustments.
3. Management had to give a one-month notice to MTUC before it could lay-off workers. Also, the employers notified the union about any vacancies. The union provided the job matching and placement services.
4. A non-binding code of conduct stipulated that retrenchment should be the last resort and very importantly recommended that any sacrifice should be equitably distributed across the hierarchy. Severance pay was imposed. Employers could begin to effect savings and the employees were expected to take a lead in suggesting such opportunities.
5. In several court cases challenging retrenchments, the law penalized the firm if it had defaulted in the code of conduct.

Evidently sustainable democracy and growth both need the participation of workers' associations for various reasons.

There is evidence that responsible participation between the labour, management and government is indeed possible and failure to harness this synergy can lead to turmoil as in South Korea.

The questionnaire submitted to 779 employees as part of the survey undertaken in the latter part of this study is based on this consideration. It also evaluates the state of the employees union and the possible relationship of union presence and bargaining strength to insecurity.

6.8 Conclusion

The chapter developed the theme of trade unions in the context of insecurity in the post-restructuring period, making a point that the existence of strong trade unions with a range bargaining influence does have an impact on the insecurity of employees. Workers and employees can neglect unions only at the cost of rising insecurity and associated problems discussed in the previous two chapters. Taking up the situation in the developed countries and developing countries, the chapter went on to highlight how the decline in trade unions is both a cause and effect of rising insecurity. The cumulative causations induced by flexible labour markets pose a grave threat, but also a new opportunity for trade unions to reinvent themselves. And the seminal role that can well be played by these institutions in improving distribution and macro-economic performance is also indicated. They have been fighting the battle of 1 per cent against the 99 per cent for so long that their cumulative experience and wisdom will be the backbone of any political transformation in the interest of workers.

The central theme that can be reiterated at this point is that labour markets are key institutions through which the contours and cohesiveness of society are shaped. It is the labour market wherein the various structural, political, social and technological forces that drive the process of economic development intersect and where the effects of these are directly felt on jobs, working conditions, and incomes. It is where the economic well-being of individuals and families is determined and their social values and relationship to society as a whole are moulded. Labour markets function within social power structures and ultimately impact the fundamental issue of distribution of the social product.

It is through the labour markets that both the stimulus to economic growth and the process of social justice could largely operate. And the extent of increase in gainful employment opportunities provides the crucial bridge between economic growth and efficiency on the one hand and social justice on the other.... Economic reforms are bound to falter without enough popular support, unless they meet this latter test (Bhaduri 1996).[65]

Notes

1. N. Bacon (1999): 'Union Derecognition and the New Human Relations: A Steel Industry Case Study', *Work Employment and Society*, 13.1, pp. 1-17.

R.B Freeman (1995): The Future of Unions in Decentralized Collective Bargaining Systems: US and UK Unionism in an Era of Crisis', *British Journal of Industrial Relations*, 33, 4, pp. 519-36.
G. Gall (1998): 'The Changing Relations of Production: Union Derecognition in the UK Magazine Industry', *Industrial Relations Journal*, 129, 2, pp. 151-61.
2. N-M. Riley (1997): 'Determinants of Union Membership: A Review', *Labour* 11, 2, pp. 265-301.
3. OECD (1985): *Economic Outlook*, December 1985, OECD, Paris, p. 41.
4. *Economist* (2005): 22 September-8 October.
5. M. Dumont, Glen Ray and Peter Willeme (2006): 'Does Internationalization Affect Union Bargaining Power?: An Empirical Study of Five E.U. Countries', *Oxford Economic Papers*, vol. 58, no. 1.
6. Joyce Kolko (2000): 'Restructuring the Working Class 1988', in Harry Dahms (ed.), *Transformations of Capitalism*, Macmillan Press.
7. Peter Fairbrother and Charlotte Yates (2003): 'The Unions in Crisis', in P. Fairbrother and C. Yates (eds.), *Trade Unions in Renewal: A Comparative Study*, Continuum, London, New York.
8. Palo Sasmita (2004): 'Changing Collective Bargaining Structure', *Indian Journal of Labour Economics*, vol. 47, no. 7, p. 20.
9. R. Taylor (1994): *The Future of Trade Union*, Andre Deutsch, London.
Gray N. Chaison et al. (1993): 'Unions and Legitimacy: A Conceptual Refinement', *Research in the Sociology of Organization*, vol. 12, pp. 139-66.
10. *International Herald Tribune* (1985): Report, 23 January.
11. Peter Fairbrother and Charlotte A.B. Yates (2003): 'The Unions in Crisis', in Peter Fairbrother and Charlotte Yates (eds.), *Unions in Renewal: A Comparative Study*, Continuum, London, NY.
12. A. Flanders (1970): *Management and Union*, Faber, London.
John Dunlop (1993): *Industrial Relation System*, Harvard University Press, Cambridge.
13. H. Clegg (1960): *A New Approach to Industrial Democracy*, Basil Blackwell, Oxford.
H. Clegg (1979): *The Changing System of Industrial Relations in Great Britain*, Basil Blackwell, Oxford.
14. T. Kochan and Paul Osterman (1994): *The Mutual Gain Enterprise*, HBS Press, Boston.
15. M. Parker and J. Slaughter (1988): *Choosing Sides: Unions and the Team Concept*, South End Press, Boston.

16. Kim Scipes (1993): 'Understanding the New Labour Movement in the Third World: The Emergence of Social Movement Unionism', *Critical Sociology*, vol. 19, pp. 81-101.
17. R. Freeman and J. Medoff (1984): *What Do Unions Do*, Basic Books, New York.
    R.A. Dahl (1998): *On Democracy*, Yale University Press, New Haven.
18. R. Nathanson et al. (1999): *Union Response to a Changing Environment: The New Histadrut - The General Federation of Labour in Israel*, International Institute of Labour Studies, ILO, Geneva.
19. A.V. Jose (2000): 'The Future of the Labour Movement: Some observations on Developing Countries', *Indian Journal of Labour Economics*, vol. 43, no. 1.
20. D. Bhattacherjee (1999): 'Organized Labour and Economic Liberalization - India: Past, Present and Future' - Discussion Paper, *International Institute for Labour Studies*, ILO, Geneva.
21. HO-Keun Song (1999): 'Labour Unions in the Republic of Korea: Challenge and Choice', Discussion Paper, *International Institute for Labour Studies*, ILO, Geneva.
22. E. Webster and G. Adler (2001): 'Towards a Class Compromise in South Africa's Troubled Transition' - Paper presented at *14th World Congress of Sociology*, 26 July-1 August, Montreal.
23. P. Bassett and A. Cave (1993): *All for One: the Future of the Unions*, Fabian Pamphlet 559, London.
24. John Kelly (1998): *Rethinking Industrial Relations*, Routledge, London.
25. M.A. Hogg and Abrams Dominic (1998): *Social Identifications: A Social Psychology of Inter Group Relation and Group Process*, Routledge, London.
26. N.D. Kondratieff (1926): 'The Long Waves in Economic Life', *Review* 2, 4, pp. 519-52.
27. K. Bronfengbrenner (1993): 'Seeds of Resurgence: Successful Union Strategies for Winning Certification Election and First Contracts in the 1980s and Beyond', PhD dissertation, Cornell University.
28. K. Bronfengbrenner (2003): 'The American Labour Movement and the Resurgence in Union Organizing', in Peter Fairbrother and C.A.B. Yates (eds.), *Trade Unions and Renewal: A Comparative Study*, Routledge, London, New York.
29. T. Boeri, A. Brugiavini and L. Calmfors (2001): *The Role of Trade Unions in the 21st Century*, Oxford University Press, Oxford.

30. J. Storey (1995): *Human Resource Management: A Critical Text*, Routledge, London.
31. E. Webster and G. Adler (2001): 'Towards a Class Compromise in South Africa's Troubled Transition: Bargained Liberalization and Consolidation of Democracy', Paper presented at the *14th Congress of Sociology*, Montreal, 26 July-1 August.
32. A.V. Jose (2000): 'The Future of the Labour Movement: Some Observations on Developing Countries', *Indian Journal of Labour Economics*, vol. 43, no. 1.
33. B.J. Silver (2003): *Forces of Labour: Cambridge Studies in Comparative Politics*, Cambridge University Press, New York.
34. Ibid.
35. *People Democracy October* (2005): 'Whom do they serve?', 16 October, pp. 1-2.
36. Piven Francis and Richard Cloward (2005): 'Power Repertoires and Globalization', *Politics and Society*, 28(3), September, pp. 413-30.
37. Sarath Davala (1994): 'New Economic Policy and Trade Union Response', *Economic and Political Weekly*, vol. 29, no. 8, February, pp. 406-8.
38. Praveen Jha (2005): 'States Growing Intolerance Towards Labour in India: A Note Based on Some Recent Developments', *Indian Journal of Labour Economics*, vol. 8, no. 4, pp. 897-916.
39. E.A. Ramaswamy (2000): *Managing Human Resources*, Oxford University Press, New Delhi.
40. Pranab Bardhan (2002), 'The Political Economy of Reform in India', in Mohan Rakesh (ed.), *Facets of the Indian Economy*, Oxford University Press, New Delhi, pp. 123-35.
    Pranab Bardhan (2000): 'Social Justice in Global Economy', *Economic and Political Weekly*, vol. 39, nos. 5-6, pp. 54-62.
41. Ajeet N. Mathur (1991): 'Industrial Restructuring and Union Powers', *ILO-ARTEP*, New Delhi.
42. Barbara Harris-White (2003): *India Working: Essays on Society and Economy*, Cambridge University Press, Cambridge.
43. R. Nagaraj (2004): 'Fall in Organized Manufacturing Employment', *Economic and Political Weekly*, vol. 39, no. 30, July, pp. 3387-90.
44. E.A. Ramaswamy (1998): *Workers Consciousness and Trade Union Response*, Oxford University Press, New Delhi.
45. Arnab Bhattacharjee and Saibal Ghosh (2003): 'Strikes and Public Policy: Indian Evidence', *Indian Journal of Labour Economics*, vol. 46, no. 4.

46. Sarosh Kuruvilla et al. (2002): 'Trade Union Growth and Decline in Asia', *British Journal of Industrial Relations*, vol. 40, no. 3, September, pp. 431-61.
47. D. Bhattacharjee (1987): 'Union Types Effects on Bargaining Outcomes in Indian Manufacturing', *British Journal of Industrial Relations*, vol. 25, no. 2, July, pp. 147-266.
    S. Das (1989): 'A Note on Trade Union Density in India', *Working Paper, Department of Collective Bargaining*, Cornell University, Ithaca.
48. A.K. Sengupta (2003): 'Decline of Trade Union Power in India', *Indian Journal of Labour Economics*, vol. 46, no. 4.
49. D.K. Srivastava (2001): 'Trade Union Situation in India: Views of Central Trade Union Organizations', *Indian Journal of Industrial Relations*, vol. 36, no. 4, April, pp. 463-78.
50. N. Sundramurthy (1994): 'NEP and Trade Union Response', *Economic and Politics Weekly*, June, pp. 1551-2.
51. D. Bhattacharjee (1987): 'Union Types and Effects on Bargaining Outcomes in Indian Manufacturing', *British Journal of Industrial Relations*, vol. 25, no. 2, July, pp. 147-266.
52. Mark Holmstrom (1978): *South Indian Factory Workers: Their Lives and their World*, Allied Publishers, New Delhi.
53. E.A. Ramaswamy and F.B. Schiphorst (2000): 'Human Resource Management, Trade Unions and Empowerment: Two Cases from India', *International Journal of Human Resource Management*, vol. 11, no. 4, August, pp. 664-80.
54. R. Nagaraj (1994): Wages and Employment in Manufacturing Industry: Trends, Hypothesis and Evidence', *Economic and Political Weekly*, vol. 29, no. 4, January, pp. 48-52.
55. S.K. Bhaumik (2002): 'Coping With Economic Liberalization: Alternative Trade Union Strategies', *Indian Journal of Labour Economics*, vol. 45, no. 4, pp. 1338-46.
56. Kim Moody (2002): 'Why not in USA?: Around the World Mass Political Strikes Challenge the Effects of Globalization', *Labour Notes* February.
    K.R. Shyam Sunder (2003): 'Industrial Conflicts in India in the Reform Period', *Indian Journal of Labour Economics*, vol. 46, no. 4.
57. A. Kalhan (2005): 'Social Movement Unionism', *Teachers of the World*, January-March.
58. E.A. Ramaswamy (2000): *Managing Human Resources*, Oxford University Press, New Delhi.

59. *The Economic Times* (2006): 'Its Hire and Fire at State SEZs', 16 June. *Frontline* (2006): 'Zone of Conflict', 30 June. *Business India* (2006): 'Irrational Zones', 4 June.
60. LPH (2006): *Indian Factories and Labour Report,* Law Publishing House, New Delhi. Commissioner of Labour (2006): *Labour Gazette,* Office of the Commissioner of Labour, Government of Maharashtra.
61. D. Rodrik (1999): *The New Global Economy and Developing Countries: Making Openness Work,* Overseas Development Council, Washington DC.
62. Campbell Duncan (2000): 'Social Dialog and Labour Market Adjustment in East Asia after the Crisis', in Harry Dahms (ed.), *The Transformations of Capitalism, Society and State in Modern Times,* Macmillan Press, London, pp. 485.
63. Government of Thailand (1997): *The Eighth National Economic and Social Development Plan 1997-2001,* National Economic and Social Development Board, Bangkok.
64. *Economist* (2007): 'Sweden One Year On', 15-21 September, p. 62.
65. A. Bhaduri (1996): 'Employment, Labour Market Flexibility and Economic Liberalization in India', *Indian Journal of Labour Economics,* vol. 39, no. 1.

CHAPTER 7

Conclusion

> When one admits that nothing is certain one must, I think, also admit that some things are much more nearly certain than others.
>
> BERTRAND RUSSELL

It is nearly certain that globalization and restructuring have altered the labour market in the OECD countries since the late 1970s; and similar changes have permeated labour markets in the developing world over the last two decade. Recent changes in the labour markets can only be understood in a historical perspective.

Flexibilization of the production process is the cause of insecurity and the broad frame within which alterations in labour markets can be described. Chapter 3 finds more than half the sampled Mumbai workers in the organized sector experiencing insecurity, evidence of insecurity among young workers is greater, but all the insecurity in the sample cannot be attributed to globalization; a good deal of policy liberalization, industrial relocation and weakening of trade unions had occurred before 1991. Chapter 4 dealt with the significance of human skill base in global competition and the adverse impact of restructuring, flexibilization and insecurity on skill formation. Chapter 5 discussed the connotations of the new human resource management policies and its relationship with flexibilization (particularly flexibilization of labour costs) and insecurity. Chapter 6 emphasized the close relationship between the existence of trade unions, social dialogue and alleviation of insecurity. This chapter contains a distillation of the observations made from the investigation undertaken in Chapter 3.

In this chapter, Section 7.1 is a summary of the main conclusions, Section 7.2 suggests some policies, and Section 7.3 discusses the limitations of the study and makes suggestions for future such surveys.

7.1 Conclusions from the Study

This was a predominantly organized labour market sample, only 10 per cent of the sampled employees were employed in enterprises employing less than 50 workers and 79 per cent of them were unionized. Yet, 28 per cent were contingent of some kind, 10 per cent were contingent workers (contract, casual, *badli*, temporary) – the most insecure kind. Another 18 per cent were part-time workers. Recent studies of the corporate sector have estimated that the contingent labour in the sector is now as high as 40 to 85 per cent.[1] This is an indication of high levels of flexibilization in the organized sector. Trade union leaders confirmed this informally. The present study is underestimating them because of its focus on core workers located within factories and establishments. The claim of inflexibility in India's organized sector labour markets seems somewhat exaggerated.

Nearly one-fourth of the employees had actually experienced high to severe insecurity in the past (PEI) due to retrenchment and spells of unemployment. This compares with the experience of workers in very flexible labour markets like the USA. There, in a survey conducted in 1994 (when unemployment was at 6.5 per cent of workforce) one-fourth of those surveyed had said that they had personally experienced lay-offs, pay-cuts and decrease in hours of work available. Americans, at middle age, were dropping out of the workforce in increasing numbers to upgrade their skills. When insecurity was more comprehensively measured in terms of increase in working hours, nominal wage loss, time spent finding next job and so on, then almost 61 per cent of the sample had experienced high insecurity (CPEI). However, their ability to retain some jobs inside the organized sector may be attributed to higher skill and experience levels.

When one examines the trends in past experience of insecurity (PEI) it increases in the younger workers significantly, indicating a rising trend in recent times towards flexibilization in the organized sector.

Half of those sampled, i.e. workers currently employed in the organized sector claim to have experienced some spell of unemployment over the last 14 years.

Of this sample of employees, 49 per cent feared that they could lose their present job as well. Fifty per cent had already experienced some spells of unemployment since 1991, which for 24 per cent of them had lasted for one or two years. Sixty-seven per cent of the employees reported a reduction in staff strength in their current workplace and an almost equal number reported that job grades were being reduced. Fifty-seven per cent said that outsourcing was increasing, while 61 per cent said that the use of non-permanent workers was on the rise in their factory/establishment. This trend towards increasing flexibilization in the Indian organized sector confirms the finding of earlier studies quoted.

In the last 14 years, a sizeable proportion (39 per cent) of the surveyed workers had experienced some form of informalization such as shift away from a unionized workplace to a non-unionized one, from regular to temporary or self-employed.

Confirming global and national trends, insecurity was found to be higher among the younger (19-32 age group) employees. If the number of atypical/peripheral workers grows, the issue of their income security, training, upskilling and future employability will become important. Human Capital Theory tells us that job loss is permanent loss of firm-specific human capital. Unemployment precludes the accumulation of human capital and brings about a deterioration of existing human capital unless every phase of unemployment is accompanied by reskilling or upgrading skills. Past unemployment is also often the best indicator of future unemployment and wage scarring possibilities.

However, in the sampled population, the objective possibilities of getting another job with similar terms and conditions had not deteriorated progressively or drastically over the period for the majority over the period under consideration. This is despite the fact that there was a steep rise in unemployment and casualization and Informalization of those employed in the region according to the 2001 census. The higher skill/job experience base of the sample, and the rapid growth of the service sector, even though the manufacturing sector declined in the region, perhaps explains this.

Some further explanation why this sampled lot have survived

could be found in the fact that 56 per cent of the employees reported that they had upgraded their skills/qualifications over the period. Fifty-four per cent reported that they received training on the job or on new machines. Three-fourths of the sample had reported introduction of some new technology at the workplace. This points to the trend of technological up-gradation in the post-liberalization period.

The study found that HRM policies at the firm level have changed significantly. Firms employ a mixture of high and low road policies including work intensification, outsourcing, use of contingent workers, introduction of new technology, training, performance appraisals for core workers, performance-related pays and so on. Eighty-one per cent of the surveyed employees reported significant changes in the HRM policies at the workplace with a clear majority of employees (66 per cent) reporting high to medium levels of flexible work practices. This trend in flexible work practices is also amply supported by earlier studies quoted in chapter 3. Work intensification is the most favoured HRM policy.

It needs to be stated that majority of the workers reported experience of low road adverse kind of HRM practices. The public sector not only reported more change in the HRM practices but it also fared better than the private sector in the quality of HRM changes experienced by workers.

Work intensification has risen. This is clear from the responses. More than two-thirds report (79 per cent in the service sector) said that they were required to do additional jobs, 67 per cent reported that staff strength had been reduced and 66 per cent said job grades had been compacted. A third of the workers also reported longer working hours.

In the context of the above, an unanticipated finding was that past experiences of insecurity and the current experience are both directly related to upskilling/improvement of qualifications. Increasing insecurity may be causing the sampled employees to enhance their market value by investing in their own skills and education. The explanation may lie in the fact that there exist opportunities for only those who are better skilled in the small organized sector. Both insecurity and opportunity seem to be the motivating factors promoting this rational choice. Own savings were the most common source of financing skill upgradation for 61 per cent of the employees, followed by training sponsored by the firm.

There is, however, analogous evidence (from other secondary sources) that contingent employment inhibits systematic improvement of on-the-job skills.

The significant fact here is that the employees surveyed were all literate to begin with; only 11 per cent of them were non-matriculates. Thirty-four per cent of them were graduates and above and another 9 per cent were vocationally qualified. Majority of them were in reasonably comfortable wage categories (when compared to the informal or unorganized sector) of above Rs. 5,000 per month.[2] It was also found that those who had higher basic education were more likely to seek and receive further skill upgradation, training, higher wages and so on in a virtuous cycle confirming theory. This highlights parallel observations made by other researchers that educated individuals adapt more easily to changes in economic conditions, use assets more effectively, exploit new income opportunities faster, and decode available information to their advantage more easily.[3]

More than three-fourths of the sample was unionized. Their members rated the unions as having moderate to high range of bargaining influence. Then, do unions instill a higher level of security in their members? There is evidence to suggest that restructuring in the presence of strong unions creates pressures to train and upgrade workers instead of hiring new ones and firing old ones. Union members are more likely to receive training than non-union members, and unions can avert the low skill/cheap labour trajectory.

Public sector employees, employees of large firms and firms that are introducing rapid technological change are all more likely to receive training. Such firms are represented in the sample.

The situation could be very different in the informal sector, where both entry-point skills, lower wages, higher levels of insecurity of both income and employment could all cumulate to cause an adverse situation for skill upgradation. A study of human capital formation and insecurity in the informal sector (statistically more significant) is therefore important to provide an insight into insecurity and skill formation.

Income security seems more critical than job security for skill upgradation. The availability of affordable training is as important. Majority of employees (51 per cent) used their own savings and public institutions to upgrade their skills even though there is an extensive private sector presence in the vocational training sector. But upskilling in the absence of job security will create low returns on investments in job-related skills. (The preference in that case would be for more generic kind of skills.) The situation would be worse if employment security itself was declining. Also, substantial degree of income security in the absence of employment security would be difficult anywhere.

Hire- and fire-policies are known to reduce the incentives of employees to invest in firm-specific skills. There are no substitutes for on-the-job training even though vocational courses pass on that problem and the cost to the employees. Training sponsored by the firm continues to be important in the sample. As demand for skilled workers increases firms will have to invest more in creating those skills at the workplace. However, the data does indicate some tendency of very secure workers to ignore the need for skill upgradation and resulting efficiency gains. A middle way is required to motivate skill upgradations that are focused on high road HRM policies at the firm level.

Overwhelming majority (81 per cent) of the workers who feared job loss attribute their current insecurity to management policies. Few attribute it to rising domestic and global pressures. 'Attribution' is an explanation for an event in terms of causes, reasons, and mechanisms. Trade unions play an important role in informing and educating workers about national and global labour market trends. However, the perception of the worker remains mainly and directly impacted by their managements. When managements fail to communicate, clarify and justify their policies then the levels of mistrust and insecurity seem to rise. This is also supported by studies quoted earlier where firms in the same industry, in the same country (UK), over the same period of restructuring time had distinctly different HRM practices and worker responses. Policies of the management emerge as the single most important factor in creating insecurity.

Unions also impact the current levels of insecurity (CEI) experienced by employees. A lower (47 per cent) percentage of unionized workers feared job losses compared to non-unionized workers, fifty-six per cent of whom feared a job loss. But the levels of CEI remained high overall, which has to be understood in the background of past experiences of unemployment and redundancy, where 53 per cent of the sample had experienced some form of insecurity. Unions play a crucial role in informing their members about threats and opportunities in a globalizing economy. But, for unions to survive in the new circumstances they may have to emphasize means to help workers develop current and adaptable skills.[4] In a flat world, the set of skills workers acquire will determine those who survive in the labour market.

Finally there is clear evidence of the existence of a low skill trap. For an employee, there is a direct link between basic education and likelihood of skill upgradation after joining the workforce. There is also a relationship between basic education, past experience of insecurity and response to insecurity. Those with higher basic education respond to job insecurity by improving their skills. Public policy interventions are clearly needed to forestall the trap by expanding and improving basic schooling.

7.2 Policy Suggestions to Avoid a Race to the Bottom from the Bottom

Race to the bottom has been seen typically as downward pressure on developed country labour standards as a result of competition from the developing, low-wage, poor-regulation countries. Recently, the perspective has shifted to developing countries competing with each other for global market shares and its impact on their labour standards.[5]

Globally all countries seem to be heading towards flexibility, often citing pressures of globalization and competitive liberalization but some towards a capital-dominated flexibility and others towards a slightly negotiated flexibility.[6]

Active Labour Market Policies (ALMP) have emerged as an important tool to deal with structural adjustment and labour market changes in industrial countries. They cover a wide range of measures intended to improve the quality of labour on the supply side through training and re-training the workforce including the contingent labour. On the demand side ALMP focus on direct job creation, public works programmes, and promoting sunrise industries. The significance of the demand side is most often underplayed in the high-skill society paradigm so much so that critics have pointed at the possible emergence of the over-education syndrome. This is likely in the developing world where policies to support orderly industrial upgradation are not being framed.[7] On the delivery side, ALMP carry out job matching and search services. The intent is to improve employability, productivity, and income for employees; to reduce the procurement cost for employers; and socially to promote inclusion and participation.[8]

The debate on policy often compares the active measures with the so-called passive measures such as legislative barriers to severance, insurance, and social transfers that mitigate the financial needs of the unemployed. The passive initiatives are imperative; however, they do not improve employability. Metaphorically, the passive schemes are likened to safety net with implied dependencies. The disincentive from the workers' point of view is the limiting duration of unemployment support. The active measures are likened to 'trampoline-bounce' that is politically more appealing and has a theoretical rationale in labour markets that are often characterized by unequal information, high transaction costs, and the frequent market failures.

Active programmes (specifically retraining) are expected to become increasingly important for promoting employability, to enhance the national competitive-skill advantage, and towards providing greater equality of opportunity. Do such programmes do any good? In many instances the results are mixed because design and implementation of effective programmes requires balancing of a host of complex issues like securing participation of complementary public and private role-players, optimal resource allocation, targeting, delivery, monitoring, evaluation, anticipation of future shifts in demand, identification and quantification of skill sets, and feedback. All this presupposes considerable capacity and maturity of administration. The nature and the role of such active programmes obviously depend on the development stage of the national economy and its institutions; and then again, the culture matters a great deal. Most of what is known about ALMP is from the experience of industrialized OECD countries. Coordination between active and passive labour policies can maximize benefits. Germany, Japan, Norway, and Spain have integrated systems and Canada is in the process of doing so. In the UK, as an experiment, employment officials interviewed the unemployment insurance claimants. According to the OECD 1994 report, it was found that for some reason even a minimal contact reduced the number of claims.[9] Coordinating benefit distribution with job search assistance can save administrative cost.

The East Asian countries during the crisis of 1997-9 implemented some of these policies, but no country has yet made active measures an imperative policy instrument. All the same, the developing countries need to consider these policies attentively. As these economies integrate globally, respond to the long-term requirements of development, and anticipate any future economic shifts and crisis, ALMP will become essential. Japan, for example, has had a comprehensive experience in ALMP implemented since Second World War during periods of acute unemployment, rapid growth, downturn, and severe recession.

The successful models of ALMP and the high skill models suggest the following points of state (policy) intervention are:

1. Support for institutions and systems that strengthen labour market governance and social dialogue. Social dialogues between strong worker and employer organizations are known to help in increasing productivity and building cohesive societies.[10]
2. Create disincentive for cheap labour policy preference in the registered organized sector to begin with. Such firms benefit from many tax advantages especially when they operate in backward areas, EPZs and SEZs. They are in a financial position to develop a stakeholder culture instead of a 'stockholder takes

all' cult. They ought to be involved in socially responsible projects of developing human capital. The examples of EPZs provided in this study are an indication of the low quality of employment, skills and training available to workers in such zones in India. On the other hand, the examples of successful high skill models in South-East Asia in Chapter 3 are a clue to the possibility of changing that trajectory.

3. Fiscal incentives/rewards for firms to maintain levels of employment and improve on-the-job training, and off-the-job firm-sponsored training. This will increase employee productivity as well as the firm's commitment to its workers and also force the firms to upgrade their HRM planning and link it to their business strategy. Over time, this will propel high skill growth trajectories.
4. Increase subsidies and regulate quality of public-funded education/training at all levels, since it is the most favoured form of learning. This will also keep the cost of skilled labour low and competitive.[11]
5. Generate effective coordination of data collection and market intelligence in the labour market like the longitudinal microdata available in the OECD countries. For example, in the UK, the British New Earnings Survey Panel provides a random sample of 1 per cent of working people. Companies are legally obliged to provide details of wages and hours of work from their payroll records along with numerous other quality-of-work-life-related details. This provides high sample coverage, qualitatively rich research material and low response bias.[12]
6. In addition both demand and supply side numbers for different skill types in the labour market ought to be consistently and continually published by a centralized labour market data generating authority.

7.3 Limitations of the Study

The study was limited primarily by the non-cooperation of managements whose employees were the subject of this research. Related limitations stem from the primary difficulty of obtaining a wider sample. Lack of management cooperation limits the ability to seek confirmation and clarifications from the managers for instance regarding their HRM practices, union participation and so on. As mentioned earlier, the sample had to be restructured after inordinate delays by the managements in responding to permission for survey.

Extensive field study is time consuming and expensive, involving travel, training of surveyors and data validation. Non-cooperation of managements adds to the costs and delays. These stumbling blocks can be overcome by public policy directives, making management cooperation obligatory, particularly if researchers approaching managements are from recognized public-funded institutions of higher education and research. This will go a long way in encouraging a culture of fruitful field-based research on labour.

Second, the method of questionnaires cannot completely eliminate the possibility of subjectivity and perception of respondents. Anomalies were found in the responses and rejection rates were fairly high. Coupled with non-access to management views and clarifications, cross-checks and validations were not feasible to the desired level (which led to an even higher rejection rate). This was particularly again the case regarding the actual human resource policies of the organization, in comparison to the workers' perception. Some issues therefore could not be free of haziness up to the end.

Many respondents for example had ambiguous responses and thought that they could keep their current job till retirement, yet while answering another question they felt they could lose their current job. It would have helped to know why and which policy of the managements in the past or present made them uncertain.

Third, since it was an attempt to adapt studies undertaken in OECD countries to India, the adaptations of instruments, key concepts and their operationalization to local conditions did throw up some difficulties. One of the issues that became problematic was the absence of information about the entry-level skills/ educational qualifications of employees. This created problems for evaluating the skill upgradations that took place specifically in the post-employment phase. Intuitive solutions had to be generated based on the age of the respondents.

Two areas emerge for further investigation. Using the HRM issues listed in the questionnaires in the present study, detailed micro-level studies of firm-level policies, with inputs from both the managements and employees need to be undertaken and linked to the issues of growth of the firms, insecurity of employees, their productivity and skill upgradation. Firms can then be compared for the outcomes that their policies generate. Determining the best practices could then serve a useful policy purpose. This will also provide valuable insights into the interrelationships of the correlates of the hypothesis as well.

Further the same study needs to be modified for the informal, tiny sector where the majority of 'the employed' work. In this sector, the relationship between greater insecurity, lower incomes and its impact on skill formations can provide important insights.

Notes

1. Sarath Davala (ed.) (1992): *Employment and Unionization in Indian Industry*, Friedrich Ebert Stiftung, New Delhi.
   S.K. Bhaumik (1998): 'The Labour Movement in India: Present Problems and Future Prospects', *The Indian Journal of Social Work*, 59, 1, pp. 147-66.
2. B. Harris-White (2004): *India Working, Essays on Society and Economy*, Cambridge University Press, Cambridge.
   D. Turnham, Bernard Salome and A. Schwarz (1990): *The Informal Sector Revisited*, OECD, Paris.
3. T.W. Schultz (1975): 'The Value of Ability to Deal with Disequilibria', *Journal of Economic Literature,* 13, no. 3, pp. 827-46.
4. J.T. Delaney (2006): 'The Flattening of Industrial Relations', *Industrial and Labour Relations Review*, vol. 59, no. 3, pp. 497-501.
5. Nancy H. Chou and R. Kambur (2006): 'The Race to the Bottom from the Bottom', *Economica*, vol. 3, no. 290, pp. 193-228.
6. P. Littlewood, Ignace Glorieux and Ingrid Jonsson (2004): *The Future of Work in Europe*, Ashgate, Burlington.
7. James Heinz (2006): 'Low Wage Manufacturing and Global Commodity Chain: A Model in Unequal Exchange Tradition', *Cambridge Journal of Economics*, 30, pp. 507-52.

8. G. Betcherman and A. Dar (2001): 'Active Labour Market Policies', in Blanchard Gordon and Rizwanul Islam (eds.), *East Asia Labour Markets*, ILO, Geneva.
9. Ibid.
10. Juan Somavia, Director General ILO (2006): 'Employment in Asia', *The Hindu*, 30 August.
11. Mark Gladstein, Mashe Justman and Volker Meier (2005): *The Political Economy of Education-Implications for Growth and Inequality*, MIT Press, Massachusetts.
12. R.A. Hart (2006): 'Worker Job Matches, Job Mobility and Real Wages', *Economica*, May, no. 73, pp. 287-98.

CHAPTER 8

Epilogue

8.1 The Disposable Worker on the World Stage

At the beginning of the last century observers in industrialized, developed countries described the 'degradation of work' as simple, repetitive tasks on assembly lines. By the middle of the century the assembly-line factories and new services were generating more such jobs but with wages that raised the standard of living and created a 'middle class'. By the end of the twentieth century something in the world of work had changed fundamentally. Social scientists were reporting an actual scarcity of 'decent work' and were talking of 'capitalism without work'. Some observers were even suggesting that the Luddites of early nineteenth century might have been correct when they wrecked machines fearing they were taking away people's work. The rate at which workers are getting displaced by technological change today is faster than the rate at which the system can compensate by creating new and adequate number of jobs in other sectors. Technologically displaced workers are not reabsorbed. The drive towards automation and robotics is worsening their foreboding. But it appears that 'technological' change is only part of the difficulty embedded in political economy, a part that economists are willing to discuss more readily.[1]

8.2 The Great Recession of 2008 Spun into a Job Crisis

'Decent work' by classification is work where compensation covers the full cost of social reproduction and does not compel the worker into debt. The beginning of the twenty-first century actually found millions of working peoples lip into both greater debt and work-related insecurity. At this stage the Great Recession of 2007-8 emerged. The most unmistakable social consequence was flaring insecurity and inequality – parallel but correlated phenomena. The prolonged social protest 'Occupy Wall Street' drew international attention to the wealth of the top 1 per cent of society as against the rest 99 per cent. (In the USA, they said, the top 1 per cent owned 33 per cent of the wealth and Warren Buffet, the second richest man in the world, stated that he paid lower tax rate than his secretary.) Trade unions joined the youth in public protests; the movement had reverberations in Africa, America and Europe. Millions marched streets and occupied public spaces against what they perceived as the injustice imposed by the government policies on working people in the aftermath of the recession. Banks were bailed out, but indebted people were left to face foreclosures and arrest warrants. No job-creating public spending was introduced. Private sector and most specifically the financial sector emerged as the dominant infrangible sector. And eventually the movement subsided under media blackout and considerable state repression.

Inequality again became the talking point in 2014 with the publication of Piketty's *Capital in the 21st Century* (Harvard University Press). An unusual theme for a bestseller, it made the point again that inequality is bound to grow further and this would weaken freedom and democracy.

What happened to security, inequality and labour markets worldwide (from the point of view of the workers) after 2008 can basically be understood against the background of chapters 1 and 2. It is through the labour market that the questions of distribution and inequality are advanced and that is where the trouble began, persisted and accelerated after 2008.

By 2008 the fact of declining employment elasticity of growth all over the globe from 1991-2003 (Kapsos 2005)[2] was generally recognized. The relationship between job creation and economic growth had become weak. (The same is not true in an economic slowdown. Job losses rise rapidly.) Before the recession set in an expanding service (business consultancy, brokerage, education, IT, ICT, PR, marketing, hospitality, nails, tattoos, beauty, fitness, personal services, above all financial services, etc.) sector generated more jobs and value addition than the traditional sectors. A structural transformation that reduced jobs in the secondary and related sectors had almost concluded in the developed world reducing permanently the availability of traditional/organized sector industrial employment. This structural change in many OECD countries (and oddly in developing countries like India as well) had moreover overlapped with cut-backs in public funding of education, grounding and training for new skills, housing, health care and shrinkage of public-sector jobs. Real wages had stagnated. The bargaining strength of trade unions had declined thereby disabling most coping mechanisms for the lower and middle classes. This was ascribed to an ideological shift now referred to as neoliberalism. In his influential scrutiny of neoliberalism as it developed from the late 1970s, Harvey (2005) says:

> Neo liberalism seeks to strip away the protective coverings that embedded liberalism allowed and occasionally nourished. The general attack against labour has been two-pronged. The powers of trade unions and other working class institutions are curbed or dismantled within a particular state (by violence if necessary). Flexible labour markets are established. State withdraws from social welfare provision and technologically induced shifts in job structures that render large segments of labour force redundant, complete the domination of capital over labour in the marketplace. (p. 168)

The responsibility of the state and employer is shifted on to a 'personal responsibility system' till individual security becomes 'tied to the affordability of financial products embedded in risky financial markets'.[3]

By 2010 social scientists were recognizing that 'The global financial crisis of 2007 has cast its long shadow on the economic fortune of many countries, resulting in what is often called the Great Recession'[4] (Verick and Islam, 2010, p. 4). Soon after the Great Recession set in, it was widely known that it began as a sub-prime crisis in the booming American financial sector in 2007, became a full-blown global economic slowdown over 2008 and eventually got entrenched as an enduring job crisis. Economic growth slowed down in the OECD countries, and it pulled down many other countries. Even after the global economic crisis stabilized, job markets did not recover because the depressing effect on labour markets came in the backdrop of previous long-term trends of structural and technological changes in an increasingly globalized, neoliberal world. The consequences are manifest. Across the spectrum, scholars and reports from the ILO, UN and World Bank have documented the deleterious impact of the Great Recession on labour markets.

In the preface to his book *Free Fall*, Stieglitz (2010) says,

> In the Great Recession that began in 2008, millions of people in America and all over the world lost their homes and jobs. Many more suffered the anxiety and fear of doing so.... A crisis that began in America soon turned global, as tens of millions lost their jobs worldwide – 20 million in China alone – tens of millions fell into poverty. (p. xi)[5]

In the globalized economy developing countries could not avoid the slowdown; China and India seem to have avoided a major slump in growth. China launched a huge stimulus package and India could manage with a smaller one.

The executive summary of an ILO publication of 2011 began thus:

> The Great Recession of 2008–09 was the worst since the Second World War. The financial crisis that emerged in the United States in mid-2007 quickly transformed into a credit crunch and a dramatic collapse in trade flows. The result was a loss of jobs and livelihoods for millions around the world. The tragic consequences at the aggregate level, however, were juxtaposed with incredible diversity across regions and countries.[6]

It was a set back and slowdown from which the global economy is yet to recover in a sustained manner in terms of the quality and quantity of employment available.

In India, labour-related data is too inadequate to make a clear statement about the quality and number of jobs lost or recovered later. The reasons can be found in the size of the informal sector and the inadequate concern and policy involvement with issues of the labour market. The government commissioned a Labour Bureau study that put the job losses at about 500,000 but there as yet seems no documented evidence of a long-term impact on the labour market.

Unemployment was expected to rise after the Great Recession of 2008 and it did but impacted different countries and age, sex, gender and educational attainment groups differently, within each country. In some countries like Germany and Japan for example working hours and terms were adjusted quickly to protect employment. For certain sectors like export and manufacturing, unemployment rose quickly. Being relatively protected, education, health and other the social sectors were slow to change.[7]

Most governments undertook some fiscal and monetary stimulus soon after the crisis. These were intended to encourage growth by stimulating consumption, cheap credit and supporting the financial system. Consequently the fiscal stimulus focussed on tax cuts and capital expenditures and not directly with public-sector expansion or direct job creation. There is no significant increase in countries pursuing active labour market policies based on shared experiences or simply by a rising long-term social protection expenditures. It is hard to imagine why the job crisis should outlive the economic crisis unless the policy response has been wholly inadequate.

The ILO-WB Inventory of Policy Response (2012) calculations based on policy budgets show that for the high-income countries (and these countries were the worst affected by the recession) the 'largest share of the budget (56 per cent) went to enhance credit flows, 19 per cent for direct job creation and 13 per cent for support of SMEs, 9 per cent for stabilising employers to retain jobs. For lower and middle income the largest share, two-thirds, went to direct job creation, 15 per cent to employers subsidies to retain jobs, 13 per cent to enhanced credit'.[8]

The same report notes that the actual sectoral budget of $ 2.4 trillion to address the recession, across 77 countries, shows that the financial sector received half, manufacturing came a weak second with $ 240 billion, education $ 120 billion, exports and infrastructure received little attention.

Monetary policy became more complex and leaned towards quantitative easing (QE) whereby central banks (USA, ECB) bought bonds from the public by printing currency to ease money supply. Majority of the countries surveyed undertook a fiscal stimulus. Fiscal stimulus in adopting countries verged on $ 5.5

trillion in PPP terms. The three largest economies affected by the crisis, USA, China and Japan all deployed a fiscal stimulus of more than $ 1 trillion each. High-income countries relied more on tax cuts (59 per cent and 39 per cent) on expenditure stimulus. Low and middle income countries relied more on expenditure increase (71 per cent). Although a variety of differences in the labour market outcomes are evident, for example, some countries with more active labour market policies like Germany, Japan and Korea had the least unemployment in the aftermath while others like the USA had higher rates.

Few countries that were able to deploy public works in the crisis already had the systems to do so, like Mexico's Temporary Works Programme that could be extended in 2009. Kenya, Turkey and Kazakhstan also adopted public works. India too had a public works programme (MNREGA) that it could use.

The findings of the policy response go on to suggest policy areas that require further attention, like active labour market institutions, work sharing, wage subsidies, social insurance, social assistance, training, social dialogue to avoid violation of labour rights, participation of labour in major policy decisions and market-information systems. The list is virtually the whole arsenal of policy that directly deals with labour issues and all of that seems to require further attention even in 2012! This report was the result of a request from the G20 summit in London (2009). In the same year the ILO conference with participants from all member states adopted a Global Jobs Pact with a portfolio of key crisis response policies and the objective to reduce the time lag between economic growth and employment growth. But even in 2015 job recovery did not accelerate. The path followed so far – competitive quantitative easing in monetary policy as the favoured policy – in the post-crisis world it seems, is not remarkably different from the way that led up to the crisis.

ILO's 'World Employment and Social Outlook Report, Trends 2015' infers that the situation in labour markets will remain grim in the future. It says:

> The world economy continues to expand at rates well below the trends that preceded the onset of the global crisis in 2008 and is unable to close

the significant employment and social gaps that have emerged. The challenge of bringing unemployment and underemployment back to pre-crisis levels now appears as daunting a task as ever, with considerable societal and economic risks associated with this situation.

This report finds that the global employment outlook will deteriorate in the coming five years. Over 201 million people were unemployed in 2014 around the world, over 31 million more than before the start of the global crisis. And, global unemployment is expected to increase by 3 million in 2015 and by a further 8 million in the following four years 2014-18[9] (p. 9). It goes on to say that the situation is particularly severe for youth between 15-24 years of age (three times higher unemployment than their adult counterparts) and persists despite increasing educational attainment. The situation is likely to pose social risks.

After a brief recovery, unemployment is likely to worsen in many emerging economies as well. Worldwide the number of vulnerable and informally employed will rise to 1.44 billion. In South Asia and Sub-Saharan Africa three out of four workers are in vulnerable employment. The report estimated that

> Global employment grew at an average annual rate of 1.7 per cent between 1991 and 2007. However, since the outbreak of the crisis, employment growth has slowed to 1.2 per cent per annum between 2007 and 2014. On current trends, unemployment will continue to rise as the labour force expands. Going forward, job creation is expected to remain at this lower growth rate over the medium term, causing a widening of the global jobs gap in 2019. If new labour market entrants are taken into account, 280 million jobs will need to be created over the coming five years to close the crisis-related global jobs gap and to absorb the increase in the labour force. (p. 12)

Even as 2015 draws to a close, there is no indication of a vigorous critique of the relationship between growth and employment. Questioning the weak relation may lead to active policy interventions to address insecurity, create livelihoods and jobs. The reason may well be veiled in the subverting effect of rising inequalities on democratic processes. Since issues of distribution are addressed directly through the labour markets, Piketty is incisive when he urges economists to put the distribution question back at the heart of economic analysis (p. 15). 'Since 1970's, income inequalities have increased significantly in the rich countries, especially in the United States, where the concentration of income in the first decade of the twenty-first century regained – indeed, slightly exceeded – the level attained in the second decade of the previous century'.[10] He asserts that

> The history of distribution of wealth has always been deeply political, and it cannot be reduced to purely economic mechanism.... The history of inequality is shaped by the way economic, social and political actors view what is just and what is not, as well as by the relative power of those actors and the collective choices that result. (p. 20)

In that sense, the 2008 recession and its aftermath was an artefact of neoliberalism experimentation. Noble prize winner Stiglitz (2010) notes that 'despite mounting job losses in the first nine months of 2008, a loss of some 1.8 million jobs, with 6.1 million Americans working part-time (because they could not get a full-time job).... The administration refused to help homeowners, it refused to help the unemployed, and it refused to stimulate the economy through standard measures...' (p. 29). The giveaways were to banks and old manufacturing firms and not enough to home owners. The same preference is evident in Graber's (2014) account of the post-recession period.

Typically the World Bank's World Development Report (2013) did not shy away from the concern; it was suitably titled 'Jobs'.[11] With a long foreword on the historical, cultural and universal importance of jobs/work, it went on to reiterate that 'jobs are instrumental to achieving economic and social development ... they are central to reducing poverty, increasing productivity and social cohesion.' It aims to take the centrality of jobs in the development process as the starting point ... and tackle the most pressing problems policy makers are asking; like should countries frame their development strategies around growth or focus on jobs? What comes first: jobs or skills, etc., etc. And finally the three-stage approach it suggests, reiterates a well-entrenched neoliberal doctrine all over again, that the private sector needs an ever enabling environment to create new jobs which policy should provide along with investments in human capital, rule of law and appropriate labour market policies. It does not recommend stronger labour laws or labour market institutions or unions but something called 'voice' and extended protection for the weakest among the workers, CSR and private sector accountability, so that growth can translate into employment opportunities.

Theirs' seems to be a concern limited to the developing world; will the developed world focus entirely on finance, weaponry, research and development? What happens to industrial jobs and adequate decent jobs in the developed world where unions are increasingly restless with stagnant wages? Even as unemployment has started falling somewhat in some countries like the UK and USA, real wages remain strangely stagnant.

From the perspective of labour markets, it seems that at the moment, hegemony of neoliberal ideology and financial capital is complete. As long as the supremacy of financial capital reigns labour markets will remain neglected. It hardly matters anymore what the problem is; the solutions offered from international organizations to federal governments are still the same with rare exceptions. Instead, for European countries that have not been able to recover from the crisis like Greece, Spain and Portugal austerity measures are being recommended by multilateral institutions like the IMF and their partners in the EU, despite the fact that the recession had accelerated a free fall in employment. Up to 25 per cent of Greek workforce was unemployed in July 2015 when a new austerity schedule was forced upon them to deal with the sovereign debt crisis.

Is the world any closer to a coordinated action on the decent job front? Not yet it seems and it is not so because in this era of globalization the nation states are individually effete and incapable of coordinated action. The policy response to the Great Recession essentially in support of finance capital has just disproved that.

Graeber (2014) describes the hiatus thus:

In 2011 after a wave of popular movements swept out of Middle East and found echoes all over the world, thousands across Europe and North

America also began insisting that (some kind of conversation about) the basic questions raised in 2008 be addressed. They were met with a brief spate of attention, and then violent suppression and media blackout. And all this despite the fact that the world economy appears to be tumbling inexorably towards the next great financial catastrophe – the only real question being just how long it will take.[12] (p. 17)

If democracy in essence is the abolition of class domination, then liberal democracy seems to have achieved precisely the opposite so far. It appears as though the empire – global network of interests of finance capital and corporations – has further consolidated its grip over the state. For extensive domestic policy alterations to occur, ideological shifts have to challenge the hegemony of neoliberal discourse as well as harmonise and connect with new and like-minded political organizations at the national level. Moreover no country today can deal comprehensively with its decent job deficit in isolation as policies in one country impact others in the web of financial flows and global supply chains. Consequently the scale of change will have to be wide, regional if not global and almost simultaneous. Making it work out that way will be most challenging, calling for Zizek's (1999) 'art of the impossible – that changes the parameters of what is considered possible in the existing constellation'.[13]

8.3 Meanwhile the Bottom Tilted Further: India in the World

Chapters 1 and 2 laid the background and other chapters described the situation of trade unions, skill development, HRM in the world and India as well. After the Great Recession, employment in export- and tourism-oriented industry was the first to decline; other sectors like finance followed. The impact on labour markets however remains less clearly measured and discussed in post-recession India than in China or other East Asian countries. This continues despite the fact that its economy is more globally integrated than it had ever been since Independence.

The most instantaneous effect of the Great Recession in India was the withdrawal of funds by foreign institutional investors to cover losses made in other markets.[14] That grabbed all the headlines. The stock market index and exchange rates fell sharply. Monetary policy was tuned rapidly to deal with the crisis with sharp reduction in repo rates, Cash Reserve Ratios and SLR to ease the liquidity situation and new schemes to stabilize the financial system which had experienced a huge in- and out-flow of funds. On the fiscal expenditure side the Sixth Pay Commission hiked salaries of all government employees substantially; rural employment guarantee, farm loan waivers and other safety nets were in place to boost domestic demand.

But the impact of the recession or the counter-cyclical policy on employment was and has still not been established. Various surveys also report very low levels of unemployment, lower than most OECD countries. According to the fifth annual employment-unemployment survey at all-India level of the Labour Bureau, about 77 per cent of the households were reported to be having no regular wage/salaried person. It said the unemployment rate was estimated to be 5 per cent at all-India level under the UPS (Usual Principal Status) approach. Unemployment rate was 4.9 per cent in 2013-14, 4.7 per cent in 2012-13, 3.8 per cent in 2011-12 and 9.3 per cent in 2009-10. Labour Bureau did not bring out any such report for 2014-15.

The Labour Bureau was entrusted by the Ministry of Labour and Employment with the task of estimating the effect of the economic slowdown on employment in India. The Report (2009) was prepared on a small sample based on fieldwork for over a month using questionnaires; the estimates for the period October-December 2008 are an eye opener.[15] According to its estimates there was a loss of 500,000 jobs during October-December 2008. (The worst affected were the export-oriented like gems and jewellery, textiles, transport and automobiles.)

Scholars are of the opinion that employment in 2009 increased by over a million jobs in the domestic sector (textile and BPO/IT sector).[16] The Census of India however does reports that unemployment grew from 6.8 per cent in 2001 to 9.6 per cent in 2011.

Although GDP growth rate recovered and the average for the Eleventh Plan period 2007-12 worked out to 8 per cent. The slowdown in growth in India did kick in after 2012-13. GDP estimates ranged between estimates of 5.5 and 6.5 per cent.

In India issues of employment are compounded by various factors, for example the fact that employment elasticity of growth declined in the post-liberalization period. Additionally there has been an absolute decline in employment in the agriculture sector for the first time since Independence. It began in the period 2004-5 and intensified after 2010.[17] Rate of growth of employment to GDP slowed down (been slowing down) to almost zero (0.02 per cent) during 2005-10. (Total employment and regular salaried employment increased somewhat in the post-2010 period but the long-term trend is not very encouraging.)

According to Ghani (2013), the share of the unorganized sector as defined by the National Commission for Enterprises remains persistently high in India despite growth and structural changes in the economy and some recent growth in the organized sector employment.[18]

Low unemployment rates in India therefore do not reflect the tightness of labour markets. The nature of employment is poor and wages flexible in the vast informal employment sector and at least half of the organized sector employment is also informal. (Younger people are opting for more education resulting in some slowing down of labour-market growth rate.) But the slow growth of employment worsens the quality and terms of employment that is available even for the better educated. This, in turn, impacts skill development and productivity in a vicious cycle. It also polarises the market favouring those with high skills in regular employment in the organized sector.

Others have also repeated the observation about slow growth of employment and declining percentage of employment in the organized sector which has traditionally been dominated by public sector employment in India. In the private sector, organized sector employment growth is slower than anticipated by the supporters of liberalization and has declined as a proportion of employment between the mid-1980s and mid-2000; it has reduced in absolute numbers too, according to the HDI Report. The trend changed after 2004-5 but that phenomenon was also marked by an overall decline in LFPR, with no clear explanation except the greater enrolment of younger people in education (in a certain age group of young people) and the withdrawal of women for reasons perhaps like domestic needs. The rise in real wages and decline in poverty were proposed as an explanation for this withdrawal. It is more likely that labour force is discouraged and inclined to withdraw with the reduction in public-sector jobs, increase in contractual jobs everywhere and work intensification within the private sector.

The rise in real wage at the entry and lower levels of private establishments is actually an illusion. Hourly wages have not risen as much. If intermittent spells of unemployment are included then the real annual wage shrinks. Further if contractual wage labour is paid a certain wage on paper, their real take-away is less to the extent that they have to pay the sub-contracting agency. In India these labour contractors/agencies combine extraction, commissions and strong-arm tactics to control labour that they supply to larger firms. Almost all young workers – skilled, semi-skilled and unskilled – are being hired through these labour agencies. Among the workers, they call it the 'New Landlordism'. Casual workers at the bottom of the pyramid are worse off in all respects. Absence of any social security, pensions and benefits attached to duration of employment also discourage young workers from entering the labour force; instead they persist with education in the hope that at higher levels of education the terms of employment may improve. Depressing terms of employment also discourage young workers specially women from entering the labour market and staying in it. Otherwise it is hard to imagine that with high levels of inflation and heightened labour market insecurity for male earners there should be such a counter-intuitive tendency for female labour force to withdraw. And paradoxically (ten million graduates, post-graduates and technical degree holders amounting to 15 per cent of highest level of education were unemployed/looking for jobs, according to the 2011 census) despite the evidence of poor returns to higher education and the indifferent quality of considerable higher education there is just no let-up in the demand for higher education and skills. Nor is there a reduction in the political rhetoric on skill formation. Unless it is deeply subsidized that phenomenon itself could be another cause of rising debt. Indian banks have accumulated sizeable NPAs in the education sector and they have been rising in the last few years.[19] This is a pattern that has first emerged in America where debt-driven expensive, private education has been the mainstay of improved skills.

Low rates of unemployment and high rates of poverty, at one-third of population (by the meanest standards of poverty measurement), tell their own story about the working poor and the nature of employment - much of it being informal, self-employment, or on casual, informal contract basis.

The categories used by the NSSO (like usual and subsidiary status, weekly status) are quite unique and strictly incomparable to developed countries or even to previous years because they do not tell us anything about the quality of jobs except the degrees of impermanence. In India only the total absolute number of unemployment rises as the labour force grows.[20] What will not be measured can perhaps be ignored more easily. In India the policy response post-recession in the form of direct job creation was not significant. There were no urban counterparts of MNREGA (which was in place well before the recession). Urban areas would have logged more job losses, aggravating urban poverty.

8.4 Flimsy Labour Market Institutions

Not only is the data flimsy, but evidence indicates (and scholars largely agree) that the institutional framework in India for the labour market has been largely intact in the post-liberalization period mainly because labour laws are observed more in the breach. Labour laws have not in any way hindered growth in the post-liberalization period. Large informal sector and growth in labour force have together worked as consistent external factors to discourage and dilute trade union pressures for implementation of relevant protective laws.

The state in India (largely pro-growth and pro-elite in the post-liberalization period) has often reintroduced the argument in the public domain that rigid labour laws have come in the way of large-scale manufacturing in India. This is done periodically despite no evidence to clinch the argument for further deregulation of the labour market.[21]

If rigidity of labour laws is indeed a problem then the intermittent episodes of unrest, strikes and lockouts in the new industrial zones near Delhi called Gurgaon and Manesar from 2006-12, for example, would have had entirely different features. Some of these strikes have featured in the *Wall Street Journal* besides the national media. The Honda auto workers who struck work in 2006 were led by temporary workers. It was alleged that Maruti-Suzuki had been reducing the number of permanent workers (permanent workers are the highest skilled) and all the conflicts had been dominated by very young, casual and temporary workers who constituted 70 per cent of the workers; they were asking for simple recognition of their base union. The other demands were for more permanent staff, reduction in work intensification and better wages. The strike received support from many other neighbouring industrial workers unions.[22] This industrial zone is largely a post-liberalization formation where almost all the large MNCs and Indian companies have either offices or factories but workers there are still struggling for recognition of their base unions.

Two acts of the pre-liberalization period, the Industrial Disputes Act (IDA) 1947 and the Contract Labour (Regulation and Abolition) Act (CLRA) 1970 were in the news recently. The first one requires firms employing more than 100 workers to secure government permission before retrenchment of permanent workers or closure. The second one attempts to control the practice of keeping workers on a contractual basis (hire and fire) without the benefits of permanent status like paid leave, gratuity, increments, bonus, etc.

The Economic Survey 2014-15 lists the reform actions initiated by the new government. It also mentions (p. 9) 'Facilitating Presidential assent for labour reforms in Rajasthan, setting an example for further reform initiatives by the states; and consolidating and making transparent a number of labour laws.' It was expected that other state governments would follow the process of competitive deregulation to attract investments.

Yet another booth to supply cheap, young, skilled labour in

the market was opened by the recently proposed amendments to the Child Labour (Prohibition and Regulation) Amendment Bill, 2012 (it will have to be cleared by Parliament) allowing them to work in family enterprises, non-hazardous enterprises and farms after 14 years of age. The number of hazardous industries has been reduced to 3 from 83. Under the garb of so-called family enterprise adolescents can be made to work in areas what was earlier considered hazardous. Although fines and penalties for violation have been increased there is no institutional augmentation to strengthen implementation.

Similarly according to newspaper reports[23] the amendments to the Apprenticeship Act 1961 will make it easier for employees to hire low-cost apprentices. It drops the clause that mandates imprisonment of company directors that fail to implement the Apprenticeship Act of 1961 and does away with an amendment proposed by the earlier government mandating employers to absorb at least half of its apprentices in regular jobs. It extends these flexibilities to 500 new trades and vocations under the scheme, including skills for services sectors like IT-enabled services.

Similarly proposed amendments to Labour Laws Act 1988 will allow companies to hire more employees without having to comply with labour law requirements as the ministry has proposed that companies with 10-40 employees will now be exempt from provisions that mandate them to furnish and file returns on various aspects. The current threshold is up to 10-19 employees. The proposed amendment will however double provisions for overtime while improving safety conditions. It is not clear if adequate state institutions and manpower even exist to supervise implementation at the firm level.

Trade unions were preparing an 'All India' strike in September 2015 to oppose these laws and there have been 15 such strikes since 1991 and participation has been strong and rising particularly among the newly-organized sectors. Such trade union actions seem to stall the process of deregulation but not reverse it. It continues more rapidly by stealth, or at a slower pace by legislation.

In the absence of regulatory apparatus to improve conditions of wage or work and the presence of external pressures on real wages to fall these amendments are inclined to push up the supply of cheap labour with obvious consequences for sliding labour markets. The dominant political ideology in India too, it would appear at this juncture, is swinging further away from considering development as a process of securing decent jobs, livelihoods, skills, human capabilities and strengthening socio-economic security. The domination of capital over the production process seems to be thorough here, as in the developed world.

The Interment of NCEUS

While organized/formal sector workers (who are the main subject of this book) are struggling to protect the rights of the working people in post-liberalization India they are a numerical minority. This aspect of the Indian labour market has received less attention in this book. Central to the issue of work in the metros of India today are the informally employed within the unorganized sector who are permanently insecure. This sector is by definition relatively unreported and unquantified in a definitive way, yet it is many times the size of the organized sector in terms of work/employment. It would be inappropriate to end without mentioning the extensive, pioneering, documentation done by the National Commission on Employment in the Unorganized Sector set up in 2004 under the first UPA government (2004-8). The terms of reference of the commission, as its name suggests, required them to explore the underbelly of employment in India. They were set up to define, measure the nature, size, scope and magnitude of the unorganized sector enterprises and employment therein, suggest measures to support enterprises in the face of declining growth rate of employment in the organized sector. They were to suggest measures to support this sector and quality of employment therein with innovations in credit, skill formations, social security measures for workers and better labour administration. Immense amounts of data, reports, policy recommendations and legislative bills came out of that commission like the National Policy on Street Vendors, Unorganized Sector Workers Bill, Conditions of Work and Promotion of Livelihood, financing of enterprises in the unorganized sector, creation of National Fund for the Unorganized Sector, technological upgradation and creation of clusters and growth poles in various regions of the country. Their reports were the basis of some policy announcements and other reports were under review for action. Its conclusions on the working poor, particularly its finding that 77 per cent of the population was living on a per capita, per day expenditure of Rs. 20 that did place them above the poverty line (of Rs. 12 per day per capita in 2004-5) but only marginally so did grab national attention. They had projected a labour force of 551 million by 2017. Of these 92 per cent would continue to be employed as informal workers, and 86-7 per cent would be working in the unorganized sector. Only 6 per cent would work in the organized sector. Since official unemployment levels in India are low, by implication the unorganized sector would continue to absorb the working poor who, it is now evident, cannot be absorbed in the organized sector! The fact that this is the national trajectory after decades of high growth did become a turning point in the debate on liberalization, globalization, growth, efficiency and equity. However, the drive to address issues of working people in a comprehensive, consistent, long-term manner is absent. The National Rural Employment Guarantee Act of 2005 was one main outcome of the period. It guaranteed manual employment of 100 days per adult citizen, per family, per year at a minimum wage within a 5 km radius of their residence within 15 days. This became the main form of supporting the income of working poor and preventing mass distress migrations to the metropolises. To an extent it was successful in doing so wherever it was implemented well. This was followed by Unorganized Workers Social Security Act 2008 which critics had panned for ambiguous coverage and negligible benefits based on worker contribution.

Although the website (obviously unattended) seems to suggest that the commission still exists, its last report is dated 2009 when it completed its term. Many of its ideas and recommendations regarding improving conditions of employment in the unorganized sector remain part of current policy rhetoric about insurance, pensions, social security for unorganized sector workers, credit for start-ups and skill training for workers. However, a coherent estimation of the benefits of this form of social security or an actionable plan that will follow a road map to improve conditions of work seems to have evaporated along with the entire project of national plans.

Notes

1. D. Weldon (2015): 'Are the Robots Taking Enough Jobs?', http://www.bbc.co.uk/news/business-34846356
2. S. Kapsos (2005): 'The Employment Intensity of Growth: Trends and Macroeconomic Determinants', International Labour Office, Employment Trends Unit, Employment Strategy Department, ILO, viewed on 1 August 2013 http://www.ilo.org/wcmsp5/groups/public/---ed_emp/emp_elm/documents/publication/wcms_143163.pdf
3. D. Harvey (2005): *A Brief History of Neoliberalism*, Oxford University Press, Oxford, New York.
4. Sher Verick and Iyanatul Islam (2010): 'The Great Recession of 2008-2009: Causes, Consequences and Policy Responses', IZA Discussion Paper No. 4934, May.
5. J.E. Stiglitz (2010): *FREEFALL*, Norton paperback, NY, USA, 2010.
6. I. Islam and S. Verick, eds. (2011): *From the Great Recession to Labour Market Recovery*, Palgrave Macmillan.
7. B. Barakat, J. Holler, K. Prettner and J. Schuster (2010): *The Impact of the Economic Crisis on Labour and Education in Europe*, Vienna Institute of Demography, Austrian Academy of Sciences, Working Paper 6.
8. ILO–World Bank (2012): Inventory of Policy Response to Financial and Economic Crisis, ILO-WB, Geneva and Washington DC.
9. ILO (2015): World Employment and Social Outlook Trends 2015, ILO, Geneva.
10. T. Piketty (2014): Capital in the Twenty First Century, The Belknap Press of Harvard University Press, USA.
11. World Bank (2013): 'Jobs', World Development Report 2013, Washington DC.
12. David Graeber (2014): 'Debt, the first 5000 Years', Melville House, London.
13 S. Zizek (1999): The Ticklish Subject: The Absent Centre of Political Ontology, Verso, London, p. 243.

14. R.K. Bhatt (2011): 'Recent Global Recession and Indian Economy', *International Journal of Trade, Economics and Finance*, vol. 2, no. 3, June, pp. 212-17.
15. Labour Bureau (2009): Report on the Effect of the Economic Slowdown on Employment in India, For Ministry of Labour and Employment, Government of India, Chandigarh, India.
16. T.S. Papola (2013): 'Employment Growth during the Post Reform Period', *Indian Journal of Labour Economics*, vol. 56, no. 1, pp. 1-13.
17. Santosh Mehrotra, Ankita Gandhi, Partha Saha and Bimal Kishore Sahoo (2013): 'Turnaround in India's Employment Story, Silver Lining Amidst Joblessness and Informalization?', *Economic and Political Weekly*, 31 August, vol. XLVIII, no. 35.
18. Ejaz Ghani, R. William Kerr and S.D. O'Connell (2013): 'The Exceptional Persistence of India's Unorganized Sector', Policy Research Working Paper 6454, The World Bank, Poverty Reduction and Economic Management Network, Economic Policy and Debt Department, New York.
19. *The Hindu* (2015): 'Student Loans Dry up as Bad Debts Climb at Banks' (Mohit Saha), 25 November, p. 16.
20. Institute of Human Development (2014): Indian Labour and Employment Report 2014, Academic Foundation, New Delhi, p. 179.
21. A. Roychowdhury (2014): 'Recent Changes in Labour Laws, An Exploratory Note', *Economic and Political Weekly*, vol. XLIX, no. 41, pp. 14-17.
22. Gurgaon Workers News: See the site http://gurgaonworkersnews.wordpress.com/
23. *Economic Times* (2014): Modi's vision for labour reforms move a step forward as Cabinet approves amendments to three laws, 31 July.

APPENDIX I

Survey Data Tables

The following tables are a distribution of sample respondents by the indicated category or cross categories. The tables are broadly organized into groups like personal details of the respondents, experience of insecurity, skills, need for further skill upgradation, human resource management changes at the firm level, trade unions and miscellaneous tables. Occasionally tables from one group are placed in another group for comparison, correlation or for elucidation. Terminology used is defined and explained in Chapter 6, Section 6.4 titled 'Key Concepts and Their Operationalization'.

1. Personal Details

Table 1A: Distribution by Age

Age	*Frequency*	*Per cent*	*Cumulative per cent*
19	4	0.5	0.5
20	8	1	1.5
21	9	1.2	2.7
22	5	0.6	3.3
23	12	1.5	4.9
24	10	1.3	6.2
25	29	3.7	9.9
26	29	3.7	13.6
27	34	4.4	18.0
28	36	4.6	22.6
29	39	5.0	27.6
30	37	4.7	32.3
31	23	3.0	35.3
32	35	4.5	39.8
33	26	3.3	43.1
34	30	3.9	47.0
35	43	5.5	52.5
36	26	3.3	55.8
37	31	4.0	59.8
38	29	3.7	63.5
39	29	3.7	67.3
40	47	6.0	73.3
41	21	2.7	76.0
42	31	4.0	80.0
43	14	1.8	81.8
44	17	2.2	84.0
45	31	4.0	87.9
46	19	2.4	90.4
47	6	0.8	91.1
48	14	1.8	92.9
49	11	1.4	94.4

(contd.)

Table 1A (*contd.*)

Age	*Frequency*	*Per cent*	*Cumulative per cent*
50	9	1.2	95.5
51	6	0.8	96.3
52	7	0.9	97.2
53	2	0.3	97.4
54	6	0.8	98.2
55	4	0.5	98.7
56	1	0.1	98.8
57	4	0.5	99.4
58	4	0.5	99.9
60	1	0.1	100.0
Total	779	100.0	

Note: 1. Age Mean = 35.6, Median = 35, and Mode = 40.

Table 1B: Distribution by Gender

Gender	*Frequency*	*Per cent*	*Cumulative Per cent*
Female	188	24.1	24.1
Male	591	75.9	100.0
Total	779	100.0	100.0

Table 1C: Distribution by Education

Education Level	*Frequency*	*Per cent*	*Cumulative Per cent*
Under X	88	11.3	11.3
X	196	25.2	36.5
XII	159	20.4	56.9
Vocational diploma	72	9.2	66.1
Graduate	203	26.1	92.2
Others	61	7.8	100.0
Total	779	100.0	100.0

2. Experience of Insecurity

Table 2A: Distribution of Past Experience of Insecurity (PEI) by Scale of PEI

PEI scale	*Frequency*	*Per cent of 779 surveyed*	*Per cent of 412 – experienced PEI*
1 – Nil	367	47.1	-
2 – Low	227	29.1	55.1
3-4 – High	179	22.9	43.4
5 – Severe	6	0.8	1.5
Total	779	100.0	100.0

Notes: 1. PEI includes period of unemployment, job losses due to management decision.
2. PEI scale: NIL = 1, Low = 2, High = 3 or 4, Severe = 5. Details in Chapter 6, Section 6.4.
3. PEI experience of High + Severe: 22.9 + 0.8 = 23.7 per cent of the sample and 34.5 + 8.9 = 43.4 per cent of those affected.
4. Those that experienced some PEI: 779-367= 412.

Table 2B: Distribution of Past Experience of Insecurity by Age Category

	Past experience of insecurity category				
	Nil	*Low*	*High*	*Severe*	*Total*
Age category	81	122	71	1	275
< 32 yrs per cent in row	29.5	44.4	25.8	0.4	100.0
Age category	254	104	106	5	469
32-50 yrs per cent in row	54.2	22.2	22.6	1.1	100.0
Age category	32	1	2	0	35
51-60 per cent in row	91.4	2.9	5.7	0.0	100.0
Total count	367	227	179	6	779
Per cent within age category	47.1	29.1	23.0	0.8	100.0

Notes: 1. PEI includes period of unemployment, job losses due to management decision.
2. PEI scale: NIL = 1, Low = 2, High = 3 or 4, Severe = 5. Details in Chapter 6, Section 6.4.

Table 2C: Distribution of Past Experience of Insecurity by Skill Upgradation

PEI level	*Yes Upgraded*	*Per cent of Yes in Row*	*Per cent Yes of 779 Surveyed*	*No*	*Per cent No Out of Row*	*Total of Rows*
Nil	174	47.4	22.3	193	52.6	367
Low	125	55.1	16.0	102	44.9	227
High	130	72.6	16.7	49	27.4	179
Severe	4	66.6	0.01	2	33.3	6
Total	433	-	-	346	-	779

Notes: 1. PEI scale: NIL = 1, Low = 2, High = 3 or 4, Severe = 5. Details in Chapter 6, Section 6.4.
2. PEI includes period of unemployment, job losses due to management decision.
3. Effort rises with PEI, but at severe level, people seem to give up.
4. Insecurity seems to induce a fight back reaction by attempting skill-upgradation.

Table 2D: Distribution of Past Experience of Insecurity by Gender

Gender	*Past experience of insecurity category*				
	Nil	*Low*	*High*	*Severe*	*Total*
Female	49	80	59	-	188
Per cent within gender	26.1	42.6	31.4		100.0
Male	318	147	120	6	591
Per cent within gender	53.8	24.9	20.3	1.0	100.0
Total count	367	227	179	6	779
Per cent within category	47.1	29.1	23.0	0.8	100.0

Notes: 1. PEI scale: NIL = 1, Low = 2, High = 3 or 4, Severe = 5. Details in Chapter 6, Section 6.4.

2. PEI includes period of unemployment, job losses due to management decision.
3. Also fewer escape with nil experience.
4. Females experienced higher PEI at low and high scale.

Table 2E: Distribution of Comprehensive Past Experience of Insecurity (CPEI) by Scale

CPEI Scale	*Count*	*Per cent of 399*	*Per cent of 779 Surveyed*
Low	156	39.1	20.0
Higher	243	60.9	31.2
Some CPEI			
Low + Higher	399	-	51.2
Nil	380	-	48.8
Total	779		

Notes: 1. CPEI scale: NIL = 1, Low = 2, High = 3 or 4, Severe = 5. Details in Chapter 6, Section 6.4.

2. CPEI includes PEI + changes in compensation, working hour changes, time to find new job, and time spent in current job.
3. Over half, i.e. 51.2 per cent experienced some CPEI, and almost one-third (31.2 per cent) a high level of burden.

Table 2F: Distribution of Comprehensive Past Experience of Insecurity (CPEI) by Acquisition of New Skills Since 1991

CPEI scale	*Yes*	*No*	*Total*
Low	109	47	156
Per cent in column	39.8	37.6	39.1
High	165	78	243
Per cent in column	60.2	62.4	60.9
Total	274	125	399
Per cent in column	100.0	100.0	100.0

Chi-Square Tests

	Value	*df*	*Asymp. Sig. (2-sided)*	*Exact Sig. (2-sided)*	*Exact Sig. (1-sided)*
Pearson Chi-Square	0.171b	1	0.679		
Continuity Correction	0.092	1	0.762		
Fisher's Exact Test				0.740	0.382

Notes: 1. Computed only for a 2 × 2 table.

2. 0 cells (.0 per cent) have expected count less than 5. The minimum expected count is 48.87.
3. CPEI includes PEI + changes in compensation, working hour changes, time to find new job, and time spent in current job.
4. CPEI scale: NIL = 1, Low = 2, High = 3 or 4, Severe = 5. Details in Chapter 6, Section 6.4.

Table 2G: Distribution by Current Experience of Insecurity

(Do you think you can lose the current job?)

	Frequency	*Per cent*	*Cumulative per cent*
Yes can lose	381	48.9	48.9
No will not	398	51.1	100.0
Total	779	100.0	

Notes: 1. Current Experience of Insecurity (CEI) is fear of current job loss.
2. Nearly half 48.9 per cent fear job loss.

Distribution of Current Experience of Insecurity by Unionized and Non-Unionized Employees

	Total	*Can lose job*	*Per cent*
Unionized	612	286	46.7
Not unionized	167	95	56.9

Notes: 1. Current experience of Insecurity (CEI) is fear of job loss.
2. Trade unions or associations do seem to provide a sense of security to the employees and 10 per cent fewer unionized worker fear a job loss.

Table 2H: Distribution by Terms of Employment in Current Job

Terms of Employment	*Frequency*	*Per cent*	*Cumulative Per cent*
Full-time and permanent	565	72.5	72.5
Full-time and temporary	38	4.9	77.4
Part-time and permanent	139	17.8	95.3
Part-time and temporary	15	1.9	97.2
Contract labour, casual, *badli*, etc.	22	2.8	100.0
Total	779	100.0	100.0

Table 2I: Distribution of Employment Benefits in Current Job

Employment benefits	*Cases*	*Column response per cent*
Provident fund	611	78.4
Employment card	231	29.7
Continuous wages	509	65.3
Lay-off wages	88	11.3
Total	779	184.7

Table 2J: Distribution by Expectancy of Job Retention Period (Do you think you can keep the current job for next period?)

Valid	*Frequency*	*Per cent*	*Cumulative per cent*
Zero response	9	1.2	1.2
Till retirement	320	41.1	42.2
At least 10 years	95	12.2	54.4
At least 5 years	172	22.1	76.5
At least 1 year	141	18.1	94.6
Less than 1 year	42	5.4	100.0
Total	779	100.0	-

Table 2K: Distribution by the Most Important Threat Facing Job Security

Valid	*Frequency*	*Per cent*	*Cumulative per cent*
Imported cheaper substitutes	96	12.3	12.3
Increasing domestic competition	193	24.8	37.1
Labour policies of the management	237	30.4	67.5
Labour policies of the government	209	26.8	94.4
Policies of the trade union	12	1.5	95.9
Your own skills are inadequate	32	4.1	100.0
Total	779	100.0	

Note: Order of most important threat: management 30 per cent, government 27 per cent, domestic 25 per cent, imports 12 per cent.

Table 2L: Distribution by the Second Most Important Threat Facing Job Security

Valid	*Frequency*	*Per cent*	*Cumulative per cent*
Imported cheaper substitutes	145	18.6	18.6
Increasing domestic competition	158	20.3	38.9
Labour policies of the management	235	30.2	69.1
Labour policies of the government	195	25.0	94.1
Policies of the trade union	20	2.6	96.7
Your own skills are inadequate	26	3.3	100.0
Total	779	100.0	

Note: Order of second-most important threat: management 30 per cent, government 25 per cent, domestic competition 20 per cent, and imports 18.6 per cent.

Table 2M: Distribution by Experience of Informalization of Employment

Informalization	*Frequency*	*Per cent of 779 surveyed*
Nil	478	61.36
Some	301	38.64

Note: Informalization is change of job-status from unionized to non-unionized or fulltime to casual/part-time or from wage earner to self-employment. Intensity is the number of such changes in the job-status.

Distribution by Intensity of Informalization

Informalization Intensity	*Frequency*	*Per cent of 301*	*Per cent of 779*
Nil	478	-	61.3
Any 1 type informalization Yes	173	57.47	22.2
Any 2 type informalization Yes	98	32.55	12.6
All 3 type informalization Yes	30	9.9	3.9

Note: All surveyed = 779, those who experienced informalization = 301 (38.6 per cent).

Table 2N: Distribution by Experience of Informalization by Industry Type

Informalization Intensity	*Industry type*		*Total*
	Manufacturing	*Service*	
Nil	170	308	478
Per cent in column	88.5	52.5	61.3
Any 1 type informalization Yes	13	160	173
Per cent in column	6.8	27.3	22.2
Any 2 type informalization Yes	4	94	98
Per cent in column	2.1	16.0	12.6
All 3 type informalization Yes	5	25	30
Per cent in column	2.6	4.3	3.9
Total	192	587	779
Per cent in column	100.0	100.0	100.0

Chi-square test

	Value	*df*	*Asymptotic sigma (2-sided)*
Pearson Chi-square	77.888[a]	3	.000

Notes: 1. 0 Cells (.0 per cent) have expected count less than 5. The expected minimum count is 6.84.

2. Informalization is change of job-status from unionized to non-unionized or full-time to casual/part-time or from wage earner to self-employment. Intensity is the number of such changes in the job-status.

Table 2O: Distribution of Experience of Informalization by Sector

Informalization Intensity	*Sector type*		*Total*
	Public	*Private + Cooperative*	
Nil	130	347	477
Per cent in column	73.9	58.0	61.6
Any 1 type informalization Yes	16	157	173
Per cent in column	9.1	26.3	22.4
Any 2 type informalization Yes	18	77	95
Per cent in column	10.2	12.9	12.3
All 3 type informalization Yes	12	17	29
Per cent in column	6.8	2.8	3.7
Total	176	598	774
Per cent in column	100.0	100.0	100.0

Chi-square test

	Value	*df*	*Asymptotic sigma (2-sided)*
Pearson Chi-square	29.968[a]	3	.000

Notes: 1. 0 Cells (.0 per cent) have expected count less than 5. The expected minimum count is 6.59.

2. Informalization is change of job-status from unionized to non-unionized, full-time to casual/part-time, and from wage earner to self-employment. Intensity is the number of changes in the job-status.

Table 2P: Distribution of Experience of Informalization by Age Group

Age Group	*Experience of Intensity of Informalization of Employment*				*Total*
	Zero Yes	*One Yes*	*Two Yes*	*Three Yes*	
18-25 count	52	15	6	4	77
Per cent in age group	67.5	19.5	7.8	5.2	100.0
26-30 count	72	65	30	8	175
Per cent in age group	41.1	37.1	17.1	4.6	100.0
31-35 count	64	49	39	5	157
Per cent in age group	40.8	31.2	24.8	3.2	100.0
36-40 count	101	33	17	11	162
Per cent in age group	62.3	20.4	10.5	6.8	100.0
Above 40 count	189	11	6	2	208
Per cent in age group	90.9	5.3	2.9	1.0	100.0
Total count	478	173	98	30	779
Per cent in age group	61.4	22.2	12.6	3.9	100.0

Chi-square test

	Value	*Df*	*Asymptotic sigma (2-sided)*
Pearson Chi-square	151.23[a]	12	.000

Notes: 1. 1 Cell (5.0 per cent) have expected count less than 5. The expected minimum count is 2.97.

2. Informalization is change of job-status from unionized to non-unionized or full-time to casual/part-time or from wage earner to self-employment. Intensity is the number of such changes in the job-status.

Table 2Q: Distribution of Experience of Informalization by Type of Informalization

Shift in Job-type or Work	*Cases*	*Per cent of 301 who Experienced*
Unionized to non-unionized	154	51.2
Full-time to part-time or temporary or casual	193	64.1
Paid job to self-employment	112	37.2
Totals for 301 who experienced some	459	152.5

Table 2R: Distribution by Mobility (Job Changes) since 1991

Job changes	*Frequency*	*Per cent of 779 Surveyed*
No change	381	48.9
Yes change	398	51.1
Total	779	100.0

Distribution by Intensity of Mobility

Job Changes	*Frequency*	*Per cent of 779 Surveyed*	*Per cent of 398 who Changed Jobs*
No change	381	48.9	-
1 or 2	248	31.8	62.3
3 or 4	101	13.0	25.37
5 or 6	25	3.2	6.28
More than 6	24	3.1	6.03

Table 2S: Distribution by Involuntary Mobility: Job Changes due to Management Decision

Jobs Changed due to Firm's Action	*Frequency*	*Per cent of 779 Surveyed*	*Per cent of 398 who Changed Jobs*
Nil = voluntary	130	16.7	32.7
1 or 2	206	26.4	52.0
3 or 4	38	4.9	9.4
5 or 6	19	2.4	4.7
More than 6	5	0.1	1.2

Notes: 1. Job changed by 398 and only 130 changed voluntarily.
2. Job change due to management: 268/398 = 67.3 per cent of those who changed, and 268/779 or 34 per cent of all respondents.
3. Voluntary: 130/398 = 32.7 per cent of those who changed and 130/779 = 16.7 per cent of all surveyed.

Table 2T: Distribution by Voluntary Mobility (Job Changes on Employee Initiative)

Job Changes	*Frequency*	*Per cent of 130 who Changed Voluntarily*
Low 1-2	96	73.6
High 3-4	31	23.8
Very High 5-6	3	2.6
Total	130	100.0

Note: Voluntary: 130/398 = 32.7 per cent of those who changed and 130/779 = 16.7 per cent of all surveyed.

Distribution by Intensity of Mobility (Voluntary + Involuntary)

Job changes	*Frequency*	*Per cent of all 779 Surveyed*	*Per cent of 398 who Changed Jobs*
No change	381	48.9	-
Low 1 or 2	248	31.8	62.3
High 3 or 4	101	13.0	25.37
Very High 5 or 6	25	3.2	6.28
More than 6	24	3.1	6.03

Table 2U: Distribution of Mobility by Age

Age category	*Mobility Category*				
	Nil	*Low*	*High*	*Very High*	*Total*
< 32 years	199	58	16	2	275
Per cent in age category	72.4	21.1	5.8	0.7	100.0
32-50 years	349	85	32	3	469
Per cent in age category	74.4	18.1	6.8	0.6	100.0
51-60 years	34	1	-	-	35
Per cent in age category	97.1	2.9			100.0
Total count	582	144	48	5	779
Per cent in mobility category	74.7	18.5	6.2	0.6	100.0

Table 2V: Distribution of Mobility by Gender

Gender	*Nil*	*Low*	*High*	*Very High*	*Total*
Female count	124	45	15	4	188
Per cent within gender	66.0	23.9	8.0	2.1	100.0
Male count	458	99	33	1	591
Per cent within gender	77.5	16.8	5.6	0.2	100.0
Total count	582	144	48	5	779
Per cent within category	74.7	18.5	6.2	0.6	100.0

Table 2W: Distribution by Change in Compensation Compared to Earlier Job

Compensation compared to earlier job	*Frequency*	*Per cent of 398 who Changed Jobs*
Increased substantially	35	8.8
Increased	156	39.1
Nearly same	187	46.9
Decreased	16	4.1
Decreased substantially	4	1.0

Table 2X: Distribution by Change in Working Hours Compared to Earlier Job

Working hours Compared to Earlier Job	*Frequency*	*Per cent of 398 who Changed Jobs*
Decreased substantially	17	4.3
Decreased	30	7.5
Nearly same	227	57.0
Increased	95	23.9
Increased substantially	29	7.2

Table 2Y: Distribution by Time Spent Finding Next Job

Time to find Next Job	*Count*	*Per cent of 779*	*Per cent of 398 who Changed Jobs*
Decreased substantially	66	8.5	16.6
Decreased	81	10.4	20.4
Nearly the same	148	19.0	37.2
Increased	95	12.1	23.9
Increased substantially	9	1.2	2.3
Not applicable – no job change	380	48.8	-

Note: Time decreased for 16.6 + 20.4 = 37 per cent, and increased for 23.9 + 2.3 = 26.2 per cent.

Table 2Z: Distribution of Skill Upgradation by Past Experience of Insecurity

(New skills acquired since 1991)

Insecurity Category	*Yes*	*No*	*Total*
Nil	174	193	367
Per cent in column	40.2	55.8	47.1
Low	125	102	227
Per cent in column	28.9	29.5	29.1
High	130	49	179
Per cent in column	30.0	14.2	23.0
Severe	4	2	6
Per cent in column	0.9	0.6	0.8
Total	433	346	779
Per cent in row	55.6	44.4	100.0

Chi-square test

	Value	*Df*	*Asymptotic sigma (2-sided)*
Pearson Chi-square	31.309[a]	3	.000

Note: 2 Cells (25.0 per cent) have expected count less than 5. The expected minimum count is 2.66.

Table 2AA: Distribution of Past Experience of Insecurity by Gender

Gender	*Past Experience of Insecurity Category*				
	Nil	*Low*	*High*	*Severe*	*Total*
Female	49	80	59		188
Per cent within gender	26.1	42.6	31.4		100.0
Male	318	147	120	6	591
Per cent within gender	53.8	24.9	20.3	1.0	100.0
Total count	367	227	179	6	779
Per cent within gender	47.1	29.1	23.0	0.8	100.0

Notes: 1. PEI scale: NIL = 1, Low = 2, High = 3 or 4, Severe = 5. Details in Chapter 6, Section 6.4.
2. PEI includes period of unemployment and job changes due to management decision.
3. Female experience higher PEI at Low and High levels.
4. Also fewer females escape Nil experience of PEI.

Table 2BB: Distribution by Years of Unemployment Since 1991

Years Unemployed since 1991	*Frequency*	*Per cent*	*Cumulative per cent*
Nil	390	50.1	50.1
1-2	187	24.0	74.1
3-4	110	14.1	88.2
5-6	49	6.3	94.5
More than 6	43	5.5	100.0
Total	779	100.0	

3. Skills

Table 3A: Distribution by Acquisition of New Skills Since 1991

New Skills Acquired since 1991	*Frequency*	*Per cent*	*Cumulative per cent*
Yes	433	55.6	55.6
No	346	44.4	100.0
Total	779	100.0	

Table 3B: Distribution by Institution Category Used for Skill Upgradation

Where New Skills were Acquired	*Frequency*	*Per cent of 705 All Training Instances*	*Per cent of 433 who Upgraded Skills*
With organization where employed	310	44.0	71.6
Public institution college/ university	387	54.9	89.4
Private training institution	108	15.3	24.9
Total	705	100.0	-

Notes: 1. Training instances = 705, people who upgraded = 433, upradations per person = 1.63.
2. With-firm: 310/433 = 71.6 per cent.
3. With-public institutions: 387/433 = 89.3 per cent.
4. With-private institutions: 108/433 = 24.9 per cent.

Table 3C: Distribution by the Cost of Skill Upgradation

Who bore the Cost?	*Cases*	*Per cent of 779*	*Per cent of 433 who Upgraded*
Employer/organization	206	26.4	47.6
Own savings	263	33.8	60.7
Bank loan	92	11.8	21.2
Total cases	561	-	-

Note: Total surveyed = 779; who upgraded = 433.

Table 3D: Distribution of New Skill Acquisition by Education Level

(Have you up-graded your skills since 1991)

Education Level	*Yes and Per cent in Column*	*No and Per cent in Column*	*Total*	*Per cent Yes in Row*	*Per cent No in Row*
Under X	22	66	88	25.0	75.0
	5.1	19.1	11.3		
X	70	126	196	35.7	64.3
	16.2	36.4	25.2		
XII	89	70	159	56.0	44.0
	20.6	20.2	20.4		
Vocational	53	19	72	73.6	26.4
	12.2	5.5	9.2		
Graduates or others	199 46.0	65 18.8	264 33.9	75.4	24.6
Total	433	346	779	-	-
	100.0	100.0	100.0		

Chi-square test

	Value	*df*	*Asymptotic sigma (2-sided)*
Pearson Chi-square	116.073[a]	4	.000

Notes: 1. 0 Cells (0.0 per cent) have expected count less than 5. The expected minimum count is 31.98.
2. Basic education has a consistent and progressive influence on skill upgradation.
3. 25 per cent of under-X and 75.4 per cent of graduates upgraded their skill.

Table 3E: Distribution of Need to Further Upgrade Skills for Continued Employability

Valid	*Frequency*	*Per cent*	*Cumulative per cent*
Yes	379	48.7	48.7
No	400	51.3	100.0
Total	779	100.0	-

Table 3F: Distribution of Desire to Change Discipline/Profession

Valid	*Frequency*	*Per cent in Column*	*Cumulative Per cent*
No response	146	18.7	18.7
Yes	151	19.4	38.1
No	482	61.9	100.0
Total	779	100.0	

4. Need for Upgradation

Table 4: Distribution of Need for Upgradation by Education Level

Education level	*Yes*	*No*	*Total*
Under X	12	76	88
Per cent in column	3.2	19.0	11.3
X	55	141	196
Per cent in column	14.5	35.3	25.2
XII	77	82	159
Per cent in column	20.3	20.5	20.4
Vocational	48	24	72
Per cent in column	12.7	6.0	9.2
Graduates or others	187	77	264
Per cent in column	49.3	19.3	33.9
Total	379	400	779
Per cent in row	48.7	51.3	

Chi-square Test

	Value	*df*	*Asymptotic sigma (2-sided)*
Pearson Chi-square	137.805[a]	4	.000

Note: 0 Cells (0.0 per cent) have expected count less than 5. The expected minimum count is 35.03.

Table 4A: Distribution of Need for Further Upgradation by Past Upgradation

Prior Upgrade Status	*Count*	*Need Further Upgrade*		*Do Not Need Further Upgrade*	
		Count	*Per cent in row*	*Count*	*Per cent in row*
Earlier up-gradation	433	297	68.6	136	31.4
Per cent in column	55.6	78.4		34.0	
No earlier up-gradation	346	82	23.7	264	76.3
Per cent in column	44.4	21.6		66.0	
Total	779	379		400	
Per cent Yes of 779 surveyed		48.7			

Chi-square test

	Value	*df*	*Asymptotic sigma (2-sided)*	*Exact Sig. (2-sided)*	*Exact Sig. (1-sided)*
Pearson Chi-square	155.144[b]	1	.000		
Continuity correction[a]	153.353	1	.000		
Fisher's exact test				.000	.000

Notes: 1. Computed only for a 2 × 2 table. 0 Cells (0.0 per cent) have expected count less than 5. The expected minimum count is 168.34.

2. Earlier upgraded = 433, of these 297 want further upgradation: 297/433 = 68.6 per cent.
3. Not upgraded earlier = 346, and of these 82 want upgradation: 82/346 = 23.7 per cent.

Table 4B: Distribution of Need for Further Upgradation by Age

Age Group	*Need Further Upgrade*		*Do not Need Further Upgrade*		*Total*	
	Count	*Per cent*	*Count*	*Per cent*	*Count*	*Per cent*
18-25	54	14.2	23	5.8	77	9.9
26-30	77	20.3	98	24.5	175	22.5
31-35	89	23.5	68	17.0	157	20.1
36-40	77	20.3	85	21.2	162	20.8
> 40	82	21.7	126	31.5	208	26.7
Total	379	100.0	400	100.0	779	100.0

Chi-square Test

	Value	*df*	*Asymptotic sigma (2-sided)*
Pearson Chi-square	26.966[b]	4	.000

Note: 0 Cells (0.0 per cent) have expected count less than 5. The expected minimum count is 37.46.

Table 4C: Distribution of Income by Education Level

Income Level ->	*V*	*IV*	*III*	*II*	*I*	*Total*
Graduate or more	85	51	46	12	9	203
Per cent in row	42.0	25.0	23.0	6.0	4.0	
Vocational	15	24	15	11	7	72
Per cent in row	21.0	33.0	21.0	15.0	10.0	
XII		16	57	54	32	159
Per cent in row	0	10.0	36.0	34.0	20.0	
X		14	52	54	76	196
Per cent in row	0	7.0	27.0	28.0	39.0	
Under X		4	24	24	36	88
Per cent in row	0	5.0	27.0	27.0	41.0	
Others – ignored						61

Notes: 1. Salary category: V > Rs. 40000, IV 20000-40000, III 10000-20000, II 5000-10000, I < 5000.

2. Education does lead to higher incomes. 42 per cent graduates are in salary scale V, while 41 per cent under X are in the lowest scale I.

Table 4D: Distribution of Upgradation by Education and Income

(Number of upgrade/number of employees in salary category)

Salary Category->	*V*	*IV*	*III*	*II*	*I*	*Total Upgrades*
Graduates	84/85	51/51	49/46	25/12	23/9	232/203
Upgrade per cent	98.8	100.0	106.5	208.3	255.6	114.3
Vocational	16/15	23/24	20/15	12/11	13/7	84/72
Upgrade per cent	106.7	95.8	133.3	109.1	185.7	116.7
XII	0 /0	10/16	21/57	29/54	39/32	99/159
Upgrade per cent	0.0	62.5	36.8	53.7	121.9	62.3
X	0/0	13/14	7/52	29/54	16/76	65/196
Upgrade per cent	0.0	92.9	13.5	53.7	21.1	33.2
Under X	0/0	3/4	4/24	6/24	8/36	21/88
Upgrade per cent	0.0	75.0	16.7	25.0	22.2	23.9
Others-ignored 61						

Notes: 1. Salary categories: V > Rs. 40000, IV 20000-40000, III 10000-20000, II 5000-10000, I < 5000.

2. Better educated try hardest to upgrade when they are in lower salary scale, e.g., 255.6 per cent for graduates in scale I upgraded.

3. Under X: when incomes are low in scale I and II only 22-4 per cent upgraded (vicious cycle), but in scale IV 75 per cent upgraded.

Table 4E: Distribution of Upgradation by Education + Income

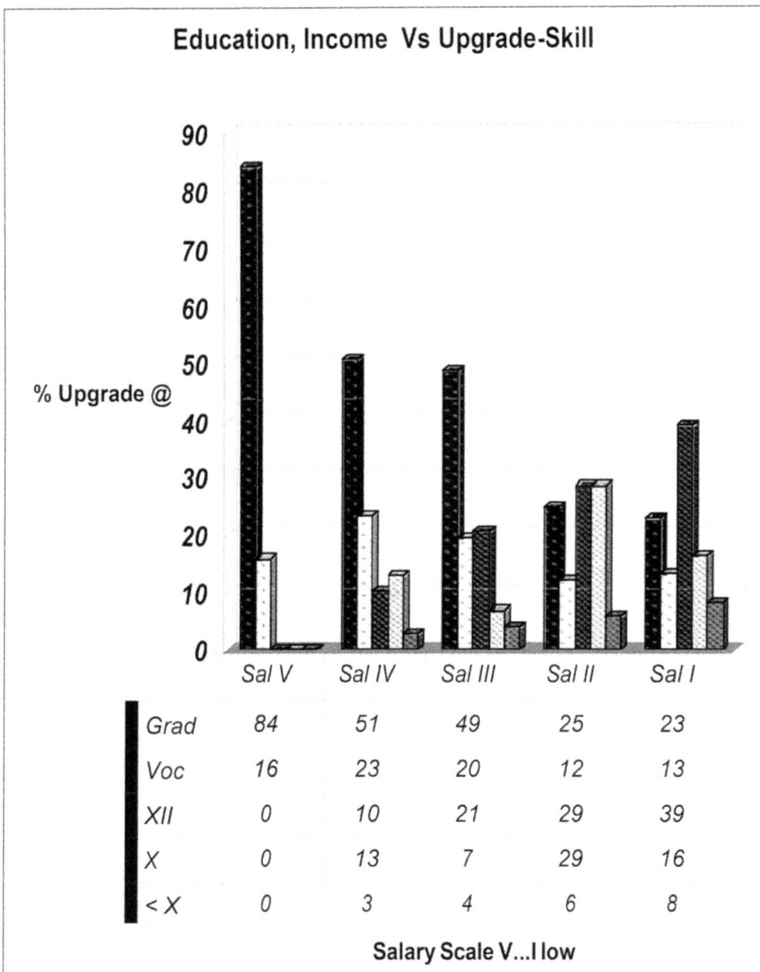

	Sal V	Sal IV	Sal III	Sal II	Sal I
Grad	84	51	49	25	23
Voc	16	23	20	12	13
XII	0	10	21	29	39
X	0	13	7	29	16
< X	0	3	4	6	8

Table 4F: Distribution of Need for Further Upgradation by Gender

Gender	*Need Upgradation*		*Do not need Upgradation*		
	Count	*Per cent in row*	*Count*	*Per cent in row*	*Total*
Female	122	64.9	66	35.1	188
Male	257	43.5	334	56.5	591
Total	379	48.7	400	51.3	779

Chi-square Test

	Value	*df*	*Asymptotic Sigma (2-sided)*	*Exact Sig. (2-sided)*	*Exact Sig. (1-sided)*
Pearson Chi-square	26.166[b]	1	.000		
Continuity correction a	25.316	1	.000		
Fisher's Exact Test				.000	.000

Notes: 1. Computed for a 2×2 table.
2. 0 Cells (0.0 per cent) have expected count less than 5. The expected minimum count is 91.47.

Table 4G: Distribution of Need for Further Upgradation by Industry Type

Type	*Yes*	*Per cent of All Yes*	*No*	*Per cent of All No*	*Sector Total*	*Per cent of Yes in Sector*
Manufacturing	34	9.3	146	36.8	180	18.8
Service	332	90.7	251	63.2	583	56.9
Total	366	100.0	397	100.0	763	-

Chi-square Test

	Value	*df*	*Asymptotic Sigma (2-sided)*	*Exact Sig. (2-sided)*	*Exact Sig. (1-sided)*
Pearson Chi-square	79.815[b]	1	.000		
Continuity correction	78.297	1	.000		
Fisher's Exact Test				.000	.000

Notes: 1. Computed for a 2×2 table.
2. 0 Cells (0.0 per cent) have expected count less than 5. The expected minimum count is 86.34.

Table 4H: Distribution of Need for Further Upgradation by Sector

Sector	*Yes*	*Per cent of All Yes*	*No*	*Per cent of All No*	*Sector Total*	*Per cent Yes in Sector*
Public	118	31.5	58	14.5	176	67.0
Private + cooperative	257	68.5	341	85.5	598	43.0
Total	375	100.0	399	100.0	774	-

Chi-square Test

	Value	*df*	*Asymptotic Sigma (2-sided)*	*Exact Sig. (2-sided)*	*Exact Sig. (1-sided)*
Pearson Chi-square	31.540[b]	1	.000		
Continuity correction a	30.584	1	.000		
Fisher's Exact Test				.000	.000

Notes: 1. Computed for a 2 × 2 table.

2. 0 Cells (0.0 per cent) have expected count less than 5. The expected minimum count is 85.27.

5. Human Resource Management (HRM)

Table 5A: Distribution by HRM Changes in Workplace (High-Road)

Changes in Workplace (Yes)	*Cases*	*Per cent of 750 Valid*
New machine or technology	566	75.46
Firm gave sufficient training on job or new machinery	407	54.26
Sufficient safety training	309	41.2
Training is linked to promotion	286	38.1
Performance appraisal exists	504	67.2
Payment is linked to performance	275	36.66
Promotion is linked to performance	351	46.8
Worker's participation in quality circles, teams – increased	259	34.5
Direct communication by management with employees	268	35.73
Worker participation in management has increased	298	39.73

Table 5B: Distribution by HRM Changes in Workplace (Low-Road)

Further Changes in Work Conditions (Yes)	*Cases*	*Per cent of 761 Valid*
Compensation is on individual basis	338	43.6
Voluntary retirement has been offered	345	45.33
Workers are employed but rendered idle	230	30.22
Job grades have been reduced	502	65.96
Most workers are required to do additional duties	602	79.1
Staff strength has decreased	509	66.88
Outsourcing has increased	436	57.29
Use of non-permanent staff has increased	466	61.23
Frequency of legal proceeding between employer, employees has increased	242	31.8
Relocation of plant/office has occurred	204	26.8

Table 5C: Distribution of Comprehensive HRM Changes in Work Place (High + Low-Road) by Scale

Scale of Comprehensive Experience of HRM Changes	*Frequency*	*Per cent*
Low	152	19.5
Medium	497	63.8
High	130	16.7
Total	779	100.0

Notes: 1. Out of 10 points Low scale is 2-3, Medium 4-6, and High 7-10.
2. Medium + High Scale of comprehensive HRM experience: 63.8 + 16.7 = 80.5 per cent.

Table 5D: Distribution of High-Road HRM Changes by Scale

Scale of High-Road HRM Changes	*Frequency*	*Per cent*
Low	321	41.2
Medium	272	34.9
High	186	23.9
Total	779	100.0

Notes: 1. Out of 10 points Low scale is 2-3, Medium 4-6, and High 7-10.
2. Medium + High Scale: 34.9 + 23.9 = 58.8 per cent.

Table 5E: Distribution of Low-Road HRM Changes by Scale

Scale of Low-Road HRM Changes	*Frequency*	*Per cent*
Low	201	25.8
Medium	365	46.9
High	213	27.3
Total	779	100.0

Notes: 1. Out of 10 points Low scale is 2-3, Medium 4-6, and High 7-10.
2. Medium + High scale: 46.9 + 27.3 = 74.2 per cent.

Table 5F: Distribution of High-Road HRM (HRHRM) Changes by Sector

Scale of HRHRM Changes	*Public*		*Private*		*Row Total*	*Per cent of 774 Valid*
	Count	*Per cent of Public*	*Count*	*Per cent of Private*		
Low	63	35.8	257	43.0	320	41.3
Medium	77	43.8	193	32.3	270	34.9
High	36	20.4	148	24.7	184	23.8
Total	176	100.0	598	100.0	774	100.0

Notes: 1. Out of 10 points Low scale is 2-3, Medium 4-6, and High 7-10.
2. High + Medium in public sector: 43.8 + 20.4 = 64.2 per cent.
3. High + Medium in private sector: 32.3 + 24.7 = 57.0 per cent.
4. Overall in both sectors: 34.9 + 23.8 = 58.7 per cent.

Sector	*HRHRM changes*			*Total*
	Low	*Medium*	*High*	
Public count	63	77	36	176
Per cent in column	19.7	28.5	19.6	22.7
Private + cooperative count	257	193	148	593
Per cent in column	80.3	71.5	80.4	77.3
Total	320	270	184	774

Chi-square Test

	Value	*df*	*Asymptotic Sigma (2-sided)*
Pearson Chi-square	7.885[a]	2	.019

Notes: 1. 0 Cells (0.0 per cent) have expected count less than 5. The expected minimum count is 41.84.
2. Out of 10 points Low scale is 2-3, Medium 4-6, and High 7-10.
3. Public sector Medium + High: 113/176 = 64.2 per cent vs. private Medium + High: 341/598 =57 per cent.
4. Public sector is 7 per cent better in High-Road HRM changes.

Table 5G: Distribution of Low-Road Human Resource Management (LRHRM)

Changes by Sector

Scale of LRHRM changes	*Public*	*Per cent of Public*	*Private*	*Per cent of Private*	*Total Row*	*Per cent of 774 Valid*
Low	38	21.6	162	27.1	200	25.8
Medium	71	40.3	292	48.8	363	46.9
High	67	38.1	144	24.1	211	27.3
Total	176	100.0	598	100.0	774	100.0

Notes: 1. Out of 10 points Low scale is 2-3, Medium 4-6, and High 7-10.
2. Low-Road HRM in Public sector – Medium + High: 138/176 = 78.4 per cent.
3. Private medium + High: 436/598 = 72.9 per cent.
4. Public sector is 5.5 per cent higher in Low-Road HRM changes.

Sector	*Low-Road HRM Changes*			*Total*
	Low	*Medium*	*High*	
Public count	38	71	67	176
Per cent in change category	19.0	19.6	18.8	22.7
Private + cooperative count	162	292	144	598
Per cent in change category	81.0	80.4	68.2	77.3
Total	200	363	211	774

Notes: 1. Out of 10 points Low scale is 2-3, Medium 4-6, and High 7-10.
2. Public Medium + High = 138/176 = 78.4 per cent.
3. Private Medium = 436/598 =.72.9 per cent.

Table 5H: Distribution of Comprehensive HRM Changes by Sector (High + Low-Road)

Scale of Comprehensive HRM Changes	*Public*	*Per cent of Public*	*Private + Cooperatives*	*Per cent of Private*	*Total*	*Per cent of 774 valid*
Low	19	10.8	132	22.1	151	19.5
Medium	126	71.6	369	61.7	495	64.0
High	31	17.6	97	16.2	128	16.5
Total	176	100.0	598	100.0	774	100.0

Sector	*All HRM changes*			*Total*
	Low	*Medium*	*High*	
Public count	19	126	31	176
Per cent in column	12.6	25.5	24.2	22.7
Private + cooperative count	132	369	97	598
Per cent in column	87.4	74.5	75.8	77.3
Total	151	495	128	774

Chi-square Test

	Value	*df*	*Asymptotic Sig. (2-sided)*
Pearson Chi-square	11.103[a]	2	.004

Notes: 1. 0 Cells (0.0 per cent) have expected count less than 5. The expected minimum count is 29.11.
2. Out of 10 points Low scale is 2-3, Medium 4-6, and High 7-10.
3. Both types of HRM changes in public sector of Medium + High scales = 89.2 per cent vs. 77.9 per cent in private sector.
4. For the sample Medium + High Scales = 80.5 per cent.

Table 5I: Distribution of Job Retention Expectancy Period by Comprehensive HRM Changes

Can you keep Your Job for Next?	*All HRM changes*			*Total*
	Low	*Medium*	*High*	
No response	2	5	2	9
Per cent in column	1.3	1.0	1.2	1.2
Till retirement	62	192	66	320
Per cent in column	40.8	38.6	50.8	41.1
At least 10 years	10	63	22	95
Per cent in column	6.6	12.7	16.9	12.2
At least 5 years	27	128	17	172
Per cent in column	17.8	25.8	13.1	22.1
At least 1 year	47	82	12	141
Per cent in column	30.7	16.5	9.2	18.1
Less than 1 year	4	27	11	42
Per cent in column	2.6	5.4	8.5	5.4
Total	152	497	130	779

Chi-square Test

	Value	*df*	*Asymptotic Sig. (2-sided)*
Pearson Chi-square	44.077[a]	10	.000
Valid cases	779		

Note: 2 cells (11.1 per cent) have expected count less than 5. The expected minimum count is 1.50.

Table 5J: Distribution of Job Retention Expectancy Period by Scale of High-Road HRM Changes

Can you keep your job for next?	*High-Road HRM changes*			*Total*
	Low	*Medium*	*High*	
No response	1	5	3	9
Per cent in column	0.3	1.8	1.6	1.2
Till retirement	117	118	85	320
Per cent in column	36.4	43.4	45.7	41.1
At least 10 years	26	39	30	95
Per cent in column	8.1	14.3	16.1	12.2
At least 5 years	76	55	41	172
Per cent in column	23.7	20.2	22.0	22.1
At least 1 year	84	38	19	141
Per cent in column	26.2	14.0	10.2	18.1
Less than 1 year	17	17	8	42
Per cent in column	5.3	6.3	4.3	5.4
Total	321	272	186	779

Chi-square Test

	Value	*df*	*Asymptotic Sig. (2-sided)*
Pearson Chi-square	35.975[a]	2	.000

Note: 0 cells (0.0 per cent) have expected count less than 5. The expected minimum count is 90.97.

Table 5K: Distribution of Current Experience of Insecurity by Scale of Low-Road Human Resource Management Changes

Can Lose Current Job?	*Experience of Low-Road HRM Changes*			
	Low	*Medium*	*High*	*Total*
Count in category	74	176	131	381
Percentage of 381	18.4	46.2	34.4	100.0

Can Lose Current Job?	*Low-Road HRM Changes*			*Total*
	Low	*Medium*	*High*	
Yes	74	176	131	381
Per cent in column	36.8	48.2	61.5	48.9
No	127	189	82	398
Per cent in column	63.2	51.8	38.5	51.1
Total	201	365	213	779

Chi-square Test

	Value	*df*	*Asymptotic Sig. (2-sided)*
Pearson Chi-square	25.352[a]	2	.000

Notes: 1. 0 cells (0.0 per cent) have expected count less than 5. The expected minimum count is 98.31.

2. Current Experience of Insecurity (CEI) is fear of job loss.
3. Among the 381 who fear job loss 80.6 per cent have experienced medium to high scale of low road HRM changes.

Table 5L: Distribution of Current Experience of Insecurity by Comprehensive HRM Changes (High + Low-Road)

Yes Can Lose Job	*Experience of Comprehensive HRM Changes*			
	Low	*Medium*	*High*	*Total*
Count in category	78	252	51	381
Per cent of (381) Yes can lose	20.5	66.1	13.4	100.0

Yes can lose job		*Experience of Comprehensive HRM changes*			
		Low	*Medium*	*High*	*Total*
Yes	Count	78	252	51	381
Per cent in Column		51.3	50.7	39.2	48.9
No	Count	74	245	79	398
Per cent in Column		48.7	49.3	60.8	51.1
Total		152	497	130	779
		100.0	100.0	100.0	100.0

Chi-square Test

	Value	*Df*	*Asymptotic Sig. (2-sided)*
Pearson Chi-square	5.866[a]	2	.053

Notes: 1. 0 cells (0.0 per cent) have expected count less than 5. The expected minimum count is 63.58.

2. Among 381 who fear job loss 78.5 per cent experienced medium to high levels of comprehensive HRM changes.
3. Current experience of insecurity (CEI) relates to fear of job loss.

Table 5M: Distribution of Current Experience of Insecurity by High-Road HRM Changes

Yes Can Lose Job	*Experience of High-Road HRM Changes*			
	Low	*Medium*	*High*	*Total*
Count in category	82	250	49	381
Per cent (381) Yes can lose job	21.5	65.6	12.9	100.0

Notes: 1. Among 381 who fear job loss 78.5 per cent have experienced medium and high scales of high road HRM changes.
2. Current experience of insecurity (CEI) relates to fear of job loss.
3. Differences between CEI among high and low road HRM changes are small because firms adopt a mix of both types.

Table 5N: Distribution by Incidence of Human Resource Management Practices

Changes in Workplace (Yes)	*Per cent*
Most workers are required to do additional duties	79.1
New m/c or technology introduced	75.46
Performance appraisal exists	67.2
Staff strength has decreased	66.88
Job grades have been reduced	65.96
Use of non-permanent staff has increased	61.23
Outsourcing has increased	57.29
Firm gave sufficient training on job or new m/c	54.26
Promotion is linked to performance	46.8
VRS has been offered	45.33
Compensation is on individual basis	43.6
Sufficient safety training	41.2
Worker participation in management has increased	39.73
Training is linked to promotion	38.1
Payment is linked to performance	36.66
Direct communication by management with employees	35.73
Worker's participation in quality circles, teams – increased	34.5
Frequency of legal proceeding between employer, employees has increased	31.8
Workers are employed but rendered idle	30.22
Relocation of plant/office has occurred	26.8

Note: Organizations employ a mixture of High and Low-Road HRM practices, and hence the distribution, of CEI by Low and High-Road separately, does not show significant difference.

Table 5O: Distribution of Expectancy of Job Retention Period by Low-Road HRM Changes

Can you Keep Your Job for Next?	*Low-Road HRM Changes*			*Total*
	Low	*Medium*	*High*	
No response	6	2	1	9
Per cent in column	3.0	0.6	0.5	1.2
Till retirement	90	148	82	320
Per cent in column	44.8	40.5	38.5	41.1
At least 10 years	21	45	29	95
Per cent in column	10.4	12.3	13.6	12.2
At least 5 years	49	71	52	172
Per cent in column	24.4	19.5	29.4	22.1
At least 1 year	32	81	28	141
Per cent in column	15.9	22.2	13.1	18.1
Less than 1 year	3	18	21	42
Per cent in column	1.5	4.9	9.9	5.4
Total	201	365	213	779
	100.0	100.0	100.0	100.0

Chi-square Test

	Value	*Df*	*Asymptotic Sig. (2-sided)*
Pearson Chi-square	32.394[a]	10	.000

Note: 3 cells (16.7 per cent) have expected count less than 5. The expected minimum count is 2.32.

Table 5P: Distribution of Flexible Work Practices (FWP) by Scale

Scale of FWP	*Frequency*	*Per cent*
Nil	69	8.9
Low	189	24.3
Medium	389	49.9
High	132	16.9
Total	779	100.0

Notes: 1. Scale of FWP: Low = 1, Medium = 2, High = 3.
2. FWP includes many forms of work intensification like grade compaction, multi-tasking.
3. Flexible work practices at Medium + High scales = 521/779 = 66.88 per cent.

Table 5Q: Distribution of Flexible Work Practices by Industry Type

Type	*Total*	*FWP has Occurred*	*Per cent in Row*	*Per cent of 556 Experienced FWP*
Manufacturing	180	94	52.2	17.0
Service	583	462	79.2	83.0
Others (16)	-	-	-	-
Total	763	556	72.8	100.0

Notes: 1. Others =16 responses could not be classified into only manufacturing or service.
2. FWP includes many forms of work intensification like grade compaction, multi-tasking.

6. Trade Unions

Table 6A: Distribution by Trade Union Membership

Member of Trade Union	*Count*	*Per cent of 779, All Surveyed*
Yes	612	78.6
No	167	21.4
Total	779	100.0

Table 6B: Distribution by Membership of Federated and Non-federated Trade Unions

Union Status	*Count*	*Per cent 612 Union Members*	*Per cent of 779, All Surveyed*
Union is Federated	472	77.1	60.6
Union is not federated	140	22.9	18.0
No union	167	-	21.4

Table 6C: Distribution of Trade Union Membership by Gender

Gender	*Union Member*	*Per cent*	*Not Union Member*	*Per cent*	*Total*
Female	127	68	61	32	188
Male	485	82	106	18	591
Both genders	612	77	167	23	779

Table 6D: Distribution by Union Bargaining Issues

Union Bargains For	*Cases*	*Per cent in Row*
Training on job	395	59.8
Length of working day or work time	436	66.0
How to measure work performance	271	41.0
Promotion related to length of service	335	50.7
Wages	593	89.7
Bonus	511	77.3
Outsourcing of work earlier done in the firm	329	49.8
Reduction in staff	356	53.9
Introduction of new machinery	277	41.9
Training on new technology	333	50.3

Table 6E: Distribution by Scale of Union Bargaining

Scale of Union Bargaining	*Frequency*	*Per cent*
Nominal	132	16.9
Low	123	15.8
Medium	285	36.6
High	239	30.7
Total	779	100.0

Note: Bargaining scale: Out of 10 issues Low deals with 2-3, Medium 4-6, and High 7-10. Refer to Chapter 6, Section 6.4.

Table 6F: Distribution of Current Experience of Insecurity by Membership of Trade Union

Union Members	*Count*	*Can Lose Job*	*Per cent in row*
Yes	612	286	46.7
No	167	95	56.8
Yes + No	779	381	48.9

Note: Current experience of insecurity (CEI) relates to fear of job loss.

7. Miscellaneous

Table 7A: Names of Organizational Units

Agnes Pathan 3D PLM
Auto Windows
B.E.S.T.
Barista Coffee Bar
BKO Industries
Bombay Retreading Service
Carriage Workshop
CEAT Tyres
Central Railway Workshop – Matunga
Datta Meghe College of Engineering
DHL
E.M.U P-O-PH Workshop – Matunga
Events Ten
Gemetic
Geometric Software
Godrej and Boyce Soaps
Grindlays Bank – Fort
Hindustan Lever
Hutch
Intelinet
Intelnet, Emmay H.R.
IT Services Company
J.S.O.
Jai Hind College
Joast Company
KEM Hospital
M/s Apar Industries Ltd.
McDonald Restaurant

contd.

Table 7A (contd.)

McDonalds – Colaba
Maharashtra Rolling Mills
Modisons Private Ltd.
Nanavati Hospital
Nationalized Commercial Bank
President Hotel
Punjab National Bank
Sahakari Cooperative
Savari Dibba Maramat Factory C.R.
Software Solutions
Universal Parcel Service
Standard Chartered Bank
Sub-central Workshop
Tata Consultancy Services
Unideritend Ltd.
Zoroastrian Automobile

Table 7B: Distribution of Responses by Sector

Sector	*Frequency*	*Per cent*	*Cumulative Per cent*
Nil	5	0.6	0.6
Public	176	22.6	23.2
Private	559	71.8	95.0
Cooperative	39	5.0	100.0
Total	779	100.0	

Table 7C: Distribution of Responses by Size of Workforce

Workforce Size	*Frequency*	*Per cent*	*Cumulative Per cent*
0	2	0.3	0.3
1-49	76	9.8	10.0
50-99	111	14.2	24.3
100-999	276	35.4	59.7
1,000-4,999	146	18.7	78.4
5,000 and above	168	21.5	100.0
Total	779	100.0	

Table 7D: Distribution by Size of Organisation

Size	*Frequency*	*Per cent*	*Cumulative Per cent*
Small	168	21.6	21.6
Medium	301	38.6	60.2
Large	310	39.8	100.0
Total	779	100.0	

Note: Size as subjectively described by employee.

Table 7E: Distribution of Respondents by Type of Industry

Industry Type	*Frequency*	*Per cent*
Metal and metal products	95	12.2
Mechanical Engineering	77	9.9
Paper and paper products	10	1.3
Plastic and plastic products	15	1.9
Chemicals and products	40	5.1
Construction and Civil engineering	15	1.9
Textiles and products	11	1.4
Leather and products	9	1.2
IT, communication, BPO	123	15.8
Banking and Financial service	158	20.3
Services	265	34.0
Total	779	103.6

Note: Some responses fall in more than one category.

Table 7F: Distribution of Respondents by Length of Service in Current Job

Years in Current Job	*Frequency*	*Per cent*	*Cumulative Per cent*
More than 8	412	52.9	52.9
6-8	93	11.9	64.8
4-6	89	11.4	76.3
2-4	116	14.9	91.1
Less than 2	69	8.9	100.0
Total	779	100.0	

Table 7G: Distribution of Respondents by Current Job Description

Current Job Description	*Frequency*	*Per cent*	*Cumulative Per cent*
Professional, technical	193	24.8	24.8
Administrative, executive	38	4.9	29.7
Clerical and related	120	15.4	45.1
Sales	51	6.5	51.6
Production	143	18.4	88.8
Transport equipment, operator, labourer	59	7.6	96.4
Other workers	28	3.6	100.0
Total	779	100.0	

Table 7H: Sample Statistics

	Age	*Past Experience of Insecurity*	*Mobility*
N	779	779	779
Mean	35.6	1.83	0.34
Median	35.00	2.00	0.00
Mode	40	1	0
Std. Deviation	8.25	0.94	0.68
Range	4	4	4
Minimum	19	1	0
Maximum	60	5	4

Table 7I: Distribution of Respondents by Change in Working Hours in Current Job

Working Hours in Current Job	*Frequency*	*Per cent*	*Cumulative Per cent*
Decreased substantially	15	1.9	1.9
Decreased	53	6.8	8.7
Nearly the same	420	53.9	62.6
Increased	235	30.2	92.8
Increased substantially	56	7.2	100.0
Total	779	100.0	

Table 7J: Distribution of Respondents by Change in Income in Current Job

Change in Income in Current Job	*Frequency*	*Per cent*	*Cumulative Per cent*
Increased substantially	49	6.3	6.3
Increased	370	47.5	53.8
Nearly the same	308	39.5	93.3
Decreased	38	4.9	98.2
Decreased substantially	14	1.8	100.0
Total	779	100.0	

Table 7K: Distribution of Respondents by Salary Scale in Current Job

Salary Scale in Current Job (Rupees per Month)	*Frequency*	*Per cent*	*Cumulative Per cent*
Less than 5,000	152	19.5	19.5
5,000-10,000	352	45.2	64.7
10,000-20,000	181	23.2	87.9
20,000-40,000	74	9.5	97.4
More than 40,000	20	2.6	100.0
Total	779	100.0	

Table 7L: Distribution of Skill Upgradation by Change in Salary in Current Job

Salary Change	*Count*	*Upgraded*	*Per cent Upgrade in Row*
Substantial increase	49	47	95.9
Some increase	370	214	57.8
Nearly same	308	129	41.8

Survey Questionnaire

Job Security Survey 2005-6

1. Personal Information

1.1 Age ☐☐ years

1.2 Gender – Tick only one box Female ☐ Male ☐

1.3 Education – Tick only one box

Under VII ☐ X ☐ Vocational Diploma ☐ Graduate ☐

Other (please specify) ____________________

2. Job Status since 1991

2.1 How many jobs you have changed since 1991 – Tick only one box

Nil ☐ 1 or 2 ☐ 3 or 4 ☐ 5 or 6 ☐ More than 6 ☐

2.2 If you have changed jobs then Number of jobs lost, due to firm/organization decisions during last 10 years – Tick only one box

Nil ☐ 1 or 2 ☐ 3 or 4 ☐ 5 or 6 ☐ More than 6 ☐

2.3 If you have changed jobs then, for you, the time spent in finding the next job has – Tick only one box

Decreased substantially ☐ Decreased ☐ Nearly the same ☐

Increased ☐ Increased substantially ☐

2.4 How long you have been in current job – Tick only one box

More than 8 years ☐ 6-8 years ☐ 4-6 years ☐ 2-4 years ☐

Less than 2 years ☐

2.5 Have any job changes from 1991 resulted in any of the following?

- Tick as many as applicable

1. Shift from Unionized to non-Unionized Yes ☐ No ☐
2. Shift from full-time to part-time or temporary or casual
   Yes ☐ No ☐
3. Shift from paid job to self-employed Yes ☐ No ☐

2.6 Compared to earlier jobs your total compensation has – Tick only one box
Increased substantially ☐ Increased ☐ Nearly the same ☐
Decreased ☐ Decreased substantially ☐

2.7 Compared to your earlier jobs how your working hours have? – Tick onle one box
Decreased substantially ☐ Decreased ☐ Nearly the same ☐
Increased ☐ Increased substantially ☐

2.8 Have you acquired new skills and or qualifiaction since 1991?
Yes ☐ No ☐

2.9 If yes, Where did you acquire the new skills/qualifications – Tick as many as relevant
Within the organisation/firm where you were employed ☐
Public institution/University/College ☐
Private Training Institution ☐

2.10 Who has borne the cost of new skill/qualification acquisition – Tick as many as relevant
Employer organization ☐ Own Savings ☐ Bank Loan ☐

2.11 Do you require to further upgrade your skill for continued employability?
Yes ☐ No ☐

2.12 If yes, does it mean you have to change over to a new discipline/profession?
Yes ☐ No ☐

3. Your Present Job

3.1 Present Job Description – Select the closest and Tick only one box
1. Professional, Technical & Related ☐
2. Administrative, Executive, Managerial ☐
3. Clerical and related ☐
4. Sales ☐
5. Services ☐
6. Production ☐
7. Transport Equipment Operators, Labourers ☐
8. Workers not classified above ☐

3.2 Terms of Present Job/Service – Tick only one box
Full-time and permanent ☐
Part-time and permanent ☐

Full-time and temporary ☐
Part-time and temporary ☐
Contract labour, Casual, Badli, etc. ☐

3.3 Which of the following employees benefit you have NOW? – Tick as many as relevant

Provident Fund ☐ Employee Card ☐
Continuous Wages ☐ Lay-off wages ☐

3.4 Do you think you can, If you want to, keep the current job for the next? – Tick only one box

Till retirement ☐ At least 10 years ☐ At least 5 years ☐
At least 1 year ☐ Less than 1 year ☐

3.5 Which of the following changes in the working conditions have taken place in the present job – Please Tick as many as you know/are applicable

1. New machinery or technology has been installed Yes ☐ No ☐
2. Firm has given sufficient training on job or new machines Yes ☐ No ☐
3. Sufficient safety training is given Yes ☐ No ☐
4. Training is linked to promotion Yes ☐ No ☐
5. Performance appraisal exists Yes ☐ No ☐
6. Payment is linked to productivity/is incentive based Yes ☐ No ☐
7. Promotion is linked to performance Yes ☐ No ☐
8. Worker participation in quality circles, teams, programmes has increased Yes ☐ No ☐
9. Direct communication by management with employee has increased Yes ☐ No ☐
10. Your frequency or ease of meeting senior management has increased Yes ☐ No ☐
11. Worker participation in management has increased Yes ☐ No ☐

3.6 Futher changes in the working conditions have taken place in present job – Tick as many as you know/are applicable

1. Payment is now piece rate; earlier it was on time rate (per day, week, month) Yes ☐ No ☐
2. Payment and conditions of employment are based on individual contracts Yes ☐ No ☐

3. VRS has been offered Yes ☐ No ☐
4. Workers are employed but rendered idle Yes ☐ No ☐
5. Job grades have been reduced (work intensification) Yes ☐ No ☐
6. Most workers are required to do additional duties Yes ☐ No ☐
7. Length of service per worker has decreased Yes ☐ No ☐
8. Staff strength has decreased Yes ☐ No ☐
9. Outsourcing has increased Yes ☐ No ☐
10. Use of non-permanent workers has increased Yes ☐ No ☐
11. Frequency of legal proceeding between employer, employees has increased Yes ☐ No ☐
12. Relocation of plant/offices has occurred Yes ☐ No ☐

3.7 Your working hours, in this job – Tick one box
Decreased substantially ☐ Decreased ☐ Nearly the same ☐
Increased ☐ Increased substantially ☐

3.8 Has your income in the present job – Tick one box
Increased substantially ☐ Increased ☐ Nearly the same ☐
Decreased ☐ Decreased substantially ☐

3.9 Your Monthly salary per month in the current job is – Tick one box
Less than 5000 ☐ 5000-10000 ☐ 10,000-20,000 ☐ 20,000-40,000 ☐
More than 40,000 ☐

4. State of the Employee Union

4.1 Are you a member of any Union? Yes ☐ No ☐

4.2 If yes, is your Union federated to a central Union? Yes ☐ No ☐

4.3 If yes, does your Union bargain for the following – Please Tick as many as you know

1. Training on job Yes ☐ No ☐
2. Length of wroking day or work time Yes ☐ No ☐
3. How to measure work or performance Yes ☐ No ☐
4. Promotion related to length of service Yes ☐ No ☐
5. Wages Yes ☐ No ☐
6. Bonus Yes ☐ No ☐
7. Outsourcing of work earlier done in the firm Yes ☐ No ☐
8. Reduction of staff Yes ☐ No ☐
9. Participation in quality circles, teams, programmes Yes ☐ No ☐
10. Introduction of new technology, machinery Yes ☐ No ☐
11. Training on new technology, machines Yes ☐ No ☐

4.4 Most important threat facing your job security? – Tick only one box

1. Imported substitutes that are cheaper Yes ☐ No ☐
2. Increasing domestic production Yes ☐ No ☐
3. Labour policies of the Management Yes ☐ No ☐
4. Labour policies of the Government Yes ☐ No ☐
5. Policies of the Trade Union Yes ☐ No ☐
6. Your own skills are inadequate Yes ☐ No ☐

4.5 Number – Two threat facing your job security? – Tick only one box

1. Imported substitutes that are cheaper Yes ☐ No ☐
2. Increasing domestic production Yes ☐ No ☐
3. Labour policies of the Management Yes ☐ No ☐
4. Labour policies of the Government Yes ☐ No ☐
5. Policies of the Trade Union Yes ☐ No ☐
6. Your own skills are inadequate Yes ☐ No ☐

5. Miscellaneous

5.1 Name of the Firm/organization

Area/Locality

5.2 Industry Type – Tick as many as relevant

1. Metal and metal products ☐
2. Mechanical engineering ☐
3. Paper and paper products ☐
4. Plastic and plastic products ☐
5. Chemical and chemical products ☐
6. Construction and civil engineering ☐
7. Textile and textile products ☐
8. Leather and leather products ☐
9. IT, Communication, BPO ☐
10. Banking & Financial Services ☐
11. Services ☐
12. Others (please specify) ____________________

5.3 Sector Public ☐ Private ☐ Cooperative ☐

5.4 Size of the Total workforce is? – Tick only one box

1-49 ☐ 50-99 ☐ 100-999 ☐ 1000-4999 ☐ 5000 & above ☐

5.5 Size of Assets in crores? – Tick only one box

Tiny ☐ Small ☐ Medium ☐ Large ☐

Bibliography

Abraham, K.S. (2005): 'What We Don't Know Could Hurt Us: Some Reflections on the Measurement of Economic Activity', *Journal of Economic Perspectives*, vol. 19, no. 3, pp. 3-18.

Acemogul, D. (1998): 'Why do New Technologies Complement Skills?: Directed Technical Change and Wage Inequality', *Quarterly Journal of Economics*, vol. 113, pp. 1055-89.

Ackroyd, S. et al. (1998): 'The Japanization of the British Industry', *Industrial Relations Journal*, vol. 19, no. 1, p. 23.

ADB (1997): *Emerging Asia: Changes and Challenges*, ADB, Manila.

Ahluwalia, Montek S. (2000): 'Economic Performance of State in Post-Reform Period', *Economic and Political Weekly*, vol. 35, no. 19, 6 May.

Albert, M. (1993): *Capitalism against Capitalism*, Whurr Publishers, London.

Amsden, A. (1989): *Asia's Next Giant: South Korea and Late Industrialisation*, Oxford University Press, New York.

Amy, L.R. (1964): 'Diversified Manufacturing Business', *Journal of Royal Statistical Society*, Series A, vol. 127.

Armstrong, M. and Angela Baron (2002): *Strategic HRM*, Chartered Institute of Personnel and Development, CIPD House, London.

Arulampalam, W., P. Gregg and M. Gregory (2001): 'Introduction. Unemployment Scarring', *The Economic Journal*, vol. 111, no. 475, pp. F577-84.

Arulampalam, W. (2001): 'Is Unemployment Really Scarring?', *The Economic Journal*, vol. 111, no. 475, pp. F585-606.

Ashton, D. and J. Sung (1994): *The State, Economic Development and Skill Formation: A New East Asian Model*, Centre for Labour Market Studies, University of Leicester.

Ashton, D. et al. (1996): *Work Skills in Britain*, Warwick University, Skope.

Bacon, N. (1999): 'Union Derecognition and the New Human Relations: a Steel Industry Case Study', *Work Employment and Society*, vol. 13, no. 1, pp. 1-17.

Baker, K. and K. Christensen (1998): *Contingent Work: American Employment Relations in Transition*, Cornell University Press, Ithaca.

Bardhan, Pranab (2002), 'The Political Economy of Reform in India', in Mohan Rakesh (ed.), *Facets of the Indian Economy*, Oxford University Press, New Delhi, pp. 123-35.

______ (2000): 'Social Justice in Global Economy', *Economic and Political Weekly*, vol. 39, nos. 5-6, pp. 54-62.

Barro, J.R. and Salai-Martin (1995): *Economic Growth*, McGraw-Hill, New York.

Bassett, P. and A. Cave (1993): *All for One: The Future of the Unions*, The Fabian Society, London.

Baumohl, Bernard (1993): 'When Downsizing Becomes Dumb Sizing', *Time Magazine*, 15 March.

Beatson, M. (1995): *Labour Market Flexibility*, Employment Development, London.

Beck, U. (1992): *Risk Society: Towards a New Modernity*, Sage, London.

______ (2000): *What is Globalization?*, Polity Press & Blackwell, London.

Becker, G.S. (1964): *Human Capital*, Chicago University Press, Chicago.

______ (1993): 'The Economic Way of Looking at Life', *American Economic Review* 109(3): 385-409.

Bell, Daniel (1976): *The Coming of Post-Industrial Society*, Basic Books, New York.

Bell, Judith (1993): *Doing Your Research Project*, Open University Press, Buckingham, Philadelphia.

Best, M. (1990): *The New Competition: Institutions of Industrial Restructuring*, Cambridge Polity Press, Cambridge.

Betcherman, G. and A. Dar (2001): 'Active Labour Market Policies', in G. Betcherman and R. Islam (eds.), *East Asian Labour Markets and the Economic Crisis*, ILO, Geneva.

Beynon, H. (1997): 'The Changing Practices of Work', in R.K. Brown (ed.), *The Changing Shape of Work*, MacMillan, Basingstoke.

Bhaduri, A. (1996): 'Employment, Labour Market Flexibility and Economic Liberalization in India', *Indian Journal of Labour Economics*, vol. 39, no. 1, pp. 13-22.

Bhatt, P.R. (2003): 'Changes in Workforce Structure in India', *Indian Journal of Labour Economics*, vol. 46, no. 4, pp. 877-86.

Bhattacharjee, Arnab and Saibal Ghosh (2003): 'Strikes and Public Policy: Indian Evidence', *Indian Journal of Labour Economics*, vol. 46, no. 4, pp. 725-36.

Bhattacharjee, D. (1999): 'Organized Labour and Economic Liberalization – India: Past, Present and Future', Discussion Paper, International Institute for Labour Studies, ILO, Geneva.

Bhattacharya, B.B. and S. Sakthivel (2003): 'Economic Reforms and Jobless Growth in India in the 1990s', *Indian Journal of Labour Economics*, vol. 46, no. 4, pp. 845-76.

Bhaumik, S.K. (2003): 'Unemployment in India: The Post Liberalization Era', *Indian Journal of Labour Economics*, vol. 46, no. 1, pp. 69-94.

——— (2003): 'Casualisation of the Workforce in India, 1983-2002', *Indian Journal of Labour Economics*, vol. 46, no. 4, pp. 907-26.

——— (2002): 'Coping With Economic Liberalization: Alternative Trade Union Strategies', *Indian Journal of Labour Economics*, vol. 45, no. 4, pp. 1338-46.

——— (1998): 'The Labour Movement in India: Present Problems and Future Prospects', *The Indian Journal of Social Work*, vol. 59, no. 1, pp. 147-66.

Birada, R.R. and S.T. Bagalkoti (2001): 'Changing Facets of Employment in Rural India: Emerging Issues & Challenges', *Indian Journal of Agricultural Economics*, vol. 56, no. 3, July-September.

Blanchard, Gordon and Rizwanul Islam (2001): *East Asia Labour Markets*, ILO, Geneva.

Blanchard, K., J.P. Carlos and A. Randolph (1999): *The Three Keys to Empowerment*, Berret-Koehler, San Francisco.

Blanchard, O.J. (2004): 'Macroeconomic and Policy Implications of Shifts in Relative Demand for Skills', in D.J. Snower and G. Dehesa (eds.), *Globaliztion and Skills*, Cambridge University Press, Cambridge.

Bluestone, B. and Bennett Harrison (1982): *The Deindustrialization of America*, Basic Books, New York.

Blundell, Richard et al. (1999): 'In the Human Capital Investment', *Fiscal Studies*, vol. 20, no. 1, pp. 1-23.

BMR Development Authority (1995): Draft Regional Plan for BMR: 1996-2011.

Boeri, T., A. Brugiavini and L. Calmfors (2001): *The Role of Trade Unions in the 21st Century*, Oxford University Press, Oxford.

Bootle, Roger (2001): *Money for Nothing*, Oxford University Press, London.

——— (1996): *The Death of Inflation*, Nicholas Brealey, London.

Bound, J. and G. Johnson (1992): 'Changes in the Structure of Wages in the 1980s: An Evaluation of Alternative Explanation', *American Economic Review*, 82, pp. 371-92.

Bowen, W.G. (1964): *Economic Aspects of Education: Three Essays*, Princeton University Press, Princeton.

Bowman, M.J. (1966): 'The Human Investment Revolution in Economic Thought', *Sociology of Education*, 39(2), Spring, pp. 111-37.

Braveman, H. (1974): *Labour and Monopoly Capital*, Monthly Review Press, New York.

Brecher, J. and Tim Costello (1994): *Global Village or Global Pillage*, Southend Press, Boston MA.

Breman, Jan (1996): *Footloose Labour in India's Informal Economy*, Cambridge University Press, Cambridge.

Broadbent, J. et al. (1998): 'The End of Profession?', in J. Broadbent, M. Dietrich and J. Robert (eds.), *The End of Profession?: The Restructuring of Professional Work*, Routledge, London.

Bronfengbrenner, K. (2003): 'The American Labour Movement and the Resurgence in Union Organizing', in Peter Fairbrother and C.A.B. Yates (eds.), *Trade Unions and Renewal: A Comparative Study*, Routledge, London, New York.

______ (1993): 'Seeds of Resurgence: Successful Union Strategies for Winning Certification Election and First Contracts in the 1980s and Beyond', Ph.D. dissertation, Cornell University, Ithaca.

Brown, C. et al. (1993): 'Becoming a High Performance Work Organization: The Role of Security, Employee Involvement and Training', *International Journal of Human Resource Management*, vol. 4, no. 2, pp. 247-75.

Brown, Paul (1987): *Schooling Ordinary Kids: Inequality, Unemployment and the New Vocationalism*, Routledge, London.

Brown, Philip, Andy Green and Hugh Lauder (2001): *High Skills*, Oxford University Press, Oxford.

Brown, R.K. (1997): 'Flexibility and Security: Contradictions in the Contemporary Labour Market', in Brown (ed.), *The Changing Shape of Work*, MacMillan, Basingstoke.

Burgess, S. and H. Rees (1996): 'Job Tenure in Britain 1975-92', *The Economic Journal*, 106, pp. 334-44

Burgess, S. (1994): 'Where did Europe Fail: A Disaggregated Experiment of Net Job Generation in USA and Europe', London: Discussion Paper 192, Centre for Economic Performance, London School of Economics, London.

Burke, R.J. and C.L. Cooper (2000): *The Organization in Crisis: Downsizing, Restructuring and Privatization*, Blackwell, Oxford.

Business India (2006): 'Irrational Zones', 4 June.

Cadene, P. and Mark Holmstrom (1998): *Decentralized Production in India*, French Institute of Pondicherry and Sage, New Delhi and London.

Caplinsky, R. (1993): 'Is Flexible Production Relevant to Less Developed Countries', *OECD Development Center Working Paper*, OECD, Paris.

Cappelli, P., ed. (1999): *Introduction in Employment Practices and Business Strategy*, Oxford University Press, New York.

Cappelli, P. et al. (1997): *Change at Work,* Oxford University Press, New York.

Cappelli, P. (1995): 'Rethinking Employment', *British Journal of Industrial Relations*, vol. 33, no. 34, pp. 563-602.

Carr, E.H. (1990): 'History as Progress', in *What is History?*, Penguin Books, England.

Castells, Manuel and Yukio Aoyama (1997): 'Paths Towards the Informational Society: Employment Structure in G-7 Countries, 1920-1990', *International Labour Review,* 133 (1), pp. 325-30.

Castells, Manuel and Alejandro Portes (1989): 'World Underneath: the Origins, Dynamics and Effects of the Informal Economy', in Alejandro Portes, Manuel Castells and Lauren A. Benton (eds.), *The Informal Economy: Studies in Advanced and Less Developed Countries,* Johns Hopkins University Press, Baltimore, viii, pp. 327-30

Catt, H. and Patricia Scudammore (1997): *Solving Skills Shortages*, Kogan Page, London.

Chaddha, G.K. (2004): 'Human Capital Base of the Indian Labour Market, Identifying Worry Spots', *Indian Journal of Labour Economics*, vol. 47, no. 1, pp. 3-38.

Chadha, Vikram (2004): 'Changing Structure of Scientific and Technical Workforce in India's Industrial Sector', *Indian Journal of Labour Economics*, vol. 47, no. 3, pp. 281-92.

Chaison, Gray N. et al. (1993): 'Unions and Legitimacy: A Conceptual Refinement', *Research in the Sociology of Organization,* vol. 12, pp. 139-66.

Chandavarkar, Rajnarayan (1994): *The Origins of Industrial Capitalism in India: Business Strategies and the Working Classes in Bombay, 1900-1940*, Cambridge University Press, London.

Cheng, L. (1999): 'Globalization and Woman's Paid Work in Asia', *International Social Science Journal,* no. 160, UNESCO.

Chou, Nancy H. and R. Kambur (2006): 'The Race to the Bottom from the Bottom', *Economica*, vol. 3, no. 290, pp. 193-228.

Christopherson, Susan (1987): 'Workforce Flexibility: Implications for Women Workers', *ISSR Working Paper* 3 (2).

Clegg, H. (1979): *The Changing System of Industrial Relations in Great Britain*, Basil Blackwell, Oxford.

_____ (1960): *A New Approach to Industrial Democracy*, Basil Blackwell, Oxford.

Collinson, D. and M. Collinson (1995): 'Corporate Liposuction and the Re-Masculinisation of Management', Keynote address at Gender and Life in Organizations Conference, University of Portsmouth, Portsmouth.

Commissioner of Labour (2006): *Labour Gazette*, Office of the Commissioner of Labour, Government of Maharashtra.

Confederation of British Industry (1996): *Flexible Labour Markets*, CBI, London.

Cooper, R. (1995): *When Lean Enterprises Collide*, Harvard Business School Press, Boston.

Cooper, C.L. and R.J. Burke (2002): 'Introduction: The New World of Work', in Cooper and Burke (eds.), *The New World of Work*, Blackwell, Oxford.

Crouch, C. (1997): 'Skill Based Full Employment: The Latest Philosopher's Stone', *The British Journal of Industrial Relations*, vol. 35, no. 3, pp. 367-84.

Cutler, T. (1992): 'Vocational Training and British Economic Performance: A Further Installment of the British Labour Problem', *Work Employment and Society*, 6(2), June, pp. 161-83.

D'Souza, Errol (2004): 'Wage Disparity and Human Capital Accumulation', *Indian Journal of Labour Economics*, vol. 47, no. 4, pp. 677-82.

_____ (2002): 'Firm Nation and Training', *Indian Journal of Labour Economics*, vol. 45, no. 4, pp. 2134-43.

D'Souza, K. et al. (1997): *Empowering Workers Through Human Resource Development*, Allied Publishers, New Delhi.

Dahl, R.A. (1998): *On Democracy*, Yale University Press, New Haven.

Dahms, Harry (2000): 'Introduction', in Harry Dahms (ed.), *The Transformations of Capitalism, Society and State in Modern Times*, MacMillan Press, London.

Daly, A., D. Hitchins and K. Wagner (1988): 'Productivity Machinery and Skills in a Sample of British and German Manufacturing Plants', *National Institute of Economic Review*, 111, February, pp. 48-61.

Danford, Andy (1999): *Management Techniques and British Workers*, Mansell, London, New York.

Daniel, W.W. (1987): *Workplace Industrial Relation and Technological Change*, Frances Printer and Policy Study Institute, London.

Das, K. and Panayiotopoulos (1996): 'Flexible Specialization: New Paradigm for Industrialization for Developing Countries', *Economic and Political Weekly*, vol. 31, no. 52, 28 December, pp. 57-61.

Das, S. (1989): 'A Note on Trade Union Density in India', Working Paper, Department of Collective Bargaining, Cornell University, Ithaca.

Datar, M.K. (2004): 'Human Capital Approach and Indian Labour Market: The Case of Information Technology Industry', *Indian Journal of Labour Economics*, vol. 47, no. 4, pp. 825-32.

Datt, Gaurav (1999): 'Has Poverty Declined Since Economic Reforms?: Statistical Data Analysis', *Economic and Political Weekly*, vol. 34, no. 50, December.

Davala, Sarath (ed.) (1992): *Employment and Unionization in Indian Industry*, Friedrich Ebert Stiftung, New Delhi.

Deardel, L. (1998): 'Ability, Family, Education and Earning in Britain', Institute for Fiscal Studies: Working Paper, no. 98/14.

Delaney, J.T. (2006): 'The Flattening of Industrial Relations', *Industrial and Labour Relations Review*, vol. 59, no. 3, pp. 497-501.

Department of Commerce (1999): *21st Century Skills for 21st Century Jobs*, US Government Printing Office, Washington.

Deshpande, L. et al. (2004): *Liberalization and Labour: Labour Flexibility in Indian Manufacturing*, Institute for Human Development, New Delhi.

Deshpande, Sudha (2003): 'Changing Employment Structure in Large States in India: What do NSSO Data Show?', *Indian Journal of Labour Economics*, vol. 46, no. 4, pp. 811-44.

Deshpande, Sudha and L.K. Deshpande (2002): 'Reform and Labour Market in India', Institute of Applied Manpower Research, *Reform and Employment*, Concept, New Delhi.

Deshpande, S. and L.K. Deshpande (1998): 'Impact of Liberalization on Labour Markets in India', *Economic and Political Weekly*, vol. 33, no. 22, 14 May.

Deshpande, Sudha, Guy Standing and Lalit Deshpande (1998): *Labour Flexibility in a Third World Metropolis: A Case Study of Bombay*, Commonwealth Publishers, New Delhi.

Dex, S. and A. McCulloch (1997): *Flexible Employment*, MacMillan, Basingstoke.

Dickens, R. and D.T. Ellwood (2000): 'Wither Poverty in Britain and United States', Center for Economic Performance Report, no. 506, London School of Economics, London.

Dickinson, James (1986): *From Poor Law to Social Insurance: The Periodisation of State Intervention in the Reproduction Process*, Routledge, London.

Diwan, Ritu (2004): 'Captive Workers in Captive Small Scale Factories', *Indian Journal of Labour Economics*, vol. 47, no. 4, pp. 1039-52.

Doeringer, P. and M.J. Piore (1971): *Internal Labour Markets and Manpower Analysis*, Heath and Co, Lexington, MA.

Dore, R. (2000): *Stock Market Capitalism: Welfare Capitalism, Japan and Germany Versus the Anglo Saxon*, Oxford University Press, Canada.

Dreze, J.H. and Henry Sneessens (1997): 'Technological Development, Competition from Low Wage Economies and Low Skilled Unemployment', in D.J. Snower and G. Dehesa (eds.), *Unemployment Policy*, Cambridge University Press, Cambridge.

Drucker, Peter (1993): *Post-capitalist Society*, Butterworth Heinemann, London.

Dumont, M., Glen Ray and Peter Willeme (2006): 'Does Internationalization Affect Union Bargaining Power?: An Empirical Study of Five E.U. Countries', *Oxford Economic Papers*, vol. 58, no. 1, pp. 77-102.

Duncan, Campbell (2000): 'Social Dialog and Labour Market Adjustment in East Asia after the Crisis', in Harry Dahms (ed.), *The Transformations of Capitalism, Society and State in Modern Times*, MacMillan Press, London.

Dunlop, John (1993): *Industrial Relations Systems*, Harvard Business School Press, Boston.

Edwards, P., M. Collinson and C. Reese (1998): *The Determinants of Employee Responses to Total Quality Management: Six Case Studies, Organization Studies*, 19/3, pp. 449-75.

Elbaum, B. et al. (1979): 'The Labour Process, Market Structure and Marxist Theory', *Cambridge Journal of Economics*, 3(3), September, pp. 227-30.

Elliot, L. and D. Atkinson (1998): *The Age of Insecurity*, Verso, London.

Emmott, Bill (2005): 'The Sun Also Rises' – www//economist.com/survey/audio, p. 56.

Engberg, E. (1993): 'Union Responses to the Contingent Work Force', in D.S. Cobble (ed.), *Women in Union: Forging a Partnership*, ILR Press, Ithaca, New York.

Engineer, Mahrukh (1999): *Liberalization and Human Resource Management: Challenges for the Corporation of Tomorrow*, Response Books, New Delhi.

European Commission (1993): 'Growth Competitiveness and Employment: The Challenges and the Way Forward into the 21st Century', *Bulletin of the European Community*, Supplement 6/93, Brussels.

Faber, H. (1993): 'The Incidence and the Cost of Job Loss 1982-91, Bookings Papers on Economic Activity', *Microeconomics*, pp. 73-132.

Fairbrother, Peter and Charlotte A.B. Yates (2003): 'The Unions in Crisis', in Peter Fairbrother and Charlotte Yates (eds.), *Unions in Renewal: A Comparative Study*, Continuum, London, New York.

Fallon, T. and R. Lucas (1991): 'Impact of Changes in Job Security Regulation in India and Zimbawe', *World Bank Economic Review*, vol. 5, no. 3, pp. 121-34.

Far Eastern Economic Review (1985): 19 December, p. 57.

Felstead, A. et al. (1998): 'Insecurity at Work: Is Job Insecurity Really Much Worse than Before', *New Economy*, 5, pp. 180-4.

FineGold, D. and S. Soskice (1998): 'The Failure of Training in Britain: Analysis and Prescription', *Oxford Review of Economic Policy*, vol. 4, no. 3, pp. 21-53.

Flanders, A. (1970): *Management and Union*, Faber, London.

Forrester, P. (1994): 'Flexibility, Politics and Strategy: In Defense of the Model of the Flexible Firm', *Work Employment and Society*, vol. 8, no. 2, pp. 221-42.

Frank, Thomas (2004): *What's the Matter with Kansas?*, Metropolitan Owl, New York.

Fraser, J.A. (2001): *White-collar Sweat Shops: The Deterioration of Work and its Rewards in Corporate America*, W.W. Norton, New York.

Freeman, R.B. (1995): 'The Future of Unions in Decentralized Collective Bargaining Systems: US and UK Unionism in an Era of Crisis', *British Journal of Industrial Relations*, vol. 33, no. 4, pp. 519-36.

Freeman, R. (1993): 'Labour Market Institutions and Economic Performance', *Economic Policy*, vol. 3, no. 1, April.

______ (1993): 'Labour Market Institutions and Policies: Help or Hindrance to Economic Development', *Annual Conference on Development Economic – 1992*, Supplement to the World Bank Research Observer, March.

Freeman, R. and J. Medoff (1984): *What Do Unions Do*, Basic Books, New York.

Frontline (2006): 'Zone of Conflict', 30 June.

Fugio, Mitarai (2005): 'Survey of Japan', *Economist*, 8-14 October, p. 4.

Gall, G. (1998): 'The Changing Relations of Production: Union De-recognition in the UK Magazine Industry', *Industrial Relations Journal*, vol. 129, no. 2, pp. 151-61.

Gallie, D. (2004): 'Skill Gender and the Quality of Employment: In the Recomposition of Skills and Employment', *Work Employment and Society*, 4 (2), pp. 211-21.

______ (1991): 'Patterns of Skill Change: Upskilling, Deskilling or the Polarization of Skills', *Work Employment and Society*, 5 (3), pp. 319-51.

Gallie, D. et al. (1998): *Restructuring the Employment Relationship*, Oxford University Press, Oxford.

Gallie, D. and M. White (1993): *Employee Commitment and the Skill Revolution*, Policy Studies Institute, London.

Garrhan, P. and T. Stewart (1992): *The Nissan Enigma-Flexibility at Work in Local Economy*, Mansell, London.

Gemmell, Norman (1996): 'Evaluating the Impacts of Human Capital Stock and Accumulation on Economic Growth: Some New Evidence', *Oxford Bulletin of Economics and Statistics*, Special Issue on Human Capital in Economic Development, vol. 58, no. 1, February.

Gladstein, Mark, Mashe Justman and Volker Meier (2005): *The Political Economy of Education: Implications for Growth and Inequality*, MIT Press, Massachusetts.

Glynn, S. and H. Gospel (1993): 'Britain's Low Skill Equilibrium: A Problem of Demand?', *Industrial Relations Journal* 24(2), June, pp. 112-25.

Goddard, J. (1998): 'Review of Change at Work', *British Journal of Industrial Relations*, vol. 36, no. 3: 501-3.

GOI (2003): *Report of the Second National Commission on Labour*, Ministry of Labour.

______ (2002): *Report of the Second Commission on Labour*, vol. II, Ministry of Labour, pp. 34, 43-4.

______ (2001): *Report of the Working Group on Skill Development and Training*, Government of India, New Delhi.

______ (1999): *Report - Ministry of Human Resource Development*, Dept. of Youth Affairs.

______: *Tenth Five Year Plan*, Government of India, Chapter 2.4.

Gopal, M.G. (1994): 'India: Economic Liberalization and the Legal System', World Bank Working Paper, Washington.

Gosling, A. et al. (1997): 'The Dynamics of Low Pay and Unemployment in Early 1990s Britain', Institute for Fiscal Studies, Working Paper, London.

Government of Thailand (1997): *The Eighth National Economic and Social Development Plan 1997-2001*, National Economic and Social Development Board, Bangkok. http://www.nesdb.go.th/nesdb_en/main.php.

Granovetter, M. and R. Swedberg (1994): *The Sociology of Economic Life*, Westview, Boulder, Colorado.

Gray, J. (1995): 'The Undoing of Conservatism', in J. Gray (ed.), *Enlightenment Wake: Politics and Culture at the End of the Modern Age*, Routledge, London.

Green, F. (1992): 'On the Political Economy of Skill in Advanced Industrial Nations', *Review of Political Economy*, 4(4), pp. 413-35.

Greenbaum, Joan (2004): *Windows on the Work Place*, Cornerstone Publications, New Delhi.

Greg, Paul and Genevieve Knight (2000): 'Job Insecurity in the British Labour Market', in Heery Edmond and John Solomon (eds.), *Insecure Work Force*, Routledge Press, London.

Gregg, P. and J. Wadsworth (1996): *'Feeling Insecure', Employment Audit*, Autumn, London: Employment Policy Institute.

Gregory, M. and R. Jukes (2001): 'Unemployment and Subsequent Earning . . . Estimating Scarring Among British Men 1984-94', *The Economic Journal*, vol. 111, no. 475, pp. F607-25.

Guest, David (2000): 'Management and the Insecure Workforce', in Edmund Heery and John Salmon (eds.), *The Insecure Workforce*, Routledge, London, New York.

——— (1997): 'Towards Jobs and Justice in Europe: A Research Agenda', *Industrial Relations Journal*, vol. 28, no. 4, pp. 344-52.

Guest, D.E. (1999): 'Human Resource Management: The Workers Verdict', *Human Resource Management Journal*, vol. 9, no. 2, pp. 5-25.

——— (1989): 'Personnel and HRM, Can You Tell the Difference?', *Personnel Management*, January, pp. 48-51.

Guest, D.E. and N. Conway (1997): *Employee Motivation and the Psychological Contract*, Institute of Personnel and Development, London.

Hammer, J.S. (1996): 'The Public Economics of Education', *Draft for*

Comments, Public Economics Division, Policy Research Department, WB, Washington.
Handy, Charles B. (1984): *The Future of Work*, Basil Blackwell, Oxford.
Hardt, Michael and Negri Antonio (2000): *The Empire*, Harvard University Press, Cambridge, MA, pp. 461-2.
Hargreaves, P. and Peter Jarvis (1998): *The Human Resource Development Handbook*, Kogan Page, London.
Harris, N. (1995): 'The Reproduction of Labour Force', in N. Harris (ed.) *The New Untouchables: Immigration and the New World Worker*, I.B. Tauris Publishers, London, pp. 157-85.
Harrison, Bennet (1994): *Lean and Mean . . . the Changing Landscape of Corporate Power in the Age of Flexibility*, Basic Books, New York, pp. 125-6.
Harris-White, B. (2003): *India Working: Essays on Society and Economy*, Cambridge University Press, London.
Hart, R.A. (2006): 'Worker Job Matches, Job Mobility and Real Wages', *Economica*, May, no. 73, pp. 287-98.
Harvey, David (1989): *The Conditions of Post Modernity: An Enquiry into the Origins of Cultural Change*, Basil Blackwell, Oxford.
______ (1993): 'Class Relations, Social Justice and Politics of Difference', in Michael and Pile (eds.), *Place and Politics of Identity*, Routledge, London.
Heckman, J. and C. Pages (2000): 'The Cost of Job Security Regulation, Evidence from Latin American Labour Market', Working Paper 7773, http://www.nber.org/papers/w7773
Heery, Edmund and John Salmon, eds. (2000): *The Insecure Workforce*, Routledge, London, New York.
Heery, Edmund and Abbott Brian (2000): 'Trade Union and the Insecure Work Force', in Heery and John Salmon John (eds.), *The Insecure Work Force*, Routledge, London.
Heery, Edmund and John Salmon (2000): 'The Insecurity Thesis', in Heery Edmund and John Salmon (eds.), *The Insecurity Thesis*, Routledge, London.
Heinz, James (2006): 'Low Wage Manufacturing and Global Commodity Chain: A Model in Unequal Exchange Tradition', *Cambridge Journal of Economics*, 30, pp. 507-52.
Hill, S. (1991): 'Why Quality Circles Fail and Total Quality Management Might Succeed', *British Journal of Industrial Relations*, vol. 29, no. 4, pp. 541-68.

Hindustan Times (2006): 'Shortage of Skilled Blue-collared Cotton Textile Workers Hindering Growth of the Industry in India', 10 June.
Hitoshi, Ota (2004): 'Flexible Work Organization, Human Resource Practices', *5th Asian Regional Congress of the International Industrial Relations Association (IIRA)* held from 23-6 June 2004, at Seoul, South Korea.
Hoare, Stephen and A. Jolly (1999): *Skills and Training Handbook*, Association of Directory Publishers, http://www.adp.org./
Hogg, M.A. and Abrams (1998): *Social Identification: A Social Psychology of Inter Group Relation and Group Process*, Routledge, London.
Holmstrom, B.R. and J. Tirole (1989): 'The Theory of the Firm', in R. Schmalensee and R.D. Willig (eds.), *Handbook of Industrial Organization*, North Holland, Amsterdam.
Holmstrom, Mark (1978): *South Indian Factory Workers: Their Lives and their World*, Allied Publishers, New Delhi.
Hutton, W. (1995): *The State We're In*, Johnathan Cape, London.
ILO (2006): *Director Generals Report on the 95th International Labour Conference*, ILO, Geneva.
——— (2006): *Report of the International Labour Conference*, ILO, Geneva.
——— (2005): *World Employment Report 2004-05*, ILO, Geneva.
——— (2004): 'A Fair Globalization: Creating Opportunities for All', *Report of the World Commission on the Social Dimensions of Globalization*, ILO, Geneva.
——— (2000): 'Income Security and Social Protection in a Changing World', *World Labour Report*, 2000, ILO, Geneva.
——— (1999): *Decent Work: Report of the Director General*, ILO, Geneva.
——— (1999): *World Employment Report*, ILO, Geneva.
——— (1998): 'Employability in the Global Economy and How Training Matters', *World Employment Report 1998*, Bureau of Public Information, September, ILO, Geneva.
——— (1997): *World Employment: National Policies in a Global Context*, ILO, Geneva, 1996/7.
——— (1995): *World Employment Report*, ILO, Geneva.
ILO–FAAT (1996): *Indian Economic Reforms and Labour Policy*, ILO, FAAT, New Delhi.
Inoki, T. (1987): 'Skill Transfer and Economic Organization', in K. Koike and T. Inoki (eds.), *Skill Formation in Japan and South East Asia*, University of Tokyo Press, Tokyo.
International Herald Tribune (1985): A Report, 23 January.

Jarvis, Peter (2000): 'The Age of Learning', in Peter Jarvis (ed.), *Continuing Education at the University of Surrey*, Oxford University Press, London.

Jha, Praveen (2005): 'States Growing Intolerance Towards Labour in India: A Note Based on Some Recent Developments', *Indian Journal of Labour Economics*, vol. 8, no. 4, pp. 897-916.

Johnson, C. (1982): *MITI and the Japanese Miracle: Growth of Industrial Policy 1925-1982*, Stanford University Press, Stanford.

_____ (1995): *Japan – Who Governs?: The Rise of Developmental Stage*, W.W. Norton, New York.

Jonathan, Wadsworth (2000): 'Insecurity at Work', in Heery Edmond and John Solomon (eds.), *Insecure Work Force*, Routledge Press, London, pp. 39-55.

Jose, A.V. (2000): 'The Future of the Labour Movement: Some Observations on Developing Countries', *Indian Journal of Labour Economics*, vol. 43, no. 1.

Joshi, H. and Vijay Joshi (1976): *Surplus Labour and the City: A Case Study of Bombay*, Oxford University Press, Mumbai.

Kalhan, A. (2005): 'Social Movement Unionism', in *Teachers of the World*, January-March, vol. 6, no. 7, pp. 6-9.

_____ (2004): 'Life Long Learning for What?', in *Teachers of the World*, July-September, vol. 5, no. 7, pp. 4-8.

Kang, Soon-Hie et al. (2001): 'World Bank and ILO', in G. Betcherman and R. Islam (eds), *East Asian Labour Markets*, pp. 126-37.

Kelly, John. (1997): 'Industrial Relation: Looking to the Future', *British Journal of Industrial Relations*, 33, 3, pp. 393-8.

_____ (1998): *Rethinking Industrial Relations*, Routledge, London.

Kennedy, P. (1993): *Preparing for the Twenty-first Century*, Random House, New York.

Kenny, M. and R. Florida (1993): *Beyond Mass Production: The Japanese System and its Transfer to the USA*, Oxford University Press, New York.

Kirk, J. and M.L. Miller (1985): *Reliability and Validity in Qualitative Research*, Sage, California.

Kochan, T. and Paul Osterman (1994): *The Mutual Gain Enterprise*, HBS Press, Boston.

Kochan, T. et al. (1986): *The Transformation of American Industrial Relations*, Basic Books, New York.

Kolko, Joyce (2000): 'Restructuring the Working Class 1988', in Harry

Dahms (ed.), *Transformations of Capitalism*, Palgrave MacMillan, London.

——— (1988): *Restructuring the World Economy*, Pantheon, New York.

Kondratieff, N.D. (1926): 'The Long Waves in Economic Life', *Review* 2, 4, pp. 519-52.

Korgaonkar, Chanda P. (1995): *Workers and Working Conditions in EPZs in India: A Case Study of SEEPZ*, INTUC, New Delhi.

Krugman, Paul (2005): 'The Drop out Puzzle', in *The Hindu*, 19 July.

——— (1994): 'Inequality and the Political Economy of Eurosclerosis', Discussion Paper 8, Centre for Policy Research, London.

Kundra, Ashok (2000): *The Performance of India's Export Promoting Zones: A Comparison with the Chinese Approach*, Sage, New Delhi.

Kundu, Amitabh (1997): 'Trends and Patterns of Female Employment in India: A Case of Organized Informalization', *Indian Journal of Labour Economics*, vol. 40, no. 3, July-September, pp. 1785-93.

——— (1993): 'Urban Informal Sector: An Overview of Macro Dimensions, Socio Economic Correlates and Policy Perspectives in India', in H. Nagamine (ed.), *Urban Informal Sector Employment: A Cross National Comparison Study*, Institute for Regional Planning.

Kuruvilla, Sarosh et al. (2002): 'Trade Union Growth and Decline in Asia', *British Journal of Industrial Relations*, vol. 40, no. 3, September, pp. 431-61.

Kuruvilla, Sarosh (1999): 'Impact of Globalization on Economies and IR/HR Systems: Theory and Evidence', in A. Sivananthiran and C.S. Venkata Ratnam (eds.), *Globalization and Labour Management Relations in South East Asia*, ILO–SAAT, New Delhi, pp. 11-64.

Kuttner, R. (2000): 'The Role of Government in Global Economy', in W. Hutton and A. Gidden (eds.), *On the Edge: Living with Global Capitalism,* Jonathan Cape, London.

Lam, Alice (1996): 'Work Organisation, Skill Development and Utilisation of Engineers', in R. Crompton, D. Gallie and K. Purcell (eds.), *Changing Forms of Employment*, Routledge, London, New York.

Lane, C. (1990): 'Vocational Training, Employment Training and New Production Concepts: Some Lessons for Britain', *International Review Journal*, vol. 21, no. 4, pp. 247-59.

Latack, J.C. and R.B. Dozier (1986): 'After the Axe Falls: Job Loss as a Career Transition', *Academy of Management Review*, 11, pp. 375-92.

Lauder, H. (1999): 'Competitiveness and Low Skill Equilibrium: A

Comparative Analysis', *Journal of Education and Work*, vol. 12, no. 3, pp. 281-94.

Lawless, Paul (1998): 'The Policy Challenge', in Paul Lawless, Ron Martin and Sally Hardy (eds.), *Unemployment and Social Exclusion*, Jessica Kingsley Publishers & Regional Studies Association, London.

Lazonick, W. and M. O'Sullivan (2000): 'Maximizing Shareholder Value: The New Ideology for Corporate Governance', *Economy and Society Journal*, vol. 29, no. 1, pp. 13-35.

Leadbeater, S.R.B. (1993): *The Politics of Textiles: The Indian Cotton Mill Industry and the Legacy of Swadeshi*, Sage, New Delhi.

Lee, Eddy (2001): *Export Promoting Zones and Industrial Employment in Asia*, ILO-ARTEP, Bangkok.

Legge, K. (1998): 'Flexibility: The Gift-wrapping of Employment, Degradation', in P. Sparrow and M. Marchington (eds.), *Human Resource Management: The New Agenda*, Pitman Publishing, London.

______ (1995): 'Human Resource Management: Rhetorics and Realities', *Journal of Management Studies*, 34(2), pp. 315-17.

Leisink, P. (1997): 'New Union Constituency Call for Differentiated Agenda and Democratic Participation', *Transfer*, 3, pp. 534-50.

Littlewood, P., Ignace Glorieux and Ingrid Jonsson (2004): *The Future of Work in Europe*, Ashgate, Burlington.

Lokshahi, Hakk Sanghatana (1996): 'Murder of the Mills: An Enquiry into Bombay's Cotton Textile Industry and its Workers', CED, Lokshahi Hakk Sanghatana, Mumbai, p. 6.

LPH (2006): *Indian Factories and Labour Report*, Law Publishing House, New Delhi

Luttwak, E. (1994): 'Why Fascism is the Wave of the Future', *London Review of Book*, 7 April.

Mamgain, Rajendra and Vandana Parashar (2000): 'Enhancing Employability of Youth through Education and Training', *Indian Journal of Labour Economics*, vol. 43, no. 4, pp. 757-80

Marchington, M. and P. Parker (1990): *Changing Patterns of Employee Relations*, Harvester Wheatsheaf, Hemel Hempfteadt, London.

Martin, Carnoy (1999): 'The Family, Flexible Work and Social Cohesion at Risk', *International Labour Review*, vol. 138, no. 4, pp. 411-29.

Martin, Ron (1998): 'Regional Dimensions of European Unemployment Crisis', in Lawless Paul, Ron Martin, Sally Hardy (eds.), *Unemployment and Social Exclusion*, Jessica Kingsley Publishers & Regional Studies Association, London.

Mathur, A. and R.P. Mamgain (2004): 'Human Capital Stocks: Their Levels of Utilization and Economic Development in India', *Indian Journal of Labour Economics*, vol. 47, no. 4, pp. 655-76.

Mathur, Ajeet N. (1991): 'Industrial Restructuring and Union Powers', ILO-ARTEP, New Delhi.

Maurice, Marc et al. (1980): 'Societal Differences in Organizing Manufacturing Units', *Organization Studies*, 1, pp. 59-86.

Mehrotra, Santosh (2005): 'Human Capital or Human Development?', *Economic and Political Weekly*, vol. 40, no. 4, 22 January, pp. 300-405.

Millward, N. (1994): *The New Industrial Relations*, Policy Studies Institute, London.

Millward, N. et al. (1992): *Workplace Industrial Relations in Transition*, Aldershot, Dartmouth.

Mitchell, M.F. (2005): 'Specialization and the Skill Premium in the 20th Century', *International Economic Review*, vol. 46, August, pp. 935-55.

MMRDA (1995): *Draft Regional Plan for Mumbai Metropolitan Region 1996-2011*, October.

Moody, Kim (2002): 'Why not in USA? Around the World Mass Political Strikes Challenge the Effects of Globalization', *Labour Notes*, February.

Morris, J. and B. Wilkinson (1995): 'The Transfer of Japanese Management to Alien Institutional Environments', *Journal of Management Studies*, vol. 32, no. 6, pp. 719-30.

Moser, C.A. and G. Kaltron (1971): *Survey Methods in Social Investigation*, Heinemann, London.

Marchington, M. (2007): 'Involvement and Participation', in J. Storey (ed.), *Human Resource Management: A Critical Text*, Thompson Learning, London, p. 2008.

Mukherjee, Dipa (2004): 'Informal Manufacturing Sector in India: Pre- and Post-Reform Growth Dynamics', *Indian Journal of Labour Economics*, vol. 47, no. 2, pp. 293-310.

Munck, R. (2002): *Globalization and Labour*, Madhya Books, Delhi.

Nagamine, H. (2004): *Urban Informal Sector Employment: A Cross National Comparative Study*, Research Institute for Regional Planning and Development, Nagoya, 1st pub. 1993.

Nagaraj, R. (2004): 'Fall in Organized Manufacturing Employment', *Economic and Political Weekly*, vol. 39, no. 30, July, pp. 3387-90.

——— (2000): 'Indian Economy since 1980: Virtuous Growth or Polarization', *Economic and Political Weekly*, vol. 35, no. 32, 5 August, pp. 2831-39.

______ (1995): 'India in the Era of Economic reforms', *Indian Journal of Labour Economics*, vol. 24, May, pp. 16-25.

______ (1994): 'Wages and Employment in Manufacturing Industry: Trends, Hypothesis and Evidence', *Economic and Political Weekly*, vol. 29, no. 4, January, pp. 48-52.

Nathanson, R. et al. (1999): *Union Response to a Changing Environment: The New Histadrut - The General Federation of Labour in Israel*, International Institute of Labour Studies, ILO, Geneva.

National Technical Manpower Information System (1998): *Annual Technical Manpower Reviews*, Institute of Applied Manpower Research, New Delhi.

Neetha, N. (2004): 'Education and Skill Development of Workforce in NOIDA Export Processing Zone', *Indian Journal of Labour Economics*, vol. 47, no. 2, pp. 269-80.

______ (2004): 'Employment Conditions and Quality: A Study of Small Enterprises in NOIDA Export Promoting Zone', *Indian Journal of Labour Economics*, vol. 47, no. 4, pp. 1083-91.

Neef, D. (1998): *The Knowledge Economy*, Butterworth-Heinemann, Oxford.

New York Time (1994): 'Reports on Employment Scenario', 10, 28 March, 6 May.

Nickell, S. (2004): 'Poverty and Worklessness in Britain', *The Economic Journal*, vol. 14, no. 494, March, *The Journal of the Royal Economic Society*.

Nickell, S., P. Jones and G. Quintini (2002): 'A Picture of Job Insecurity Facing British Men', *The Economic Journal*, vol. 112, no. 476, pp. 1-27.

Nolan, J.P., I.C. Wichert and B.J. Burchell (2002): 'Job Insecurity and Psychological Well Being and Family Life', in Edmund Heery and John Salmon (eds.), *The Insecure Workforce*, Routledge, London, New York.

OECD (1998): *Human Capital Investment: An International Comparison*, OECD, Paris.

______ (1997): 'Is Job Insecurity on the Increase in OECD Countries?', *Employment Outlook*, OECD, Paris.

______ (1997): *Employment Outlook*, OECD, Paris.

______ (1994): *The OECD Job Study: Fact, Analysis, Strategy*', OECD, Paris.

——— (1993): *Green Paper: European Social Policy Options for the Union*, COMPOM 551, OECD, Paris.

——— (1985): *Economic Outlook*, December, OECD, Paris.

Oliver, N. and B. Wilkinson (1988): *The Japanization of British Industry*, Blackwell, Oxford.

Osterman, Paul (2000): 'Work Reorganization in an Era of Restructuring: Trends in Diffusion and Effects on Employee Welfare', *Industrial and Labour Relations Review*, vol. 53, no. 2, January, pp. 179-96.

——— (1994): 'How Common is Workplace Transformation and Who Adopts it', *Industrial and Labour Relations Review*, vol. 47, no. 2, January, pp. 173-88.

Ota, Hitoshi (2005): 'Flexible Work Organization, Human Resource Practices and Worker Perception in India: A Case Study of Bangalore City', *Indian Journal of Labour Economics*, vol. 48, January-March, pp. 115-29.

Ozaki, Muneto (1999): *Negotiating Flexibility: The Role of the Social Partner and the State*, ILO, Geneva.

Ozveren, E. (2005): 'Polyani Chayanov and Lessons for the Study of the Informal Sector', *The Journal of Economic Issues*, vol. 39, no. 3, September, pp. 765-76.

Panchamukhi, V.R., Nagesh Kumar and Ram Upendar Das (2004): 'Economic Reforms and Implications for Labour Markets', in R. Agarwal, N. Kumar and Ribond Michelle (eds.), *Reforms Labour Markets and Social Security in India*, Oxford University Press, New Delhi.

Panda, Hrushikesh (2001): 'Technology, Factor Substitution and Employment Generation at the Firm Level: A Case of Automobile Industry in India', *Indian Journal of Labour Economics*, vol. 44, no. 2, pp. 205-21.

Pankaj, Joshi (2002): 'An Introduction to Urban Regeneration of the Harbour of Mumbai', in Darryl D'Monte (ed.), *Ripping the Fabric the Decline of Mumbai and its Mills*, Oxford University Press, New York.

Parker, M. and J. Slaughter (1988): *Choosing Sides: Unions and the Team Concept*, South End Press, Boston.

Penn, R., M. Rose and J. Rubery (1994): *Skill and Occupational Change*, Oxford University Press, Oxford.

People's Democracy (2005): 'Whom do they Serve?', 16 October, pp. 1-2.

Pigato, M. et al. (1997): *South Asia's Integration into the World Economy*, World Bank, Washington DC.

Piore, M. and C. Sabel (1984): *The Second Industrial Divide: Possibilities of Prosperity*, Basic Books, New York.

Piven Francis and Richard Cloward (2005): 'Power Repertoires and Globalization', *Politics and Society*, 28(3), September, pp. 413-30.

Polanyi, Karl (1957): *The Great Transformation*, Beacon Press, Boston.

Porter, M.E. (1980): *Competitive Strategy: Technique for Analyzing Industry and Competitors*, Free Press, New York.

Psacharopoulous, G. (1981): 'Return to Education', *Comparative Education*, vol. 17, pp. 321-41.

Psacharopoulous, G. and H.A. Patrinos (2002): 'Returns to Investment in Education: A Further Update', Policy Research Paper 2881, World Bank, Washington DC.

Psacharopoulous, G. and M. Woodhall (1985): *Education for Development*, Oxford University Press, New York.

Ramaswamy, E.A. (2000): *Managing Human Resources*, Oxford University Press, New Delhi.

_____ (1998): *Workers Consciousness and Trade Union Response*, Oxford University Press, New Delhi.

Ramaswamy, E.A. and F.B. Schiphorst (2000): 'Human Resource Management, Trade Unions and Empowerment: Two Cases from India', *International Journal of Human Resource Management*, vol. 11, no. 4, August, pp. 664-80.

Ramaswamy, K.V. (1999): 'The Search for Flexibility in Indian Manufacturing', *Economic and Political Weekly*, vol. 34, no. 30, 6 February, pp. 363-8.

Rani, U. (2004): 'Technology and Skill Transfer in Auto Component Firms of the National Capital Region', *Indian Journal of Labour Economics*, vol. 47, no. 4, pp. 1067-82.

Ray, P.K. (2002): 'Decent Work in the Informal Sector: Training Issues', *Indian Journal of Labour Economics*, vol. 45, no. 4, pp. 1163-73.

Reddy, V.R.K. (1991): *Labour Policy 2000: Proceeding of the Seminar, 3-4 October 1991*, Friedrich Ebbert, Stiftung, New Delhi.

Reed, A. (2001): *Innovations in Human Resource Management*, Chartered Institute of Personnel and Development, CIPD House, London.

Rees, G. et al. (1997): 'History, Place and the Learning Society: Towards a Sociology of Life Time Learning', *Journal of Education Policy*, vol. 12, no. 6, pp. 485-97.

Rhinehart, J. et al. (1994): 'Reunifying Conception and Execution of Work Under Japanese Production Management?: A Case Study', in Tony Elger and Smith Chris (eds.), *Global Japanization? The*

Transnational Transformation of the Labour Process, Routledge, London, pp. 152-74.

Rifkin, Jeremy (2004): *The End of Work: The Decline of the Global Labour Force and the Dawn of the Post Market Era*, Penguin, New York, 1st pub. 1996.

Riley, N.-M. (1997): 'Determinants of Union Membership: A Review', *Labour*, vol. 11, no. 2, pp. 265-301.

Robinson, Peter (2000): 'Insecurity and the Flexible Work Force, Measuring the Ill Defined', in Heery and Solomon (eds.), *The Insecure Work Force*, Routledge, London.

Rodrik, D. (1999): *The New Global Economy and Developing Countries: Making Openness Work*, Overseas Development Council, Washington DC.

Rousseau, D.M. (1996): 'Changing the Deal while Keeping the People', *Academy of Management Executive*, vol. 10, pp. 50-61.

Roy, Sudita (1998): 'Lags in Employment Adjustment and Inter-industry Differential . . . an Analysis Using Dynamic Inter-related Factor Demand Function', Discussion Paper, no. 199, IGIDR, Bombay.

Sangma, P.A. (1991): *A Statement*, Union Minister of State for Labour, GOI.

Sasmita, Palo (2004): 'Changing Collective Bargaining Structure', *Indian Journal of Labour Economics*, vol. 47, no. 7, pp. 1159-73.

Schene, K.F. and Matthew Job Slaughter (2001): *Globalization and the Perceptions of American Workers*, Institute for International Economics, Washington.

Schmitz, H. (1989): 'Flexible Specialization: A New Paradigm of Small Scale Industrialization', Institute of Development Studies, Paper no. 324, pp. 27-33.

Schoenberger, R. (1982): *Japanese Manufacturing Techniques*, The Free Press, New York.

Schuler, R.S. and S. Jackson (1987): 'Linking Competitive Strategy with Human Resource Management Practices', *Academy of Management Executive*, vol. 1, no. 3, pp. 209-13.

Schultz, T.W. (1975): 'The Value of Ability to Deal with Disequilibria', *Journal of Economic Literature*, vol. 13, no. 3, pp. 827-46.

——— (1961): 'Investment in Human Capital', *American Economic Review*, vol. 51, pp. 1-17.

Scipes, Kim (1993): 'Understanding the New Labour Movement in the Third World: The Emergence of Social Movement Unionism', *Critical Sociology*, vol. 19, pp. 81-101.

Screeck, W. (1989): 'Skill and the Limit of Neo Liberalism: The Enterprise of the Future as the Place for Learning', *Work, Employment Society*, vol. 3, no. 1, pp. 89-104.

Secombe, W. (1986): 'Marxism and Demography, Family, Economy and State: The Social Reproduction Process under Capitalism', in J. Dickinson and Bob Russell (eds.), *Social Welfare*, Routledge, London, pp. 56-84.

Sen, Abhijit (1996): 'Economic Reforms, Employment and Poverty', *Economic and Political Weekly*, vol. 31, nos. 35-7, Special Number, pp. 213-22.

Sen, Amartya (1985): *Commodities and Capabilities*, Oxford University Press, New Delhi.

Sengupta, A.K. (2003): 'Decline of Trade Union Power in India', *Indian Journal of Labour Economics*, vol. 46, no. 4, pp. 685-702.

Seth, V.K. (2002): 'Primitive Flexible to Modern Flexible Manufacturing and the Process of Skilling and Deskilling of Labour', *Indian Journal of Labour Economics*, vol. 45, no. 4, pp. 1175-93.

Shaikh, Juned (2005): 'Worker Politics, Trade Unions and the Shiv Sena's Rise in Central Bombay', *Economic and Political Weekly*, 30 April-6 May, vol. 40, no. 18, pp. 1893-1900.

Sharma, Alakh and S.K. Sasikumar (1996): *Structural Adjustments and Labour*, V.V. Giri National Labour Institute, Noida (mimeo).

Shyam Sundar, K.R. (2005): 'Labour Flexibility Debate in India', *Economic and Political Weekly*, vol. XL, no. 22, 23 May, no. 23, 28 June, pp. 4-10.

______ (2005): 'State in Industrial Relations System in India: From Corporatist to Neo Liberal', *Indian Journal of Labour Economics*, vol. 48, no. 4, December, pp. 917-37.

______ (2003): 'Industrial Conflicts in India in the Reform Period', *Indian Journal of Labour Economics*, vol. 46, no. 4, pp. 287-303.

______ (2003): 'Flexibility and Rigidity in Labour Market . . . Towards Balanced Prospective', *Journal of Indian School of Political Economy*, vol. 15, no. 3, pp. 679-88.

Silver, B.J. (2003): *Forces of Labour: Cambridge Studies in Comparative Politics*, Cambridge University Press, New York.

Singh, Surjit (2002): 'Education Skills and Training Some Perception', *Indian Journal of Labour Economics*, vol. 45, no. 4, pp. 1079-90.

Sinha, P. et al. (1994): *Voluntary Retirement Schemes and Workers Response*, Maniben Kara Institute, Friedrich Ebert Stiftung, New Delhi.

Smith, D. (1997): *Job Insecurity versus Labour Market Flexibility*, Social Market Foundation, London.

Sodi, J.S. (1997): *Industrial Relations and Human Resources Management in Transition*, Sri Ram Centre for Industrial Relations and Human Resource, New Delhi.

Sohlamon, A. and David Turnham (1994): 'What can the Developing Countries Learn from the OECD Labour Markets', Technical Paper 93, OECD, Paris.

Soloman, Robert (1999): *Transformations of the World Economy*, Macmillan Press, London

Solow, Robert M. (2005): *What is Labour Market Flexibility? What is it Good for?* Internet site www://. Britac.uk/pubs/src/keynes97/text. html.

Somavia, Juan, Director General, ILO (2006): 'Employment in Asia', *The Hindu*, 30 August.

Song, HO-Keun (1999): 'Labour Unions in the Republic of Korea: Challenge and Choice', Discussion Paper, International Institute for Labour Studies, ILO, Geneva.

Srinivas, Ravi K. (1992): 'Underclass, Hi-Technology and Los Angeles Uprising', *Economic and Political Weekly*, 24-31 October, pp. 2388-98.

Srivastava, D.K. (2001): 'Trade Union Situation in India: Views of Central Trade Union Organizations', *Indian Journal of Industrial Relations*, vol. 36, no. 4, April, pp. 463-78.

Standing, Guy (1999): *Global Labour Flexibility: Thinking Distributive Justice*, Macmillan Press, London.

——— (1997): 'Globalization, Labour Flexibility and Insecurity: In the Era of Market Regulation', *European Journal of Industrial Relations*, vol. 3, no. 1, pp. 43-55.

Steedman, H. (1987): 'Vocational Training in France and Britain: Mechanical and Electrical Craftsmen', *National Institute Economic Review*, 126, December, pp. 57-71.

Steedman, H. and K. Wagner (1987): 'A Second Look at Productivity, Machinery and Skill in Britain and Germany', *National Institute Economic Review*, 122, November, pp. 84-95.

Stiglitz, J.E. (2002): 'Employment, Social Justice and Societal Well-being', *International Labour Review*, vol. 141, nos. 1-2, pp. 9-29.

Storey, J. (1995): *Human Resource Management: A Critical Text*, Routledge, London.

______ (1992): *Developments in the Management of Human Resources*, Blackwell, Oxford.

Storey, J. et al. (1993): 'The New Agenda and Human Resource Management: Round Table Discussion with John Edmondson', *Human Resource Management Journal*, vol. 4, no. 1, pp. 63-70.

Storey, J. and K. Sisson (1993): *Managing Human Resources and Industrial Relations*, Milton Keynes Open University Press, Buckingham.

Stredwick, J. and Steve Ellis (1998): *Flexible Working Practices: Techniques and Innovations*, Institute of Personnel and Development, London.

Streeck, Wolfgang (1997): 'German Capitalism: Does Information Technology Exist, Can Information Technology Survive', *New Political Economy*, vol. 2, no. 2, pp. 237-53.

______ (1992): *Social Institutions and Economic Performance*, London, Sage.

______ (1989): 'Skills and the Limits of Neo Liberalism: Enterprise of the Future as a Place of Learning', *Work Employment and Society*, vol. 3, no. 1, pp. 89-104.

Sundram, K. (2001): 'Employment-Unemployment Situation in the Nineties: Some Results from NSS 55th Round Survey', *Economic and Political Weekly*, vol. 36, no. 11, March, pp. 931-40.

Sundramurthy, N. (1994): 'NEP and Trade Union Response', *Economic and Politics Weekly*, June, pp. 1551-2.

Tabak, F. and M.A. Crichlow (2000): *Normalization: Process and Structure*, John Hopkins University Press, Baltimore and London, pp. 133-65.

Taylor, R. (1994): *The Future of Trade Union*, Andre Deutsch, London.

Teasdale, P. (1998): 'Incidence And Repeat Spells of Unemployment: An Analysis Using Claimant Data', *Labour Market Trends*, vol. 106, no. 11, pp. 555-62.

The Economist (2007): 'Sweden One Year On', 15-21 September, http://www.economist.com/node/9803876.

______ (2005): 'The Great Job Switch', 1-7 October.

The Economic Times (2006): 'Its Hire and Fire at State SEZs', 16 June.

Tilak, J.B.S. (2002): 'Education in Unequal World', in Monees Raza (ed.), *Educational Planning: A Long Term Perspective*, Concept Publishing Company, New Delhi.

Torrington, D.P. (1989): 'Human Resource Management and the Personnel Function', in J. Storey (ed.), *New Perspectives on Human Resource Management*, Routledge, London.

Turnbull, Peter and Victoria Wass (2000): 'Redundancy and the Paradox of Job Insecurity', in Heery Edmond and John Salmon (eds.), *Insecure Work Force*, Routledge Press, London, pp. 57-77.

Turnham, D., Bernard Salome and A. Schwarz (1990): *The Informal Sector Revisited*, OECD, Paris.

UNDP (2001): *Human Development Report 2001*, Oxford Universty Press, New York.

——— (2001): *Making Technology Work for Human Development*, Oxford Universty Press, New York.

——— (1996): *Human Development Report 1996*, Oxford Universty Press, New York.

Unni, Jeemol and U. Rani (2003): 'Changing Structure of Workforce in the Unorganized Manufacturing', *Indian Journal of Labour Economics*, vol. 46, no. 4, pp. 983-97.

——— (2004): 'Technical Change and Workforce in India: Skill Based Growth', *Indian Journal of Labour Economics*, vol. 47, no. 4, pp. 683-92.

US Bureau of Labour (1989): *Labour Statistics Report*, US Department of Labour, Bureau of Statistics, USA.

——— (1988): *Labour Statistics Report*, US Department of Labour, Bureau of Statistics, USA.

US Congress, Joint Economic Committee (1986): *The Concentration of Wealth in the United States: Trends in the Distribution of Wealth among American Families*, Washington DC, 1986.

Venkat Ratnam, C.S. (2004): *Negotiated Change, Collective Bargaining, Liberalization and Restructuring in India*, Response Books, Sage, New Delhi/London.

——— (1997): 'Collective Bargaining and Flexibility in India', Paper presented for Labour Law and Labour Relations Branch, ILO, Geneva.

Visaria, Pravin (2002): 'Workforce and Employment in India 1961-94', in B.S. Minhas (ed.), *National Income Accounts & Data Systems*, Oxford Universty Press, New Delhi.

Vuuren, T. et al. (1991): 'Employee Reactions to Job Insecurity', in J. Hartley et al. (eds.), *Job Insecurity: Coping With Jobs At Risk*, Sage, London.

Wachtel, Howard (1986): *Money Mandarins: The Making of a New Supra National Economic Order*, Pantheon, New York.

Wade, R. (1990): *Governing the Market: Economic Theory and the Role of the Government in East Asian Industrialization*, Princeton University Press, Princeton,

Wayne, J. (1986): 'Function of Social Welfare in a Capitalist Economy', in Dickinson and Russell (eds.), *Social Welfare*, Routledge, London, pp. 56-84.

Webster, E. and G. Adler (2001): 'Towards a Class Compromise in South Africa's Troubled Transition: Bargained Liberalization and Consolidation of Democracy', Paper presented at the 14th Congress of Sociology, Montreal, 26 July-1 August.

Wever, K.S. (1998): 'International Labour Revitalization: Enlarging the Playing Field', *Industrial Relations*, vol. 37, no. 3, pp. 388-407.

Wickham, J. (1997): 'Part-time Work in Ireland and Europe', *Work-Employment and Society*, vol. 11, no. 1, pp. 133-51.

Wilkinson, B. et al. (1995): 'The Iron Fist in a Velvet Glove: Management and Organization in Japanese Manufacturing Transplants in Wales', *Journal of Management Studies*, vol. 32, no. 5, pp. 819-30.

Williamson, O.E. (1985): *The Economic Institution of Capitalism: Firms Markets and Relational Contracting*, Free Press, New York.

Womack, J. et al. (1990): *The Machine that Changed the World: The Triumph of Lean Production*, Macmillan, New York.

World Bank (1999): *Knowledge for Development: A Report*, World Bank, Washington DC.

______ (1993): *The East Asian Miracle*, World Bank, Washington DC.

Wright, Martyn (1998): *Managing Competitive Crisis*, Cambridge University Press, Cambridge.

Yates, M.D. (2003): 'Naming the System: Inequality and Work in the Global Economy', Monthly Review Press, New York.

Zagha, R. (1999): 'Labour and India's Economic Reforms', in J. Sachs, A. Varshney and N. Bajpai (eds.), *India in the Era of Economic Reforms*, Oxford University Press, New Delhi.

Zeitlin, J. (1979): 'Craft Control and the Division of Labour: Engineers and Compositors in Britain 1890-1930', *Cambridge Journal of Economics* 3(3), September, pp. 263-74.

Index

For Product Safety Concerns and Information please contact our EU representative GPSR@taylorandfrancis.com
Taylor & Francis Verlag GmbH, Kaufingerstraße 24, 80331 München, Germany

www.ingramcontent.com/pod-product-compliance
Ingram Content Group UK Ltd.
Pitfield, Milton Keynes, MK11 3LW, UK
UKHW022114190926
475702UK00013B/1433
* 9 7 8 1 0 3 2 6 5 3 1 9 8 *